Business Insurance

7th Edition

DEARBORN™
A **Kaplan Professional** Company

This publication is designed to provide accurate and authoritative information in regard to the subject matter covered. It is sold with the understanding that the publisher is not engaged in rendering legal, accounting, or other professional service. If legal advice or other expert assistance is required, the services of a competent professional person should be sought.

This text is updated periodically to reflect changes in laws and regulations. To verify that you have the most recent update, you may call Dearborn at 1-800-423-4723.

© 1976, 1981, 1985, 1987, 1991, 1995, 2000 by Dearborn Financial Publishing, Inc.®

Published by Dearborn Financial Institute, Inc.

All rights reserved. The text of this publication, or any part thereof, may not be reproduced in any manner whatsoever without written permission from the publisher.

Printed in the United States of America.

First printing, September 2000

Library of Congress Cataloging-in-Publication Data

Business Insurance.--7th ed.
    p.cm.
      ISBN 0-7931-4190-7
      1. Business life insurance--Law and legislation--United States. 2. Business life insurance--United States.
   KF1180.B8 B87 2000
   368.8'1'00973--dc21
                                              00-060361

Contents

ACKNOWLEDGMENTS	**ix**

CHAPTER 1
INTRODUCTION TO BUSINESS INSURANCE — 1

The Business Market	2
Selling Business Insurance	2
Types of Business Organizations: An Overview	6
Business Insurance Prospects	8
Target Marketing	12
Rapport Building	18
Data Gathering	20
Qualifying Business Insurance Prospects	28
Approaching Business Insurance Prospects	29
Summary	31
Questions for Review	31

CHAPTER 2
HOW BUSINESSES ARE TAXED — 33

Internal Revenue Code	33
Sole Proprietorships	33
Partnerships	41
Corporations	43
Summary	49
Questions for Review	49

CHAPTER 3
ANALYZING FINANCIAL STATEMENTS — 51

Obtaining Financial Statements	52
Types of Financial Statements	53
Balance Sheet	53
Income Statement	58
Statement of Cash Flows	61

Accounting for Insurance Cash Values, Policy Loans and Premiums	62
Interpreting Financial Data	63
Insurance Needs as Revealed in Financial Statements	66
Finding the Premium Dollars in Financial Statements	75
Summary	79
Questions for Review	80

CHAPTER 4
THE SOLE PROPRIETOR — 81

The Sole Proprietorship Market	81
What Happens When a Proprietor Dies?	82
Liquidation of the Proprietorship	93
Case Study: Ms. Green	95
Family Retention	96
Case Study: Mr. Blue	99
Selling the Business to an Employee	101
Case Study: Mr. Brown	103
The Proprietorship Purchase Agreement	105
Summary	106
Questions for Review	115

CHAPTER 5
THE PARTNERSHIP — 117

The Partnership Market	117
Partnership Structure and Operation	118
When a Partner Dies	120
Planned Liquidation	123
Case Study: Ms. Bacon and Mrs. Black	124
Reorganization with Deceased's Heirs	126
Case Study: The Glasses—Father and Son	127
Sale to Surviving Partners	127
Types of Partnership Purchase Agreements	130
The Funding Insurance	135
Valuation of Partnership Interests	137
Tax Considerations in Partnership Purchase Agreements	139
The Professional Partnership	142
Summary	142
Three Sample Buy-Sell Agreements	143
Questions for Review	160

CHAPTER 6
THE CORPORATION — 161

Opportunities in the Corporate Markets	161
Introduction to the Corporate Form	162
Tax Advantages of Incorporation	165
Liquidation	167
Case Study: Mr. Barnett	170
Family Retention of Incorporated Business	171
Sale of the Deceased's Interests	173
Insured Buy-Sell Agreement	176
Summary	184
Questions for Review	184

CHAPTER 7
OTHER FORMS OF INCORPORATION — 187

Introduction to the S Corporation	187
What Is an S Corporation?	188
Taxation of Shareholders	189
Advantages and Disadvantages of S Corporations	193
S Corporation Buy-Sell Agreements	194
Key-Executive Insurance	194
Section 1244 Stock	195
The Professional (Personal Service) Corporation	195
What Is a Professional Corporation?	196
Employee Benefits for Professionals	197
Tax Problems of Incorporation	198
Buyout Agreements in Professional Corporations	201
The Limited Liability Company	201
Summary	205
Questions for Review	206

CHAPTER 8
THE CORPORATION—
CROSS-PURCHASE OR STOCK REDEMPTION — 207

The Agreement	207
The "Wait-and-See" Buy-Sell Agreement	213
Some Final Thoughts	213
Summary	223
Sample Stock Purchase Agreements	223
Sample Cross-Purchase Agreement	224
Sample Stock Redemption Agreement	230
Sample "Wait-and-See" Buy-Sell Agreement	237
Questions for Review	244

CHAPTER 9
SECTION 303 REDEMPTIONS — 247

Introduction to Section 303	247
Qualified Stock for Redemption	248
Tax Consequences	249
Case Study: Acme Mfg., Inc. and Zephyr Distributors, Inc.	250
Case Study: Four Corporations	252
Life Insurance to Assure a Section 303 Redemption	253
Section 303 Redemption Agreements	254
A Suggested Section 303 Sales Approach	255
Case Study: Mr. Brown and ABC Electronics Corporation	260
Distribution of Property Other Than Cash	262
Summary	263
Sample Agreements and Resolutions	264
Questions for Review	274

CHAPTER 10
KEY-EXECUTIVE LIFE INSURANCE — 275

Human Values in Business	275
Mechanics of the Plan	278
Case Study: Three Key Employees	281

Taxation of Key-Executive Life Insurance	282
Effect of Key-Executive Insurance on Valuation of Stock	288
An Undersold Market	288
Summary	289
Resolution of Board of Directors	290
Questions for Review	292

CHAPTER 11
NONQUALIFIED DEFERRED COMPENSATION PLANS — 293

Deferred Compensation Plans	293
The Deferred Compensation Agreement	301
The "Insured" Plan in Action	303
Case Study: Deferred Compensation Plan	304
The Question of Majority Shareholders	305
Other Tax Issues	307
Summary	308
Questions for Review	321

CHAPTER 12
SALARY CONTINUATION PLANS — 323

Plan Overview and Design	324
Case Study: Salary Continuation Plan	325
Tax Aspects of the Life Insurance-Funded Plan	329
ERISA and Salary Continuation Plans	331
Reasonable Compensation Considerations	333
Summary	334
The Salary Continuation Agreement	335
Questions for Review	352

CHAPTER 13
SPLIT-DOLLAR PLANS — 353

Basic Split-Dollar Plan	353
Advantages of the Split-Dollar Plan	356
Variations on Basic Split-Dollar Plans	357
Tax Considerations	367
Major Uses of Split-Dollar	374
Summary	379
Sample Split-Dollar Insurance Agreements	380
Questions for Review	394

CHAPTER 14
GROUP TERM LIFE INSURANCE — 395

Overview of Group Term Life	396
Eligibility and Amount of Coverage	397
Current Taxation of Employees	399
Conversion Privilege	405
Group Insurance and Buy-Sell Agreements	405
Group Life Insurance on Less Than Ten Lives	405

Summary	407
Group Term Insurance Documents	408
Questions for Review	416

ANSWER KEY TO QUESTIONS FOR REVIEW — 417

Acknowledgments

We wish to acknowledge Paul J. Winn, CLU, ChFC, who prepared the current revision of this text. A published author, he is a former agent, agency head and home office executive who now writes and edits training programs for financial services professionals.

Steve Froiken, Editor

1
Introduction to Business Insurance

The market for business insurance is large—and growing. This chapter introduces the course and gives an overview of the types of business organization that constitute the market. Sources of prospects, methods of qualifying prospects and approaches to prospects are all examined.

As an insurance professional, you are reading this course because you have just entered—or are at least thinking about entering—the business insurance market. You may be wondering:

- What's this market like?

- What are the opportunities?

- Who are the prospects?

- How do I reach them?

- What are their needs?

In this chapter, you will receive a profile of this dynamic, exciting market, the needs of business clients and the opportunities they present. Then, in the chapters that follow, you will learn the technical specifics of how to work in the business market.

■ THE BUSINESS MARKET

When most of us think about business, images of large, multinational corporations such as IBM and General Motors come to mind. These giants may be prospects; however, the real opportunity lies within what is known as the small business market. These are closely held (privately owned) companies, typically owned and managed by a limited number of individuals.

Some small businesses have as many as 250 employees; others are "mom and pop" family businesses with as few as two or three people on the payroll. Some have been in existence for generations; others have sprung up and thrived as a result of the entrepreneurial spirit that has swept the country in the last decade and shows no sign of slowing.

These small businesses are the backbone of our economy—in terms of sheer numbers as well as payroll. According to the U.S. Treasury Department, there are now more than 6 million small businesses (defined as having 100 or fewer employees) operating in this country. That number is up from 4.5 million in 1980, with more new businesses being formed each year.

Economically, these small businesses wield a great deal of clout, not just because of their numbers but also due to their economic contributions. The total payroll for all businesses in the United States is as follows:

Size of Company	Payroll
Under 20 employees	$647 billion
20 - 99 employees	$747 billion
100 - 499 employees	$730 billion
500 - 999 employees	$240 billion
1,000 or more employees	$485 billion

A look at these data shows that companies with fewer than 100 employees have payrolls totaling $1,394 billion a year, or nearly half the total payroll in this country. Collectively, it is safe to say that small business is big business.

■ SELLING BUSINESS INSURANCE

In general, the field of business insurance offers tremendous opportunities for the insurance agent: larger sales, more premium and commission dollars and a generally high level of persistency. Furthermore, when you sell business insurance, you are completing the insurance sales cycle by taking care of your client's total insurance needs—both personal and business. The transition from the sale of personal insurance to business insurance is largely a shift in emphasis; the buyer's motives, the procedure and the prospects are the same. If you have successfully sold personal insurance, you should have no difficulty presenting the insurance solutions to a businessperson's business problems.

ILL. 1.1 ■ *Business Establishments by Number of Employees*

- 86.7% Under 20 employees
- 11.0% 20-99 employees
- 2.0% 100-499 employees
- .02% 500-1,000 employees

Statistical Abstract of the United States, 1999.

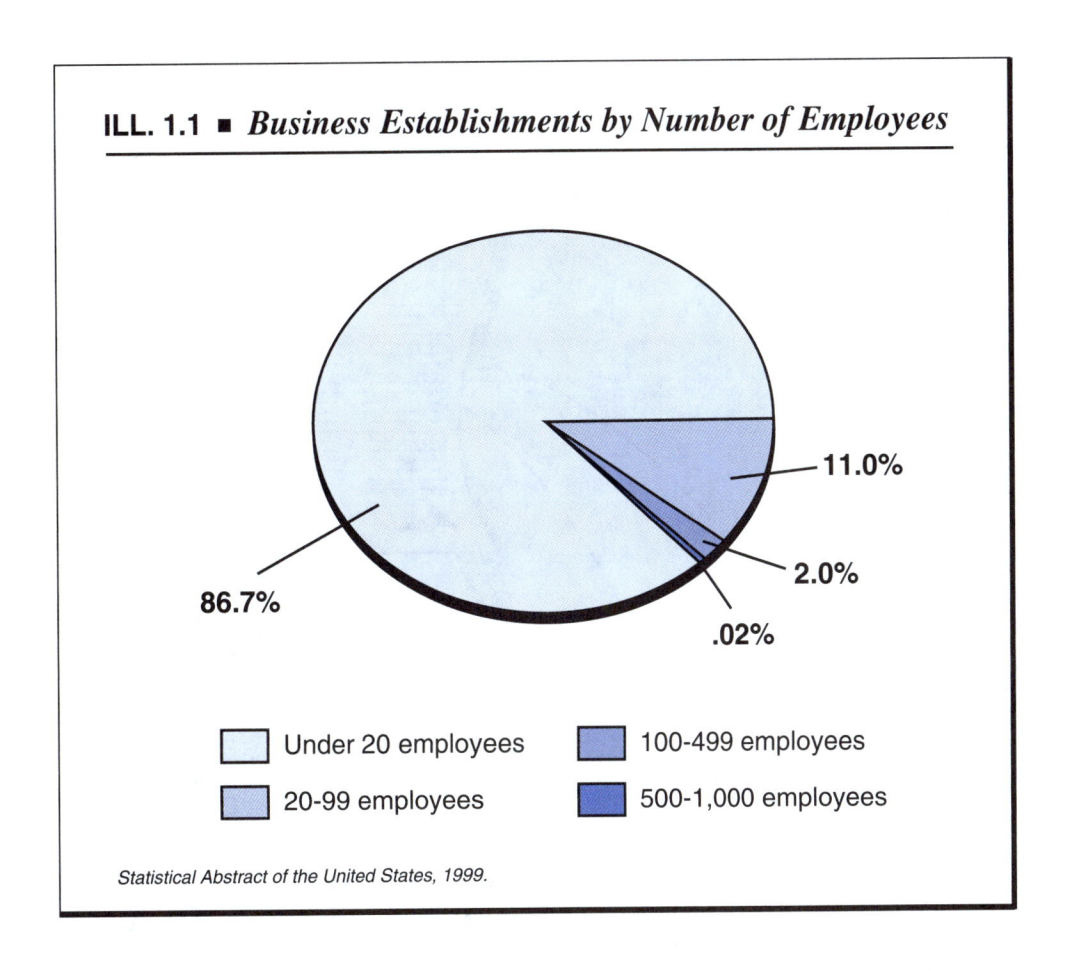

With the majority of small businesses, the welfare of the family and the business are interrelated. The continued financial well-being of families depends not only on the flow of income from the wage earners, but also on the continued good health of the businesses in which they are engaged.

The fortunes of small businesses and the families that own them often rise and fall together. You should be eager to talk to business owners about business needs as you are to discuss family needs with these same people. Further, many businesspeople are approached about business insurance more easily than about personal insurance. The need for insurance of all types is a fact of business activity. Also, the dollar amounts sent for business life insurance premiums are relatively small when compared with other business expenses such as salaries and wages, occupancy, cost of goods and supplies, and services.

The Role of Life Insurance

Business profits are a product of human activity. In some instances, such as a professional partnership, a partner's mental ability to handle a client's needs produces the profit. In other cases, the combination of mental ability with manual skill and raw materials produces the profits. Wipe out the property assets of a business and the business is stalemated until these assets can be replaced. Wipe out the human assets—especially key persons—and the business will find it cannot produce profits until new personnel have taken over.

ILL. 1.2 ■ *How Life Insurance Meets Business Needs*

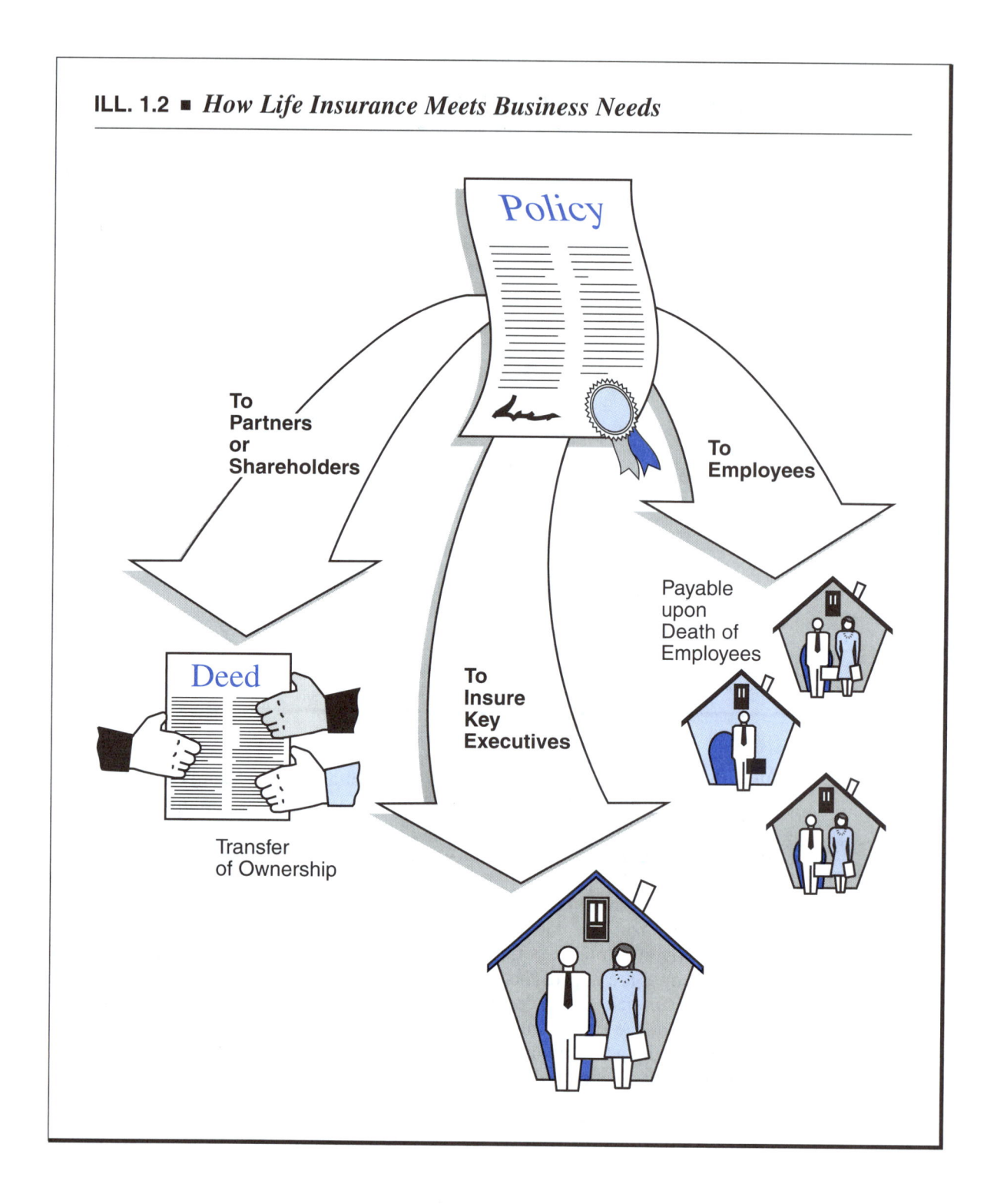

Life insurance serves three major roles in the business setting. One role is that of a funding medium. Life insurance, for example, is used to fund a buy-sell agreement to transfer ownership between partners or stockholders or to fund a deferred compensation plan.

A second role of life insurance is that of business interruption insurance, covering the human values in a business rather than the property values. Life insurance cannot prevent the interruption of business activity caused by death and disability; however, life insurance can indemnify the business for the losses these interruptions create.

The last role of life insurance in business is one of protection. Life insurance can be used to protect the employees and their families from the problems associated with death, disability and retirement.

More specifically, life insurance can play a key role in three vital areas: (1) transferring ownership of a business interest; (2) insuring key executives; and (3) providing employee benefits.

Transferring Ownership

The death (or permanent disability) of a business owner, if it does not cause the termination of the business itself, will at least cause changes in ownership and management personnel. And often it can create havoc not only within the business but also in the deceased business owner's estate.

Life insurance proceeds can indemnify the business organization and its owners against some or all of those losses. In those cases in which co-owners or employees desire to carry on the business, life insurance proceeds can give them the money to purchase the deceased's interest. In other cases, when the new business manager is a spouse, grown child or other member of the decedent's family, life insurance proceeds can pay the decedent's debts, costs and taxes, and otherwise permit the heirs to carry on a viable business. On the other hand, sometimes the best thing for all concerned may be an orderly liquidation of the business. Here again life insurance proceeds an be helpful, offsetting the dollar loss that occurs when a business is liquidated at the death of an owner.

Key-Executive Coverage

Small businesses are guided to success by a handful of key people. Often, these key people are largely responsible for the firm's good credit, its product line or its goodwill. The death of such a person is bound to leave its mark upon the business—an interruption at the least, termination at the worst.

To offset some or all of these losses, a business can carry life insurance on its key people. This insurance, payable to the business, indemnifies it against the loss of these key people. Disability insurance also may be purchased to give key-employee protection to a firm. Families of key employees may also be beneficiaries of key employee life insurance.

Employee Benefits

Life insurance also has its place in the area of employee benefits. These benefits may be limited to key officers and personnel, or they may be made available to all permanent, full-time employees.

Employee benefits may take a variety of forms. For example, individual life policies may be purchased to provide death benefits for an employee's spouse. Life policies also can be used to provide a deferred compensation plan for the employee or to fund a pension or profit-sharing plan. Under a split-dollar policy, a selected employee could obtain a larger insurance benefit than the employee could otherwise afford.

Another employee benefit is group life insurance. These contracts can be purchased as group term life insurance to provide a benefit for a group of employees, and as group permanent insurance—either as an extra benefit or as part of a pension or profit-sharing plan.

Obviously, the business uses of life insurance are many and varied. At one time or another, a large percentage of businesses will purchase one or more of these plans of insurance. Therefore, all the business owners in your area are potential clients. Furthermore, you will be offering them a tremendous service, one that will benefit not only them but also their employees and families.

TYPES OF BUSINESS ORGANIZATIONS: AN OVERVIEW

Before you can understand the business insurance problems of your prospects and offer solutions for them, you first must understand and be able to distinguish the three basic types of business organizations: sole proprietorships, partnerships and corporations.

We will examine each of these types of businesses in greater detail later in the course; for now, we will discuss some of their distinguishing features.

Sole Proprietorships

The sole proprietorship is a business owned by one person. Many retail outlets operate as sole proprietorships, as do many service businesses and professional practices.

A major advantage of the proprietorship business form is simplicity. There are no complicated articles of incorporation to prepare, no fees to pay, no public notice to give or documents to record (unless the business is conducted in a name other than that of the owner). Other advantages of proprietorships include the flexibility and freedom of action enjoyed by their owners—they make their own decisions without having to seek the approval of others; they can abandon old fields of endeavor, enter new ones or introduce new methods of operation into their work with complete freedom.

However, there are some disadvantages to a sole proprietorship form of business. One is that a sole proprietor and his or her business are not separate entities. The owner shares in both the assets and the liabilities of the business. A second disadvantage, and probably the greatest, is that sole proprietorships end with the death of their owners. If sole proprietors want their businesses to be continued by the family or an employee, they must make the business and insurance arrangements before death. These arrangements and the role the agent plays in implementing them are discussed in detail in Chapter 4.

Partnerships

A partnership is simply a business owned by two or more individuals. This type of business organization enables them to strengthen their own effectiveness by working with others whose assets and talents complement their own. An agreement among partners need not be written, although a written agreement is preferable.

Any change in a partnership creates a new firm. A new member cannot be brought into the business without the consent of each existing member. Nor can a partner sell his or her interest to a third party without the consent of each co-partner. The death of a partner automatically dissolves the partnership, unless otherwise provided in a written agreement.

From a legal standpoint, there are two classes of partnerships: general and limited. The differences between these two classes will be covered in detail in Chapter 5, but the basic difference is in how much personal liability a partner must assume for the partnership's debts.

Besides the legal classes of partnerships there are two business classifications—commercial and professional. These classifications are determined by the nature of the partnership's assets and are discussed in Chapter 5.

Corporations

Unlike a proprietorship or a partnership, a corporation is a business vested with a completely separate tax and legal personality apart from its owners.

It is created by individuals who contribute cash or other assets in exchange for a piece of ownership. Ownership is in the form of stock, which is evidenced by stock certificates.

Corporate owners, known as shareholders, possess certain rights due to their ownership status:

- the right to vote their shares at stockholder meetings;
- the right to elect the board of directors;
- the right to share in the distribution of profits (dividends);
- the right to transfer their stock freely;
- the right to inspect the corporate books and records; and
- the right to share in any surplus assets after a corporation is terminated.

Because the corporation is a separate legal entity, shareholders are not personally liable for the corporation's debts in the absence of fraud or other special circumstances. Their liability is limited to their initial capital investment plus any amount invested subsequently. Professional corporations, however, differ somewhat in this area in that a professional is subject to unlimited liability for any malpractice. Also, in small corporations, limited liability often is illusory because the shareholders often must guarantee personally the debts of the corporation.

Finally, as a separate legal entity, the corporation is taxed separately, with its own federal and state tax rates. However, under federal law, certain corporations may elect to be taxed similarly to partnerships. These are called S corporations and will be discussed in a later chapter.

An even newer development in organizational entities, the limited liability company, permits taxation of a business as either a corporation or a partnership, and combines many of the advantages of both forms of organization. Limited liability companies are treated in more detail in Chapter 7.

A close corporation is characterized by a small number of shareholder-owners who actively manage the business. Its stock is not traded or sold publicly; thus, its ownership remains *closed*. Although the close corporation seems to be run almost like a partnership, the characteristics of limited liability for the shareholders and the corporation's status as a separate legal entity distinguish it from a partnership. Close corporations will be explored in more detail in later chapters.

BUSINESS INSURANCE PROSPECTS

Many of your present policyowners and contacts will constitute a good portion of your business insurance prospects. In fact, as we noted earlier, the primary market for business insurance is not "big business," but "small business." Every insurance professional has some sort of contact with small businesses in the community—the clothing store, hardware store, auto supply store, barbershop or hair salon, restaurants and cafes, and so on. The owners of these businesses are your prospects.

As mentioned at the beginning of this chapter, there are literally millions of businesses in this country. To get an idea of the sheer numbers in your area, just open the Yellow Pages of your phonebook or drive down the street. Prospects are everywhere.

Working with Small Business Owners

One good reason for making small businesses your prime market is that the owners are generally easy to approach. There is little bureaucratic red tape to fight your way through. This is because the small business owner usually is actively involved in the day-to-day running of the business. As the key decision maker, he or she rarely needs to go through a lengthy approval process within the company; the decision is his or hers alone to make. Your recommendations can be implemented immediately.

ILL 1.3 ▪ *Comparing the Proprietorship, Partnership and Corporation*

Points	Proprietorship	Partnership	Corporation
Creation and Organization	By voluntary action of the individual. Ordinarily no formalities.	By voluntary agreement of the parties.	By consent and authorization of law, after compliance with the statutory formalities.
Relation of owners to business	The business and its owner are *not* separate entities. The person and the business are the same. Personal and business assets are merged.	Association of owners, managed by general partners. Business conducted in firm's name; partner acts as principal for self and agent for associates. Assets may be in firm's name; but partners are co-owners as tenants in partnership.	The business and its stockholders are separate entities. The corporation is a legal unit unto itself, capable of owning its own assets and acting in its own right. Managed by directors and officers.
Liability of owners for firm debts	Complete	Complete; but with the right to have firm assets first applied to firm debts, and with rights of contribution between partners.	Limited to capital contribution unless shareholder personally guarantees corporate debt.
Capital facilities	No legal limitations on the amount of capitol; but as a practical matter, capital is limited to the resources of the individual owner.	No legal limitations on the amount of capital; but as a practical matter, capital is limited to the individual resources of the partners and what they are willing to contribute.	Legally limited to the capital authorized in the articles of incorporation. This can be increased or diminished only by amendment of the articles as permitted by law. Practically, capital is limited to the amount the stockholders are willing to invest.
Sharing of profits	All belong to the individual owner	Shared equally, in the absence of special agreement	Shared indirectly through dividends declared by directors out of profits and apportioned among the outstanding shares of stock.

ILL 1.3 ▪ *Comparing the Proprietorship, Partnership and Corporation (Cont.)*

Points	Proprietorship	Partnership	Corporation
Taxation	Taxed as the individual owner is taxed. Business income is his or her income.	Income taxed to partners as individuals.	Taxed as a separate unit, usually with special license and franchise taxes. Some close corporations can elect S corporation taxation and be taxed as partnerships.
Period of legal life	Limited to life of individual owner	Ends with winding up of affairs following dissolution on death of any member unless prior contrary agreement.	Perpetual, unless limited by terms of charter, by-laws or statute.
Effect of owner's death	Business passes into owner's estate with other personal assets	Business automatically dissolved, and must be liquidated and reorganized, unless prior contrary agreement. Deceased partner's interest passes to his or her estate.	Business continues its independent legal existence, with the deceased stockholder's shares passing to his or her estate and through it to heirs.

Most successful small business owners readily understand their needs when they are explained to them; in fact, many are already acutely aware of them. If you tell your story competently, the owners will listen because they know that it means much to them personally—in terms of both the business and their family. They need business insurance, so the responsibility for providing it falls squarely on your shoulders. In fact, whether the vast majority of American business organizations will be sold business insurance or passed by will depend almost entirely upon the activity or inactivity of you and agents like you in making your day-to-day contacts.

Where to Begin

Where do you find business insurance prospects? There are several natural places to start:

1. *Existing clients who own businesses.* Review your client files. If you have a client for whom you have already done personal insurance work, requesting a meeting to discuss business insurance needs is a logical next step. Not only do you already know something about this individual, but you should have no trouble getting an appointment. Also, if

you've done a good job for this client in the past, he or she will be more than willing to work with you.

2. *Businesses with which you do business.* Do you have a favorite restaurant? A service station you use regularly for gas and auto work? A clothing store whose owner has learned to recognize you by face, if not by name? A lawn service? Plumber? Electrician? These are the people who have done business with you in the past, with you as the buyer. Especially if you're a preferred customer, they'll give you the opportunity to tell your story.

3. *Cold canvassing.* Cold canvassing entails dropping by local businesses in your area without an appointment. The purpose of this initial meeting is simply to get acquainted and, if possible, arrange a time for a meeting.

4. *Telephone directory.* An often underrated source, the phone book contains the names of virtually every business in your area.

5. *The Chamber of Commerce and business associations.* Members of the Chamber of Commerce represent some of the most prominent business owners in your community. Consider joining your local Chamber and becoming actively involved. The people you will meet are the kind of people you're looking to do business with.

6. *Referred leads.* Referred leads produce the best kind of qualified prospects. Even more so than in the personal markets, members of the business community rely on word of mouth and place high value on referrals. Many small businesses operate on a network basis with other businesses. Once you have made a business owner a satisfied client, ask about the company's suppliers.

7. *Community involvement.* Becoming active in your community boosts your profile and enhances your professional prominence. Becoming active can include coaching or sponsoring a little league team, making speeches for local organizations and conducting seminars, perhaps sponsored by your bank.

8. *The financial section of your local newspaper.* Make a habit of reading the financial news, which reports information about business expansions, mergers, new corporations, promotions and the like. This kind of information can give you door-openers to appointments.

For the greatest long-term success in the life insurance business, and especially in the business market, there are few approaches to client development that can equal target marketing for effectiveness. By using a target-marketing approach, the agent focuses his or her attention and marketing efforts on particular groups of people who are connected with each other with the intention of developing a relationship with them.

The groups of people on which the successful target-marketing agent focuses are those that:

- are appropriate for the agent in light of his or her experience, interests and temperament;
- can be reached by the agent;
- communicate with each other;
- have similar characteristics; and
- have generally common needs.

Interestingly, although target marketing can—and ought to—be learned by every agent serious about the profession of life insurance selling, the finest agents always have employed its principles and techniques. Often these agents used the techniques of target marketing without realizing they were doing it.

■ TARGET MARKETING

Target marketing is a process, and, like any process, it requires time and effort to complete successfully. As a result, reaping the unquestionable rewards of target marketing efforts doesn't happen immediately.

Successful target marketing involves a number of important steps. Those steps involve:

- identifying potential markets;
- researching identified markets to determine their viability;
- analyzing the market data developed and selecting one or more markets;
- creating market development plans; and
- implementing market development plans and strategies to cultivate the members of the market and network among them.

Identifying Potential Markets

The agent who chooses to work entirely within selected target markets can effectively be involved in up to four markets. Involvement in more than four target markets often means that the opportunities offered by one or more of the markets are being neglected. The result of that neglect by the agent is usually that the market or markets fail to live up to their potential.

An important key to selling successfully in target markets lies in finding markets and people with whom you enjoy working and want to be associated. Identifying potential markets is the first step in target marketing. Because it is important that you enjoy working with the people in the market, the first place to find business markets is among your current business clients.

Look through your book of clients and separate those existing clients that are business owners—sole proprietors, partners or stockholders in close corporations. Once you have identified your business clients, consider each and ask yourself if you would like to work with business owners like him or her. If the answer is no, you probably should not consider working in that market. If the answer is yes, however, call the client and arrange a meeting to talk about specializing in that industry. If you are able to identify five or more clients in different markets in which you would consider working, your initial market identification exercise may be completed. In that case, you can begin researching those markets, beginning at your client meetings.

Unfortunately, not every agent can identify existing clients who can provide information about their industry. In that case, the best approach for most agents without existing business clients is to contact the chamber of commerce, consult a local reference librarian to obtain lists of local associations, or look at a telephone directory. Hundreds of associations serving small businesses may exist in a medium-size city, such as the state plumbing contractors' association, the local homebuilders' association or the association of electrical contractors.

Other ideal sources of information about potential markets include:

- the secretary of state's office, which maintains a list of registered associations and organizations in the state;

- the local department of economic development. Normally this office maintains excellent demographic and economic information;

- the local small business association; and

- the state directory of association meeting planners.

Although these information sources can help any agent begin target marketing, it is not complete. A reference librarian or chamber of commerce executive likely will be able to suggest many other sources.

Once you have identified at least five market segments to target, you need to determine whether they would be good markets in which to work. In other words, you need to remove your sales "hat" and begin researching.

Researching Potential Markets

For many in sales, research seems to be one of those dull, lifeless activities best left to others. After all, aren't the most productive sales people fast-paced and action-oriented? While many good agents thrive on such a fast pace, the best agents often combine high energy with thoughtfulness and insight.

The single greatest reason why target marketing has disappointed agents in the past is because the markets were not right for them. Adequate early research into the markets being considered before committing your time and resources to them can often avoid this disappointment.

The primary function of market research is to gather enough information about the market to decide whether the market is right for you. To reach that decision, you usually need to determine five things about the market. Those five things are:

1. *Is there a fit between the market's needs and your products?* If the members of the market are not interested, do not need or are unable to qualify for the benefits that are provided by your products, sales to them are unlikely.

2. *Is the market large enough (either now or in the future) to justify your resource expenditure?* The necessary resources to penetrate a market can be significant in terms of time and money. If the sales potential is limited because the market is small or shrinking, it may not represent the best use of those resources.

3. *Do the market members have the wherewithal to buy your products in sufficient quantity to make market penetration worthwhile?* Even if the market members both need and want your products, they must be able to afford them. Is the industry economically strong? Are the market members earning substantial incomes? Is the market subject to strong economic swings?

4. *Is there much competition in the market?* Competition may be good because it makes us sharper, but if the market already is being served by skilled, competent agents it is generally more difficult for a brand new agent to become productive. A rule of thumb that some productive agents have used in assessing the extent of market competition is that a market of 200 members will generally support one competent agent.

5. *Can you reach the members?* Although market selection should be based on your research results in all of the areas, this is usually considered the single most important criterion in assessing the viability of a market. If you can't reach the members, you can't sell. Reaching the members, however, means more than contacting them. It includes their interaction with each other. Markets in which you are likely to be most productive are those in which the members communicate and interact frequently and regularly. That interaction and communication—the more the better—can include the following:

    – social gatherings;

    – business meetings;

    – an association magazine or newsletter;

    – trade shows; and

    – seminars.

Communication and interaction among market members is important for the agent because it provides the opportunity to make his or her name known to the members. Reaching the members is also facilitated by the willingness of the association that serves the market to accept you as a member on some basis. Depending on the rules of the association, you may be able to become a member, such as an associate member or a vendor member.

Obtaining this type of information is relatively easy. If you have existing clients in the markets that you are considering—either business or personal insurance clients —they often will be willing to talk to you about their industry. Frequently, clients will be flattered by your interest in their opinions and eager to share their insights. If you don't have existing clients in these markets, getting the information is still not difficult.

Often the best way to obtain information about a market is to contact the executive director of the association that serves it. That usually means the association's executive director. Association executives are typically responsible for managing the day-to-day affairs of the association and acting as the principal spokesperson or public relations person for the organization. It is in this latter role that the association executive can be most helpful in your market research. Regardless of whether your initial market introduction was through an existing client, you will want to interview the association executive, who usually is happy to share available demographic and economic information that affects the membership.

Doing the proper amount of research in a market requires that you interview more than just one or two individuals. It is suggested that you interview at least five market members and ask identical questions. This will allow you to gain a more complete understanding of the market. Additionally, the market members interviewed often are willing to give you the names of other market members and may become your first clients in the market.

When you have interviewed enough market members and have gained enough knowledge to assess the market, you need to summarize the results of your interviews in the five categories and decide whether to enter the market. The fundamental question to answer at this stage is whether the anticipated sales results are worth the time and money required to adequately penetrate the market. If the answer to that question is yes, your focus needs to shift from market research to developing your plan for penetrating the market. That means you must decide on strategies for developing the market.

Developing the Market

The objective of creating and implementing market development strategies is ultimately to sell your products to market members. To do that most effectively, the agent needs to position himself or herself as a resource—someone who brings value to the members.

Timing and sequence are extremely important in positioning. Simply stated, you must position yourself appropriately before attempting to sell to the members. Two reasons exist for this:

1. Your attempts to secure appointments and make sales to the market members are likely to be more effective if your reputation as a reliable resource is firmly established; and

2. Trying to sell to members before establishing your reputation could be counterproductive—it may create a feeling among the membership that your motivation is solely to create value for yourself rather than for the members. Engendering such a feeling among the membership would be disastrous to working in the market.

The timing and sequence requirements have two consequences for an agent that may be considered somewhat less desirable. The first consequence is that your initial sales within the market may not occur for about six months. The second consequence is that while you are waiting to begin selling in the market, you must implement your positioning strategies, and implementation may consume a substantial amount of your time, talents and money. Don't be put off by these consequences, however. Your successful penetration of a viable business market can result in selling success that exceeds your record. Let's turn our attention, now, to the how to of market development.

Developing a market calls for creating and implementing an overall strategy. You should begin by identifying particular strategies to use in the chosen market. Although a market may offer unique penetration opportunities, several methods are common to many markets for cultivating the market and networking among its members. Keeping in mind that people prefer to do business with those who they know and like, it will be clear why and how these strategies work.

Networking Within Your Market

By networking you are creating visibility within the market. Accordingly, networking strategies are ones that make you visible.

One of the first networking opportunities is to join the association that serves the market. Many associations restrict their full membership to those who are working in the field. However, these same associations may offer associate or vendor memberships that often will permit the agent to do everything a full membership would permit except to vote for the board members of the association.

The cost of joining the association often represents the agent's first direct target marketing cost. It is not unusual for association membership to cost from $300 to $500 annually. If you, as an agent, are committed to doing what is necessary to penetrate the market, the dues should be an acceptable expense. However, if you don't see yourself becoming immersed in the market —and that means attending meetings, joining committees and being involved in the organization—target marketing may not be for you. If that is the case, you may want to use those funds differently.

Joining the association that serves the market that you want to penetrate is just the beginning of networking. You need to be with the members. Many associations have monthly business meetings—often preceded by a cocktail hour and(or) dinner—at which they present a program of interest to the membership. You should attend those meetings. A relationship can change immensely with a prospect when breaking bread together. Furthermore, attending association meetings introduces the issues that are important to the members and provides you with knowledge about subjects that interest them.

Associations often have standing committees that usually have difficulty recruiting members to staff them. Consider your strengths, and offer to join a committee that can benefit from them. Once you join a committee, however, you should be prepared to work. In other words, while an important objective is to meet the members in a non-sales setting, don't join a committee and then fail to support its mission.

To work most effectively in the market, you need to know as much as possible about issues that concern the members. When you have gotten to know several of the centers of influence in the market, consider inviting them to become members of your personal board of advisors. As an agent, you share many of the problems and concerns of other small businesses. Just as any business might have a board of directors to guide and counsel its management, your board of advisors can help you focus on the market and advise on changes that may affect your business. In addition, because they come from your market, they can be a source of regular referrals to other members.

Some agents have a board of advisors that meets formally once each calendar quarter for dinner. The agent pays for the meal, and afterward, the board discusses strategies and suggestions to help the agent. Usually, the agent speaks with the members regularly between these formal meetings to obtain referrals or learn about changes.

Associations often have newsletters or magazines for members of the organization that the agent can use as a tool of communication. Agents sometimes write articles of interest to members that appear in the association magazine. If writing articles is not your forte, contact the company that you represent to see if its public relations department will write one for you. In addition, consider advertising in the magazine or newsletter. It will show that you support the association and will help spread your name among the members.

Many opportunities can help the target-marketing agent build visibility. You also should consider doing some or all of the following networking activities:

- participating in trade shows;

- sponsoring and speaking at a program for the members;

- providing free coffee and donuts at an association-sponsored seminar;

- providing a free beer and soda cart at the association's annual golf outing;

- sending financial and business newsletters with your name on the masthead; and

- creating and giving out a brochure outlining your services.

Implementing the visibility-building strategies that are appropriate for your market can pay enormous dividends, including giving you entree as a respected resource to its members. When you have implemented your market development and networking strategies and are recognizable to members, it is time to begin selling—and that means securing appointments.

Even though you have increased your visibility substantially in the market, you will want to implement a system of member contact and referrals to make appointments. One time-honored approach to member contact is through mailings. While mailings seem to be unproductive in certain professional markets, they can be worthwhile in other business markets. Sequential, timed mailings sometimes can generate interest and provide a reason to call the member.

Obtaining leads is the best way to secure an appointment, especially if the person providing the lead is someone that the member respects, such as another member or a person who serves the membership, such as an attorney or accountant. An effective process to obtain names is the list method. Like all good strategies, it requires some preparation.

At the conclusion of meetings with centers of influence in the market or at the end of a sales interview, an agent using the list method will say:

> *Mr. (center of influence) there are several members that I plan to call on in the next week or so. You may even know them. I would appreciate it if you would look at this list and tell me something about them. Nothing confidential, of course. Just something that will help me break the ice with them.*

When the center of influence or client has offered comments about the names on the list, the agent should say:

> *Thank you. Knowing something about the people I will be calling on helps a great deal. If any of these people feel a need to ask someone about me, would you have any objection to their calling you?*

RAPPORT BUILDING

The process of target marketing, including the market-development strategies that you implement, will go a long way toward helping build a relationship with prospects that will promote a successful career in the business market. However, regardless of whether you choose to employ target marketing, you will need to create and build rapport with your business prospects before they will do business with you.

The Nature of Rapport

Before talking about how to build rapport, it's important that to have a clear understanding of its meaning. Rapport is being in harmony with another individual, a sense of being on his or her wavelength. Being in rapport with the prospect, we see the world in the way that he or she sees it. Such congruity makes each of us likable to the other, and when we like someone, we are more likely to do business with that person.

Being in rapport with someone doesn't mean that we always agree; it means that we have consistent values. When we have a deep rapport with a prospect, we can disagree but can bring him or her into unconscious agreement. In other words, that deep rapport enables us to influence the other person dramatically. A person who is able to create immediate and deep rapport is *charismatic*.

Just about everyone will agree that the ability to create rapport is an important skill for a life insurance agent. The more important issue is how do we create it? How do we get on someone else's wave length? Let's examine three techniques that help build rapport.

1. *Encouraging the prospect to talk.* An important first step in developing rapport with your prospect is to use open-ended questions to draw him or her out. Rapport is developed much more quickly when your prospect is talking than when he or she is listening. Although there are any number of questions that you may want to ask, an obvious question for the business owner is "How did you decide to get into this business?"

2. *Employing creative listening techniques.* Just having the prospect talk isn't enough. You need to listen to what the prospect says and to how he or she says it. Prospects often will expose their attitudes and emotions through both verbal and body language. Creative listening techniques should be employed. Giving feedback to your prospect shows that you have listened.

    Nod approval or verbalize agreement by saying: "I see what you mean." Smiling and paraphrasing your prospect's remarks will cause the prospect to feel that you are on his or her wavelength.

3. *Using mirroring techniques.* Mirroring, a technique of offering prospects a reflection of themselves, is particularly effective when building rapport. An effective form or mirroring is paraphrasing the prospect's statements. In addition to enabling you to check your perception of the prospect's remarks, it also tends to create the feeling in your prospect that you understand him or her.

Although mirroring is effective, mimicking certainly is not. In fact, if the prospect believes he or she is being mimicked, your rapport—and, possibly, your interview—will end.

The purpose of employing techniques that create and deepen your rapport with prospective clients is not to deceive. It is used to create an atmosphere of trust in which the prospective client feels free to disclose personal and business information that will allow you to better meet his or her insurance needs. Much of that disclosure occurs during the sales step that we often describe as the fact-finding or data-gathering interview.

DATA GATHERING

Gathering the necessary data from your prospective client often is seen as the most important step in the sales process. Not only does it give you insight into what he or she may buy, but also it helps to ensure that your recommendation will be suitable. In addition, the fact that a data-gathering interview was held and that the agent used a data-gathering form may be an important part of defending against a subsequent claim that a recommendation was unsuitable.

Obtaining the Data

Although data-gathering in the business market still can usefully employ indirect, open-ended questions similar to those used in the personal market, the business data-gathering interview is considerably more focused than normally found in the personal market. Part of the reason for this increased focus is the generally broader range of issues that confront the agent working with business clients. The other reason relates to the somewhat less relaxed nature of the business interview compared to the personal interview. This is a result of the fact that business is usually being conducted while the interview is taking place.

Use of a data-gathering form is important to designing the right program regardless of the market in which the agent is working; in the business market it is essential. An appropriate business-market fact finder will generally focus on four key needs of business owners:

1. Business succession

2. Key executive insurance needs

3. Attracting and retaining high-quality executives through selective benefit plans

4. Employee benefits

It is important that you not only ask the right questions, but also that you know why those questions are important. The questions to ask in each of these areas are as follows.

Business Succession

As we will discuss in considerable detail later in this book, business owners have three fundamental choices concerning how to dispose of their business interest in the event of death, disability or retirement. The choices are to sell the interest, retain the interest in the family or liquidate the interest. The questions that should be asked in the section of the fact finder on business succession are questions that are designed to help the insurance professional and the business owner realistically assess the three choices in the business owner's particular situation. As we look at the data-gathering questions, we will examine the reasons why they are important.

The first question concerning business succession should be similar to the following: What are your plans for the business if you or one of your co-owners were to die or become disabled—sell the business, liquidate the business or retain the business in the family?

This question gives the insurance professional a starting point from which to begin gathering data about the chosen method of business succession. The purpose of the following questions is to assess whether the choice is reasonable for the business.

Selling the Business Interest. If the business owner's answer is to sell the business, you should pursue this by asking the following questions:

1. Who would be the buyer of your business interest?

2. Do you have a written buy-sell agreement?

If the business owner does not have a written buy-sell agreement or can't identify a buyer, it is possible that selling the business interest isn't a realistic option. In that case, you should ask the owner if he or she would consider retaining the business interest in the family or liquidating it. Depending on the answer, you should ask the questions in the retention or liquidation sections.

If the business owner has a written buy-sell agreement, you should determine if the value recited in the agreement is still appropriate and if the agreement is funded with life insurance by continuing with the following questions:

3. How is the price at which the business interest will be purchased established in the agreement?

4. When was your buy-sell agreement updated last?

5. How have you funded your buy-sell agreement—sinking fund, life insurance or through another method?

If the buyer of the business interest subsequently sells it during his or her lifetime, the extent of basis can substantially affect tax liability. In a regular corporation, purchase of the business interest under a cross-purchase agreement will result in a stepped-up basis for the purchaser on a subsequent sale. A stock redemption in a regular corporation will not increase the co-stockholder's basis. To determine if that is likely to be important to the survivor, you should ask the following question:

6. How likely is it that the buyer of the business interest would sell it during his or her lifetime—very likely; possible, but not likely; or very unlikely?

To determine if the business value in the buy-sell agreement is appropriate, or to arrive at a business value if there is no existing agreement, it is important to have an understanding of what the owner believes that the business is worth. The next several questions are designed to elicit that information.

7. If you were interested in selling your business interest now, what is the minimum amount that you would sell it for?

8. If you were to buy your business today, what is the maximum that you would agree to pay for it?

9. When did you last have your business valued for your buy-sell agreement? What method was used to value it?

Liquidating the Business Interest. Liquidation of a business interest is generally the least desirable option following the death, disability or retirement of the business owner since it usually results in a dramatic loss in asset value. Simply stated, the value of an ongoing business is almost always greater than the book value of its individual parts.

If liquidation is the only available option, you will want to determine the extent of the asset loss and—because family members usually rely on the income provided by the business—the other income sources available to replace the income it now provides. Life insurance can be used effectively to replace both the asset loss and the income loss in the event of the business owner's death.

1. If you were able to sell your business today to a willing buyer, what do you think that you could sell it for?

2. If you had to liquidate your business entirely within the next 9 months, what do you think that you could get for it?

3. Explain what sources of income your family has other than your business?

Retain the Business Interest. Retaining the business interest in the family is sometimes the appropriate business succession solution, especially if the business interest is a majority interest. It may continue the family's income source and tends to minimize the asset loss resulting from liquidation. However, a number of issues need to be resolved, including:

- identifying the successor to run the business;

- determining the source of family income if the successor is other than the business owner's spouse;

- providing for sufficient marital assets passing by will to avoid a widow's challenge based on statutory share;

- arranging for an interim manager if the chosen successor is inexperienced;

- paying any estate settlement costs; and

- arranging for the ownership transfer.

Life insurance has obvious application when the business owner is interested in retaining the business in the family. It may be used to pay estate settlement costs, provide family income, indemnify the business on the loss of the business owner, provide marital assets, and meet other financial needs, such as the equalization of inheritance when other family members will not share in the business interest.

There may be other issues in a situation that need to be addressed. The life insurance needs in the case of business retention will be discussed more fully later in this book. The questions that you need to ask the business owner interested in retaining the business interest are as follows:

1. Who will run the business when you retire, die or become disabled?

2. What are the qualifications—experience, education or whatever else may be needed—that will enable the successor to run the business effectively?

3. How have you arranged to transfer the business to your successor—testamentary transfer at death, lifetime transfer or sale? Have the arrangements been made to carry out that intention?

4. How much do you estimate your estate settlement costs will be? How will those estate settlement costs be paid?

5. If the business will not be passed to your spouse, what income sources are available to your surviving family?

Key Executive Insurance Needs

Many great industrialists have stated that their most important assets were the managers of their organizations. People made their companies profitable, not buildings or machines or inventory. For many businesses, that hasn't changed. It is people—especially key people—that still make the difference.

When a key person is lost, regardless of the cause, the business suffers. When the loss is due to death or disability it can be especially devastating because it is often sudden and unexpected. The loss suffered by the business may result from a cessation of credit, a decrease in sales, a loss of product-development momentum or from many other causes. In addition to the profit loss, there may be increased expenses as the business seeks to replace the key executive.

The questions to ask in this area are designed to identify the key individuals, to quantify the business loss occasioned by their departure and to estimate the cost to replace them. The answer to indemnifying the business for the key executive lies in the purchase of an appropriate amount of company-owned life and disability insurance.

Several factors and approaches can be used to establish an appropriate amount of key-executive life insurance or disability insurance. Insurance companies employ a rule of thumb that limits key-executive life and disability insurance amounts they will issue to some multiple of the individual's salary. The multiple varies with insurers but is often 5 to 10 times compensation.

Let's turn to the key-executive insurance questions that need to be addressed.

1. Who are the individuals you employ that are critically important to your company's profitability? (This may include the business owner.)

2. How would you determine the loss that your business would sustain if these key individuals were to die or become disabled? (a percent of sales, a multiple of salary)

3. What costs would your business incur to recruit, attract and train a replacement for your key individuals?

Key Individual	Hiring Costs	Cost to Train	Opportunity Costs
1.			
2.			
3.			
4.			

Selective Benefit Plans

Selective benefit plans generally are provided as additional executive benefits. They may be in the form of split-dollar life insurance, executive bonus plans, selective executive retirement plans or deferred compensation plans. Because they are non-qualified plans, the employer is not required to include all employees.

The primary attraction of these benefits to the employer often hinges on two factors:

1. the employer may discriminate as to who to include and at what level; and

2. the employer may recover the costs of providing the benefits.

Although certain selective benefits may result in a tax deduction for the employer, unlike qualified plans they usually do not permit both an employer tax deduction and employee tax deferral. The questions that will help determine the appropriate selective benefit for the employer are:

1. What benefits do you want your non-qualified plan to give you and your executives?

Benefit	Level of Importance		
	High	Medium	Low
Provide retirement income benefits			
Provide preretirement death benefits			
Tax-deductible benefit costs			
Recoverable benefit costs			

	Level of Importance		
Benefit	**High**	**Medium**	**Low**
Minimize effect on executives' taxes			
Plan should be under executive control and portable			
Shield plan proceeds from estate taxes			
Allow executives to contribute			
Benefits should keep pace with inflation			
Benefits should keep pace with salaries			

2. List the executives you wish to include in a selective benefit plan.

3. What level of benefits would you like to provide for each executive's retirement, disability and pre-retirement death benefit?

4. What dollar amount would the business be willing to spend on each executive's retirement, disability, or pre-retirement death benefit?

Qualified Retirement Plans

Qualified retirement plans "qualify" for a current income tax deduction of employer plan contributions. This current income tax deduction benefit comes with certain requirements, however. An important requirement is that the plan not unfairly discriminate against lower-paid employees.

Qualified plan rules permit a certain amount of disparity between the contributions or benefits provided for plan participants based on their age and income. As a result of that permitted disparity, qualified plans may favor older and highly-paid plan participants within certain prescribed limits. This permitted disparity is often of considerable interest, especially to the smaller employer.

Since the subject of qualified plans is generally complex, the insurance practitioner should not attempt qualified plan design without a thorough knowledge of the subject. Instead, when an employer expresses interest in a qualified plan, the following questions and their answers should provide the basis for a fruitful discussion with a qualified plan professional. Qualified plan questions that should be asked include:

1. A range of qualified plans may meet your goals and objectives. To provide the basis for designing the right plan for your business, I need to understand your feelings concerning a number of key issues.

Qualified Plan Design Issues	\multicolumn{3}{c}{**Level of Importance**}
	High	Medium	Low
Allow the maximum income tax deduction			
Allow yearly adjustment of annual contribution			
Favor higher-paid participants			
Favor older participants			
Permit participants to defer part of compensation			

If the employer indicates that a desirable plan would allow the plan participants to defer compensation, you should ask questions 2 and 3 below, which relate to the likely level of employee participation and the willingness of the employer to match employee elective deferrals.

2. What percentage of your employees would be likely to defer a part of their salary?

3. Would you be willing to match a part of their deferred salary as an incentive to them to defer? If yes, what percent would you be willing to match?

If the employer continues to show interest in a qualified plan, whether or not employee salary deferral is appropriate, ask the following questions:

4. What employees should be included in the qualified plan—all employees or full-time employees only?

5. Should plan participants be required to complete a certain number of years of employment before they are fully vested in employer plan contributions?

6. Should plan participants be permitted to take loans from the plan?

7. Should plan participants be permitted to purchase life insurance in the plan?

8. Approximately what level of employer annual plan contributions would you anticipate making to the plan?

Be sure to obtain an employee census from the employer (Ill. 1.4).

ILL. 1.4 ■ *Employee Census Information*

Name	Social Security Number	Sex	Date of Birth	Date Hired	Position	Highly Compensated (h) or Key Employee (k)	Percent of Voting Stock	Annual Non-Deferred Compensation			
								Basic	Bonus	Overtime	Total

QUALIFYING BUSINESS INSURANCE PROSPECTS

Each business insurance prospect should be qualified with the same four standards used to qualify a personal insurance prospect: need, ability to pay, insurability and ability to be seen. Let's briefly review each of these in light of the business insurance setting.

Insurance Need

To make a sale, a prospect must have a business insurance need that your services can meet. This need also must be immediate. At times you can anticipate your prospect's needs before the interview through information received from outside sources or maybe from an employee or friend. A word of caution: even though you anticipate your prospect's needs, you must still listen during the interview; the prospect's interpretation of his or her needs might be quite different from your interpretation. The initial gathering of data is the first step in closing the sale. A favorable impression made at this point and reinforced at each successive meeting with the client is vitally important for a successful conclusion to the sales process.

Ability to Pay

A common myth about small business owners is that they are all affluent, fly first-class, take long vacations and drive luxury cars. In reality, the typical small business owner lives modestly, sends his or her children to the local public school and worries about paying the bills. While the incomes of small business owners tend to be above the national average, most of their assets are tied up in the business. In fact, cash flow is the number-one concern of most businesses—and in any typical year, approximately 90,000 businesses go bankrupt. So, don't assume every business you encounter is flush with cash. A prospect for business insurance must have the ability to pay.

Qualify prospects in the business market just as you would those in the personal markets—find out as much as you can in advance, and then conduct a detailed fact search. In addition, you should keep an eye on the financial news section of your local newspaper for such information. Better yet, subscribe to the Dun & Bradstreet business service, which can provide you with a financial snapshot of virtually every business in your community.

Insurability

As in the personal insurance markets, insurability is a key factor, for obvious reasons. No matter how good your plan is and no matter how willing your prospect may be to buy, uninsurability can kill the sale. On the positive side, however, an increasing number of insurers are recognizing the responsibility to meet the needs of the rapidly expanding small business market, and their underwriting guidelines reflect this. All the same, be alert to the potential problem of uninsurability when working in this market.

Ability to Be Seen

As in the personal markets, the ability to approach your business prospect and obtain an appointment on a favorable basis is critical. If you know the prospect or have a referral, all the better. Regardless, when contacting your prospect, be professional. Recognize that this person's time is valuable. Get your credentials on the table quickly. Most of all, because the owners are generally the ones who make the key decisions, go right to the top. Don't be put off or intimidated by such titles as president or vice president.

APPROACHING BUSINESS INSURANCE PROSPECTS

The most important thing to remember when approaching your business prospect is to capture his or her attention at the outset of the interview and keep it. Always know in advance what to say and how to say it. Adequate preparation before the call will pay off in increased confidence. You also will be more capable of servicing your client's business insurance needs.

Of course, the initial interview is the most difficult, because the prospect usually puts up some resistance at the idea of spending company money for insurance. One way to deal with this resistance is to talk about hypothetical cases rather than the prospect's specific situation. Or, better yet, you can explain that the purpose of the interview is to gather information for a proposal tailored to the prospect's needs. Either method allows you to present your case and allows the prospect a chance to get to know you.

Use Visual Aids

The use of visual sales aids can help you secure more interviews. "I have something to show you" has a far stronger appeal than "I have something to tell you."

Moreover, visual aids can help you get a more complete interview. Seldom willa prospect end an interview until you have finished your visual presentation. Sales visuals also can serve as an interview guide. They outline the main points of the interview and can help you find your place if you are interrupted. In addition, a visual can assist the prospect in retaining important figures.

A good general rule is to stick closely to the printed materials during the interview. By doing so, you can devote your attention to such matters as delivery, timing and reactions.

Use Available Help

Most insurance professionals are uncomfortable in their first business insurance interview. It's too much to expect that someone who is new to the business insurance area will act skillfully the first two or three times out. Inexperienced agents may make successful sales, but often in spite of themselves.

For this reason, it is probably best for you to seek the help of others. Usually, the help is of the interoffice variety. Your manager or a veteran fellow agent can help you plan your interview with a prospect. Ask them to discuss with you not only what you will say to the prospect, but also your answers to the objections most likely to come up. After the interview, the manager or veteran agent also can help you with your business insurance proposal.

If you feel you need extra help in the interview, you can ask your advisor to accompany you to the interview. You can always account for his or her presence to your prospect by explaining that he or she has a certain area of expertise that will aid in the prospect's case.

Also, a two-person sales team is often more effective when the prospect has other advisors present, such as an attorney or accountant.

Cooperate with the Client's Attorney and Accountant

Quite often, you will have to work in conjunction with the prospect's attorney and accountant. To foster the best relationship possible, stress at the outset that you are not trying to move in on their areas of expertise. Legally, you cannot prepare the forms necessary for buy-sell agreements. It is the function of the attorney to draft any business insurance agreements needed to accomplish the purpose for which the insurance is to be purchased; also, the attorney will advise the prospect of all legal consequences of the business insurance purchase. The accountant, on the other hand, establishes the accounting procedure relative to the insurance premiums, loans and cash values, when the insurance is purchased by the business. You, as an insurance professional, have the responsibility to see that life insurance policies are of a sufficient amount and the proper kind and that the ownership and beneficiary provisions conform to the legal agreements prepared by the attorney.

Very likely, your business prospect will not have a close working relationship with an attorney or accountant. At the same time, the successful completion of your work will depend on the involvement of such professionals.

Never overstep your bounds as an insurance professional by giving legal advice or attempting to develop legal documents yourself. This is illegal and not in the best interests of your clients. When necessary, bring in an attorney or accountant.

As you begin working in the business insurance market, develop a working relationship with an attorney—an individual who can be brought in to meet with clients when needed. Under this networking arrangement, the attorney benefits by an introduction to new clients. You, in turn, benefit by having a professional in your corner, so to speak; plus, you have a valuable resource for referred leads.

SUMMARY

To be successful in the business insurance market, you need two things:

1. Technical knowledge

2. Sales ability

Separately, these ingredients have no value; the ability to tie your sales techniques to your technical knowledge is what makes you a competent business insurance producer. Remember, nothing happens until the sale is made. It takes not only know-how, but also imagination and selling ability to motivate buyers to solve their business problems with the purchase of insurance.

The purpose of this course is to arm you with the knowledge and skills development needed to sell business insurance successfully. After you understand the basic factors that affect businesses and professional practices, you can vary your sales presentations to meet the individual needs and desires of the business and professional people upon whom you call.

In the next few chapters, you will be introduced to the types of business organizations, taxation of these organizations and how to read financial statements. The role of life insurance will be explained. Then, we will take a look at specific areas of business insurance, which are generally classified as fringe benefits.

CHAPTER 1 QUESTIONS FOR REVIEW

1. The business market consists of

   A. small "mom and pop" retail stores
   B. sole proprietorships with 20 or fewer employees
   C. closely held corporations with several hundred employees
   D. all of the above

2. According to the U.S. Treasury Department, the number of small businesses in this country today is

   A. 6 million
   B. 10 million
   C. 20 million
   D. 30 million

3. Life insurance in the business setting can be used to

   A. fund buy-sell agreements
   B. indemnify the company against the loss of key employees
   C. provide employee benefits
   D. all of the above

4. An organization owned by one person and started without any formality or legal document is called a(n)

   A. sole proprietorship
   B. limited partnership
   C. closely held corporation
   D. S corporation

5. When working with business prospects

   A. avoid giving legal advice
   B. be prepared to work with the prospect's other advisors
   C. be prepared to provide an attorney when necessary
   D. all of the above

2

How Businesses are Taxed

How small businesses, their owners and employees are taxed is of vital importance to an insurance agent or financial planner. Income taxation of life insurance touches almost every business insurance sale you will be making. This chapter will introduce how proprietorships, partnerships and corporations are taxed. Later chapters will highlight income tax problems peculiar to the specific topics being covered.

INTERNAL REVENUE CODE

In spite of efforts in recent years to simplify the tax laws in this country, they are a complex quagmire, full of pitfalls as well as opportunities. This situation applies especially to business owners. It is not recommended that you attempt to develop an in-depth knowledge about tax law. However, as an insurance professional, you should be aware that virtually every business insurance need is connected in some way to a client's tax situation. For this reason, it is important to acquire at least a general working knowledge of how taxes affect your business clients. The reward is increased self-confidence and, most of all, effectiveness in meeting the needs of your clients.

For now, our focus will be on general principles of income taxation that impact personal and business decisions within the three types of businesses: sole proprietorships, partnerships and corporations.

SOLE PROPRIETORSHIPS

The income taxation of a sole proprietorship is actually the income taxation of the sole proprietor as an individual. The proprietorship is not a separate tax entity the way a corporation is. This blending of personal and business assets and liabilities is important to the insurance agent or financial planner in making the business insurance sale, as you will learn. For now, the income taxation of an individual will be discussed, because this is how the sole proprietor is taxed.

Gross Income

The starting point for all income tax calculations is the individual's gross income. Gross income is defined as *"all income from whatever source derived."* Included are the following seven types of income:

1. Wages, salaries and commissions
2. Gains from the sale or exchange of property
3. Dividends
4. Interest income
5. Rents
6. Royalties and copyrights
7. Income derived from a business or profession

There are exceptions. *Not* included in gross income are:

1. Life insurance death benefits
2. Gifts and inheritances
3. Compensation for sickness or injuries
4. Interest earned on municipal bonds issues for public purposes
5. A portion of certain annuity payments

Deductions for Adjusted Gross Income

Congress has ruled that certain forms of taxpayer expense justify a reduction in gross income. The result, after deducting these expenses from gross income, is *adjusted gross income* or *AGI*.

Allowable deductions include:

- *Reimbursed employee business expenses*—If the amounts involved are included on the individual's W-2 form as wages or salary for the year, they are permitted as an adjustment.

- *Certain traditional individual retirement account (IRA) contributions*— Some individuals are allowed to deduct contributions made to a traditional IRA from their gross income.

- *Self-employed health insurance deduction*—A phased-in deduction of health insurance premiums, which permits the self-employed individual to deduct the applicable percentage of health insurance paid according to the following schedule:

Year	Applicable Phase-In Percentage
2000-2001	60%
2002	70%
2003 and later	100%

- *Keogh retirement plan/self-employed SEP plan contributions*—Deductions for amounts contributed to these self-employed retirement plans are permitted, with limitations.

- *Penalty on early withdrawal of savings*—Bank charges due to a premature withdrawal, as in the case of a certificate of deposit, are deductible, even if the loss is not connected with a trade or business.

- *Alimony paid*—Alimony payments are deductible as an adjustment against gross income.

- These deductible business-related expenses:

  - office rent, utilities and overhead

  - salaries and employee benefits

  - office supplies

  - proportionate business use of a personal car

  - 100 percent of interest paid on business loans

  - use of a home office (as a proportionate share of home expenses)

  - 50 percent of travel and entertainment expenses

  - business publication subscriptions

  - advisor's fees for tax preparation and collection of income

  - continuing education course expenses

  - professional dues and memberships

  - depreciation of capital assets

  - moving expenses

These expenses are itemized whether the individual uses the standard deduction or itemizes personal deductions.

Itemized and Standard Deductions

There are two basic types of deductions: adjustments to income, as discussed above, and *itemized deductions,* which are deductions from adjusted gross income used to calculate taxable income. Both of these serve the same purpose: to allow a taxpayer to reduce the tax base against which the progressive tax rates are applied. An individual taxpayer can opt to itemize his or her deductions *or* apply the standard deduction amount. The option that yields the greatest amount should be the one the taxpayer applies to reduce taxable income. Following is a list of some itemized deductions allowable under the current code:

- medical expenses;

- state and local income taxes and state and local real estate taxes;

- interest paid on a mortgage used to purchase a taxpayer's principal residence or a second residence;

- investment interest (i.e., interest expense on property held as an investment);

- charitable contributions; and

- casualty and theft losses.

For taxpayers who do not have itemized deductions to apply against their adjusted gross incomes, the tax laws allow a *standard deduction.* Actually, the standard deduction is available to anyone, and its use simplifies preparation of the return. However, itemized deductions should be computed first to see which deduction—standard or itemized—produces the greatest amount. The standard deduction is available to individual taxpayers only.

When a taxpayer who has an adjusted gross income exceeding a specific threshold amount, which was $128,950 for year 2000 ($64,475 for married individuals filing a separate return), the amount allowable for itemized deductions must be reduced. The formula for the reduction is at a rate of 3 percent of the excess of adjusted gross income over the threshold amount with a maximum reduction of 80 percent of the total amount of that deduction that would be otherwise allowed.

Deductibility of Medical Expenses

Employees, partners and sole proprietors may deduct medical insurance premiums and unreimbursed medical expenses to the extent that when added to all other unreimbursed medical expenses the total exceeds 7.5 percent of the taxpayer-employee's adjusted gross income.

ILL. 2.1 ■ *Calculation of Individual Income Tax*

Step 1 ← Gross Income

    minus

Step 2 ← Deductions for Adjusted Gross Income

    minus

Step 3 ← Itemized (or Standard) Deductions

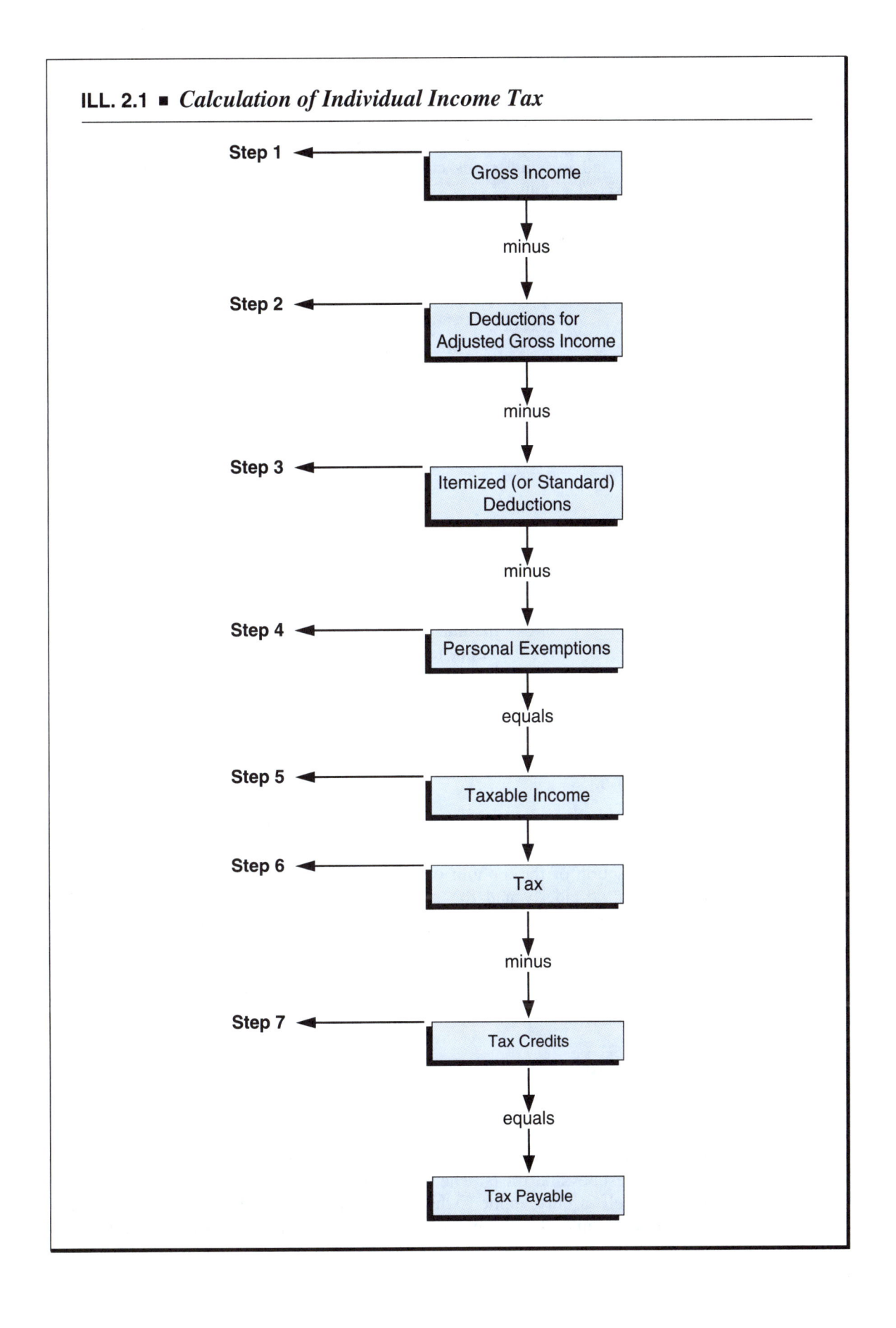

    minus

Step 4 ← Personal Exemptions

    equals

Step 5 ← Taxable Income

Step 6 ← Tax

    minus

Step 7 ← Tax Credits

    equals

Tax Payable

The Personal Exemption

A fixed dollar amount is allowed each taxpayer and eligible dependent for a personal exemption. The personal exemption is adjusted annually for inflation. For 2000, the figure was $2,800. For higher income taxpayers, the exemption is reduced and in some cases completely eliminated as income exceeds designated threshold amounts.

For 2000, the threshold amounts were as follows:

$193,400 Joint return or surviving spouse
$161,150 Head of household
$128,950 Single taxpayers (other than above)
$ 96,700 Married but filing separately

For each $2,500 (or fraction thereof) of adjusted gross income exceeding the threshold amounts, the exemption amount is reduced by 2 percent. Depending on the amount of taxpayer income, successive 2 percent reductions could completely phase out the exemptions.

Taxable Income

At this point, we can determine taxable income. The steps described so far are as follows:

```
  Gross income
- Adjustments to gross income
- Itemized deductions or the standard deduction
- Personal exemption(s)
= Taxable income
```

Tax Credits

Unlike tax deductions, which reduce the income subject to tax, a *tax credit* is a direct offset against the tax due. The result of a tax credit is a dollar-for-dollar reduction of the amount of tax to be paid. The credits available include credits for the elderly and the permanently and totally disabled, child and dependent care, the qualified adoption credit, the child tax credit and the Hope Scholarship and Lifetime Learning credits. In addition, there are general business-related credits, such as energy, rehabilitation and low-income tax credits. Remember that these tax credits are subtracted from the tax due on taxable income.

The Alternative Minimum Tax

The alternative minimum tax (AMT) is designed to ensure that individuals with above-average income and large deductions do not completely escape paying their share of income taxes. This tax is also applied to corporate taxpayers including estates and trusts. The calculation of this tax can be complicated and the tax itself is only applied when its computation yields a result higher than would be obtained by using the regular income tax calculation. In comparing

ILL. 2.2 ▪ *2000 Federal Income Tax Table*

Married, Filing Jointly

If taxable income is		Then tax is		
More than	But not more than	This	Plus this%	Of amount more than
$ 0	$ 43,850	$ 0	15%	$ 0
43,850	105,950	6,577.50	28%	43,850
105,950	161,450	23,965.50	31%	105,950
161,450	288,350	41,170.50	36%	161,450
288,350	Unlimited	86,854.50	39.6%	288,350

Single Taxpayer

If taxable income is		Then tax is		
More than	But not more than	This	Plus this%	Of amount more than
$ 0	$ 26,250	$ 0	15%	$ 0
26,250	63,550	3,937.50	28%	26,250
63,550	132,600	14,381.50	31%	63,550
132,600	288,350	35,787.00	36%	132,600
288,350	Unlimited	91,857.00	39.6%	288,350

the two methods of taxation, the AMT is essentially a lower rate applied to a larger taxable base. The larger taxable base results from the inclusion of so-called tax preference items such as certain types of: property depreciation; excess intangible drilling costs in connection with oil exploration; and tax-exempt interest on industrial development bonds.

The amount of income qualifying for the tax, which is known as the AMTI (alternative minimum taxable income) determines the applicable tax rate. If the AMTI, minus certain exemptions, is under $175,000 (or $87,500 for spouses filing separately), the tax rate is 26 percent. A 28 percent rate applies to incomes over these amounts.

Exemptions are reduced by 25 cents for each $1 of income subject to AMT that exceeds $112,500 for unmarried individuals and heads of households, $150,000 for married individuals filing joint returns and $75,000 for married individuals filing separate returns.

The AMT is also applied to corporations. This will be discussed later.

Transferring Assets or Property

In a sole proprietorship, special tax rules apply when property or assets are gifted or transferred at death. These rules are especially important when they involve succession in a family business. Quite often, the bulk of a sole proprietor's assets are tied up in his or her business, which he or she plans to pass on to a family member, either by gift during life or by will after death.

Property Transferred by Gift

When property is given gratuitously, the donor may be liable for gift taxes for amounts or property valued in excess of $10,000 per year to a family member (year 2000 figure subject to adjustment for inflation). The recipient (donee) pays no taxes on the gift at the time of transfer. However, ultimate tax consequences for the donee depend on the donor's basis in the property. As a rule, the donee's basis in the donated property is the same as the donor's basis, with some adjustments. This "carryover" basis, such as in property transferred from a father to a son, will be used to determine the taxable gain when the son eventually sells the property.

Here is a simplified example: The father buys a piece of property for $5,000. When he gives it to his son, the value is $7,000. The son's basis in the property is still $5,000, not $7,000. When the son eventually sells the property for $15,000, he is liable for tax on gain of $10,000.

Property Transferred at Death

The rules are different for property transferred at death. As a rule, the value at death is "stepped up" to the fair market value at the time of death. So, if the property in the above example were held by the father until his death, and at that time it was valued at $15,000, the son's basis would be $15,000. If he sold the property for that amount, there would be no taxable gain.

The Self-Employment Tax

Self-employed persons such as proprietors are subject to a *self-employment tax* in addition to the regular or alternative minimum income tax. This tax is payable by all self-employed individuals whose net earnings are $400 or more for each tax year.

In reality, this tax is a Social Security tax, applied to self-employment income. Payment of this tax entitles a self-employed taxpayer to the same Social Security benefits as an employed individual whose Social Security contribution is withheld and matched by the employer.

There is, however, a major difference: the self-employed individual must shoulder the entire Social Security tax, whereas employees pay only one half. To offset this disadvantage, the self-employed are able to deduct one half of the self-employment tax as a deductible business expense on Schedule C.

Taxation of Sole Proprietorships Summarized

The most important thing to keep in mind regarding sole proprietorships is that their personal and business income is taxed as one—as individuals at the individual rate. However, while the sole proprietorship is the simplest form of business, its tax situation can be fairly complex. At the same time, the opportunities for you to help the proprietorship save tax dollars and also meet its other needs are many.

PARTNERSHIPS

As a business entity, the partnership itself does not pay an income tax; instead, it merely files an information return. This return shows the distributive shares of the partners (i.e., the share that is allocated to each partner annually), who then are taxed individually under the individual income tax rules discussed above. Therefore, in general, partners are taxed similarly to sole proprietors on their share of partnership taxable income.

Every partnership required to file a return must furnish to every person who was a partner at any time during the partnership's taxable year a copy of such information shown on the return as may be required by regulation.

Miscellaneous and Administrative Partnership Tax Provisions

The tax law includes numerous provisions that govern the taxation of partners and partnerships. For example:

1. The law provides partners with rights to information and to participate in proceedings involving tax matters of other partners.

2. The law recognizes a partner's right to waive participation in audits and other tax matters at the partnership level.

3. Each partner's return must be consistent with the partnership return.

4. Windfall profit tax items (related to oil and gas exploration and development) are to be determined at the partnership level rather than the partner level.

5. The term "partner" is defined as a direct partner in the partnership and any other person whose income tax liability is determined in whole or in part by taking into account directly or indirectly the partnership items of the partnership.

Partnership Taxable Income

The partnership taxable income is found by taking gross profit or receipts and subtracting business deductions. The profits that remain are passed on to the individual partners in proportion to their interest. This channeling of business profits to partners is known as a partner's *distributive share*, and it is the distributive share that a partner must report on his or her individual tax return.

Partner's Distributive Share

A partner does not have to receive his or her distributive share for it to be income taxed—in fact, it's common for partnerships to retain profits for growth or investment—a partner is considered to receive *constructively* the amount of his or her share. If the partnership income is not in fact distributed, the partner may increase the adjusted basis of his or her partnership interest by the distributive share of partnership income. A partner's share of a charitable contribution will decrease his or her basis in the partnership, because such a contribution is nondeductible by the partnership. When an actual distribution is made, the partner's adjusted basis for his or her partnership interest is reduced again—but never below zero. Also, every time the partnership sustains a taxable loss, each partner will decrease the basis of the partnership interest by his or her distributive share of the loss.

Usually, all income and loss items are allocated equally among the partners. However, the partnership agreement may provide for other than a pro rata distribution of income and loss items. When providing for an unequal allocation under a partnership agreement, such an allocation may be disregarded if it does not have a "substantial economic effect," which means whether the allocation may actually affect the dollar amount of the partners' shares of the total partnership income or loss independently of tax consequences.

Finally, income and losses are allocable to a partner only for the portion of the partnership taxable year in which the partner is a member of the partnership.

Sale or Exchange of a Partnership Interest

If a partner transfers his or her partnership interest to another partner (not to the partnership itself) or sells the interest to an outsider, the original partner will have taxable income or loss equal to the difference between the sale price and his or her adjusted basis. This taxable income usually comes to the partner in the form of a capital gain because the sale is typically treated as the sale of a capital asset.

If the sale price of the partnership interest includes an amount attributable to unrealized accounts receivable (bills owed the partnership) or to a substantial appreciation in the value of the partnership inventory or goods, this amount will be treated as ordinary income. The IRS has defined "substantially in value" as a fair market value of 120 percent or more of the partnership's adjusted basis for the property.

Liquidation of a Partnership Interest

A partnership ends in one of two ways. It can be terminated by mutual consent of the partners or upon the death or retirement of one of the partners. Be aware that if one partner dies, the partnership automatically ends, unless a written agreement exists between the partners to the contrary. When the liquidation of partnership interests occurs between the partnership as an entity and a withdrawing partner, such as a retiree, payments to a retiring partner may be looked at in either of two ways: as a distributive share or guaranteed payment or as an exchange for the interest of the partner in partnership property.

If the payment is treated as a distributive share, two results arise. First, the amount received by the retiree will be taxed normally as ordinary income. Second, the distributive shares of the other partners will be reduced. (Remember, distributive shares decrease basis.)

If the payment is considered a "guaranteed payment," then the amount received by the retiree will be taxed to him or her as ordinary income and deducted by the
partnership. This is because "guaranteed payments" are considered to be made to those who are not members of the partnership and are determined without regard to partnership income.

If the payments are considered in exchange for the retiree's interest in partnership property, the retiree will treat the transaction as a sale, which will be taxed as ordinary income.

In some cases, the liquidation will be payments to a deceased partner's successor. Of course, the basis of these assets will be stepped up or stepped down to fair market value at the date of the partner's death (or alternate valuation date) according to the basis rules. Any income in respect of a decedent will have a carryover basis from the partnership to the recipient.

Partnership Buy-Sell Agreements

A *buy-sell agreement* can be made among the partners which provides for the purchase of a partner's share upon death, disability or retirement. Under the terms of a written buy-sell agreement, a partner's share will be purchased upon certain conditions. The purchase price, or formula to determine it, is contained in the agreement. These agreements are very often funded by life insurance.

As for tax consequences, because there is a stepped-up basis at death, there should be no income tax problems at death for the heirs selling the deceased partner's interest to either the surviving partners or the partnership.

■ CORPORATIONS

Unlike the sole proprietorship or the partnership, a corporation is itself a taxable entity and, as such, has its own gross income, deductions and tax rates.

A corporation is formed when incorporation papers are filed and registered with the state in which the corporation is headquartered. In a closely held corporation, assets are contributed by the owners, who receive proportionate shares in the business. In general, the owners or shareholders are also employees of the corporation and receive salaries. The corporation is taxed at the corporate income tax rate, and the salaries are taxed at the individual rate. An exception is the "Subchapter S" corporation (so named because of the section of the tax code that describes it). In an S corporation, income to the corporation passes through to the shareholders, where it is taxed at the individual rate (See Ill. 2.4).

ILL. 2.3 ■ *Partnership Tax Computation*

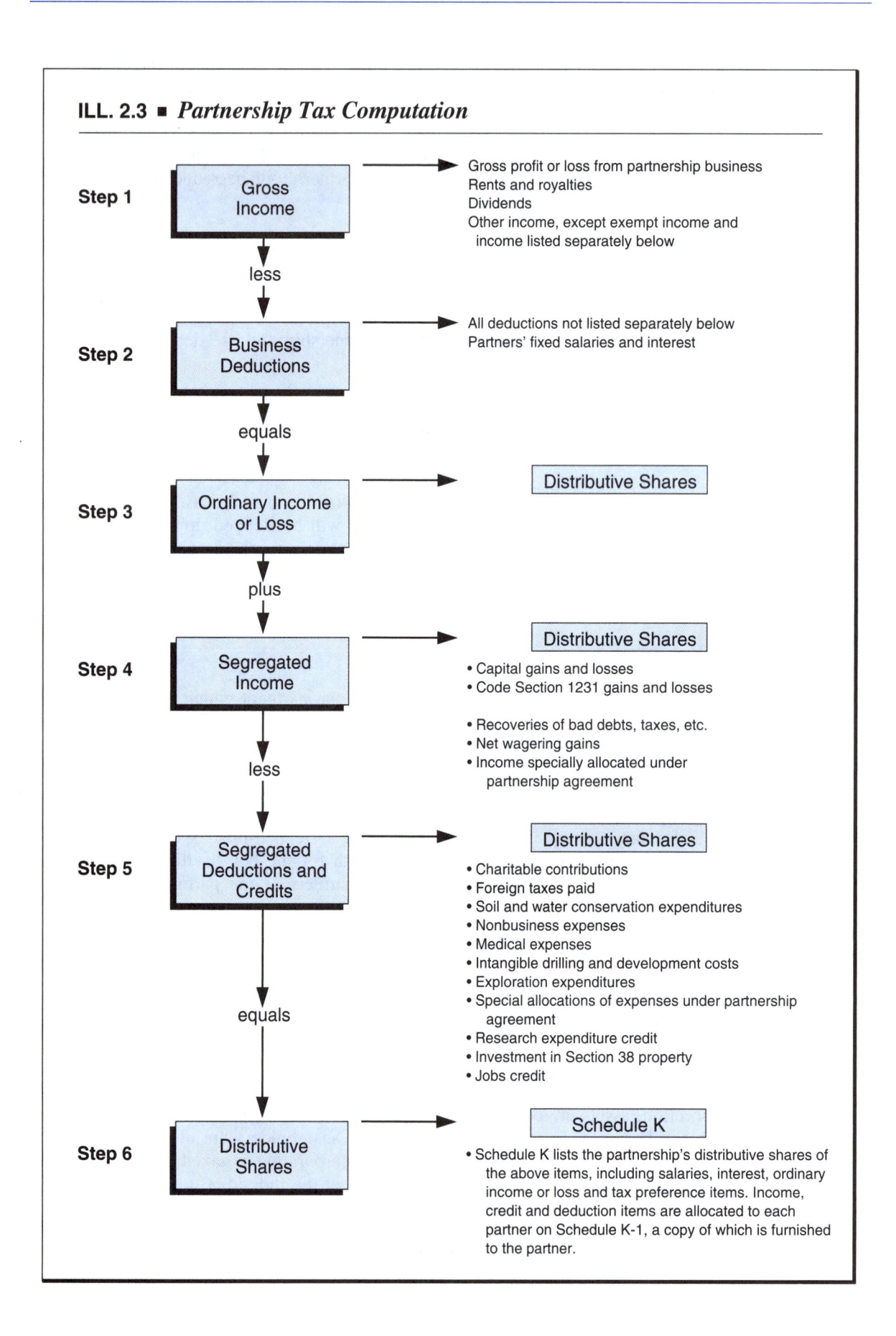

Step 1: Gross Income
- Gross profit or loss from partnership business
- Rents and royalties
- Dividends
- Other income, except exempt income and income listed separately below

less

Step 2: Business Deductions
- All deductions not listed separately below
- Partners' fixed salaries and interest

equals

Step 3: Ordinary Income or Loss → Distributive Shares

plus

Step 4: Segregated Income → Distributive Shares
- Capital gains and losses
- Code Section 1231 gains and losses
- Recoveries of bad debts, taxes, etc.
- Net wagering gains
- Income specially allocated under partnership agreement

less

Step 5: Segregated Deductions and Credits → Distributive Shares
- Charitable contributions
- Foreign taxes paid
- Soil and water conservation expenditures
- Nonbusiness expenses
- Medical expenses
- Intangible drilling and development costs
- Exploration expenditures
- Special allocations of expenses under partnership agreement
- Research expenditure credit
- Investment in Section 38 property
- Jobs credit

equals

Step 6: Distributive Shares → Schedule K
- Schedule K lists the partnership's distributive shares of the above items, including salaries, interest, ordinary income or loss and tax preference items. Income, credit and deduction items are allocated to each partner on Schedule K-1, a copy of which is furnished to the partner.

ILL. 2.4 ▪ *2000 Corporate Federal Income Tax Rates vs. Individual Rates*

Corporate

If taxable income is | | **Then tax is** | |

More than	But not more than	This	Plus this%	Of amount more than
$ 0	$ 50,000	$ 0	15%	$ 0
50,000	75,000	7,500	25%	50,000
75,000	100,000	13,750	34%	75,000
100,000	335,000	22,250	39%	100,000
335,000	10,000,000	113,900	34%	335,000
10,000,000	15,000,000	3,400,000	35%	10,000,000
15,000,000	18,333,333	5,150,000	38%	15,000,000
18,333,333	infinity	6,416,667	35%	18,333,333

Married, Filing Jointly

If taxable income is | | **Then tax is** | |

More than	But not more than	This	Plus this %	Of amount more than
$ 0	$ 43,850	$ 0	15%	$ 0
43,850	105,950	5,850	28%	39,000
105,950	161,450	21,320	31%	94,250
161,450	288,350	36,618	36%	143,600
288,350	Unlimited	77,263	39.6%	256,500

Corporate Income and Deductions

A corporation's gross income consists of the corporation's gross receipts or profits from the sale of its products or services. The income also includes any interest, dividends, rents, royalties and gains on sales or exchanges that the corporation receives.

A corporation calculates its taxable income in much the same way as an individual does. From its gross income, it subtracts its allowable deductions—business expenses (including salaries, rents, operating expenses, charitable contributions, qualified plan contributions, taxes, depreciation, interest, etc.) plus certain "special" deductions not available to individual taxpayers. For example, a corporation may be entitled to deduct a certain percentage of dividends it receives.

Unlike an individual taxpayer, a corporation has no standard deduction. The corporation's taxable income is reached by taking gross income and subtracting all deductions to reach the taxable income.

Corporate Tax Rates

In the past, corporations were taxed at a substantially lower tax rate than individuals. For this reason, incorporation was often an easy choice for business owners. Under current law, however, the rates are comparable at many income levels.

Alternative Minimum Tax

The *alternative minimum tax* (AMT), previously discussed in relation to individuals, is also applied in the corporate area. Here also, the objective is to see that corporations, through large deductions, do not evade paying their share of income taxes. The tax preference items referred to in connection with individual taxpayers also apply in the case of corporations in much the same way. There is also a basic exemption applied for businesses; however, this exemption is phased out as corporate income increases.

The corporate tax preference items are somewhat more complicated than those applied to individuals although few of these items will apply with smaller, closely held corporations. The insurance professional should be aware, however, of how the AMT in general affects the proceeds of key-person life insurance. In some cases, a portion of such proceeds will fall under AMT regulations.

In the case of corporate-owned life insurance, the inside buildup in such contracts, normally tax-free to individuals, must be included in the corporation's general earnings each year and thus enters into the computation for the AMT. There is a deduction allowed for the portion of the premium that is attributable to life insurance protection. When a death benefit is received by the corporation, the difference between the amount received as death proceeds and the cost basis for the contract is includable for AMT purposes. When a contract is surrendered in exchange for the cash value, amounts in excess of the cost basis are also includable for calculating the AMT.

Deductions

Corporations, like individuals, can deduct all ordinary and necessary expenses paid or incurred during the taxable year in carrying out their trade or business. To qualify for a deduction, an expense must meet these four tests:

1. it must be connected with the corporate taxpayer's trade or business;

2. it must be an "ordinary and necessary" expense;

3. it must be paid or incurred during the taxable year for which the deduction is claimed; and

ILL. 2.5 ■ *Corporate Tax Computation*

Step 1: Gross Income

Gross profit or loss includes:
- Receipts from sales
- Interest earned
- Rents received
- Gains from sales or exchanges of securities

less

Step 2: Business Deductions

Business expenses include:
- Interest paid
- Taxes paid
- Depreciation
- Salaries, bonuses, commissions paid
- Rents paid
- Research and development costs
- Qualified plan contributions
- Casualty losses
- 70% of corporate dividends *received* (80% where corporate recipient owns at least 20% but less than 80% of distributing corporate stocks)

equals

Step 3: Taxable Income

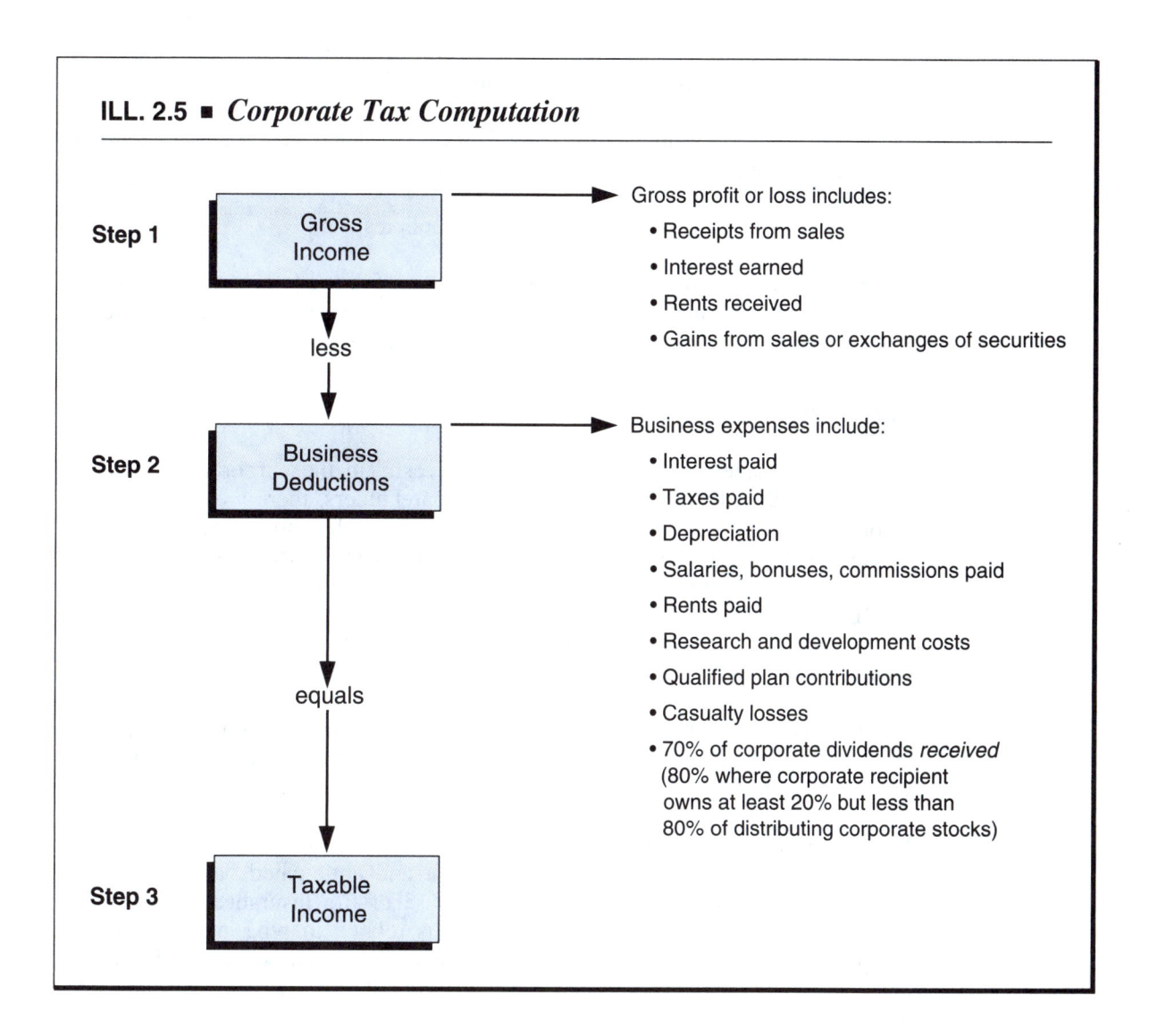

4. it must benefit the corporation making the deduction claim. (A corporation's payment of its stockholders' personal expenses is not deductible.)

Following are several deductions by category:

- the costs of organizing a corporation, expenses of temporary directors, organizational meetings, fees paid to a state for incorporation, accounting expenses and legal services;

- ordinary and necessary business expenses, paid or accrued, for personal services rendered to the corporation, such as wages, salaries, commissions, bonuses, management expenses, supplies, incidental repairs, advertising, promotion and certain rentals;

- interest paid or accrued on indebtedness;

- depreciation, amortization and depletion of business property that has a useful life of more than one year;

- various taxes imposed by federal, state and local governments incurred in the ordinary course of trade or business;

- premiums paid on certain insurance policies; and

- ordinary and necessary business expenses incurred for traveling away from home; meals and entertainment expenses, even though "directly related" to business purposes, are not fully deductible.

Accumulated Earnings Tax

To prevent business owners from "stashing cash" in the corporation, thereby avoiding taxable distributions of profits to shareholders, there are limits on the amount of money that may be retained. Unless it can be shown that this money is reasonably required for current or anticipated business needs, amounts above certain levels are subject to the accumulated earnings tax. As a general rule, the first $250,000 in retained earnings is allowed. For personal service corporations that do not typically require large amounts of capital, the accumulated earnings credit is $150,000.

The accumulated earnings tax at a rate of 39.6 percent is in addition to regular corporate income tax and applies only to excess earnings accumulated by regular, or C, corporations. This tax does *not* apply to S corporations.

When determining the amount of income subject to the tax, a credit is allowed for accumulations to meet reasonable current and anticipated business needs. For example, income retained for the purchase of life insurance, if the life insurance serves a valid business need and is related in type and amount to that need, will not be taxed. Some cases where the purchase of life insurance are considered a reasonable business need and not subject to this penalty tax are:

1. The purchase of life insurance to compensate the corporation for the loss of a key executive's service through early death is a reasonable business need. Earnings used for key-executive life insurance are a reasonable business need.

2. The accumulation of earnings to meet the corporation's obligations incurred under a deferred compensation agreement is also considered a reasonable business need.

3. The accumulation of earnings to fund a stock redemption may constitute an accumulation for a "reasonable need of the business" for purposes of promoting corporate harmony and efficiency of management or enabling a corporation to continue its accustomed practices or policies. For example, many state laws require a corporation to purchase the stock of a deceased or disqualified professional. An accumulation to fund such redemption, particularly if funded by life insurance, should be immune from the accumulated earnings tax.

Other valid business purposes for accumulated earnings include the following:

- expansion of business or replacement of a plant;
- acquisition of a business through the purchase of stock or assets;
- retirement of business debt;
- provision of necessary working capital; and
- provision of loans or investments to suppliers or customers in order to maintain the business of the corporation.

■ SUMMARY

This chapter has covered in general the tax treatment applicable to sole proprietorships, partnerships and corporations. As mentioned at the beginning of the chapter, specific income tax treatment of certain business insurance plans will be discussed in later chapters.

■ CHAPTER 2 QUESTIONS FOR REVIEW

1. When working with business owners, one should

    A. offer tax and legal advice on tax matters.
    B. acquire a detailed, in-depth knowledge of the tax code, so you can advise the client's attorney and accountant.
    C. acquire at least a working knowledge of the tax code.
    D. stay away from such topics completely.

2. The alternative minimum tax applies primarily to

    A. tax preference items.
    B. salaries and wages.
    C. accumulated earnings.
    D. all of the above

3. For Social Security, the sole proprietor

    A. does not pay into the system.
    B. contributes half as much as salaried employees.
    C. contributes the same amount as salaried employees.
    D. pays twice the amount of salaried employees.

4. A partnership is taxed

    A. as a separate legal entity.
    B. with the individual partners taxed under a "partnership taxation" rate.
    C. with the partners taxed as individuals according to their proportionate share of partnership income.
    D. the same as a corporation.

5. Under the law, corporations are discouraged from retaining excessive earnings by use of

    A. accumulated earnings tax.
    B. capital gains tax.
    C. alternative minimum tax.
    D. None of the above

3
Analyzing Financial Statements

Understanding business financial statements is essential if the insurance professional is to meet the real insurance needs of a business and its owners. Starting from the threshold of "how to obtain" financial statements, this chapter explains the meaning of the balance sheet, income statement and statement of cash flows. A special look is taken at the question of accounting for insurance cash values, policy loans and premiums. Finally, the chapter covers interpretation of financial data in terms of how financial statements can reveal insurance needs and provide the source for premium dollars.

The more information the insurance professional can obtain about a business prospect, the greater his or her chances of turning the prospect into a client. One of the most overlooked sources of information in the selling of business insurance is a company's financial statements.

A financial statement presents a picture of the company's earnings, assets and liabilities. It may be one or two pages in length or run dozens of pages, depending on the form, size and complexity of the business. Small, closely held companies create financial statements to obtain bank loans and venture capital, as well as to track their own performance. Large, publicly traded corporations provide financial statements in the form of annual reports to shareholders.

The ability to read and analyze a company's financial statement can give you keen insight into the business's financial condition—and insurance needs. But more than that, it enables you to demonstrate your professionalism and knowledge, which enhances your credibility and your prospect's confidence in your abilities.

ILL. 3.1 ■ *Three Financial Statements*

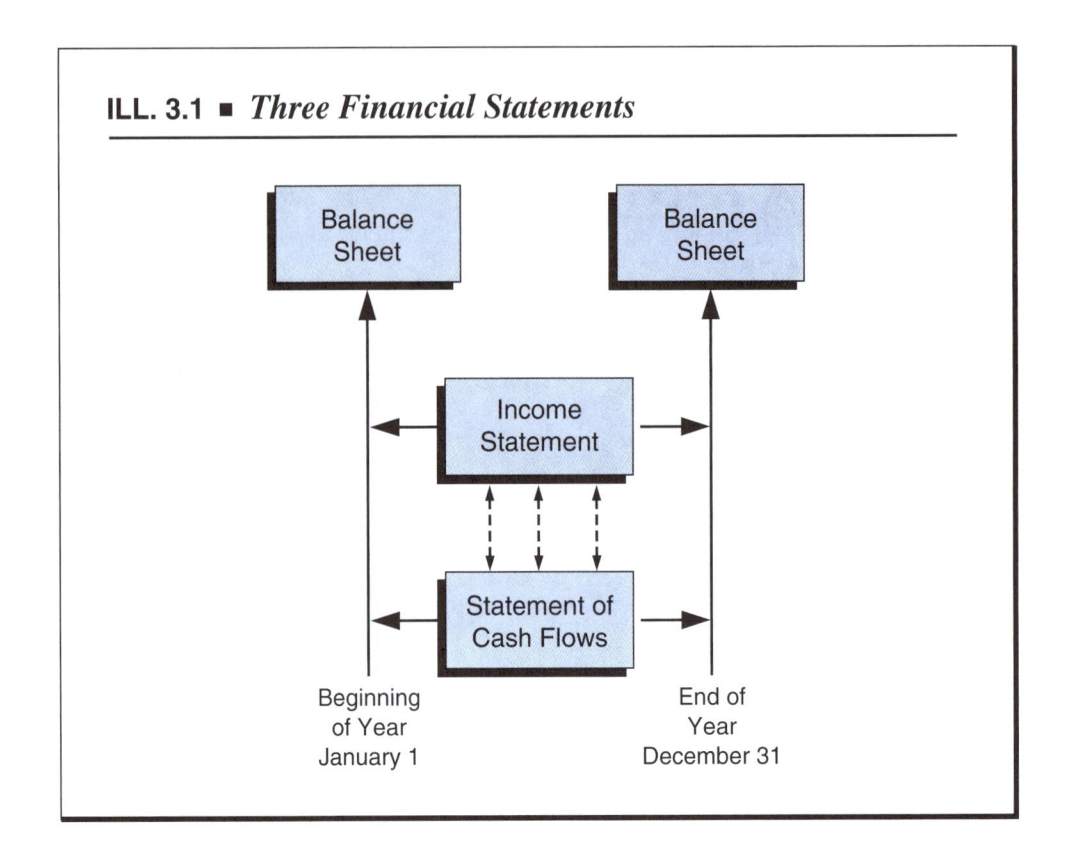

```
      Balance                    Balance
       Sheet                      Sheet
         ▲                          ▲
         │                          │
         │      Income              │
         ◄──── Statement ────►
                  ▲
                  │
         ◄──── Statement of ────►
                Cash Flows

   Beginning                    End of
    of Year                      Year
   January 1                  December 31
```

■ OBTAINING FINANCIAL STATEMENTS

When dealing with publicly held corporations, the best way to obtain a financial statement is to request a copy of the most recent annual statement. Outside sources include such services as *Dun & Bradstreet Reports,* Industry Mercantile Agencies, and financial publishers such as "Moody's Investors Service," "Fitch Industrial Stock Bulletins" and "Standard Corporation Records." It is a good idea to obtain from three to five years of past statements to help determine business growth and progress. There may have been unusual circumstances causing a highly profitable or substantially unprofitable year; having several years of statements will give you a better idea of the company's financial situation.

If your prospect is a closely held corporation or unincorporated business, public-record information may not be available. The only source is the business itself. The best approach is a direct one. In an initial fact-finding interview, request the financial statement, explaining that you need it to accurately assess the company's current situation and needs.

Keep in mind, however, that tact is required. After all, you are asking the prospect to share confidential financial information.

■ TYPES OF FINANCIAL STATEMENTS

There are three major types of financial statements, each serving a specific purpose. These are *the balance sheet, the income statement* and *the statement of cash flows*. The balance sheet is like a snapshot of the company's finances at a specific moment in time, such as at the beginning or end of a year. In contrast, income statements and statements of cash flows measure financial activity over a specific period of time.

■ BALANCE SHEET

The balance sheet, or statement of financial position, shows the financial condition of a business as of a particular date, usually the end of the business's fiscal year. A balance sheet for the hypothetical S&T Corporation is depicted in Ill. 3.2. Note that it is divided into two main sections: "Assets," which lists all the business's properties, and "Liabilities and Shareholders' Equity," which lists the sources from which these properties were obtained.

Assets

Assets are the properties owned by the business that are tangible and can be given a monetary value.

Valuation of Assets

Most business assets are listed on a balance sheet at their acquisition cost. One notable exception to this rule is a company's inventory or stock-in-trade, which generally is stated at the lower of its acquisition cost or market value. In addition to acquisition cost and market value, a third way to value assets is by their replacement cost.

There is considerable debate among concerned professionals over the merit of valuing assets at their acquisition cost, rather than at their replacement cost or market value. Convincing arguments have been made on each side. The two reasons given most often in support of acquisition cost evaluation are:

1. the method prevents manipulation or unrealistic evaluation by management; and

2. the method is consistent with conservatism, a basic accounting concept holding that accounts generally should record assets at their lower, conservative values.

Whether these two reasons justify the use of the acquisition cost method over the replacement cost method or the market value method is irrelevant for our purposes. However, it is important to realize that there are alternative valuation methods and that the acquisition cost valuation method can cause the actual value of a business to be substantially understated.

Grouping of Assets

Assets are grouped on the balance sheet according to their liquidity. The more liquid the asset, the higher its position on the balance sheet. Assets basically can be broken down into three categories: *current, fixed* and *other*.

Current Assets. *Current assets* are assets that are expected to return to cash, or to be sold or consumed within one year after completion of the company's operating cycle. Current assets can be divided into "quick" current assets and "regular" current assets.

Quick current assets are the most liquid of all business assets and include:

- cash available for immediate disbursement, without restriction;

- investments, which are not only readily marketable but also purchased for a short term of one year or less;

- accounts receivable, which are simply amounts owed to the business by its customers or clients; and

- notes receivable, which are basically the same as accounts receivable except that the amount owed is acknowledged by a note or other written instrument.

Regular current assets consist of:

- inventories, which include goods ready for sale, goods in production, raw materials and supplies.

- prepaid expenses or deferred charges, which are items paid in advance of the time in which the business charges them off as expenses. (The status of these items generally expires within a short period of time.)

Fixed Assets. *Fixed assets* are long-lived tangible and intangible assets used in production of other goods and services. Fixed *tangible* assets include land, buildings, equipment, furniture, fixtures and natural resources. Fixed *intangible* assets include such things as purchased goodwill, patents, copyrights, trademarks, franchises and the like.

Because most fixed assets wear out or depreciate, a part of their cost should be written off for as long as they are used as an expense against each period's income. The accumulated depreciation account simply represents the total depreciation subtracted to date from a fixed asset.

Other Assets. Other assets are items that do not fit any of the previously discussed categories. Generally, such items fall under one of the following two headings:

1. investments in another company, generally in the form of securities; or

2. intangible assets, including long-lived items such as the cash value of business life insurance.

ILL 3.2 ▪ *Balance Sheet S&T Corporation*

December 31, 20___

ASSETS

Current assets		$13,521	
Cash		4,386	
Marketable securities		31,625	
Accounts receivable		7,000	
Inventories		36,810	
Prepaid rent		2,800	
Prepaid insurance (fire)		2,600	
Total Current Assets			$ 98,742
Fixed assets			
Land		82,750	
Buildings	$250,000		
Less accumulated depreciation	30,000	220,000	
Machinery and equipment	$ 90,000		
Less accumulated depreciation	12,000	78,000	
Total Fixed Assets			$380,750
Other assets			
Licenses		50,000	
Purchased goodwill		28,000	
Total Other Assets		$ 78,000	
TOTAL ASSETS			$557,492

LIABILITIES AND SHAREHOLDERS' EQUITY

Current liabilities			
Accounts payable		$ 34,085	
Notes payable		5,000	
Accrued salaries and wages		8,200	
Dividends payable		15,000	
Total Current Liabilities			$ 62,285
Fixed liabilities			
Mortgage		163,900	
Bonds		45,000	
Total Fixed Liabilities			$208,900
Shareholders' equity			
Cumulative 6% preferred stock ($100 par)		65,000	
Common stock	$150,000		
Less treasury stock	25,000	125,000	
Additional paid-in capital		20,000	
Retained earnings		76,307	
Total Shareholders' Equity			$286,307
TOTAL LIABILITIES AND SHAREHOLDERS' EQUITY			$557,492

Liabilities

Liabilities constitute a firm's obligations to outsiders. These obligations can be the firm's debts or promises to provide goods or services. Liabilities are set off against a business's assets.

Valuation and Grouping of Liabilities

Liabilities are valued on the balance sheet at the current dollar amount *owed*, plus accumulated interest. The more liquid the liability, the higher its position on the liability section of the balance sheet. Liabilities can be categorized as *current* or *long term*.

Current Liabilities. *Current liabilities* are expected to be satisfied within one operating cycle of the business (paid in one year or less). They include the following:

- accounts payable, which are debts owed to creditors and vendors;

- notes payable, which are debts acknowledged by a note or some other written instrument;

- accrued expenses such as salaries and wages;

- deferred income or credits, which are amounts received by the company in advance of the time they are earned; and

- miscellaneous current liabilities, including dividends payable and estimated tax liabilities.

Long-Term Liabilities. *Long-term liabilities* are usually business obligations or debts that fall due more than a year after the balance sheet date. These include such items as mortgages, bonds, long-term loans and purchase contracts.

Owner's Equity or Capital

The difference between the company's assets and liabilities is equal to the owner's *equity* or *capital*. This difference includes not only what the owners originally invested, but also the subsequent earnings that have been left in the business. Terminology in this area differs depending on whether the business is incorporated.

Corporations

The owner's equity section of the balance sheet in a corporation is called the *shareholder's equity*. There are two main elements of shareholder's equity: paid-in or contributed capital, and retained earnings.

Paid-in Capital. *Paid-in capital* is the owner's total direct investment in the business. Paid-in capital can be divided into capital stock—preferred or common—and additional or other paid-in capital.

1. *Preferred stock* is the type of stock that pays a stated dividend and has priority over common stock in regard to assets at liquidation, receipt of dividends and other rights described on the balance sheet proper or in a footnote. If preferred stock is recorded on the balance sheet, then its par or face value, the dividend rate, and whether the stock is cumulative or noncumulative, convertible or nonconvertible, voting or nonvoting, and participating or nonparticipating, will be recorded also.

2. *Common stock* is representative of the residual ownership in the issuing corporation. Holders of common stock receive any corporate earnings and assets left after all prior claims and obligations of the corporation have been satisfied. Consequently, common stockholders bear the primary risk in the corporation. The balance sheet usually will list:

   – number of authorized shares and number issued;

   – number of shares and total value of treasury stock;

   – number of shares and total value of outstanding common stock; and

   – the par value, if any, of each share of common stock.

3. *Additional paid-in capital* or unearned income results from transactions such as sale of stock at a price greater than its par or stated value; a gift of assets or a donation of stock by stockholders; a profit from the purchase or sale of treasury stock; or recapitalization.

Retained Earnings or Earned Surplus. Basically, whatever earnings are not paid out as dividends go into the *retained earnings* or *earned surplus account* each year. These are the *cumulative* earnings retained in the business from its beginning to the present date. Sometimes these earnings are broken down to show the latest addition. A distinction is made between retained earnings and earnings accumulated beyond the reasonable needs of the business. Although the *term retained* earnings is properly the broader accounting category, the Internal Revenue Service has structured the Code to make it undesirable for a corporation to allow the retained earnings account to be larger than the amount necessary for legitimate business purposes.

Unincorporated Businesses

With regard to owner's equity, when partnerships or proprietorships are involved, the owner's or partner's original investment and subsequent retained earnings are not separated on the balance sheet. Thus, the owner's equity most often is indicated merely by the owner's or partner's name and the amount of his or her capital account.

Sometimes, a partnership or proprietorship might use a "draw account," which would be depicted on this part of the sheet. This account records amounts withdrawn from the business by the partner or owner. It is basically a simple subtraction from the partner's or owner's gross capital account to arrive at the net capital account.

INCOME STATEMENT

The *income* or *profit and loss statement* is an itemized statement of the income and expenses of an enterprise for a stated period of time. The period of time can be as short as one week or one month and as long as one year, depending on the needs of the business. Even though the income statement's uses are the same as a balance sheet's, its emphasis is different. The income statement summarizes the financial *performance* of a firm rather than its financial position or condition.

Although each company's income statement differs in format, a statement usually contains the following:

INCOME STATEMENT
THE ABC COMPANY, INC.
Year Ended December 31, 20__

INCOME

Sales and revenue	$1,475,890
Other income	25,600
Total income	$1,501,490

EXPENSES

Costs of goods sold	$ 568,335
Depreciation	42,500
Selling expenses	223,762
General and administrative expenses	188,496
Research and development	175,000
Interest	45,000
Other	12,000
Federal taxes (estimated)	129,623
Total Expenses	$1,384,716

DISCONTINUED OPERATIONS

Net gain from sale of discontinued segment	$ 22,000
TOTAL NET INCOME	$ 138,774

Income from Continuing Operations

The first item on an income statement is the company's income or source of revenue. The source of revenue can be either operating or nonoperating. Operating income may be labeled as "Sales," "Revenues" or "Fees," and includes all revenue the business has generated in the last accounting period from its ordinary operation. The next figure listed would be "Other Income" or "Nonoperating Income," which is revenue generated by means other than day-to-day operations.

Expenses from Continuing Operations

The next item on the income statement is the company's expenses. The following are the most common expenses.

Cost of Goods Sold

This expense item totals the costs a business incurs in acquiring, manufacturing and/or converting goods or products it has sold. Often this item will appear in a footnote to the income statement. The format of the schedule will vary depending on whether the firm is a manufacturing or nonmanufacturing concern.

Manufacturing Concern. A manufacturer's cost of goods sold normally includes two elements: an *acquisition cost* and a *conversion cost*.

1. The acquisition cost is simply the purchase price for raw materials plus any freight and shipping charges.

2. The conversion cost includes any direct labor, materials and manufacturing overhead that must be added to the raw materials to make finished goods.

The computation of a manufacturer's cost of goods sold is as follows:

Step 1: Work in process at start of period
    + Raw materials used during period
    + Labor and manufacturing overhead costs for period
    − Work in process at end of period
       Cost of goods manufactured

Step 2: Finished goods inventory at beginning of period
    + Cost of goods manufactured
    + Finished goods inventory at end of period
       Cost of goods sold

Nonmanufacturing Concern. A nonmanufacturing concern's cost of goods sold consists generally of acquisition costs, because a nonmanufacturing company usually does not convert raw materials into finished goods. Its inventory can be classified in one of two ways, depending on whether the company is a service organization or a merchandising organization.

1. Service companies provide basically intangible services rather than tangible goods, so they generally do not report a cost of goods sold on their income statements.

2. Merchandising companies purchase tangible finished goods and offer them for resale, so they usually have few conversion costs, if any. Then, the computation of the cost of goods sold is much simpler.

      Inventory at start of period
   + Net purchases made during period
   − Inventory at end of period
      Cost of goods sold

Depreciation. *Depreciation* is defined as the fraction of a fixed asset's total cost that has been consumed by a business during an accounting period. Assets used for business purposes (except land) can be depreciated over their useful life. The property is deemed to have no value at the end of the depreciation period.

The IRS allows several methods of depreciation. For instance, under the rules of the Modified Accelerated Cost Recovery System (MACRS), automobiles used for business are depreciated, with a maximum deduction for cars placed in service in the year 2000 of $3,060 in the first year, $4,900 in the second year, $2,950 in the third year and $1,775 in each succeeding year of the recovery period. Most machinery and equipment is depreciated over seven years. Computers, however, remain five-year property. Residential rental property is depreciated over 27.5 years and commercial real estate is depreciated over 39 years.

Other Expenses

Selling expenses are the costs of marketing a finished product or service: salaries, commissions, fees, reimbursed and direct sales expenses, advertising and promo-tional costs and any other expenses of the marketing department are included.

General and administrative expenses are operating expenses such as salaries and bonuses of nonsales personnel, rent, equipment purchases, utilities, office supplies and any other costs applicable to the general office function.

Research and development (R&D) expenses used to be lumped with general and administrative expenses, but now companies who give priority to R&D tend to list them separately.

Interest expenses include interest paid out or accrued on loans, notes and any other obligations.

Income tax liability will appear only on a corporation's (non–S corporation) income statement. In partnerships and proprietorships, the net income before taxes is transferred to the partners' or proprietor's individual tax return and charged as personal income.

Other expenses not includable elsewhere can be listed under the catch-all heading—other expenses.

Discontinued Operations

This item arises when the closing down or discontinuation of a company division or other distinct segment results in a gain or loss. The transaction must involve a whole business unit, not just an individual fixed asset or product.

ILL. 3.3 ■ XYZ Company Statement of Cash Flows
(For 12 months at year's end)

Cash flow from operating activities:

Cash received from customers	$7,549*
Cash paid to suppliers and employees	−6,601
Interest paid	0
Interest received	39
Bank fees	− 21
Income taxes paid	0
Other trading income	209
Other trading expense	− 4
Net cash from operating activities	$1,171

Cash flow from investing activities:

Proceeds from sale of equipment	
Cash purchases of equipment	$ 104
Proceeds from note receivable	− 150
Net cash from investing activities	100
	$ 54

Cash flow from financing activities:

Repayment of Debt-Bank	$ 0
Repayment of Debt-Finance Companies	0
Net cash from financing activities	0
Net Inc. in Cash and Equivalents	$1,225
Cash & Equivalents at end of previous year	727
Cash & Equivalents at end of current year	$1,952

*000 omitted.

Total Net Income (or Loss)

Total net income (or loss)—the *bottom line*—appears on the income statement after all revenues and expenses have been reported—with adjustments made for taxes, dividends, discontinued operations, extraordinary items and so on.

■ STATEMENT OF CASH FLOWS

The third type of financial report is the *statement of cash flows*. It reports the sources and uses of cash for a specific time period. Cash flow is measured in three areas as follows:

cash relating to operations
+ or −
cash relating to investing activities
+ or −
cash relating to financing activities

The result represents the net increase or decrease in cash.

Operating Activities

Operating activities include all transactions and other events that are the result of delivering or producing goods for sale and providing services.

Cash inflows from operating activities include cash receipts from the sale of goods or services and from interest and dividend income. Cash outflows for operating activities include cash payments for acquisitions of inventory, wages and benefits to employees and government taxing bodies, and interest to lending institutions and various other suppliers.

Investing Activities

Investing activities include lending money and collecting on the loans, acquiring and selling securities, and acquiring and selling productive assets such as land and equipment.

Cash inflows from investing activities include principal repayments from borrowers, proceeds from sales of loans, and receipts from sales of assets such as securities or machinery and equipment. Cash outflows for investing activities include loans made, loans purchased, and payments to acquire assets such as securities or plant, property and equipment.

Financing Activities

Financing activities include obtaining resources from owners, providing owners with a return on (of) their investment, obtaining resources from creditors and repaying amounts borrowed. Interest on borrowings, however, is an operating activity.

Cash inflows from financing activities include proceeds from the issuance of equity securities and from long- and short-term borrowings. Cash outflows for financing activities include payment of dividends, cash paid to reacquire the company's stock and repayment of amounts borrowed. Illustration 3.3 provides an example of a statement of cash flows.

ACCOUNTING FOR INSURANCE CASH VALUES, POLICY LOANS AND PREMIUMS

Insurance cash value increases, policy loans and premium payments are accounted for on financial statements by using one of several methods. For our purposes, we will focus on the most commonly used, or conventional, method. Under this method of accounting for policy values, loans and premiums, it is assumed that the business surrenders the policy at the end of the year.

Cash Value

Controversy has arisen over where to put the cash value of a policy on the balance sheet. The most widely recognized accounting practice today is to place the cash value under *Other Assets* or *Miscellaneous Assets*. The value itself is most easily figured by asking the insurance company for the cash value as of a certain date.

Policy Loans

When a bank loans money against the security of a life insurance policy, the note to the bank should be shown on the balance sheet as either a current or long-term liability, depending on the maturity date.

When the policy loan is from the insurance company, accounting practices vary. Some accountants treat it as a decrease in the equity of the policy rather than a liability, and the balance sheet shows only the excess of the cash value over the amount of the loan. Other accountants treat this loan in the same way as the loan from the bank—as a liability with the cash value being undisturbed.

Premium Payments

The accounting relative to the payment of life insurance premiums requires a recognition of expense *and* investment elements. The net premiums (gross premium minus any dividend) is an expenditure and reduces cash by this amount. Conversely, increases in policy cash values enhance the asset value of the business. The excess of premium paid over the increase in cash value is the actual insurance expense.

Of course, premiums paid for permanent individual life insurance generally are not income tax-deductible by the employer or the employee. Exceptions fall primarily in the qualified plan area, where life insurance is included as all or part of the funding vehicle for a qualified employee benefit plan. The annual premium of term insurance is simply an expense of the period. If the premiums are paid in advance, then the balance sheet would show this as an asset.

■ INTERPRETING FINANCIAL DATA

Financial statements present the data of a business, but such data must be interpreted to be meaningful to you. Analysis and comparisons to similar companies will point out the problem areas of a business. Analysis and comparison also will indicate the presence or absence of possible insurance needs. The interpretation of financial data is not a science; however, certain procedures make the task more precise.

Prior-Period Comparisons

Companies often release financial statements containing not only the current period's data, but also data of one or more previous accounting periods. Information about past performance helps reveal a company's track record and trends over time, often creating a more accurate picture of its stability and strength.

Intercompany Comparisons

This method compares the financial data of similar companies for the same time period. To be more accurate, dollar amounts should be changed to percentages.

Ratios

Analyzing certain ratios within the company, such as its liquidity, activity, leverage and profitability, are also helpful in analyzing financial statements.

Liquidity Ratios

Liquidity is defined as a company's ability to meet its current or maturing obligations.

1. *Current ratio.* This is the most traditional liquidity measurement and tends to be the most imprecise. The current ratio is found by dividing current assets by current liabilities. This results in an indication of a company's liquidity and the safety margin built up by management as a provision for unexpected demands on the firm's funds. Traditionally, a 2:1 ratio was satisfactory. Today, less emphasis is placed on a 2:1 ratio and more is given to needs of a specific business. Dun & Bradstreet publishes *Key Business Ratios* for certain industries, providing a tool for comparison. Although these ratios are not magic numbers, they do give you some idea of an average ratio.

2. *The Acid Test.* Some financial analysts, arguing that the current ratio is too imprecise, eliminate inventories, prepaid expenses and any other non-cash items from current assets and compare the remainder, "quick assets," to current liabilities. Traditionally, a 1:1 ratio was used. Today, most analysts use the acid test to compare with past accounting periods or similar industries.

Activity Ratios

Activity ratios determine how effectively a company uses the resources available to it. All activity ratios relate sales to various asset accounts except for the inventory turnover ratio.

Inventory Turnover Ratio. The *inventory turnover ratio* measures how many times in one accounting period a company is able to complete the cycle of inventory to sales to cash to inventory. It is computed by dividing the cost of goods sold by the total inventory. A note of caution: Dun & Bradstreet uses net sales instead of cost of goods sold; however, because inventory usually is carried at cost, this practice is not recommended except for industry comparison purposes.

Receivables Turnover Ratio. The *receivables turnover ratio* measures the efficiency or inefficiency of a firm's collection procedure. It is computed by dividing net sales by net receivables. Companies who do a great deal of their business on credit generally will have a lower turnover of receivables than those with a more restrictive credit policy.

Leverage Ratios

Leverage ratios indicate a company's ability to meet its long-term liabilities by measuring the debt/equity mix of its financing. A highly leveraged firm relies primarily on outside financing. A low-leveraged firm uses funds generated internally, either from operations or from a new stock issue.

Debt to Total Assets. The firm's total debt is divided by its total assets. The higher the ratio, the more leveraged a company is. Another debt ratio divides the firm's equity capital by its debt capital, with basically the same interpretive results as the other debt ratio.

Times Interest Earned. This ratio acts as a measure of how far earnings can decline before the company's ability to pay interest charges on its long-term liabilities becomes impaired. It is calculated by dividing a company's earnings before interest and taxes by its interest charges. The higher the ratio, the more solvent and less leveraged the company is. One drawback is that this ratio equates income and cash.

Profitability Ratios

Profitability ratios are concerned primarily with a firm's overall profitability, rather than one specific aspect of its operations. Two important profitability ratios measure the return on sales and investment.

Return on Sales. This ratio, also known as the profit margin, is determined by dividing a firm's net income after taxes by its sales. This ratio should be used in conjunction with return on investment.

Return on Investment. This measurement can be defined in at least three different ways:

1. *Total assets.* Return on investment can be said to equal the return on a firm's assets and is calculated by dividing the sum of a firm's net income plus interest after taxes by its total assets.

2. *Invested capital.* On the other hand, investment can be defined as a company's debt and equity. It is calculated by using the same numerator in (1) and dividing it by the sum of the firm's long-term liabilities and stockholders' equity.

3. *Stockholders' equity.* Return on investment can equal a company's net income divided by the stockholders' equity.

INSURANCE NEEDS AS REVEALED IN FINANCIAL STATEMENTS

The primary objective of this chapter is to demonstrate how financial statements might disclose the presence or the absence of various business life insurance needs. There are several indicators of need.

Funding Buy-Sell Agreements

A balance sheet often will disclose how a company's present buy-sell agreement is funded, or how a proposed insurance plan could be funded. At any rate, the presence or absence of insurance cash values on a balance sheet calls for further investigation into the prospect's business continuation plans.

Absence of Cash Values

The absence of cash values on the balance sheet might indicate that:

1. the company has neither a business continuation plan nor enough present insurance to fund one;

2. the company has a business continuation plan that is either not funded by life insurance, funded by term insurance or funded by a permanent policy that has yet to show cash values; or

3. the company has a cross-purchase business continuation plan and the policies are owned by the individual principals in the business.

Presence of Cash Values

The presence of a life insurance cash value indicates one of three things.

1. The company has some type of entity-purchase business continuation plan funded adequately by insurance.

2. The company has an entity-purchase business continuation plan, but more insurance is needed to fund the plan adequately.

3. The company has purchased insurance for some purpose other than business insurance.

Whether a balance sheet contains insurance cash values or not, you should investigate the prospect's business continuation plans. Also, you should not let the presence of an insured buy-sell agreement discourage you. In fact, when you do discover such a plan, you may be able to demonstrate the need to reassess it and the insurance funding it. Simply take the most current balance sheet and compare it to the balance sheet for the year in which the agreement was last considered. Often, such a comparison will reveal a dramatic growth in business values.

ILL. 3.4 ▪ *Balance Sheet D&E Trash Service (A Partnership)*

Assets

Cash	$ 7,500
Accounts receivable	18,000
Trucks, other equipment	74,000
Total Assets	$99,500

Liabilities and Partners' Equity

Accounts payable		$ 5,000
Notes payable		16,000
Partners' equity		
D	$39,250	
E	$39,250	$78,500
Total Liabilities and Partners' Equity		$99,500

Buy-Sell Valuation

You should determine exactly how much insurance a prospect needs. We've already mentioned one way to determine how much *additional* insurance is needed in an *existing* plan: Whatever amount business values have increased is the amount of additional coverage needed. In the case of a *new* plan, one of the easiest ways of determining the value of the enterprise is simply to use the book value or the owners' equity. The illustrations that follow are examples of different insurance needs. In them, we deliberately have chosen small figures so that the concepts can be grasped quickly. In actual sales situations, the numbers involved may be substantially larger. The principles, however, are the same. In Ill. 3.4, D and E are 50/50 owners of a service partnership. The partners' equity is $78,500.

D and E might have divided the partners' equity, $78,500, and insured themselves for $39,250 each. However, each felt he should share the cash account, $7,500, after first deducting the accounts payable, $5,000. The underwriter, therefore, suggested that the minimum insurance be $76,000 or $38,000 on each life. The $76,000 was arrived at by first deducting the cash not needed to cover the accounts payable, $2,500.

Although using book value (or owners' equity) is one of the simplest ways to calculate how much life insurance is needed for a buy-sell agreement, it also can be one of the most inaccurate. A thorough discussion of the pros and cons of various valuation methods is beyond the scope of this course. However, you should be aware that book value often is used best as a starting point in business valuation, or in combination with other methods.

Presence of a Key Executive

The presence of a key executive in a business can be revealed by the standard methods of interpreting financial statements and by outside evidence. Suppose, for instance, that you have examined the balance sheet of a local discount store

ILL. 3.5 ■ *Balance Sheet RST Manufacturing Corp.*

Assets	As of Preceding Year	As of Current Year
Cash	$ 10,000	$ 10,000
Accounts receivable	26,000	34,000
Inventory	41,000	58,000
Fixed assets	220,000	220,000
Other assets	25,000	25,000
Total Assets	$322,000	$347,000
Liabilities and Partners' Equity		
Accounts payable	$ 8,000	$ 10,000
Accrued liabilities	6,000	6,000
Notes and mortgages payable	100,000	95,000
Capital stock	150,000	150,000
Retain earnings	58,000	86,000
Total	$322,000	$347,000

and have found a current liquidity ratio of four-to-one. In checking the Dun & Bradstreet ratios, you would find that this ratio is well above the median current ratio for discount stores throughout the nation. It therefore indicates the presence of a key executive.

Outside evidence might reveal that this key executive is an excellent merchandise buyer, is able to write traffic-pulling ads, is a wizard at store arrangement and display or is an excellent financial manager. Would not the store suffer a major loss if he or she died? Certainly this key executive is worth something to the store. You should explore the need for insuring the executive.

A Deficient Current Ratio

While a firm with a better-than-average current ratio is an obvious candidate for key executive insurance, some agents who sell business insurance reason that even a company with a deficient current ratio is a prospect for such coverage. By a deficient current ratio, we mean one that falls below the standard for that industry or one that is lacking when compared to current ratios of previous accounting periods of this company. The reasoning goes that such life insurance coverage helps to quiet the fears of creditors, who wonder whether there will be sufficient assets after the death of the key executive to pay them. A life insurance policy payable to the company will assure sufficient capital should such a person die.

The difficulty with this approach is that a company short on working capital generally is looking for a more immediate answer to its problems. Unless its creditors insist upon it, the company likely will not buy life insurance until such time as the current ratio is adequate.

Comparison of Balance Sheet Items

Other tests that might indicate the presence of a key executive in a business involve prior-period comparisons of various balance sheet items. Illustration 3.5 compares two balance sheets of the RST Manufacturing Corp. You will note the big investment in fixed assets. At the end of the current year, the fixed assets were $220,000 and the stockholders' equity was $236,000 (capital stock, $150,000; plus retained earnings, $86,000). For every $1.07 of stockholders' equity, therefore, there was $1 of fixed assets.

In order for the retained earnings to have increased by $28,000 in one year, someone must have managed the enterprise very carefully. He or she must have pushed sales while simultaneously "riding herd" over the inventory and accounts receivable. There is no other way to explain this growth in retained earnings. The corporation certainly will want to retain this person's services and indemnify itself against his or her loss.

Valuing the Key Executive

Whether you use ratios, comparisons, outside evidence or a combination of each, once you've uncovered a key executive and have convinced a prospect of the need for key executive insurance, you still have one major problem. How much insurance should you recommend?

There is no set rule for measuring a key executive's value. Fortunately, three valuation methods take much, but not all, of the guessing out of this measurement task. They are: (1) the contribution-to-earnings method; (2) the salary test; and (3) the combination method. All are based upon information revealed in a firm's financial statements, and all have some drawbacks. But, when used correctly, they can yield satisfactory approximations of a key executive's value to a business.

Contribution to Earnings. Basically, the computation is based upon two figures: the average book value or stockholders' equity for the past five years and the average net income before taxes for the same period.

1. The average book value is multiplied by some percentage that represents a fair return if the money were invested elsewhere by the owners.

2. The product then is subtracted from the average five-years' income to obtain that portion of business income attributable to management.

3. The difference then should be multiplied by the number of years it would take to find and train new management. This product represents the value of the management that could be indemnified with the proper life insurance.

As an example, let us suppose that a firm has an average book value of $450,000 and an average income before taxes of $75,000. Further, it considers 7 percent to be a fair return and estimates that it might take four years to replace the current management. The steps in computing "management value" are:

ILL. 3.6 ■ *Combination Method (Sample Calculation)*

Average annual net earnings:		
Salaries to owners	$180,000	
Dividends paid	10,000	
Additions to retained earnings	<u>30,000</u>	$220,000
Less:		
Estimated replacement salaries for		
owners' routine duties	120,000	
Earnings on net worth of $200,000		
at 8 percent	<u>16,000</u>	<u>136,000</u>
Annual earnings attributable to		
managerial expertise		<u>84,000</u>
Portion attributable to key executive		
(1/3)		$ 28,000
		× <u> 5</u>
Value of key executive (replacement		
needs five years to acquire managerial		
expertise)		<u>$140,000</u>

1. Average book value × fair return = investment elsewhere

    $450,000 × 7% = $31,500

2. Average income − fair return = management portion

    $75,000 − $31,500 = $43,500

3. Management portion × replacement years = management value

    $43,500 × 4 = $174,000

A further computation would have to be made to divide the management value among the members of the management group. The result would be the value of the individual members of the management group.

The Salary Test. In this method, first determine the salary of the key executive in excess of what would be paid if someone else were hired to do his or her routine duties. The "excess" salary then is multiplied by the number of years it would take to find and train a replacement.

As an example, if an executive is being paid $80,000 per year and a replacement to perform his or her routine duties could be found for $45,000, then that key executive's managerial talents are worth $35,000. Furthermore, if it would take five years to find and train a replacement, the key executive's total worth would be $175,000.

A Combination Method. As a general rule, the more difficult the valuation method, the more accurate the answer. Of course, this doesn't always hold true. But when it does, it's primarily because the more sophisticated methods generally consider a greater number of variables.

With this in mind, we recommend the use of the combination method illustrated in Ill. 3.6. As you can see, it combines the two methods previously discussed.

In some cases, the amount of insurance suggested by the above method will require a greater premium than the prospect can afford—especially if the use of permanent insurance is recommended. Therefore, you should be as flexible as possible when making your proposal. If a lesser amount of insurance is undesirable, a combination permanent-term plan might be the answer to your prospect's needs.

Some Words of Caution. None of the valuation methods discussed here or elsewhere in this course are foolproof. They all contain variables whose values are subjective. Chief among these are the fair return percentage, length of recruiting/training period, and the "routine" salary figure. For this reason—with your help and their other financial advisers—your prospects should be encouraged to determine the value of these variables for themselves.

A Qualified Pension or Profit-Sharing Plan

The income statement also can be an extremely valuable sales aid, especially if you want to sell qualified pension or profit-sharing plans. All you need to do is to reconstruct a prospect's current income statement and show the tax savings that would have resulted had a pension or profit-sharing plan been in effect.

Consider the effect that a pension plan would have had upon the income statement of the Delightful Department Store in Ill. 3.7. We have assumed that the stockholder employees would have enjoyed two-thirds of the benefits to be purchased initially.

You will note that, while the pension plan contribution was $10,000, the store would have saved $2,500 in income tax by installing the plan ($11,825 minus $9,325). The store's out-of-pocket cost then for its $10,000 contribution would have been $7,500.

When, as we have shown above, you combine this tax savings with the fact that the stockholder employees will be the major beneficiaries of the plan, you've made the two most telling arguments for installing the plan.

While you should be aware of your prospect's preference for either a pension or a profit-sharing plan, the balance sheet and income statement often can indicate which would be better for a company. A good cash position with years of consistent profits normally favors a pension plan. Because definite retirement benefits are being purchased in a pension plan, the corporation must be capable of sustained contributions. A profit-sharing plan, on the other hand, is favored by those companies with fluctuating profits, because the company's contributions can be adjusted accordingly.

ILL. 3.7 ▪ *Delightful Department Stores, Inc., Income Statement (Reconstructed)*

	Actual Statement Year Ended Dec. 31	If Plan Had Been in Effect
Net Sales	$525,000	$525,000
Cost of goods sold	342,000	342,000
Gross profit	$183,000	$183,000
Expenses:		
Selling and delivery	$ 47,000	$ 47,000
Buying	17,000	17,000
Building rental	21,000	21,000
General and administrative:		
PENSION PLAN CONTRIBUTION	–0–	10,000
Other	33,000	33,000
Total	$118,000	$128,000
Net income from operations	$ 65,000	$ 55,000
Other income (expense) net	2,300	2,300
Net income before income tax	$ 67,300	$ 57,300
Income Tax*	$ 11,825	$ 9,325

*2000 corporate rates

Split-Dollar Insurance

When a company's statement of changes in financial position reveal that the business has more sources of funds than it is using in its current operations, it might consider using such excess cash to join with its key people or its rising young employees in the purchase of *split-dollar insurance*. Such a plan has numerous advantages both to the employee and to the company. Let's take a minute to review these advantages.

Advantages to the Employees

A split-dollar plan enables employees to have adequate coverage at times when they are less likely to be able to afford it. It also enables them to obtain this coverage at the lowest possible cost. In addition, a split-dollar plan represents a hedge against employees becoming uninsurable in the future, and it may permit them to continue the coverage after retirement.

Advantages to the Business

Through split-dollar, a company can provide an incentive plan with no direct cost other than the loss of earnings that might accrue if the money were invested elsewhere. This loss—if any—usually is offset by increased employee satisfaction. Also, because a split-dollar plan is informal and requires no governmental approval, the company can be selective among its employees and keep the plan on a confidential basis. Finally, when a company owns a split-

ILL. 3.8 ■ *Split-Dollar Illustration*

EMPLOYEE COST | **100,000 LIFE INSURANCE EMPLOYEE CONTRIBUTION**

at retirement

100,000 LIFE INSURANCE
- **EMPLOYEE RECEIVES POLICY**
- **COMPANY RETRIEVES ITS INVESTMENT**

dollar policy on an employee, it has a growing and readily available reserve fund to call upon for business needs and emergencies. When the insured employee retires, the company can use the cash value of the policy to establish a special retirement plan for the employee. The employer may also make a gift of the policy to the retiree, after reclaiming a portion of the cash value to recover the company's investment in the contract.

A Section 303 Redemption

Financial statements also can help you spot an excess of accumulated earnings and capital impairment problems that indicate the corporation is self-insuring a Section 303 redemption plan.

Under old law, Section 303 permitted a stockholder to bail cash out of a corporation without the money paid out being taxed as ordinary income, although it may have resulted in a capital gain. Under current law, all gains are taxed as ordinary income. Further, with a stepped-up basis, it is entirely possible that there will be no gain at all under a Section 303 redemption. In any event, the need for cash to redeem stock remains. The corporation should have enough cash or liquid assets, such as life insurance, to redeem stock within the statutory period following a stockholder's death. If the company doesn't have enough assets or if it is attempting to self-insure such a redemption, you might want to point out the advantages of using life insurance to fund a Section 303 redemption. Section 303 stock redemptions are discussed in detail in a later chapter.

Instant Cash. Life insurance provides quick cash for a quick redemption. Further, the company's cash account need not be depleted to fulfill the plan if the insurance purchased is sufficient.

Increase in Equity. Life insurance proceeds under such a plan effectively increase the stockholders' equity in the company to the extent the proceeds exceed the cash value. The value of the deceased's shares is increased, which may make it easier for the estate to meet the "35 percent of the adjusted gross estate" test. A Section 303 redemption is available only if the value of the stock exceeds 35 percent of the value of the decedent's adjusted gross estate.

Decrease in Tax Troubles. By using life insurance to fund a Section 303 redemption, a company reduces the possibility of accumulated earnings difficulties—and a resultant penalty tax. The cash value of a policy will be less than the amount that the corporation would have to accumulate in retained earnings to self-insure the redemption.

Eases Capital Impairment Problems. Many states have a statute that prohibits partial redemptions unless they are made out of retained earnings and will not result in an impairment of capital. Life insurance makes possible a redemption that otherwise would be barred by such a statute.

A Deferred Compensation Agreement

Even the footnotes of financial statements can reveal insurance needs. Consider, for example, *deferred compensation.* It is the practice of modern accounting to disclose deferred compensation arrangements in the balance sheet footnotes. You might find that the promised benefit isn't funded or that there is no pre-retirement death benefit. In either situation, you can make a strong case for the purchase of life insurance as a funding vehicle.

If no deferred compensation plan exists, propose that the company install one. After all, the same business that might suffer if a key executive died also would suffer if the executive left for a better job. The deferred compensation plan can offer corporations an effective means of attracting and retaining key employees.

Insure Corporate Loans

If the financial statement reveals that a firm is highly leveraged (with a high debt/equity ratio), chances are it needs life insurance to cover its indebtedness. Life insurance can also be used to secure new loans. In many cases in which the lending institution requires that the principals be insured before it grants an unsecured loan, the customer will come to you. But even in those cases in which the loan is secured by the company's assets, the repayment of the loan depends upon earnings, which in turn depend on the performance of management.

In some instances the shareholders of a corporation are personally liable for corporate debts. Examples would be found in close corporations where the shareholders are the principals of the firm and have been required to sign for corporate debt. When this situation exists, the debt must be discharged before the personal representative can settle the estate. The need for life insurance to assure payment of the debt is clear. So, when you obtain financial statements, question your prospects carefully about their corporate loans whenever possible.

FINDING THE PREMIUM DOLLARS IN FINANCIAL STATEMENTS

The financial statements that disclose the need for a business insurance sale often will show the source of the insurance premium. You should not accept easily the objection that there is "no cash." Here are some sources of premium dollars that a knowledge of financial statements will uncover.

Cash Account

While it may be self-evident that the cash account is a source of premiums, the reason for emphasizing it is to contrast it with what is not cash. The figure on the sample income statement in Ill. 3.7, "Net Income Before Income Tax," is not necessarily cash, and neither is the retained earnings account on the balance sheet. In many cases most of these sums already have been spent or committed to purchase more inventory, expand the accounts receivable, buy some fixed asset or pay the principal on some debt. That this occurs with great regularity is evidenced by the number of businesses that have to borrow money to pay the income tax generated by a "good" year.

Cash flow may not be the answer, either, to the problem of funding premium dollars. Many companies with above-average cash flow also may be burdened with above-average debt. If substantial payments on the principal are required, little, if any, money could remain for insurance premiums.

Conversion of Current Assets

Many businesses experience trouble with excessive inventories and accounts receivable at two contrasting periods of time. One occurs during periods of greatly increasing sales. During this time, inventories often expand faster than sales. Many of the sales may be on open account, but much of the inventory may have been purchased for cash. As a result the business could be short of cash.

The second period of excessive inventories and receivables can occur immediately after a down-turn in sales. Inventory may have been expanded with the expectation of even greater sales. Not only may sales drop, but collections may slow. Again, cash could be short.

If the turnover ratios that we discussed previously are applied to the inventory and accounts receivable, the business owner can see that the inventory and receivables turnover has slowed. If he or she further relates the net income for the period to the total assets employed and compares that with like periods, the business owner is likely to see a poorer return on his or her investment.

Showing the business owner the extent of the problem often is easier than getting him or her to reduce inventory or watch receivables. For instance, many retail establishments feel that they "must have the item in stock" if they are to get the customer's repeat business. There is, however, a big difference between having one or two of a slow-moving item in stock, and one or two dozen. If the retailer reduces inventory in this fashion, there soon will be enough cash for the needed life insurance.

Again, many businesspeople exercise no real control over their accounts receivable. On sales items that initially generate little profit, can the firm afford to carry the purchaser on open account for three to six months? The business owner should know what the industry-wide level of receivables turnover is or the level that past experience indicates the business should maintain. When these levels are exceeded, the business owner should not be afraid to stiffen collection procedures, as well as put some customers on a cash-only basis.

One collection policy that can speed up collections is a "credit terms" policy that offers buyers a cash discount if payment is made within a specified period of time. A common credit terms policy is "2/10, net 30." This means that a 2 percent cash discount is allowed if payment is made within ten days, and that full payment is due within 30 days in all cases.

Naturally, if a business can increase its receivables turnover, it will have more cash to pay the premiums on needed insurance.

Conversion of a Fixed Asset

There are many cases in which a fixed asset can be sold readily and advantageously to provide the cash to pay life insurance premiums. Many manufacturing concerns, for instance, have a number of expensive machines that were used at one time but are not used in the current production process. The company could sell this machinery while it still has a value and contract out any small amount of work still performed with it.

In this same vein, many retailers and wholesalers own expensive delivery trucks. These vehicles may be only partially utilized. The business owners should investigate the costs of either renting delivery vehicles instead of owning them or contracting out the delivery work to a firm specializing in this business.

Any business that owns real estate should check carefully to see whether this property is utilized efficiently. You will find that in some cases excess real property was bought for an expansion of the business that may never have taken place. In other cases, there may be unused space for an area contracted by a business for its operations. Therefore, a sale or rental of this real estate should be considered.

When making your recommendations, you should realize that any purchase of life insurance will require a recurring annual premium, while the sale of a fixed asset may provide the client with only the first premium. The prospect, however, possibly could save on installment loans it currently is paying for machines or vehicles, or it could make additional sums available by renting its facilities. Also, if the sum gained from a sale was large enough, the client might be able to prepay a number of premiums. Understand, though, that you may have to tell your prospect, "Sell this item, get healthy and then buy my proposal."

It is evident that, in order to help the prospect, you must make the most of your powers of observation and also have a good overall knowledge of the prospect's business operations. However, your original thoughts on where the prospect can save money must be stimulated by your knowledge of financial statements.

Depreciation

The *depreciation* process offers two major opportunities for finding premium dollars: excess accumulated depreciation reserves, and tax savings generated by accelerated depreciation deductions.

Depreciation Reserves

One way to determine whether the annual increase in a company's depreciation reserve account is a potential source of premium dollars is to check whether the prospect's place of business and its machinery and other equipment are in good repair. If so, you can ask your prospect if he or she is arresting the depreciation of the business with an effective repair policy. Should the answer be yes, you've found a prime source of premium dollars. Incidentally, you can also tell the business that the proposed life insurance will insure the depreciation of the firm's human life value just as the repair policy is taking care of the depreciation of the physical plant.

Accelerated Depreciation Deductions

A company's current tax deduction for depreciation and cost recovery also might result in a tax savings that could be used for life insurance premiums. A business can take significant cost recovery deductions after a capital item is purchased. The capital expenditure really does double duty: it purchases the actual machinery or equipment while providing tax savings that can be used to buy business life insurance.

External Financing

Borrowing to pay life insurance premiums is a strategy used by two different types of insurance buyers.

Firms Short on Cash

First are those firms whose financial statements indicate to them that they cannot purchase permanent life insurance, pay the full premium and still retain enough cash in the firm to operate efficiently. Of course, one alternative might be to purchase term insurance now, with plans to convert it in the future. Another might be to purchase only as much permanent coverage as the company can presently afford.

Both of these options have serious limitations. If term insurance, for example, is *not* converted, it will expire. And there are no guarantees that the company will be able to acquire coverage then, at any price. If extended term contracts providing coverage on a renewal basis to age 95 or age 100 are used, the policyowner may find it substantially less expensive to purchase one of the many flexible premium forms of permanent insurance instead. In regard to the second alternative, half a loaf indeed may be better than none. But what's really needed in most business insurance situations is complete, not partial, coverage. Therefore, whenever possible, a company short on cash might want to use a minimum deposit plan or bank loan to buy permanent insurance in an amount that will provide adequate coverage. It should be noted, however, that if a minimum deposit plan is used, interest on policy loans in a business situation is income tax-deductible only on total policy loans per employee for amounts up to $50,000.

It should be noted, however, that the deductibility of policy loan interest is severely limited. There is a general rule of non-deductibility of policy loan interest, with a limited policy loan interest deduction permitted for indebtedness on company-owned life insurance covering a key person.

Under the key person exception to the general rule prohibiting the policy loan interest deduction, policy loan interest under a life insurance policy covering a key person is deductible to the extent that the indebtedness does not exceed $50,000. This limited exception is further limited by the definition of key person and the amount of interest that may be deducted.

A *key person* is defined as an officer or 20 percent owner of the company. The number of employees who can be treated as key persons is limited to the greater of:

- five individuals; or

- the lesser of 5 percent of the total officers and employees or 20 individuals.

Generally, all members of a controlled group are treated as a single taxpayer for purposes of determining a 20 percent owner and for applying the $50,000 limit.

An interest limitation also needs to be considered. Interest in excess of the *applicable rate of interest* cannot be deducted. The applicable rate of interest for any month is Moody's Corporate Bond Yield Average—Monthly Average Corporates published by Moody's Investor.

Constant Borrowers

The second category of minimum deposit buyers includes the company that constantly borrows on all its assets to purchase additional assets. This type of buyer generally has no desire to build cash values for emergencies or for very real future needs such as purchasing the shares of uninsurable stockholders or funding a deferred compensation agreement. Life insurance is viewed as filling one purpose—indemnification.

A borrowing plan that may be employed actually involves no policy loans at all and, thereby, avoids the problem of nondeductibility of policy loan interest. It assumes that the purchaser is active in the money market each year, borrowing, for instance, to purchase inventory or finance accounts receivable. The company does not borrow to pay its insurance premiums. It pays the full premium each year and lists the increasing cash value on the balance sheet as an asset. When it borrows for inventory or accounts receivable purposes, naturally the banker cannot overlook the asset values of the insurance policy. Of course, in order not to jeopardize the interest deduction on its general credit line, the business should not borrow solely at those times when insurance premiums are due, or borrow sums equal to either the premium due or the cash value increase. Even then, the plan might be subjected to close scrutiny by the IRS.

Other Sources

Just as it was impossible to list every conceivable insurance need you might find in a company's set of financial statements, so it is with sources of premium dollars. However, the sources discussed here, along with additional ones, revealed by a careful study of a company's financial statements, should help you, in many cases, to overcome the objection that there is no cash. Establishing the insurance need should guarantee you the sale.

■ SUMMARY

Because of the vast number of companies in the United States and the increase in the total assets of these companies, prospects for selling from financial statements are not difficult to find.

The information presented in this chapter can be used effectively to make business insurance sales. It is important to keep in mind, however, that the study of a business's financial statements is not something that can be dropped once the initial sale has been made. Instead, a periodic review should be made of your clients' financial statements to determine whether their insurance coverages are of the proper amount, type and form.

Mastering the skill of reading and analyzing financial statements may take a bit of work and time. At first glance, they may be confusing, especially because of the many varieties of financial statements. In fact, as you begin, you may want to enlist the help of a friend or associate in banking or accounting.

But keep in mind that a company's financial statement contains a wealth of information. The time and effort you invest in learning how to work with these valuable documents will return multiple dividends to you in the form of sales and client-building opportunities.

■ CHAPTER 3 QUESTIONS FOR REVIEW

1. A basic working knowledge of financial statements is important to an agent for all the following reasons EXCEPT

    A. this knowledge demonstrates the agent's professionalism to the prospect

    B. a sale is impossible without this ability

    C. financial statements often reveal potential and immediate needs solvable by the agent

    D. analysis of financial statements help in making reasonable recommendations

2. Financial information about unincorporated businesses can be obtained from

    A. their annual report

    B. Dun & Bradstreet Reports

    C. the businesses themselves, by request

    D. all of the above

3. On a company's balance sheet, all the following are included as assets EXCEPT

    A. shareholder's equity

    B. inventories

    C. accounts receivable

    D. licenses and patents

4. A company's income statement summarizes its

    A. financial position

    B. financial performance

    C. projected future profitability

    D. all of the above

5. Presence of life insurance cash values on a company's balance sheet may indicate that

    A. the business has no business continuation plan

    B. if the business has a continuation plan, it is not funded by insurance

    C. the business has a key executive insurance plan

    D. all of the above

4

The Sole Proprietor

This chapter examines the proprietorship market. Topics include what happens when a proprietor dies, liquidation of the proprietorship and family retention of the business. The presentation concludes with an examination of the proprietorship purchase agreement.

The largest, most overlooked—and yet most approachable—member of the business community is the sole proprietor. Too often, insurance professionals focus all their attention on partnerships and small corporations, neglecting the vast sole proprietorship market.

In this chapter, we will first look at the sole proprietorship structure and potential as a market for you. Then we will address problems faced by sole proprietors at their deaths, as well as three positive options: (1) liquidation of the business; (2) family retention; and (3) selling of the business as a going concern, perhaps to an employee. Overall, we'll look at the role life insurance can play in helping sole proprietors and their families.

THE SOLE PROPRIETORSHIP MARKET

The primary advantage of the sole proprietorship form of doing business is simplicity. Becoming a proprietor requires no formal filing of papers or registration other than a local business license. In turn, its simple structure offers the insurance professional a number of unique opportunities:

1. It is the dominant business form in this country. That nearly three out of every four businesses in this country are sole proprietorships attests to their popularity.

ILL. 4.1 ■ *Number of Businesses in the U.S.*

- Sole Proprietorships: 17.0 million
- Corporations: 4.6 million
- Partnerships: 1.7 million

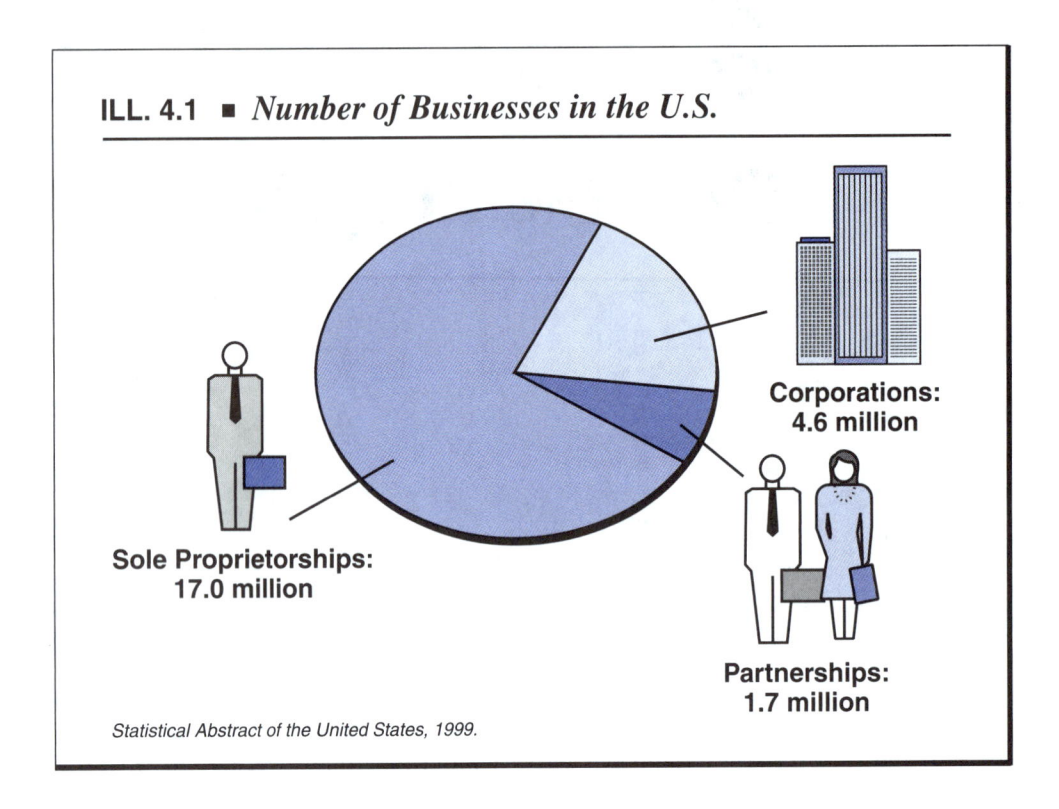

Statistical Abstract of the United States, 1999.

2. The financial resources and insurance needs of the business are tied closely to those of the family. In fact, legally, personal and business financial matters are generally indistinguishable. If you are comfortable working with families, you will find working with sole proprietors very similar.

3. The owners are approachable. Many sole proprietors count on outside resources and advisors to help them with many aspects of the business. If you know how to approach them, they will not just listen to what you have to say; they will act on your recommendations.

WHAT HAPPENS WHEN A PROPRIETOR DIES?

Upon the death of the sole proprietor, the estate is treated in the same manner as the estate of any other decedent. Unless specific assets pass by trust, contract or survivorship, they will be included in the proprietor's probate estate and subject to the estate administration process. Since the proprietor's business is not an entity apart, his or her business assets and liabilities also are subject to the estate administration process.

The value of the property included in the gross estate is the fair market value of the property at the date of the decedent's death or at an alternate valuation date six months later, if so elected. The alternate valuation date may be used only if its use decreases both the value of the gross estate and the estate tax liability. Fair market value is the price at which the property would change hands between a willing buyer and a willing seller, neither being under any compulsion to buy or sell and both having reasonable knowledge of all relevant facts.

Business Valuation

When valuation of a business is left to the IRS after the death of the sole proprietor, it opens the door to litigation with the IRS. Valuation may mean different things to different people, but to the IRS, valuation is based on a consideration of all relevant facts, especially the following factors:

- the nature of the business and the history of the enterprise from its inception;

- the economic outlook in general and the condition and outlook of the specific industry in particular;

- the book value of the stock and the financial condition of the business;

- the earning capacity of the company;

- the dividend-paying capacity;

- whether the enterprise has goodwill or other intangible value;

- sales of stock and the size of the block to be valued; and

- the market price of stocks of corporations engaged in the same or a similar line of business whose stocks are actively traded in a free and open market, either on an exchange or over the counter.

There are many reasons why the sole proprietor must have some idea of the value of his or her business. Among them are the following:

- when obtaining loans, a higher, yet realistic, value could result in increased credit;

- knowing the value of the business will help defend the reasonableness of salary and other fringe benefits;

- a price must be determined for the business if it is to be sold upon death, disability or retirement; and

- for estate planning purposes, the higher the value, the greater the potential estate tax.

When we look at the estate administration process, the importance of a realistic business valuation becomes clear.

Special Closely Held Business Provisions

One of the important aspects of estate administration is the calculation and payment of any federal estate taxes due. The need to create liquidity to pay these estate taxes is often the reason why family-owned businesses face the prospect of being sold upon the death of the business owner. A significant part of the need for insurance on the life of the business owner arises out of this need for liquidity.

Because a substantial amount of the life insurance sold to business—although certainly not all of it—is designed to pay estate taxes, it is important that the life insurance practitioner clearly understand the preferential estate tax treatment accorded closely held business interests. Three of the important provisions relate to the:

- greater exclusion granted to certain closely held business;
- special use estate tax valuation under which certain closely held business are valued; and
- extended period that certain businesses are granted to make payment of estate taxes.

Because these three provisions may affect a client, let's spend a few minutes examining them.

Estate Tax Exclusion for Closely Held Business

Certain family-owned businesses enjoy an increased exclusion from a business owner's federal estate. The increase in the exclusion in excess of the amount of the exclusion that the estate of any decedent is entitled to is equal to the lesser of the:

- adjusted value of the qualified family-owned business interest includible in the decedent's gross estate; and
- excess of $1.3 million over the amount of the gross estate exempt from estate tax by the unified credit.

In simpler language, a qualified family-owned business worth $1.3 million could be entirely excluded from federal estate taxes by using both the unified credit and the special estate tax exclusion. Because the unified credit and its exemption equivalent is scheduled to increase periodically through 2006, at which time the exemption equivalent will be $1 million, the value of the special estate tax exclusion is correspondingly decreasing, as shown in Ill. 4.2.

Although, as is apparent from Ill. 4.2, the value of the special family-owned business exclusion rapidly decreases and has correspondingly less of an effect on the estate tax due as 2006 approaches, it is important that the life insurance professional be aware of it.

ILL 4.2 ■ *Value of the Qualified Family-Owned Business Exclusion*

Year	Business Value	Unified Credit Exemption Equivalent	Family-Owned Business Exclusion Amount
2000 & 2001	$1,300,000	$675,000	$625,000
2002 & 2003	1,300,000	700,000	600,000
2004	1,300,000	850,000	450,000
2005	1,300,000	950,000	350,000
2006	1,300,000	1,000,000	300,000

Not all businesses can qualify for this preferential estate tax treatment. A business must meet several requirements before it qualifies. In summary form, those requirements are:

- The business owner must be a citizen or resident of the United States at the time of his or her death.

- The business owner and his or her family must own a certain percentage of the ownership interest as follows:'

    - at least 50 percent of the ownership interest;

    - at least 30 percent of the ownership interest if 70 percent of the interests are owned by two families; or

    - at least 30 percent of the ownership interest if 90 percent of the interests are owned by three families.

- The business interest must have been included in the business owner's gross estate and passed from the business owner to a qualified heir. (A qualified heir, for this purpose is defined as a member of the decedent's family but also includes an unrelated employee who is and has been employed by the business for at least 10 years before the business owner's death.)

- The decedent or a member of his or her family must have owned the business interest for at least five of the eight years preceding the decedent's death.

- The business owner or a member of his or her family must have materially participated in the business for at least five years during the eight-year period ending on the earlier of:

- the decedent's death;

- the decedent's disability; or

- the date the decedent began receiving Social Security benefits.

(Material participation in the business is determined on a case-by-case basis depending upon a variety of factors. The principal factors considered in a determination of material possession are two: physical work and participation in management decisions.)

- Each qualified heir (or member of the qualified heir's family) must materially participate in the business for at least five years of any eight-year period within ten years of the decedent's death. A failure to materially participate in the business subjects the heir to a recapture of the estate tax benefits.

- The adjusted value of the business interest plus the value of certain lifetime gifts of the business interests made by the decedent must comprise at least 50 percent of the decedent's adjusted gross estate.

- The qualified family-owned business interest exclusion must be elected by the executor, and each person having an interest in the business must consent—by written agreement—to the recapture tax provision.

Special Use Estate Tax Valuation

The general rule concerning the valuation of property for estate tax purposes requires that it be valued at its fair market value at the time of the decedent's death or on the alternate valuation date. This requirement places an onerous estate tax burden on those estates having large amounts of real property used in a farming or other business.

To provide estate tax relief to these estates, Congress enacted legislation that permits an executor to elect special use valuation for this real property. Special use valuation is intended to value real property used in a business at approximately its value in the manner in which it is being used. So, real property used in a single business is assigned a value that reflects its business use, rather than its highest and best use—which may be as a residential development. There are two methods for valuing this property outlined in the tax code: the simplified formula method and the multiple factor method. The simplified formula is available only for valuing farmland while the multiple factor formula can be used to value non-farm use real property or farm property that does not meet the requirements for valuation under the simplified formula. Let's briefly examine each of these formulas.

The *simplified formula method* is a variation of the capitalization of earnings approach used in valuing any business. This method uses these equations.

$$\text{Gross Rental} - \text{Real Estate Taxes} = \text{Net Rental}$$

$$\frac{\text{Net Rental}}{\text{Loan Interest Rate}} = \text{Value}$$

The first step in the simplified formula method is to determine the average annual gross cash rental for comparable land used for farming. From that amount, the average annual state and local real estate taxes must be deducted. This results in a net rental figure, which is then divided by the average annual effective interest rate for all new Federal Land Bank loans. The final result is the special use value determined by the simplified formula method.

It is easy to see how the formula operates simply by adding some hypothetical values. Let's assume that the average annual gross rental for comparable farm land is $100,000 and that the average annual real estate taxes for this comparable land amounts to $25,000. The net rental simply would be the difference, or $75,000. By dividing the net rental by the effective interest rate we can obtain the value. If the Federal Land Bank interest rate were 8 percent, the value would be $937,500 ($75,000 /.08 = $937,500).

The *multiple factor method* of valuing real property is considerably less precise that the simplified method. It must be used to establish a special use valuation when valuing real property used in a non-farming business. In addition, real property used as farm land must employ the multiple factor method if elected by the executor or if the executor is unable to find comparable farm property whose rental and taxes can be used to establish a value under the simplified method.

The multiple factor method applies five factors in determining the special use value. Unfortunately, the code doesn't indicate how they are to be applied or the weight that should be given to each factor. As a result, this valuation is not often used.

The factors that apply in determining the special use value under the multiple factor method are:

- capitalization of income the property can be expected to yield for farming or closely held business purposes over a reasonable period of time;

- capitalization of the fair rental value of the land based upon its qualified use;

- assessed land values in a state that provides a differential or use value assessment law for farm land or closely held businesses;

- comparable sales of land in the same geographical area, provided that such land is far enough removed from resorts or metropolitan areas so that non-agricultural use is not a significant factor; and

- any other factor that fairly values the property for its qualified use.

Qualifying for *special use valuation* is not automatic. As we found in the case of the estate tax exclusion for closely held businesses, there are important qualifications. To qualify for special use valuation, both the real property and the estate must meet certain requirements.

The real property must meet the following six requirements to qualify for special use valuation:

1. The real property must be located in the United States;

2. The real property must have been acquired from or passed from the decedent to a qualified heir. (A qualified heir includes an ancestor, a spouse, a lineal descendant or the spouse of a lineal descendant of the decedent.);

3. The real property must have been being used at the time of the decedent's death for a qualified use by the decedent of a member of his or her family;

4. The decedent or a member of his or her family must have owned the property and used it for a qualified use for at least five years during the eight-year period ending with the date of the decedent's death;

5. The decedent or a member of his or her family must have materially participated in the operation of the business for at least five years during the eight-year period ending with the earliest of the decedent's death, disability or retirement; and

6. All persons with an interest in the property must consent to the recapture provision under which the estate tax savings are recaptured if the property is disposed of or the property ceases to be used for its qualified use in the 10 years following the decedent's death.

In addition to the requirement that the real property meet certain conditions, the decedent's estate also must meet three tests to qualify for special use valuation. Those three requirements are:

1. The decedent must have been a United States citizen or resident at the time of his or her death;

2. At least 50 percent of the adjusted value of the gross estate must comprise real or personal property that, at the time of the decedent's death, was being used for a qualified purpose by the decedent, or a member of the decedent's family, and that passes to a qualified heir of the decedent; and

3. A minimum of 25 percent of the adjusted gross estate must consist of the adjusted value of real property that passes to a qualified heir and that meets certain requirements relating to tenure of ownership and material participation.

If the property and estate meet these requirements, the Code permits a reduction in value of the property of up to $750,000 (adjusted annually for inflation).

Deferred Payment of Estate Taxes

The tax code has two provisions that provide means of deferring estate taxes. These provisions are sections 6161 and 6166 of the Internal Revenue Code, and provide, respectively, for discretionary deferrals and elective deferrals.

Section 6161

Code section 6161, providing for discretionary deferrals, gives the Secretary of the Treasury the discretion, for reasonable cause, to extend the time for payment of the estate taxes for a reasonable period, not to exceed 10 years. Although deferral is permitted for up to 10 years by the Code, the Internal Revenue Service has been reluctant to grant a deferral for longer than 12 months with possible subsequent 12-month deferrals.

Reasonable cause, which may cause the Service to grant a discretionary deferral under Section 6161, is deemed to exist if any of the following conditions apply:

- the liquid assets are located in several jurisdictions and are not immediately subject to the executor's control, even though the estate contains sufficient liquid assets to pay the estate tax due;

- the estate substantially comprises assets consisting of rights to future payments, such as annuities, royalties, contingent fees, etc.;

- the estate includes a claim to substantial assets which cannot be collected without litigation; and

- the estate does not have sufficient funds to pay the entire estate tax due without borrowing at a rate of interest higher than that generally available.

Section 6161 provides estates relatively little certainty that they can obtain a deferral since the deferral request depends upon favorable action by the Internal Revenue Service. Even if the Service grants a deferral, its reluctance to defer beyond a 12-month period minimizes the estate tax relief for the decedent's estate. Some of the shortcomings of the discretionary deferral provisions are addressed in Section 6166, the elective deferral provision.

Section 6166

Code Section 6166 provides for elective, rather than discretionary, deferrals of estate tax for estates of certain decedents. Under Section 6166, estates that qualify may elect to pay the estate tax liability attributable to the closely held business interest in 10 annual installments. In addition, the first principal installment can be deferred—and interest only paid—until the fifth anniversary of the original due date of the estate tax return. The initial four-year interest-only period combined with the 10-year amortization period effectively gives the estate 14 years to pay the estate tax due that is attributable to the business interest. Let's examine how the provision works.

Interest on the deferred estate tax is segmented into two portions: the *2 percent portion* and the *greater than 2 percent portion*. Interest at the rate of 2 percent is imposed on the 2 percent portion. The 2 percent portion is the first $1 million (indexed for inflation) in taxable value of closely held business interest. (It is the first $1 million in value in excess of the unified credit and any other exclusions.)

Interest on the *greater than 2 percent portion* is payable at the rate of 45 percent of the annual rate provided for federal tax underpayments. So, if tax underpayments call for interest to be paid at the rate of 12 percent, the greater than 2 percent portion annual interest rate would be 5.4 percent.

To qualify for estate tax deferral under Section 6166, an estate must meet certain requirements, which are that the:

- decedent must have been a United States citizen or resident at the time of his or her death;

- closely held business interest must have been included in the decedent's gross estate; and

- value of the closely held business interest must exceed 35 percent of the decedent's adjusted gross estate.

In the event that estate taxes are deferred under Section 6166, the Internal Revenue Service may, nonetheless, demand payment or acceleration of payment of the entire balance in the following situations:

- if any installment payment is not made on or before the due date;

- if funds are withdrawn from the qualifying business, or if any portion of the interest is distributed, sold, exchanged, or otherwise disposed of, acceleration may occur depending upon the type and aggregate amounts of disposition and withdrawal;

- if the estate accumulates income after the fourth taxable year of its existence; and

- if the estate fails to comply with an IRS demand that additional estate property be subject to a special estate tax lien to secure the payment of unpaid taxes and interest.

Whether the estate tax deferral is granted under Section 6161 or Section 6166, the estate tax still must be paid. And, although these sections can grant some relief with respect to the timing of payments, life insurance remains the generally most cost-effective method of paying the taxes.

The Estate Administration Process

At the proprietor's death, the business ends, and the total estate is subject to estate administration. By law, the personal representative, in the absence of a will provision to the contrary, must take possession of all assets, convert them into cash and pay all administration expenses, taxes and personal and business obligations. Remaining estate funds are then distributed to the heirs.

Estate settlement costs (administration expenses, debts and taxes) are liabilities that must be paid within a relatively short period of time. Most estate and inheritance taxes are due within nine to eighteen months after the estate owner's death; otherwise, penalties or interest charges are imposed.

Consequently, the estate must quickly find the cash to pay the estate taxes, expenses and debts.

Furthermore, in the case of the typical sole proprietor, most of the cash is tied up in the business. He or she has worked hard through the years to build the enterprise and in the process has poured in any excess earnings as well. Most business assets are represented by inventory, fixtures and other hardware—the things necessary to carry on the business. Consequently, the estate is primarily nonliquid. An executor may be forced to sell the business for half of its fair market value to raise the necessary cash to pay the estate taxes, expenses and debts. Let's examine the possible effects of estate administration.

Possible Effects of Estate Administration

The result of the administration of a sole proprietor's estate can be a forced liquidation of the business. This also results in loss of income from the business to the surviving family.

Rather than convert business assets to cash, the estate administrator can first try to sell the proprietorship as a going concern—find a buyer for the business as a whole rather than liquidate it on a piecemeal basis. A successfully operated business has a value as a going concern that generally is much greater than its book or net asset value. However, only in a few instances will it be possible to find an immediate buyer. In the vast majority of cases, liquidation is the only alternative. An unplanned liquidation may create serious problems.

Stoppage of Income

The death of a proprietor will have a decided impact on the sole proprietor's family. Not only will there be a severe reduction in the value of the business assets upon liquidation, but income that the business formerly generated will stop. At the proprietor's death, the surviving spouse and children could be left in desperate straits.

Continuation Attempts

The administrator or executor may attempt to continue the business personally in the hope of avoiding the severe financial effects on the family of the forced liquidation of the business and the stoppage of income. This course of action could be hazardous for the legal representative.

A legal representative who continues to operate a deceased proprietor's business without authority becomes personally liable to the estate's beneficiaries for all business debts and losses. On the other hand, the personal representative cannot share in any of the business profits because they inure to the benefit of the estate. Thus, for the administrator or executor, an unauthorized continuance of the business is risky.

Every small business is built by the efforts of the proprietor over a substantial period of time. The business owner knows intimately every phase of its operation, every strength and weakness of its makeup. The business, therefore,

ILL 4.3 ▪ *Typical Forced Liquidation Value of Business*

(Items from statements of leading authorities)	For illustration Alive	Dead
CASH VALUE OF MERCHANDISE	$200,000	$100,000
The National Association of Credit Men reports, concerning its studies of the amount by which business assets shrink between the owner's death and final sale: ". . . we are satisfied beyond any question of doubt, that shrinkage has been approximately 50%."		
FIXTURES AND STORE FURNITURE	$ 25,000	$ 3,000
Those items, which usually must be disposed of through second-hand dealers are sold for only a fraction of their original value, if the purchaser of the stock buys the fixtures, the purchaser often feels that they should be "thrown in" with the stock, consequently he or she will pay but little for them.		
AMOUNT OF OPEN BOOK ACCOUNTS—ACTUAL VALUE	$ 50,000	$ 25,000
"Accounts receivable to be collected by the estate representative should be discounted by at least 50% of their book values; and experience shows that at times as little as 25% is realized." [IV University of Florida Law Review 191]		
CASH ON HAND AND IN BANK	$ 5,000	$ 5,000
Total Assets	$280,000	$125,000
Less Total Liabilities	$ 30,000	$ 30,000
Net Worth	$250,000	$ 98,000

reflects, as a going concern, the ability, industry and personality of one person—its owner.

Thus, plans for the continuation of the business created after a proprietor's death are laden with dangers and uncertainties. The proprietor alone has the knowledge, experience and keen personal interest necessary to plan effectively for its disposal at his or her death. It is the proprietor who should plan the disposal of the business—not the proprietor's legal representative, the family, the courts or the statutes.

Three Alternatives

To avoid such problems, the proprietor has three alternatives in planning the disposal of the business at death:

1. take the proper legal and financial measures necessary for its *orderly liquidation*;

2. take the proper legal and financial measures for its *orderly retention* by the proprietor's family; or

3. take the proper legal and financial measures for its *orderly sale* to one or more employees, or other interested parties.

The proprietor's tax accountant determines the valuation of the business with the proprietor's help and takes into consideration tax issues affecting the potential estate; the proprietor's attorney draws up the legal documents, agreements, will, trusts and contracts for the disposition of the business and personal assets and liabilities at death; the proprietor's banker provides the trust instrument; and you, the life insurance agent, provide the cash.

Regardless of how the sole proprietor seeks to dispose of the business, keep in mind that the insurance agent has an insured plan for the business owner, Furthermore, life insurance is not labeled specifically "for business purchase only" or "for death taxes only." It is a flexible product—being a contract to deliver cash at an indefinite future date, and its purpose and application can change between now and then, if the proprietor changes estate objectives with regard to the disposition of the business.

LIQUIDATION OF THE PROPRIETORSHIP

Very often, especially when there is no experienced family member or employee who could continue the business, the sole proprietor should plan for the orderly liquidation of the business upon his or her death. While a portion of sole proprietors may be fortunate enough to sell their businesses as going concerns during their lifetime, no one should count on a lifetime sale. The sole proprietor must act now as if his or her death will terminate the business. The requirements of an orderly liquidation are a properly drawn will and adequate life insurance on the proprietor's life.

Properly Prepared Will

The proprietor's will should contain broad powers that authorize the disposition of the proprietor's business interest. It should cover the following points:

1. The executor should be given the power to sell the business at a public or private sale, to determine not only the purchase price but the mode of payment, to dispense with collateral requirements if necessary and to deal with persons related to the decedent, if necessary, in order to complete a sale.

2. The power to retain the business temporarily also should be written broadly. The executor may have to retain the business to await a sale in a more advantageous market. An essential collateral power is the ability to borrow on the security of the business assets, in order to provide working capital or to raise funds to pay estate obligations.

3. The executor also should have the power to change the form of business (i.e., allow the executor to join a partnership or incorporate the busi-

ness). A change in the business form may aid the eventual disposition of the business as a going concern.

4. The will, further, should free the executor from personal liability for whatever course of action he or she reasonably takes.

While a properly prepared will can do much to give the executor the flexibility needed to deal with the business, many problems still exist. Regardless of the capabilities of the executor, the liquidation of a business at the death of the proprietor is the worst possible method of disposing of a business. The proprietor personally is aware of this fact, for he or she probably has purchased goods at liquidation sales. The proprietor knows that buyers go to these sales looking for bargains because time favors them. The shrinkage in value is tremendous. The physical assets, inventory and fixtures are sold at a huge discount and the goodwill—that difference between the book value and the going-concern value—is lost to the family forever.

Obviously, liquidation of the business at the death of the proprietor is not something to look forward to, but at the same time it is often the best course of action. It is, therefore, up to the proprietor to take steps during life, beyond a proper will, to offset the shrinkage in value on liquidation.

Life Insurance

Life insurance on the sole proprietor will offset the shrinkage in value on liquidation, if the only alternative is to liquidate the business. Consider the following advantages of life insurance in such circumstances:

- *Life insurance will pay estate settlement costs.* Adequate liquidity must be available to meet business debts as well as overall estate settlement costs and taxes. Cash that is immediately available at death for such purposes means that the liquidation of the business need not necessarily be hurried and may proceed in an orderly fashion.

- *Life insurance will provide additional working capital for the business during the interim period of operation.* If the business is one that needs considerable working capital, the executor may need additional cash to run the business. Life insurance will enable the executor to continue the business until the best possible price for the business as a whole, or for its individual assets, can be obtained.

- *Life insurance will offset the diminishing value of the business.* As pointed out before, in almost every case, shrinkage in the value of the business will result when the proprietor's business is liquidated at death. While the shrinkage cannot be avoided, the effect can be mitigated by the purchase of life insurance. Life insurance will replace the dollars lost in the sale and provide additional income for the proprietor's family.

Now let us apply what we have learned to a practical example of a sole proprietor who plans to have the business liquidated at death. Although the figures used in this illustration are modest, the principles apply to sole proprietor situations of all sizes.

CASE STUDY: MS. GREEN

Ms. Green is the sole owner of a small but prosperous mercantile business. The business has prospered because of her own abilities and warm relationships with her customers. Through the years she has poured most of her earnings back into the business. Having no one in her family with the ability to take over the business at her death, and knowing that the goodwill of the business will die with her, she has made authorization in her will for an orderly liquidation by her executor. She feels that, given sufficient time to shop around, her personal representative will be able to dispose of the assets for about 50 percent of their present worth. Ms. Green rents her place of business; therefore, she has no business real estate. Here's a picture of the value of the business assets before her death and after death (assuming an orderly liquidation).

	Before Death	After Death
Cash value of merchandise	$25,000	$12,500
Fixtures and furniture	6,000	3,000
Accounts receivable	5,000	2,500
Total	$36,000	$18,000

Ms. Green has business debts of $4,000. She also has a $50,000 mortgage on a $100,000 home. She has $25,000 of life insurance. She has other property worth $5,000.

If Ms. Green were to die today, her estate, assuming her executor could liquidate the business assets for $18,000, would look like this:

Assets		Liabilities	
Home	$100,000	Estimated Funeral and administration expenses	$ 8,000
Personal property	5,000		
Life insurance	25,000	Mortgage on home	50,000
Business assets	18,000	Business debts	4,000
	$148,000		$62,000

Ms. Green needs $62,000 in estate liquidity to take care of the costs of settling her estate, clear up her business debts and pay off her mortgage. She also realizes that her family needs substantially more income protection than that provided by her present life insurance. Also she wants to leave the home free and clear of any mortgage.

The Solution

Ms. Green solves both her estate and her family problems by purchasing $80,000 of additional life insurance protection.

First, she earmarks $62,000 of the proceeds to pay funeral and administration expenses, the mortgage and the business debts. Until these proceeds actually are used for their intended purposes, they also will serve as a reserve to make it possible for Ms. Green's executor to continue the business until she can liquidate its assets for their best price.

The gross physical value of her business is $36,000. Ms. Green wants to leave a dollar equivalent to her family. Therefore, she next earmarks the remaining $18,000 of life insurance proceeds for her family's benefit to offset the 50 percent shrinkage value of her business assets after her death. These proceeds can be paid to them in the form of income.

The $18,000 the business assets should bring under an orderly liquidation can be used by Ms. Green in a number of ways: she can invest the money in an annuity to provide additional guaranteed lifetime income; she might use the funds to provide a higher education for the surviving children; or she might use part as an emergency fund, part as an income fund and part for education.

In any event, the $18,000 of life insurance allocated to offset the shrinkage in the business assets coupled with the $18,000 realized on the sale of the business assets enables Ms. Green to transfer a dollar value to the family equal to the physical value of the proprietorship during her life.

In summary, remember that a proprietorship will be liquidated at death when one of two situations exists: First, when there is no one in the family capable of or interested in continuing the business and no buyer exists for the business. Second, when the proprietor has not sold the business prior to his or her death. In order to ensure an orderly liquidation, a proprietor needs a properly drawn will, which gives the executor the flexibility and discretion to do all that is needed to effect the best possible disposal of the business—whether by liquidation or otherwise. Finally, a proprietor needs sufficient life insurance to pay estate settlement costs, offset the diminished value of the business and provide income for surviving family members.

FAMILY RETENTION

Not every sole proprietorship will be liquidated at the death of the owner. Some will be retained by the family of the proprietor. In businesses in which a son, daughter or spouse is actively involved, be sure to introduce the topic of family succession. In most cases, you will immediately get the attention and interest of your prospect. In fact, a surprising number of business owners talk about having a son or daughter take over the business upon their retirement or death. Unfortunately, only a fraction of these owners ever take steps to put their wishes into concrete plans.

Once the sole proprietor determines which family member will take the reins of the business, the proprietor must reduce this plan to writing. The appropriate place to provide names of successors and instructions in running the business is in a will or a trust document. Most proprietors will use a will. The proprietor should be made aware of the following issues when arranging for the smooth transition of the business.

Will Provisions

It is likely that the proprietor will name the family successor to the business as the executor of the will. Even if this is not the case, anyone who is made executor of the will should be given these discretionary powers during the period of estate administration:

- the power to retain the business interest indefinitely;

- the power to do everything required to operate the business successfully, including making repairs and capital improvements and borrowing money on the strength of the business assets;

- the power to reorganize the business, incorporate it, or merge it with another enterprise; and

- the power to borrow money—if necessary—to help the estate meet its liquidity needs.

In addition to these discretionary powers, the will also should include a provision that relieves the executor of personal liability when he or she conducts such duties in good faith.

Life Insurance Beneficiary Provisions

Provisions also must be made to ensure that adequate cash is available upon the owner's death (or retirement) to meet the company's responsibilities, provide operating funds for an orderly transition and guarantee that income or a lump sum can be paid to other family members and heirs not involved in the business.

For instance, the executor must have adequate cash to pay funeral and administration expenses, personal and business debts and death taxes. It is important to remember that directions in the will permitting a continuation of the business will not be allowed to interfere with the right of existing creditors and the tax collectors to receive their money when the proprietor dies. The executor may be forced to sell the business if the estate lacks either sufficient liquidity or nonbusiness assets that can be liquidated to raise cash. The liquidity failure can destroy the proprietor's objective—the delivery of a going business to his or her family after the owner's death.

Providing Liquidity

When we think of ways to provide the necessary estate liquidity, we immediately think of life insurance. The reason is that the hazard to be protected against—debts, estate costs and taxes at death—can be determined reasonably and what better way of providing a measurable amount of money at death than with life insurance? The proprietor can purchase no other liquid asset that creates with one premium the fund to meet these cash needs. This is why attorneys and other business planning advisers first suggest the purchase of life insurance when a liquidity need is revealed.

Life Insurance Ownership Provisions

The proprietor has several options in arranging the ownership and beneficiary provisions of life insurance to supply the necessary estate liquidity. There are three different methods.

First, the proprietor may own the insurance policy but name the estate as beneficiary. This ensures that the executor will receive the insurance proceeds directly. However, it also means that creditors of the estate can reach the proceeds because the life insurance funds become part of the probate estate. Additionally—and, possibly, more significantly—the death benefits become part of the federal gross estate, which could increase the estate's liquidity problems by increasing any estate taxes due.

Another way of keeping life insurance proceeds out of the proprietor's estate is to name his or her spouse as both owner and beneficiary of the policy on the sole proprietor's life. However, the insured cannot possess any incidents of ownership at death. "Incidents of ownership" generally means the right of the insured or the insured's estate to the economic benefits of the policy. This includes the right to change the beneficiary or to borrow against the policy cash values. As long as the insured does not retain any incidents of ownership, the mere payment of premiums by the insured will not cause the death proceeds to be included in the estate.

In community property states, if the spouse of the sole proprietor is to be the separate owner of a policy so that none of the proceeds will be included in his or her gross estate at death, care must be exercised when the policy is acquired. The IRS probably will contend that one-half of the proceeds is includable because of the insured's community interest. Courts, however, have held that if there is affirmative action on the part of the insured at the policy's acquisition to show that the insured assigned and intended the proceeds at the insured's death to be the separate property of the surviving spouse, none of the proceeds will be includable in the insured's gross estate. The specific affirmative action required to accomplish this varies from state to state, so the insurance agent should check carefully the law for the particular community property state in which he or she is working.

A third possible arrangement for the proprietor's insurance is to have the insurance owned by and payable to a trustee empowered by the will or a trust instrument (but not be required) to purchase estate assets from the executor. This purchase gives the executor the cash necessary to pay estate debts, expenses and death taxes.

Like the first method, this beneficiary arrangement assures that the executor will have the cash to meet the estate's liquidity needs. In the moderate estate, it is a superior arrangement for the insurance proceeds not to be part of the proprietor's probate estate and subject to both probate expenses and a state inheritance tax. If the trust is made irrevocable, the insurance proceeds will not incur the federal estate tax—a benefit to the policy owner.

Provisions for the Surviving Spouse

Many proprietors who plan to leave their business interest to adult sons and(or) daughters do not have sufficiently large estates apart from their businesses to provide adequately for their surviving spouses after their deaths. Without a sufficient provision for a surviving spouse, the widow or widower could be left in a desperate financial position.

The proprietor often faces a legal as well as a moral obligation to treat the surviving spouse equitably. For example, a widow normally is entitled under her husband's will to receive a share of her husband's estate at least equal to what she would have received by state law had he died without a will. Legally, therefore, the widow can elect to take her statutory share rather than the portion of his estate allotted under her husband's will.

In this situation, life insurance payable to the proprietor's estate will provide the additional funds necessary to raise the wife's share to the legal limits—when the estate assets beyond the proprietor's business interest are insufficient.

Many states now have a legal equivalent to the widow's election for widowers, and even if a state does not, most sole proprietors will feel strongly inclined to treat the widower adequately and fairly. Here again, life insurance can assure that the necessary funds will be available, allowing the business interest to be transferred to those the owner desires.

Provisions for the Other Children

Most proprietors will want to treat their other children as equitably as the child who will inherit the business. Here again, life insurance on the proprietor's life can solve the problem.

If the surviving spouse is living at the time of the life insurance purchase, the policy can be made payable to the trustee previously described. The children will be residuary beneficiaries of the trust and eventually will receive their shares at the death of the second parent.

If the spouse predeceases the proprietor and the children are adults, the children who will not receive the business can be made beneficiaries of an amount of insurance that, along with the proprietor's nonbusiness assets, gives them an amount equal to the value of the business. And, if death taxes are a factor, the children might own the policy on their parent's life.

Now let's see through an illustration how the bequest of a proprietorship to an adult family member works.

■ CASE STUDY: MR. BLUE

Mr. Blue, age 52, is a commercial photographer who has built up a quality business and clientele over the past 25 years. This has brought to his family a comfortable living. Blue's son, Tom, age 28, has worked for Blue during the past six years and has become an accomplished photographer in his own right.

Much goodwill attributed to the Blue name can be transferred to the son. Therefore, Blue naturally wants to leave the business to his son. At the same time he wants his wife to be well provided for, and his daughter, Ann, age 25, to be treated as equitably as his son, even though she is financially independent.

Blue rents his studio but has about $15,000 tied up in photography equipment, furniture and fixtures. His accounts receivable average about $5,000 and business obligations about $3,000.

If Blue were to die today, his estate picture would look like this:

Assets		Liabilities	
Home (owned jointly with wife)	$100,000	Estimated funeral and administration expenses	$ 9,000
Personal property	20,000	Mortgage on home	60,000
Life insurance (payable to wife)	60,000	Business debts	3,000
Business equipment	15,000	Personal debts	4,000
Accounts receivable	5,000		$76,000
	$200,000		

His Estate Plan

Mr. Blue, in his will, directs that his business assets—the business equipment and the accounts receivable—be transferred to his son. Giving his son the accounts receivable will impress upon customers that the business will continue to operate as a going concern. This might not be the case if the executor were directed to collect for the estate's benefit; customers might assume from the action that the business was being liquidated.

Blue's home, which is owned jointly with his wife, and his life insurance, which is to be paid to her directly, will pass outside his probate estate. Thus, only the $20,000 of personal property will pass to his wife by means of his will; the balance of his probate estate ($20,000 of business assets) will pass to his son. However, the value of property passing to her outside his probate estate is $160,000.

Additional Required

Blue needs $76,000 of estate liquidity to assure his wife that their home will be left to her unencumbered by a mortgage, that his funeral and estate administration expenses will be paid promptly, that his personal debts will be cleaned up and that his son will take over a going photography business unhampered by business debts.

Blue also wants to treat his daughter as equitably as his son; thus, he needs an additional $20,000 to leave to her at his death.

Finally, Blue realizes that his widow will need more income than that provided for her under his present $60,000 life insurance program.

To provide for these three independent requests and to guarantee a successful transfer of the business to his son, Blue purchases $160,000 of additional permanent insurance on his life, which he allocates in the following manner:

- $76,000 payable to his estate to provide his executor with the needed funds to cover the costs of funeral and administration expenses, clear the mortgage on his home and pay off his business debts and personal debts;

- $64,000 to his wife, which can provide her with additional income under the income options in the life insurance contract; and

- $20,000 for the benefit of his daughter to equalize the value of the business bequeathed to his son.

Blue retains ownership of the policy because federal estate taxes are not a factor in his case. Furthermore, he wants access to the policy's cash value in the event of business opportunities or emergencies.

Through the use of life insurance, it is possible for Blue to retain his business within the family and at the same time carry out his obligations to all family members.

Although the above solution works very well and is presented as an example of a satisfactory approach to continuing a sole proprietorship, it is not the only method available. Another approach would be for Mr. Blue to execute a buy-sell agreement with his son Tom. Buy-sell agreements are discussed in depth later in the course. For now, it is sufficient to indicate that Tom's salary would be raised by an amount necessary to pay the premiums on the insurance policy that funds the buy-sell agreement.

■ SELLING THE BUSINESS TO AN EMPLOYEE

In some proprietorships, in which the owner has no one in the family capable of running the business, the business may be continued successfully after the owner's death if an employee is ready and willing to step in and take the owner's place.

Typical of such employees are: (a) the valuable, all-purpose individual who is familiar with every facet of the operation; (b) an outstanding sales representative who is responsible for obtaining a substantial amount of the firm's business; and (c) the indispensable inside person who runs the internal operations while the owner concentrates on sales.

The sale of the business to the employee at the proprietor's death is natural in each of these instances. The employee's talent is recognized by customers, creditors and suppliers; therefore, the employee brings to the business a degree of goodwill distinct from that attributable to the owner. The business, as a result, will continue to have a going-concern value based on the goodwill created both by the efforts of the employee and the deceased proprietor.

A Two-Step Plan

A two-step plan can bring about an orderly sale of the business to an employee:

1. The employee purchases an insurance policy on the life of the employer. The employee is the owner, the premium payer and the beneficiary of the policy. If the proprietor should die, the insurance proceeds will be used to buy the business. On the other hand, if the employee has had the foresight to purchase a permanent insurance policy and the proprietor retires and wants to sell the business, the employee can use the policy's cash value to make a substantial down payment toward the purchase of the business. The balance of the purchase price would be paid in installments over a period of years.

2. A buy-sell agreement is drafted by an attorney setting forth the employee's obligation to buy and the obligation of the legal representative to sell the business interest at an agreed-on price.

Employee's Inability to Pay Insurance Premiums

An obstacle in some cases to the insured proprietorship purchase agreement is the employee's inability to pay the insurance premiums. The employee usually is younger than the owner. Although the employee may be earning a good income, the responsibility of raising a family, combined with the high cost of living and the inroads of taxation, makes the payment of insurance premiums difficult, if not impossible.

Perhaps, before the two parties consider the purchase of term insurance or a reduction of the amount of the insurance coverage, they should consider several ways in which the proprietor can share in the insurance cost.

There are at least two ways that the proprietor can help the employee pay the insurance premiums:

1. The proprietor could increase the compensation of the employee. The proprietor should take care not to make the increase in compensation equal to the insurance premium. Otherwise, the Internal Revenue Service might claim that the proprietor did indirectly what the employer is barred from doing directly—deducting premiums for life insurance that benefits the employer. Therefore the increased compensation should be more than the premium due.

2. The proprietor could loan the employee part or all of the premium. The loans could be secured by a collateral assignment of the cash value of the insurance policy. This arrangement is common in split-dollar plans, which are discussed later in this course.

When a proprietor is fortunate enough to have a capable employee ready and willing to buy the business at the proprietor's death, the proprietor should make every effort to establish the employee as the ultimate purchaser of the business. This will assure the owner's family at his or her death the sale of the business for its true worth, rather than the value of the liquidated assets. The existence of such an employee sale agreement also serves to cement the employee's tie to the business on a long-term basis.

The following example illustrates how the insured purchase-and-sale plan works to the mutual benefit of the proprietor and the employee.

CASE STUDY: MR. BROWN

Mr. Brown, age 50, owns a well-established wholesale sporting goods firm. Ten years ago he hired John Thompson, then age 25, and a well-known former college athlete, as a salesman for his firm. Because of Thompson's reputation as an athlete, his contacts in the sports world and his outstanding sales personality, he has enjoyed a financially successful career. In his ten years with the Brown Co., he also has brought many lucrative accounts to the firm.

Mr. Brown has nobody in his family to whom he can leave the business. However, he wants to avoid a liquidation of the business at his death because of the attendant losses to his family and because he knows that the business can be continued successfully after his death. Mr. Brown also would like his other employees to be assured of good employment. Brown realizes—and Thompson, too—that Thompson is the logical purchaser of the business. Thompson knows and loves the operation, has developed accounts of his own and is identified as an integral part of the Brown Co. by customers, creditors and employees.

At age 35, Thompson is in no position to buy the business if Brown were to die. However, his income is substantial and is large enough that he can afford to maintain insurance on Brown's life equal to the amount of the purchase price. Therefore, Brown's life insurance agent brings to the attention of Brown and Thompson the insured purchase-and-sale plan. They both agree enthusiastically to the plan.

Determining the Purchase Price

After discussion, the two men arrive at a purchase price of $100,000 for the business. Of this amount, $60,000 is attributable to the net assets of the business, and $40,000 recognizes the goodwill created by Brown that will remain in the company after his death.

Thompson buys $100,000 of cash value life insurance on Brown's life for a net annual premium of $3,500. With the payment of the first premium, Thompson immediately creates the full purchase price for the business.

A buy-sell agreement incorporating the purchase price, a commitment by Thompson to maintain adequate insurance on Brown's life and other provisions are prepared by their attorney. The agreement also allows for a periodic review of the purchase price.

Benefits of the Insured Buy-Sell Agreement

When it is the desire of the proprietor to sell the business at death and the wish of the employee to be the buyer, the insured buy-sell agreement offers tremendous advantages to all parties. The proprietor, the proprietor's family, the employee and the company will enjoy the following advantages.

For the Heirs

The estate receives the full purchase price at once. The severe shrinkage due to liquidation of the assets and the loss of goodwill is eliminated.

The estate is settled promptly and efficiently. The executor has cash immediately from the sale of the business to pay the costs of funeral and administration expenses, estate liabilities and death taxes.

The family is relieved of business worries. In exchange for the going-concern value of the business, the estate receives cash that may be invested in suitable, worry-free investments to provide income for the surviving spouse and children.

For the Proprietor

A buyer for the business is established. The proprietor is assured that his or her family will receive a fair price for the business at the owner's death.

For the Employee

The purchasing employee's future business career is assured—not only is the employee's current career stabilized but, come what may, he or she ultimately will own the business.

For the Company

The business is stabilized—customers, suppliers and creditors, aware that plans have been laid for the orderly continuation of the business, will be disposed favorably toward long-term business dealings with the firm.

The services of the employee will be retained—rather than eventually starting a competitive business, the employee will be eager to do a bigger and better job for his or her present employer.

In summary, two factors favor a prearranged sale at the death of the proprietor: a capable, qualified employee who would like to own the business someday, and an assurance that the business's customers or clients will accept the substitution of this employee as owner-manager. After a satisfactory resolution of these two points, life insurance needs to be purchased by the employee on the life of the proprietor, and a purchase agreement between the proprietor and the employee must be implemented setting forth the employee's duty to buy the business at the death of the proprietor and the proprietor's legal representative's duty to sell at an agreed-on price.

THE PROPRIETORSHIP PURCHASE AGREEMENT

The essence of the proprietorship purchase plan is the agreement between the sole proprietor and the purchasing employee—preferably a written agreement binding the proprietor to sell and the employee to buy the business at the proprietor's death.

Closing the Insurance Phase First

Before going into particulars of a proprietorship business insurance agreement, it is important to be aware of the priorities for purchase agreements that are a part of a life insurance sale. Normally, the life insurance is sold and placed in force first before the purchase agreement is drafted and executed. There are three reasons for doing this:

1. The insurance contracts should be tied into the purchase agreement so that the estate of the decedent will be sure of getting the cash when the time comes.

2. The attorney who drafts the agreement will need to identify the policies (by company, by number and by amount).

3. If the proprietor turns out to be uninsurable, some other provision for funding the purchase will have to be made in the agreement.

Possible Need of a Trustee

There are definite reasons for considering a trusteed agreement in the proprietorship setting. A proprietorship insured purchase agreement contains the germ of later disagreement between the proprietor and his or her employee. The agreement provides for a one-way buyout—the employee will buy and the proprietor will sell. The proprietor is interested in getting the highest possible price for the business; the employee desires to purchase it at the lowest possible price. This basic conflict may lead to a later failure of the parties to agree on an increased valuation for the business, or on a choice, alternately, of a certified public accountant to make the valuation.

If such a conflict is even a remote possibility, perhaps the parties should consider employing a trustee as an objective third party. The trustee can function as an intermediary, acting as beneficiary of the life insurance and serving as a go-between in the transfer of cash and notes for the proprietor's business interest. More important, should the parties fail to redetermine the purchase price and the death of the proprietor occurs, the trustee acts to set the purchase price for the business interest.

Valuation of the Proprietor's Interest

Problems and methods used in fixing the valuation of a business interest, including goodwill, are common to many business forms. These principles will be discussed in Chapter 5.

Tax Considerations

The income and estate taxation of insurance premiums, policy payments and proprietorship sale proceeds varies little from that applicable to partners and partnerships. Rather than repeat this discussion, we will defer a discussion of tax considerations until Chapter 5.

The Advantages of a Definite Plan

The advantages of a definite plan for the purchase and sale of the proprietor's interest at the proprietor's death may be illustrated negatively by an example of a business for which no such plan was adopted. In this case, the proprietor started an architectural firm. She had an associate, a younger woman, who came to be a very important part of the business, a truly valuable assistant. When the founder of the firm died, her heirs inherited the business. As a matter of fact, their knowledge of the business was very limited, but they nevertheless sought to run it in accordance with their own ideas. The recommendations, advice and counsel of the surviving associate were largely ignored by the heirs.

As a result, the relations between the parties became strained. The associate could see no opportunity for herself under such circumstances, and finally quit. She started a new company and took with her a talented employee from the old firm. Many of the customers of the old firm went over to the new one, because they knew the capabilities of this former associate of the deceased proprietor. The competition resulted in the early collapse of the business the proprietor left. A successful enterprise passed into the limbo of failed businesses at a complete loss of income for the deceased owner's family.

How much better it would have been for all parties concerned if the proprietor, prior to her death, had executed an appropriate business purchase plan with her associate, under which the associate could have acquired the business for a fair cash price (out of the proceeds of insurance on the proprietor's life).

SUMMARY

The following outlines the basic points covered in proprietorship business insurance agreements:

1. purpose and object of the agreement;

2. provision giving a a first offer to purchase to the employee should the proprietor desire to sell the business during his or her lifetime;

3. description of policies covered by the plan and a method for payment of their premiums;

4. provision for the purchase of the proprietor's business interest on the death of the proprietor;

5. valuation clause and formula stipulated by the parties, as well as a plan for determination of its value, if more than 12 months have lapsed since the last valuation was agreed upon, prior to the proprietor's death;

6. provision for payment of any balance if the value of the business exceeds the business valuation;

7. provision to transfer the insurance policies to the insured if business should be sold during the proprietor's lifetime, or terminated or put into bankruptcy;

8. provision for the manner of execution of the agreement—the transfer of cash and notes for the business interest;

9. provision as to what events terminate this agreement; and

10. provisions for amendment or revocation by parties, and binding the parties and their heirs and successors to the plan.

A Proprietorship Business Insurance Agreement

In this chapter and in following chapters throughout this course, you will find sample legal agreements. These model documents are intended only to illustrate the types of documents a client's attorney may draft. In no circumstance should you attempt to use these agreements, to modify them or to draft similar agreements for your clients. To do so would be to engage in the unauthorized practice of law, a procedure that carries severe legal penalties in many states. These agreements are included so that you will be aware of the basic elements present in most documents drafted for client's specific need by the client's counsel.

We have discovered that the sole proprietor's personal, financial and business affairs are more irrevocably intertwined than those of almost any other business owner. It is impossible to separate the sole proprietor's personal assets from his or her business assets. The sole proprietor is the one person who controls the destiny of the business establishment. On the sole proprietor alone lies the responsibility and effect of business planning. Failure to plan can mean the death of the business and a loss of livelihood for the sole proprietor and the sole proprietor's family.

As a life insurance agent you are in the position to approach proprietors, make them aware of the problems and recommend possible solutions. You have for sale a product—life insurance—that, with other planning instruments, can solve the problems the proprietorship form of business creates. When you multiply these problems by the number of sole proprietorships in existence, you readily can see the vast insurance market open to you.

ILL 4.4 ▪ *Sample Proprietorship Purchase Agreement*

CAUTION: This is a specimen agreement. The actual agreement used in any particular case must be prepared by a qualified attorney.

Agreements made this _____ day of _____, 20__, between John Jones (hereinafter referred to as the Proprietor), Jane Smith (hereinafter referred to as the Employee) and The _____ Bank and Trust Company of _____ (hereinafter referred to as the Trustee).

WITNESSETH:

Whereas the Proprietor, being the sole owner of an unincorporated store located at _____, and known as The _____ Department Store, is desirous of providing the Employee with an expanded opportunity in the business, and is likewise desirous of protecting his investment in this business and of ultimately disposing of it at an adequate price; and

Whereas the Employee is desirous of protecting her business future and of ultimately acquiring for herself the business herein described;

Now, Therefore, it is mutually agreed as follows:

1. If the Proprietor should desire to dispose of The _____ Department Store during his lifetime, he shall first offer in writing to sell it to the Employee. The offer shall be based on a price determined in accordance with the provisions of Paragraph 5 hereof. If the offer is not accepted by the Employee within 60 days of her receipt thereof, the Proprietor shall have a right to dispose of it to any other person but shall not sell it to any other person without giving the Employee the right, which she must exercise within another 15 days, to purchase it at a price and on the terms offered by such other person.

    A provision such as this, restricting the lifetime sale of the business, is necessary if the value set in the buy-sell agreement is to be accepted by the government as the true fair market value for federal estate tax purposes. Such a provision would also seem desirable to protect the employee in the event a competitor or some other prospective purchaser made the employer a more lucrative offer.

2. The Employee has purchased Policy No. _____ issued by the _____ Life Insurance Company on the life of the Proprietor in the sum of $_____, with the Employee as the applicant, owner and beneficiary. During the lifetime of the Proprietor and the continuance in force of this agreement, the Employee agrees to pay premiums on the policy owned by her within 20 days after the due date of each premium and promptly give proof of payment to the Proprietor. If any premium is not paid within 20 days after its due date, the Proprietor shall have the right to pay such premium and charge it against the Employee's salary account.

Alternative Paragraph No. 2—(This provision contemplates the use of a trustee.)

2. The Employee shall deposit with the Trustee, Policy No. _____ issued by the _____ Life Insurance Company on the life of the Proprietor in the sum of $_____, with the Employee as applicant and owner and the Trustee as beneficiary. During the lifetime of the Proprietor and the continuance in force of this agreement, the Employee agrees to pay premiums on the policy owned by her within 20 days after the due date of each premium and promptly give proof of payment to the Trustee and Proprietor. If any premium is not paid within 20 days after its due date, the proprietor shall have the right to pay such premium and charge it against the Employee's salary account.

ILL 4.4 ▪ *Sample Proprietorship Purchase Agreement (Cont.)*

> The employee is named the owner of the policy and is required to pay the premiums. The Trustee, of course, should be named beneficiary. If the employee fails to pay the premiums when due, the employer is authorized to make the payment and charge it against the employee's salary.
>
> A problem sometimes encountered under these plans is that the employee is unable to finance the premium payments on an adequate amount of insurance. In such an event, since it is to the distinct advantage of the proprietor to see that the plan is executed, the proprietor should be willing to assist in financing a portion of the plan during his or her lifetime. If this approach is followed, then provision would be made in the buy-sell agreement for the employee to refund he premiums the employer has paid under the plan to his estate. This refund will be made out of the life insurance proceeds when they are received.
>
> Split-dollar insurance, which is discussed later in this course, provides another possible solution to this problem.

3. This agreement shall extend to and shall include all additional policies issued pursuant hereto, such additional policies to be listed promptly in Schedule A, attached hereto.

    > Many times the value of the business will increase substantially after the buy-sell agreement is executed and before the proprietor retires or dies. This provision allows additional life insurance policies to be purchased in order to keep pace with this increase in value. Naturally, the Trustee should also be named the beneficiary of any additional policies that are taken out.

4. Upon the death of the Proprietor, his estate shall sell to the Employee and the employee shall purchase all of the Proprietor's rights, title and interest in The _____ Department Store. Said business so sold shall include all real estate, furniture and fixtures, inventories and all other tangible and intangible property, including accounts receivable and cash in bank, owned in connection with the said business by the Proprietor. Said sale shall take effect as of the date of death of the Proprietor, and the purchase price shall be computed in accordance with the provisions of Paragraph 5 of this agreement. It is agreed that upon the of the Proprietor, the Employee shall be entitled forthwith to operate the said business but title shall pass as of the close of business on the date of death of Proprietor. The Employee shall be entitled to all of the profits of the business and suffer all the losses arising between the close of business on the date of death of the Proprietor and the consummation of this agreement.

    > Here is a key provision of the agreement. Under this provision, the estate *must* sell, and the employee *must* buy. This binding agreement to sell and the corresponding obligation to buy seems preferable to the various "option" type agreements that could be used. Too, the "option" type agreements may not effectively establish a value for federal estate purposes.

5. Unless and until changed as hereinafter provided, the total value of The _____ Department Store for the purpose of determining the purchase price to be paid for the business, shall be $_____. Said purchase price has been agreed upon by the parties as representing the fair value of the business

ILL 4.4 ▪ *Sample Proprietorship Purchase Agreement (Cont.)*

including good will. Within 30 days following the end of each fiscal year, or more often if the parties so agree, the parties shall redetermine the value of the business. Said value shall be endorsed on Schedule B attached hereto. If the parties fail to redetermine said value for a particular fiscal year, the last previously stipulated value shall be determined by a certified public accountant who shall be selected by the mutual agreement of the Employee and the Legal Representative of the Proprietor. To determine said value, the accountant shall cause an examination of the status of The _____ Department Store to be made including an inventory of its assets, as of the date of death of the Proprietor. Upon the information revealed by such an examination, the accountant is hereby empowered to establish a fair and reasonable value for the business, as a going concern, determining such value by any method which he may deem appropriate. In establishing a reasonable value for the business, the accountant is by this instrument authorized to employ and act upon the advice and counsel of such appraisers and other persons as it may deem necessary and competent to pass judgment upon the true value of the business as a going concern, and shall have full discretion in accepting or discarding the recommendations of any such persons. The value fixed by the accountant pursuant to these provisions shall not be held liable in any way to any person for any finding made in good faith.

Alternative Paragraph No. 5—(This paragraph contemplates the use of a trustee.)

5. Unless and until charged as hereinafter provided, the total value of The _____ Department Store for the purpose of determining the purchase price to be paid for the business, shall be $_____. Said purchase price has been agreed upon by the parties as representing the fair value of the business including goodwill. Within 60 days following the end of each fiscal year, the parties shall redetermine the value of the business. Said value shall be endorsed on Schedule B attached hereto. If the parties fail to redetermine said value for a particular fiscal year, the last previously stipulated value shall control, except that if no valuation has been agreed upon for a period of 24 months immediately preceding the death of the Proprietor, the value of the business shall be determined by the Trustee. To determine said value, the Trustee shall cause an examination of the status of The _____ Department Store to be made including an inventory of its assets, as of the date of death of the Proprietor. Upon the information revealed by such an examination, the Trustee is hereby empowered to establish a fair and reasonable value for the business, as a going concern, determining such value by any method which it may deem appropriate. In establishing a reasonable value for the business, the Trustee is by this instrument authorized to employ and act upon the advice and counsel of such accountants, appraisers and other persons as it may deem necessary and competent to pass judgment upon the true value of the business as a going concern, and shall have full discretion in accepting or discarding the recommendations of any such persons. The value fixed by the Trustee pursuant to these provisions shall be final, and shall fully bind all parties in interest, and the Trustee shall not be held liable in any way to any person for any finding made in good faith.

> **This provision utilizes the fixed price method of valuation and sets forth the current value of the proprietorship and provides for revaluation each year. The importance of annually executing the revaluation should be impressed upon the parties to the agreement. Too often this provision is forgotten, and disputes over the value of the business subsequently develop. It is where this provision is ignored that the Trustee must act as arbitrator and determine the fair market value of the business. However, the Trustee also can serve to remind the parties each year of their obligation to revalue the business.**
>
> **The fixed price method, coupled with a revaluation provision, has many advantages. Among them are the following:**
>
> - **The price that is arrived at initially, and upon subsequent reviews, as a result of head-to-head negotiations probably will be as "fair" as possible.**

ILL 4.4 ■ *Sample Proprietorship Purchase Agreement (Cont.)*

- Such a price provision does not involve complex formulas and is free of standards and terms that, because of possible ambiguity, could lead to controversy.

- It is a flexible method that may be adjusted periodically to reflect the changing fortunes of the business.

- The parties to the agreement are able to determine readily what price will be paid for their interest and plan their estates accordingly.

- Finally, since the purchase price is a known dollar amount, it is possible at all times to keep the buy-sell agreement "funded" with adequate amounts of life insurance.

An alternate method of valuing the business at the proprietor's death is the use of some kind of "formula" approach. Under this method, the specific price to be paid for the business is not stated in the agreement. Rather, it is agreed that the value will be determined at the time of the proprietor's death under an agreed upon, stated formula. As will be noted later, some of the more common formulas used are (1) the actual book value at the time of death; (2) some method of capitalization of earnings; and (3) average book value over a stated period of time. Each of these methods has strengths and weaknesses. The important thing is to have a method set out in the agreement that appeals to all parties as a fair method of establishing the purchase price.

6. The Employee agrees that the proceeds of the policies subject to this agreement shall be applied toward the purchase price set forth above. If the purchase price so set forth exceeds the proceeds of the life insurance, the balance of the purchase price shall be paid in _____ consecutive monthly payments beginning _____ months after the date of the Proprietor's death. The unpaid balance of the purchase price shall be evidenced by a series of negotiable promissory notes made by the Employee to the order of the estate of the Proprietor with interest at _____% per annum. Said notes shall provide for the acceleration of the due date of all unpaid notes in the series on default in the payment of any note or interest thereon; and said notes shall also give the Employee the option of prepayment in whole or in part at any time.

Alternative Paragraph No. 6—(This paragraph contemplates the use of a trustee.)

6. The Employee agrees that the proceeds of the policies subject to this agreement shall be applied toward the purchase price set forth above. The Trustee shall apply the proceeds in accordance with the terms of this agreement. If the purchase price so set forth exceeds the proceeds of the life insurance, the balance of the purchase price shall be paid in ___ consecutive monthly payments beginning _____ months after the date of the notes made by the Employee to the order of the estate of the Proprietor with interest at _____% per annum. Said notes shall provide for the acceleration of the due date of all unpaid notes in the series on default in the payment of any note or interest thereon; and said notes also shall give the Employee the option of prepayment in whole or in part at any time.

Since the purchase price and the insurance coverage may not precisely keep pace with each other at all times, it is important that provision for payment of any balance in the purchase price be made. The exact terms of any notes that are to be executed should also be included in the buy-sell agreement.

ILL 4.4 ■ *Sample Proprietorship Purchase Agreement (Cont.)*

> In this connection, it should be noted that while it is desirable for the full value of the business to be covered by the insurance, this is not absolutely necessary. This plan of purchase can be of tremendous value even where the insurance provides only a substantial down payment toward the purchase price.

Additional Paragraph—(This paragraph is used in a trusted agreement and sets forth the duties of the trustee.)

The duties of the trustee are as follows:

(a) To receive and safely hold the life insurance policy described herein and any that may be added, as described in Schedule A, attached hereto; and proof of payment of all premiums paid by the Employee, as required herein.

(b) Upon the death of the proprietor to:

    (i) determine the reasonable value of the business, if necessary, as provided in Paragraph 5 herein.

    (ii) make claim for and collect the proceeds of the life insurance policies issued on the life of the Proprietor. The Trustee shall be under no obligation to institute any action to recover the proceeds of any of the policies, unless indemnified by the Employee for all expenses and attorney's fees connected therewith.

    (iii) demand and receive from the Employee any notes required to be executed by him, as required herein.

    (iv) deliver to the estate of the proprietor the proceeds of the life insurance policies collected by it; any notes required herein to be executed or delivered by the Employee and an agreement executed by the Employee, indemnifying the estate of the Proprietor against all legal liabilities of the business, provided it receives simultaneously from the estate of the Proprietor in the business described herein.

(c) Upon termination of this agreement other than by the death of the Proprietor, the Trustee shall deliver the policies described herein and in Schedule A, to the Employee. However, the Trustee shall be under no obligation to deliver such policies until it has received the compensation and reimbursement for expenses and counsel fees, if any, specified in Paragraph 8 hereof.

> When the services of a Trustee are utilized, its duties and powers should be clearly delineated in the agreement.

Additional Paragraph—(This paragraph is used in a trusteed agreement and sets forth the compensation of the trustee.)

The Trustee shall be paid as compensation a commission of _____ percent (_____%) of all moneys which it collects as proceeds of life insurance on the death of the Proprietor. If the Trustee is required to value the business of The _____ Department Store as provided in Paragraph 5 herein, the Trustee may also deduct from the insurance proceeds it collects, the expense of an audit and appraisal of the business plus the fees of any person which the Trustee employs in establishing the value. If this agreement is terminated other than by the death of the Proprietor, the Trustee shall receive a fee of $_____, for its services in terminating the trust. The Trustee shall be reimbursed for all its reasonable expenses and counsel fees. The Trustee shall have the right to resign at any time upon giving 30 days' notice to the Proprietor and the Employee, and the Proprietor and the Employee shall have the right to substitute another Trustee at any time by paying to the Trustee a fee of $_____. The Trustee's compensation, fees and expenses shall be divided and paid equally by the Proprietor and the Employee.

ILL 4.4 ▪ *Sample Proprietorship Purchase Agreement (Cont.)*

The fees the Trustee is to receive should be set out in the agreement.

7. Upon the termination of this agreement during the Proprietor's lifetime, the Proprietor shall have the right to purchase from the Employee or from her estate in case of her death, any and all of the policies insuring her life, for a price equal to the interpolated terminal reserve thereof as of the date of transfer, less any existing indebtedness charged against the policy, plus the proportionate part of the gross premium last paid before the date of transfer which covers the period extending beyond that date. The right may be exercised at any time within 60 days after the Employee's termination of employment, or within 60 days after the qualification of the Legal Representative of the deceased Employee by the payment of such price. If the right is not exercised within the time allowed, it shall lapse.

    A provision such as this that sets a definite procedure under which the proprietor is allowed to purchase the policy on his life from the employee in the event the buy-sell agreement is terminated should be included.

8. The employee shall execute and deliver to the Trustee any promissory notes required herein to be executed by her as part of the purchase price, together with a written agreement indemnifying the estate of the deceased Proprietor against all liabilities of the business. Upon payment of the purchase price to the estate of the deceased Proprietor, in cash or in cash and notes, the estate shall execute and deliver to the Trustee all documents reasonably required to evidence such purchase; and all rights of the estate in the business and assets shall thereafter belong to the Employee.

    Since the liabilities of the business are also the proprietor's personal liabilities, this provision is desirable to assure that the employee discharges any obligations for which the proprietor's estate could be held liable.

9. The agreement may be altered, amended or terminated by a writing signed by the Proprietor and the Employee, but no amendment shall be made affecting the duties of the Trustee without its consent thereto.

10. This agreement shall terminate on the occurrence of any of the following events:
    (a) mutual agreement in writing of the Proprietor and Employee, and deposited with the Trustee;
    (b) termination of the employment of the Employee, whether voluntary or involuntary, upon deposit by the Proprietor with the Trustee of a notice in writing of such termination of employment;
    (c) bankruptcy or insolvency of the Proprietor;
    (d) death of the Employee prior to the death of the Proprietor;
    (e) death of the Proprietor and Employee simultaneously or within a period of 30 days; or
    (f) at the option of the Proprietor if the Employee fails to pay the premiums within the grace period of the policy or policies of life insurance owned by her, for the purposes of this agreement, or assigns, surrenders, or borrows against said policy or policies, changes the beneficiary or makes the proceeds payable other than in a lump sum without the written consent of the Proprietor.

11. The agreement shall be binding upon the Proprietor and the Employee, their heirs, legal representatives, successors and assigns.

ILL 4.4 ■ *Sample Proprietorship Purchase Agreement (Cont.)*

12. Notwithstanding the provisions of this agreement, any life insurance company whose policies are listed herein, or in Schedule B attached hereto, is hereby authorized to act in accordance with the terms of any policies issued by it as if this agreement did not exist, and payment or performance of its contractual obligations by the insurer in accordance with the terms of any such policy shall completely discharge the insurer from all claims and demands of all persons whomsoever. Any insurer is further authorized to provide the insured proprietor with any information with respect to the policy or policies on his life owned by the Employee. No insurer shall be deemed to be a party to this agreement for any purpose.

13. The agreement shall be governed by the law of the State of _____.

IN WITNESS WHEREOF, the parties hereto have executed this agreement at _____ in the County of _____, State of _____, on the day and the year above written.

_____

_____

_____ Bank and Trust Co.

By _____

SCHEDULE A

Schedule of Additional Life Insurance Policies

Name of Company	Policy No.	Amount	Signature of Employee-Owner

SCHEDULE B

Endorsements

Date of Execution_____

Pursuant to Paragraph 5 of this agreement, the Proprietor and the Employee do hereby determine that the total value of The _____ Department Store as of this date $_____.

> Schedule B. The attorney may want to reproduce Schedule B several times in order to accommodate the parties in executing their annual revaluations.

CHAPTER 4 QUESTIONS FOR REVIEW

1. According to the 1999 Statistical Abstract of the United States, what is the number of sole proprietorships in this country?

    A. 1.71 million

    B. 3.28 million

    C. 17.0 million

    D. 22.6 million

2. When a sole proprietor dies

    A. the estate is treated like the estate of any individual.

    B. the legal representative is empowered by law to convert the business assets to cash as quickly as possible.

    C. Both A and B

    D. Neither A nor B

3. The alternatives preferred in planning the disposition of the business upon the death of the proprietor include all the following EXCEPT

    A. forced liquidation

    B. orderly liquidation

    C. family retention

    D. sale to an employee

4. The requirements for an orderly liquidation include

    A. buy-sell agreement and life insurance

    B. will and life insurance

    C. trustee and buy-sell agreement

    D. legal representative and trustee

5. If family retention is the goal of the sole proprietor, life insurance is needed to

    A. pay final expenses and administration costs

    B. provide income for a surviving spouse

    C. provide bequests for family members not actively involved in the business

    D. all of the above

5

The Partnership

This chapter discusses opportunities for insurance professionals in the partnership market. Included is an examination of the types of partnerships and partnership structure; the problems survivors (both family and business partners) face when a partner dies; and the three positive alternatives: planned liquidation, reorganization with heirs or purchase by surviving partners. Sample agreements also are provided.

A partnership is often described as a business marriage. For better or worse, richer or poorer, two or more persons pool their assets and abilities toward a common objective—profit.

In this chapter, we'll profile the partnership market, focusing on the structure of the partnership as a unique business entity. We will also look at the consequences of the death of a partner, the alternatives facing survivors and the life insurance solutions.

THE PARTNERSHIP MARKET

Today there are approximately 1.7 million active partnerships in the United States. Unlike the sole proprietor, partners see a distinct advantage to pooling their talent and their resources. This critical interdependence between partners is both its strength as a business form and its inherent weakness, in that, should anything happen to one member of the partnership team, the prosperity—in fact, survival—of the entire partnership becomes questionable.

This interdependence is generally well understood by a company's partners. To the insurance professional, it means an awareness of a need and, in turn, a golden opportunity to approach, work with and help partners protect their business and their individual families.

Why People Form Partnerships

Before we look at the types of partnerships and partnership structure, let's review a few key reasons people form partnerships.

1. *There is a need for specialization.* In our complex business environment, specialties have developed within every business and profession. Today, it is difficult for any one individual to possess all the skills and knowledge needed to build and run a successful business. That's why partners come together—one may be a product expert, another an experienced salesperson, a third a financial or business management whiz. Each brings his or her own special skill to the business.

2. *Overhead expenses can be reduced.* In a partnership, members share offices, equipment and other facilities, as well as staff and other manpower. Costly duplication of materials and personnel is eliminated. This improves operating efficiency and competitiveness and serves to keep overhead costs down.

3. *The whole is greater than the sum of its parts*—if only because the peaks and valleys of productive effort are leveled out. A multimember partnership is less susceptible to unpredictable financial fluctuations, because the business is a reflection less of one person's personality and management style than of the group's. They come together for stability and mutual support. In return, their total productivity very often dramatically outstrips that which any of the partners could create alone.

4. *Capital can be raised more easily.* Start-up costs or the purchase price of an existing business may be greater than one person can assume. Partners going into the business help reduce the initial cost.

PARTNERSHIP STRUCTURE AND OPERATION

While there are several different types of partnerships, most have several unique characteristics in common.

1. *A partnership has no specific or separate legal life.* It is formed when two or more people come together for profit. While a written agreement forming and defining the partnership is preferable, it is not necessary. All states do have laws, however, requiring partners to register the names of the owners.

2. *A partnership itself pays no income taxes.* An information return, which details the income, expenses and profits of the partnership, must be filed each year. The profits, however, are allocated proportionately among the partners, who report income on their own personal income tax returns.

3. *Individual partners can make legal commitments that are binding on all the partners.* More significantly, in general partnerships (discussed below), all partners are fully liable for all expenses and debts of the partnership. This liability goes beyond contributed cash or other assets to include all personal assets as well.

4. *A partnership dissolves when one partner dies or withdraws from the partnership.* In fact, unless there is a written agreement and plan stating otherwise, a partnership must end upon the death of a partner.

Types of Partnerships

In general, partnerships share the same above characteristics. However, several important distinctions exist between partnerships.

Partnerships can be divided into two separate classes: *general partnerships* and *limited partnerships*.

In a general partnership, each partner contributes capital to the business in the form of money, assets or services. Most importantly, each partner shares actively in the control and management of the business. Each act of the partner is attributable to the other partners.

Additionally, each partner shares proportionately in the profits of the business. Liability for debts, however, is not limited or proportionate. As stated above, each partner is personally liable for the full amount of partnership indebtedness. This liability extends not only to each partner's investment in the company, but also to all personal assets. The general partnership is the most common form; unless indicated otherwise, our discussion will focus on the general partnership.

A limited partnership is composed of both general partners and limited partners. A limited partner contributes capital to the business but has no active control or management within the business.

Similarly, a limited partner's liability extends only to the amount of contributions to the business. Personal assets are not available to creditors of the business, should insolvency occur.

Commercial vs. Professional Partnerships

Before going on, let's note the distinction between *professional partnerships* and *commercial partnerships*. The primary difference lies in the nature of their assets.

In the professional partnership, income is derived principally from the personal services rendered by the partners (doctors, lawyers, dentists, etc.), with the capital investment being almost incidental. Another feature is that, generally, only other professionals—with similar skills to those of the existing partners—can enter the partnership.

Commercial partnerships are businesses that generally have substantial inventories and(or) fixed assets representing the capital investment of the partners.

The Partnership Agreement

As we mentioned before, the agreement between the partners need not be in writing. However, for the protection of all parties, the partnership agreement should always be in writing. One reason for a written agreement is to counteract the effect of a dissolution of the partnership at the death of a partner. A written agreement can make provision for the reorganization of the partnership business at the death or withdrawal of a partner. Another reason why the partners should have a definite, written partnership agreement is that many states have laws stating that contracts or agreements that are not to be completed within one year must be in writing to bind the parties. Finally, in those states that have adopted it, the Uniform Partnership Act will control in the absence of a written partnership agreement. The provisions of the UPA rarely coincide with the wishes and desires of the partners concerning the management of their business affairs.

The insurance professional can turn all three of the above reasons into potent sales approaches to partnerships for partnership insurance. The reasons for a written agreement can be framed in the form of questions to the partners: "Are you aware . . . ?" In this way, the agent not only is moving closer to a possible life insurance sale, but also renders a truly valuable service to those partners who have not yet taken the time to reduce their partnership agreement in writing.

A written agreement should include provisions covering at least the following subjects:

- the parties to the contract;
- the firm name;
- the purpose for which the partnership has been formed;
- the investments the different parties have made and the extent of their respective interests insofar as the division of profits and losses between them is concerned;
- the rights of the parties with respect to the conduct of the business and their powers as agents for each other; and
- the arrangements for the dissolution and reorganization or termination of the partnership in the event of death of a partner or other contingencies.

WHEN A PARTNER DIES

The death of a partner dissolves the partnership. In the absence of a special agreement to the contrary, a partnership no longer exists—except for the purposes of winding up its affairs. The surviving partners, then, must either liquidate or reorganize.

Legal Duties of the Surviving Partners

The surviving partners and the business itself instantly come up against a stone wall. By law, the surviving partners are prevented from entering into any new contracts or obligations on the part of the firm. They cannot borrow money, buy new stock or equipment, or continue the business in *any* way. The surviving partners are limited in the obligations that may be incurred in the liquidation process.

Goods may be sold for cash only, unless the surviving partners assume personally the risk of the credit loss. Sales must be at the best cash price obtainable. The surviving partners cannot require the administrator or the executor of the deceased partner's estate to sign renewals of notes or firm obligations. These and other obstacles face the surviving partners in their activities with respect to the business.

The Forced Liquidation

When a partner dies and no plan about what to do with the business has been worked out in advance, the surviving partners and the deceased partner's family members face unattractive choices. Remember, the surviving partners cannot continue to operate the business.

They do have the option to attempt to come to terms with the survivors and reorganize the business. All too often, though, this attempt fails. As a result, they simply must liquidate the business, as prescribed by law, and distribute the proceeds to the surviving partners and the deceased partner's heirs.

Most attempts to reorganize fail because of the following reasons:

1. *A lack of liquidity—both in the estate of the decedent and in the business— forces a sale of the business.* The estate needs the cash to pay the decedent's debts, the estate administration, funeral and last medical expenses and the estate and inheritance taxes. The estate itself does not have the cash. Further, the partnership does not have the cash to purchase the decedent's interest and thereby provide the needed liquidity. The estate is forced to seek the liquidation of the partnership to raise the cash.

2. *The consent of the decedent's heirs to the continued investment in the enterprise cannot be obtained.* The surviving partners cannot afford to buy the decedent's interest, and the heirs will not consent to be partners in a new partnership operating the same business. (Or in the case with a professional partnership, the heir is not qualified professionally to step into the partnership.)

Even in cases in which the consent of adult heirs can be obtained, the court acting for a minor heir may step in and force a liquidation so that the minor's interest may be invested in an approved list of securities. This may happen when, because there is no will, state intestacy laws take effect. The court may look upon the children's share of the liquidated business as a "bird in the hand" and view the business risks involved in continuing the enterprise as "two birds in a bush." Liquidation may be the only answer when the minor's interest is substantial, which is often the case if both parents die in a common disaster.

3. *The surviving partner decides to liquidate the business after working with the relatives of the former partner.* What started off as at least an acceptable partnership of the surviving partners and a tractable heir ends with the partners' relations deteriorating to the point of strife. Not able to buy out the heir-partner, the surviving partner moves to liquidate the business. The unforeseen liquidation is foreseeable, if the partners open their minds today to the possibility that any one of the above events might occur. Without a plan to combat these occurrences—a plan providing both a purchaser for the partnership interest and the money to purchase—the parties may face an unplanned liquidation.

Effect of the Unplanned Liquidation

The unplanned liquidation of the business means the hurried collection of accounts receivable, the payment of outstanding obligations, the sale of the assets for whatever they will bring and the division of the balance with the heirs.

The business is sold for a fraction of its going-concern value. In most cases, the goodwill is wiped out entirely. Even if a purchaser can be found who is willing to buy the business as a unit, losses will be tremendous. In addition, accounts receivable go for a few cents on the dollar, because most of them become impossible to collect. Inventory, plant and fixtures usually go for junk prices.

Not only is a once-prosperous, profitable business gone in an instant, but also so is the income that once provided for the partners and their families. Worst off, of course, are the survivors of the deceased partner.

Three Positive Alternatives

Fortunately, with a minimum of planning, a forced liquidation need not occur. Depending on the circumstances and needs of the partners and their families, there are three positive alternatives they can select for the business. *However, they must put their plan into effect while all partners are alive.* Their alternatives are:

- planned liquidation
- reorganization with deceased's heirs
- sale to surviving partners

For the remainder of this chapter, we'll examine these alternatives individually. We'll also explore the role of the insurance professional and life insurance in the implementation of each of these alternatives.

■ PLANNED LIQUIDATION

In many cases, the best alternative upon the death of a partner is to liquidate the business and distribute remaining assets. If possible, of course, the business should be sold as a going entity; however, the reality is that this rarely is possible. Regardless, it is always best to plan for a liquidation.

The goal of a planned liquidation is to minimize the losses and protect the survivors. This can be accomplished simply and easily by taking two steps: (1) adding proper provisions in the will of each partner; and (2) making sure there is adequate life insurance on each partner.

Provisions in the Wills of the Partners

If one of the partners is called upon to liquidate the business at the death of a partner, the liquidating partner must have a flexible power to deal with the business. For example, it may be best to operate the business temporarily and await a better price for the business. On the other hand, it may be financially advantageous to close the doors immediately and call in the auctioneer.

An essential ingredient, then, is for all the partners to execute wills giving to their executors or trustees broad powers for disposing of their partnership interests. The will provisions should cover these points:

1. *A power to sell the interest.* The executor or trustee should be given the power to join with the surviving partners to sell the partnership at such time and on such terms as they both deem best.

2. *A power to retain the partnership interest for as long as the executor or trustee deems appropriate.* This clause assures the executor that the sale does not have to be made immediately after the death of the partner.

3. *The right to join with the other partners in borrowing to raise funds to pay estate obligations,* so these debts, costs and taxes do not impede the operation of the business during the period of interim continuation.

4. *A power to select some other way of disposing of the business interest.* Again, flexibility is the keynote, because the partners later may change their minds about liquidation and wish to reorganize.

5. *The power to join with the other partners to incorporate the business,* which may facilitate the temporary retention of the business and its subsequent sale.

Life Insurance

The partners still are going to take a financial beating when the business is liquidated at the death of one of them—despite suitable will provisions and the best choice of possible sales methods. They likely will not realize the market value of the partnership assets and, in most cases, they will have to forego any additional value that might adhere to the business as a going concern.

How can the partners offset this loss on the liquidation of their business? The obvious answer is life insurance. For two, three or four cents per insured dollar per year, the partners can be assured that their families will receive the "full value" of their business interests—instead of 50 cents on each dollar of inventory and equipment, or 25 cents on each dollar in accounts receivable, or nothing at all for goodwill.

Besides indemnifying the partner's family for the loss of the "going-concern" value of the business, life insurance on the partners also helps meet the cash needs of the deceased partner's estate. Life insurance provides cash for estate and inheritance taxes, attorney's and probate fees, debts, funeral and last medical expenses, and the family's personal income during the transition period. When each partner insures his or her life to meet personal family and estate needs, the surviving partner assures the other partners that estate liquidity needs will not sink the business prematurely before the best possible price can be obtained.

As mentioned in our discussion of the liquidation of a proprietor's business, the life insurance on each partner could be owned by the partner personally or by the partner's spouse. The policy beneficiary could be the partner's spouse, or it could be the partner's estate if it were his or her desire to place the insurance proceeds directly into the hands of the executor. If the partner wanted professional administration and management for the estate, a corporate trustee could be named as beneficiary.

Now let's apply the above discussion of a planned liquidation of a partnership to a practical example.

■ CASE STUDY: MS. BACON AND MRS. BLACK

Ms. Bacon, age 55, and Mrs. Black, age 52, are partners in a neighborhood gift shop. They have built up a good business with many repeat customers. In recent years, however, a shopping center has provided stiff competition and, while many loyal customers come back to shop, the business is in a slow decline.

If either Ms. Bacon or Mrs. Black had children who were interested in coming into the business, they would spend the money necessary to move to the shopping center themselves. Because neither woman has relatives who are interested in coming into the business, their intent is to operate the business in the present location until Ms. Bacon qualifies for Social Security, and then close the doors. If one of them dies in the meantime, they have agreed that the survivor would close the business.

The Estate Plan

Each partner has her attorney draft a new will. The new wills give the executors the needed power to work with the surviving partner in arranging the most advantageous sale of the business. The partners feel that, if the executor and the surviving partner are given sufficient time to shop around, the assets of the business should bring the following:

	Present Value	Liquidation Price
Cash	$ 8,000	$ 8,000
Accounts receivable	3,000	2,000
Merchandise	20,000	15,000
Furniture & fixtures	60,000	24,000
Total assets	$91,000	$49,000
Less: accounts & notes payable	10,000	10,000
Partners' capital	$81,000	$39,000

Each partner's personal estate requirements would be about $40,000. This would pay off the home mortgage and settle the other debts, the attorney's and probate fees, the state inheritance tax and funeral and last medical bills.

In addition to their objective of a planned liquidation of the partnership—which the new wills help answer—the partners have certain other objectives for their families and themselves:

1. They want sufficient cash to meet the liquidity needs of their estates;

2. They wish to make sure their families recover at least the market value of their shares from any business liquidation; and

3. They want to save for retirement.

The Insurance Solution

Bacon and Black solve their estate and family problems with the purchase of additional permanent life insurance. They each purchase $140,000 policies on their own lives.

The first $40,000 is earmarked for the executors—to pay the estate debts, costs and taxes. If these expenses are less than expected, the extra money can provide additional family income during the transition period, when the sale of the business is in process.

The balance of the insurance, $100,000, is purchased to:

1. Replace the lost value of the business when sold;

2. Provide immediate cash or long-term income for family members upon one of the partner's deaths; and

3. Establish a retirement nest egg through the policy's growing cash values.

The Mrs. Black and Ms. Bacon example indicates what is needed if the partners and their families are to experience an orderly liquidation. First, they need properly drawn wills that give their executors the discretion to work with the surviving partner to elect the best possible sale of the business. Second, they should purchase sufficient personal life insurance to pay estate settlement costs and taxes, meet the family's income needs during the estate settlement, and make up for the family the losses suffered in the liquidation of the business.

REORGANIZATION WITH DECEASED'S HEIRS

The partnership differs from the sole proprietorship in at least one very important respect. Despite the fact that some partnerships should be liquidated, in many partnerships there will remain, at the death of one of the partners, one or more persons competent and interested in reorganizing the partnership and continuing the business. Often, this will be the surviving partners, but there are situations in which the heirs of the deceased partner will want to enter the partnership and will be accepted by the other partners.

Successful retention by a family member depends on several factors. These include:

- a member of the family willing and capable of joining the surviving partner in the business;

- surviving partners willing to accept the family member as a partner;

- customers willing to permit a substitution of partners;

- sufficient cash in the estate to pay estate costs and taxes, and provide enough income for the family during the period of estate administration. (Note the Special Closely Held Business provisions discussed in Chapter 4 that may provide some estate tax relief in the case of family retention of a closely held business interest);

- sufficient "other" assets in the estate to provide an income for the surviving spouse and equal inheritances for the children not connected with the business; and

- sufficient cash reserves in the business to overcome losses during the changeover period.

To plan for the retention of the partnership interest, each partner should:

- give the executor or trustee sufficient discretion through the partner's will to allow the executor or trustee to bridge the change in ownership as smoothly as possible;

- obtain sufficient life insurance to provide for estate liquidity and provide family income during the period of estate administration; and

- make sure that the remainder of the partner's family has enough life insurance and "other" assets to provide an income for the surviving spouse and equal inheritances.

■ CASE STUDY: THE GLASSES—FATHER AND SON

Sam Glass, age 58, and his son, John Glass, age 37, are partners in Glass Auto Body. Sam has operated the business for 25 years, John has been his partner for the last 12. They employ five repair and paint workers. They work mostly for auto insurance companies. They rent the garage where the business is located. Their investment in equipment is $30,000.

Sam's wife is still living and well. He also has two daughters, both of whom are married and are outside the business.

Sam's Problem

Sam would like to see his half of the business pass to John at his death. However, there are Sam's wife and two daughters to consider. Besides his investment in the business, Sam has few other assets. He owns his home outright, has a few dollars in stocks and $20,000 of life insurance. He is reminded that his wife would not qualify for Social Security as a widow until age 60. She is now age 55. If John gets the business, what does Mrs. Glass get?

Sam's Solution

Lucky for Sam, he has some money to spend to help correct his situation. He can afford to save $400 per month to help himself out of this predicament. He decides to do the following:

1. He purchases additional life insurance—$90,000 of permanent coverage. The policy, when combined with his present insurance, will give his wife a monthly income of $700, if arranged as a life annuity.

2. Sam Glass has a new will drafted. The will permits his executor to continue the business investment indefinitely and to join with John in borrowing on the strength of the partnership assets for either the capital needs of the business or estate liquidity. The executor, under the will, also is permitted to join with John to incorporate, merge or liquidate the business.

The new life insurance leaves John free to run the business in the best manner possible—enabling him to hire additional employees to take the place of his departed father. At the same time, the incorporation of the business under the will could mean additional income to the widow in the form of corporate dividends. Eventually, the widow's stock would pass to her children. It is assumed at that time John would make an effort to buy his sisters' shares.

With the new life insurance and the new will, Sam Glass has taken the steps necessary to assure that his son can continue the business after his death.

■ SALE TO SURVIVING PARTNERS

It is probably true that at least 50 percent of all partnership interests should be purchased by either the partnership or the surviving partners at the death

> **ILL 5.1 ▪ *Advantages of the Insured Buy-Sell Agreement for ...***
>
> **Surviving Partners**
> - Prevents forced liquidation
> - Insures continuation of the business
> - Forestalls undesired reorganization
> - Guarantees the sale and sale price
> - Provides cash to make the purchase
> - Is effective and economical
> - Keeps deceased partner's spouse out of the business
>
> **Heirs of the Deceased**
> - Guarantees a full and fair cash price
> - Facilitates settlement of the estate
> - Protects the family against loss
> - Replaces lost income with a lump sum
>
> **Partners While Still Alive**
> - Ensures business stability
> - Good business investment
> - Stabilizes credit position

of a partner. In fact, if any one of the following factors is present, a partner's interest should be sold to the surviving partners or to the partnership:

1. The business requires a knowledge and skill not commonly found in nonbusiness-oriented spouses and children.

2. The partnership interest demands the full-time attention of all the partners.

3. The loss would be felt very deeply by the surviving partners.

4. There is not enough profit in the business to pay an adequate salary to a replacement and give an inactive surviving spouse his or her partnership share of profits each month.

5. There is likely to be a lack of liquidity in the partners' estates to meet estate debts, costs and taxes. (Note, however, the estate tax relief afforded closely held businesses described in Chapter 4.)

6. The business is not a safe investment when viewed from the eyes of the partners' heirs.

7. The only person who would want to buy the business interest is the other partner.

The Insured Buy-Sell Agreement

There is only one safe, simple and sure method of avoiding the hazards of liquidation of the partnership business or of reorganization under any of the plans previously described. It is an agreement under which the surviving partners are sure to buy the deceased's interest, that they will have the cash to do so, and that the estate will sell for a previously agreed-upon and fair price. Such a plan for avoidance of the problems involves two very simple steps:

1. the execution of a binding, buy-sell agreement between the partners—or the partners and the partnership—that provides for the sale of the interest of a deceased partner and its purchase by the surviving partners or the partnership, at a value agreed on by the parties in the agreement; and

2. the establishment of the funding that automatically will provide the cash at death so the surviving partners or the partnership will have the money to carry out their purchase obligations.

With respect to the first step, the partners' attorney, with the benefit of the partners' advice, can draft a fair buy-sell agreement.

With respect to the second, life insurance is the only funding plan that can assure the partners or the partnership that they will have the money needed to purchase a decedent's interest automatically at some yet unknown date in the future. Only life insurance can guarantee that the same death activating the agreement also will provide the cash to carry out the terms of the agreement.

The plan is simple itself. The partners, or the partners and the partnership, enter into a contract—either in the articles of partnership or under a separate agreement. They agree to purchase the interest of any partner who dies. And, in turn, each partner contracts to sell the partnership interest to the surviving partners or to the partnership if the partner dies. The arrangement is a definite and binding executory contract to buy and sell. A price, or method of determining the price, is set out in the agreement.

Each partner's life is insured for an amount equal to the value of his or her interest. At the death of a partner, the surviving partners or the partnership get the business interest of the deceased, and the estate gets the insurance money. The surviving partners or the partnership have purchased the partnership interest of the decedent at least in part with the life insurance proceeds.

Important Points in the Agreement

The following are important points essential to any well-organized and complete business insurance agreement. These points are not intended to be all-inclusive or exhaustive in scope. The parties and attorneys involved probably will have other provisions that they wish to include in the contract. These are the points you should remember:

- the names of all the parties;

- the purpose of the agreement;

- a provision covering the lifetime withdrawal of a partner;

- a statement that the surviving partners (or partnership, as the case may be) will buy, and the estate of the deceased partner will sell and transfer to the surviving partners the partnership interest of the decedent;

- a specified purchase and sale price, or a method to determine such for the interest of each member;

- a list of the insurance policies involved;

- when the agreement provides for the services of a trustee, whether corporate or individual, the specific duties of this trustee;

- the person to receive the insurance proceeds;

- the manner in which the surviving partner or partners; (or partnership, as the case may be) is to pay any amount by which the value exceeds the insurance proceeds;

- similarly, the procedure to be followed in case the insurance proceeds should prove to be greater than the value of the decedent's interest at his or her death;

- a stipulation that, when the partnership is terminated, the surviving partners have the right to purchase the policies owned by the partnership (or by the deceased or withdrawing partner);

- a stipulation that no partner shall exercise any rights that he or she may have under a policy made subject to the agreement;

- a provision that the estate of the decedent shall be relieved of liability for partnership debts; and

- provisions for revocation, change or termination of the agreement by consent of all the parties.

TYPES OF PARTNERSHIP PURCHASE AGREEMENTS

There are two basic types of buy-sell agreements: the *cross-purchase* and the *entity-purchase*. Either is appropriate, depending on the needs of the partners.

Cross-Purchase Plan

The cross-purchase buy-sell agreement is the more commonly used form. It is an agreement whereby the partners *individually* agree to purchase the interest of the deceased partner, and the executor of the deceased partner is directed to sell the interest directly to the surviving partners. The partnership itself is not a party to the agreement. Each partner owns, is the beneficiary of, and pays for insurance on the life of the other partner or partners in an amount approximating the individual's share of the purchase price.

For example, assume a dual partnership worth $70,000 is owned equally. Under an insured cross-purchase plan, each partner insures the life of the other for $35,000. If partner B dies, partner A would have $35,000 of insurance proceeds with which to purchase B's interest under the buy-sell agreement.

ILL. 5.2 ■ *Cross-Purchase Plan*

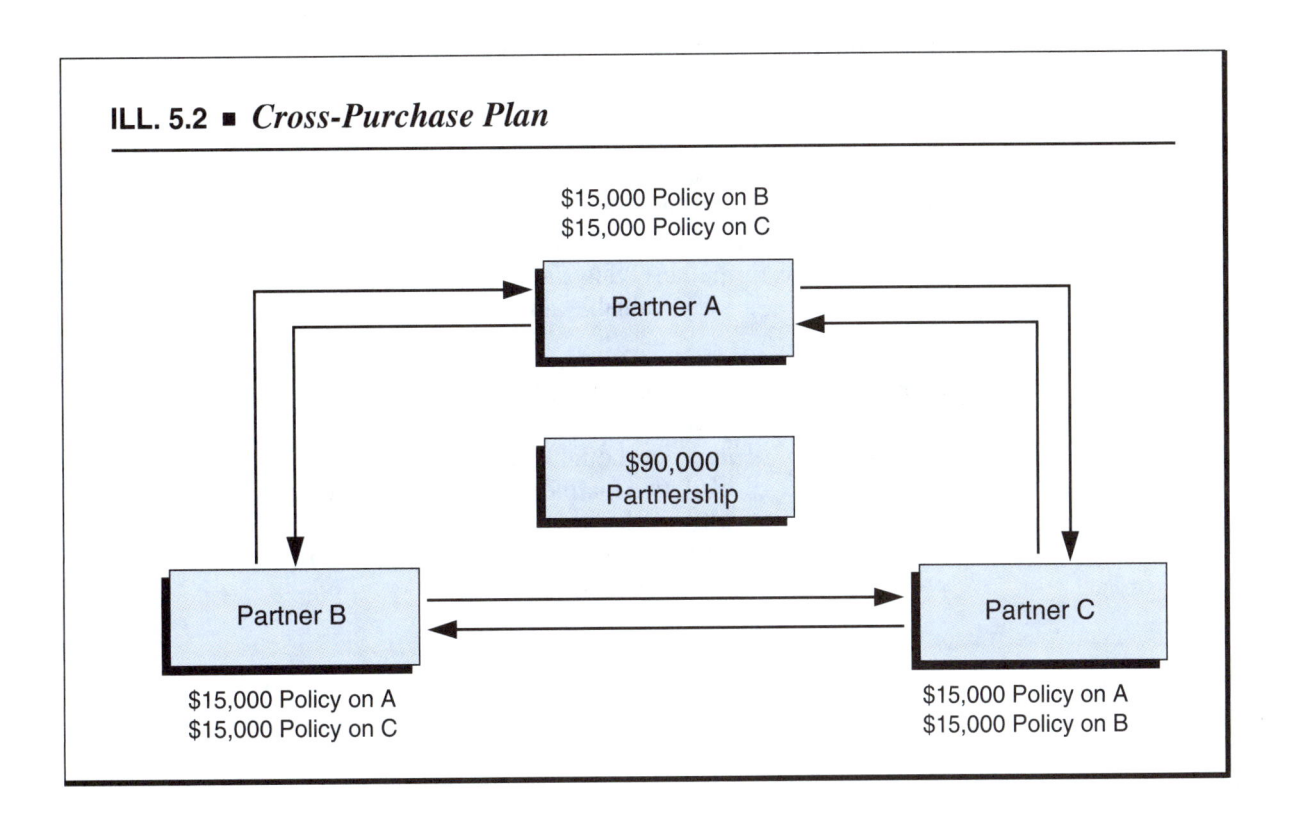

```
                    $15,000 Policy on B
                    $15,000 Policy on C

                         Partner A

                    $90,000
                    Partnership

    Partner B                              Partner C

$15,000 Policy on A                    $15,000 Policy on A
$15,000 Policy on C                    $15,000 Policy on B
```

What becomes of the policy B owned on A's life? A can buy the policy from B's estate for its cash value, or B's executor can surrender the policy, and its value at the time of death becomes a part of B's estate. The manner in which the policy is to be disposed of should be spelled out in the agreement.

Now let's assume there are three equal partners in a business worth $90,000. As shown in the illustration, A owns $15,000 on each of B and C; B owns $15,000 on each of A and C; C owns $15,000 of life insurance on each of A and B. A dies. From A's estate, B purchases one-half of A's partnership interest, using $15,000 of proceeds; C buys the other half of A's interest, also using $15,000 of proceeds. B and C now own one-half each, or $45,000 of the partnership, and A's estate has been fully compensated for its partnership interest.

Advantages of the Cross-Purchase Plan

1. *The cross-purchase plan is simple to understand.* It is relatively easy for a partner to understand that he or she owns insurance policies on the lives of the partners and that it is his or her duty to purchase their interests. On the other hand, the concept of the partnership entity may be difficult to grasp, especially because, by tradition, the partnership does not have an existence separate from that of its partners.

2. *Each partner buys only the amount of life insurance that equals his or her purchase obligations under the buy-sell agreement.* Thus, many believe that a cross-purchase plan accomplishes true equity among the partners, unlike the entity-purchase plan, in which the older or rated partner, in effect, pays part of the insurance premium on his or her own life. Also,

if a partner owns other assets that could be used as part of the purchase price, then that partner could, to that extent, underfund his or her obligation.

3. *A surviving partner, when the buyout is completed, receives an immediate step-up in basis for his or her portion of the business interest.* This means that the appreciation of the business interest that has taken place will not be taxable to the surviving partner in the event of a subsequent sale of the interest, a very valuable advantage.

Some Disadvantages of the Cross-Purchase Plan

1. *The number of policies.* Although there would only be two policies needed in the case of two partners, the number of required policies increases dramatically as the number of partners increases. The formula n × (n-1) for the number of policies needed in a cross-purchase plan produces the following results:

Number of Partners	Policies Needed
2	2
3	6
4	12
5	20

If additional policies are subsequently needed as a result or reevaluation, the number of policies may become increasingly unwieldy.

2. *The reorganization of the partnership insurance coverage is more difficult.* When the partnership is reorganized at some later date, there is a difficult administrative problem in switching the ownership of insurance policies from one partner to another. This is not, of course, necessary under the entity-purchase plan, because all policies are owned by the partnership.

3. *The disparity in ages that may occur among partners can cause widely differing premiums for the life insurance.* For example a 30-year-old partner will be paying a substantial premium to insure the life of a 60-year-old partner. The reverse will be true for the 60-year-old paying for life insurance on the 30-year-old.

Entity Plan

Under an entity plan, the partnership—rather than the individual partners—owns, pays for, and is the beneficiary of the policies on the lives of the partners in amounts equal to each partner's interest. The partnership also becomes a party to the buy-sell agreement. This type of arrangement is used, for example, when the number of partners involved would make the cross-purchase plan too cumbersome. For example, in a four-way partnership the cross-purchase plan would require 12 different life insurance plans; the entity plan would require only four.

ILL. 5.3 ■ *Entity Plan*

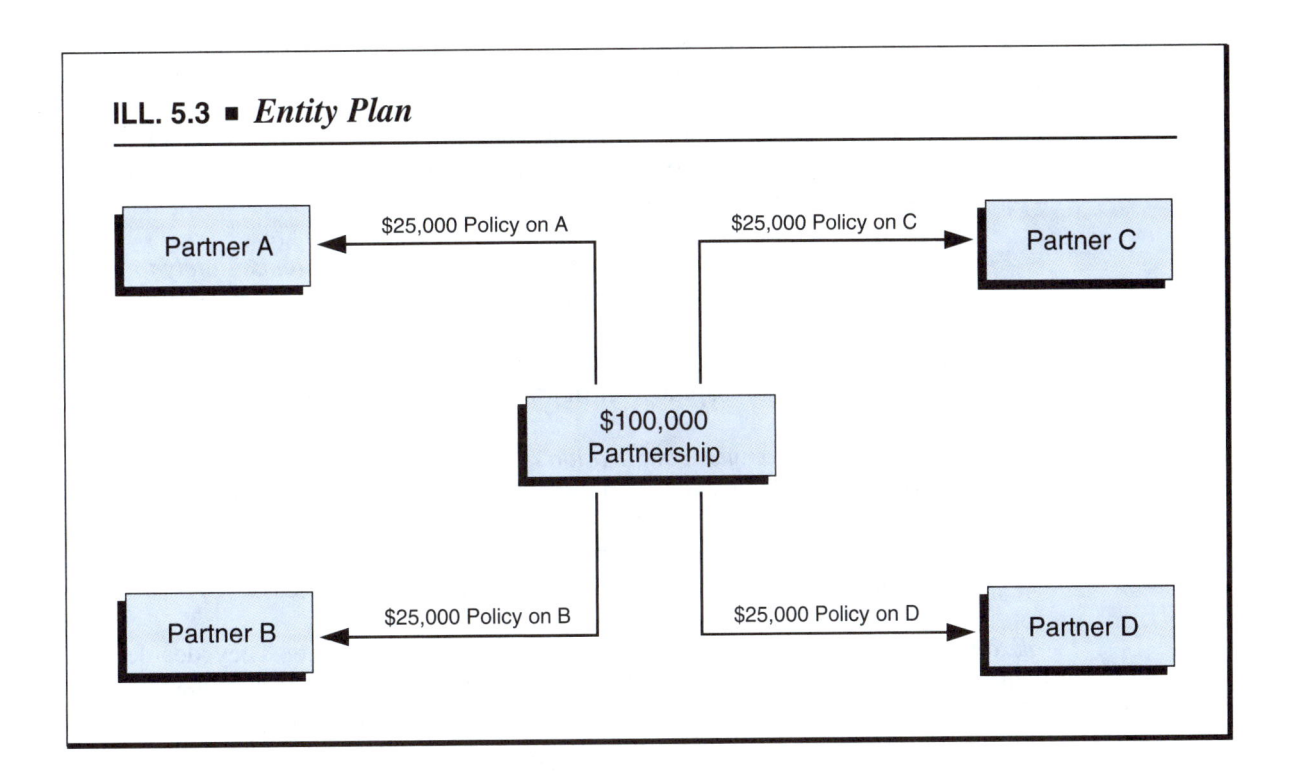

```
Partner A  ←— $25,000 Policy on A —       — $25,000 Policy on C —→  Partner C
                                    ↘   ↙
                                  $100,000
                                  Partnership
                                    ↙   ↘
Partner B  ←— $25,000 Policy on B —       — $25,000 Policy on D —→  Partner D
```

With the entity plan, when a partner dies the partnership buys this interest from the estate. It is then divided among the surviving partners in proportion to their partnership interests.

Illustration 5.3 shows a four-way partnership worth $100,000. The firm purchases $25,000 of insurance on the life of each partner. If partner A is the first to die, the firm purchases his or her interest from the estate, and the interests of partners B, C and D increase from 25 percent to 33a percent each. The firm immediately buys an additional amount of insurance on the life of each surviving partner to assure the availability of the full purchase price upon the death of the next partner.

The insurance premiums are not deductible regardless of whether they are paid by the individual partners or by the partnership, because the premium payers are directly or indirectly beneficiaries of the policies. However, the proceeds of the life insurance policies are received income tax-free.

One last point concerning the entity plan is that most life insurance companies offer a quantity discount. This, of course, means that one $50,000 policy purchased under the entity plan may cost less than four $12,500 policies under the cross-purchase plan.

Advantages of the Entity Plan

1. *It keeps the number of insurance policies to a minimum.* In the entity-purchase plan, if there are four partners, there are four insurance policies. On the other hand, if these same four partners were to agree to a cross-

purchase plan, there would be 12 policies—three on each life. It is apparent, then, that when there are a number of partners, the entity-purchase plan is easier to administer. Furthermore, most insurance companies discount their premium rates for larger-sized policies. In such an event, the partners with the entity-purchase plan will be able to take advantage of these discounts.

2. *The cash values of the insurance policies are available immediately to the partnership.* If the partnership has some immediate need for cash, the policies' cash values are available at once for loan purposes. There is no need to wait for a partner to raise his or her pro rata share of a proposed loan or capital contribution to the business.

3. *There is an automatic equalization of premium payments among the partners.* The premiums on all policies owned by the partnerships on the lives of the partners are lumped together and prorated among the partners, in the absence of an agreement to the contrary. This is, of course, advantageous to the younger partner who may earn less.

Example: A, B and C are equal partners in a clothing store. They decide to insure each other's lives fo r $25,000 each and use the entity-purchase plan. Here is how the premium distribution compares under the entity-purchase and the cross-purchase plans:

	Partner A Age 56	Partner B Age 41	Partner C Age 30
Annual premium	$1,365	$692	$ 488
Premium if cross-purchase	590	926	1,028
Prorated premium if entity purchase	848	848	848

The oldest or highest rated partner ends up paying part of the insurance premium on his or her own life. If this is objected to, the accountant might work out a formula that will charge each partner exactly for the protection each receives. Another way of offsetting the higher premium to the oldest partner is to include in the value of each partnership interest the full insurance proceeds and not just the cash value of the policies on each life. The result is that the older or highly rated partner's family is likely to recover—through the insurance proceeds—the additional premiums that partner paid during his or her life. As indicated earlier, small figures are used to clearly emphasize the concepts. The principles shown apply in business insurance sales of all sizes.

Disadvantages of the Entity Plan

1. *The insurance proceeds received by the partnership "balloon," or inflate, the partnership value.* Actually, in practice, ballooning has not been much of a problem—at least not great enough to discourage the use of entity-type agreements. Some agreements merely ignore the problem and specify a certain dollar figure for each partner's interest. Other agreements value the partnership interest a day prior to the partner's death, so that the value just includes the cash value of all insurance policies. A third way of dealing with the ballooning problem is to insure the ballooned

value by raising the insurance coverage. In the above illustration each partner, thus, would be insured for $60,000. Of course, this creates an "insurance-on-insurance" situation, which can be carried on to absurdity.

2. *The insurance cash values are open to attack by the partnership's creditors.* This alone should not deter partners from making use of the entity approach, because all general partners are liable jointly for the partnership's debts. However, if the policies were arranged in the cross-purchase manner, they still would be open to creditor attack.

3. *Life insurance cash values are a tax preference item for inclusion in alternative minimum tax calculations.* This does not mean they will invariably be taxed, but will be part of gross taxable income for the business.

THE FUNDING INSURANCE

A partnership buy-sell agreement calls for the purchase of a partnership interest upon the occurrence of certain events—at least one of which, death, is uncertain in time. Because life insurance can create with one premium today the funds needed to purchase a partnership interest at death, it is the most effective and widely used method of funding a buy-sell agreement.

Ownership and Beneficiary Provisions

It is extremely important that the partners adhere to the classic ownership and beneficiary arrangement of life insurance policies in their buy-sell agreements. If an entity-purchase plan is employed, the partnership should own the policies, pay the premiums and be the beneficiary. If the cross-purchase plan is used, each partner should own, pay the premiums for, and be the beneficiary of policies on the lives of the other partners. In general, then, those whose duty it is to purchase the interest of a deceased partner should own and be the beneficiary of the policies on that partner's life.

Trustee as Beneficiary

There are situations in which it may be advisable to use a trustee as beneficiary. The trustee acts as impartial party in completing the details of the business insurance plan. The trustee:

1. collects the money from the insurance company;

2. takes the necessary steps to determine the value of the interest of the deceased partner as set out in the agreement;

3. applies the insurance proceeds toward the purchase of that interest; and

4. sees that the proceeds, plus any notes needed to cover an excess of value, are turned over to the executor or administrator, and that they, in turn, execute the proper releases of the partnership interest.

The trusteed buy-sell agreement should be suggested when one or more of the partners decides that his or her family needs assurance or security that they will receive the insurance proceeds.

However, there are comparatively few business buy-sell agreements that are trusteed. Most attorneys and their clients apparently conclude that the written agreement, together with the classic ownership and beneficiary arrangements, are sufficient to insure a prompt and effective completion of the sale.

Who Should Pay the Premiums

Generally, the question of who should pay the premiums is answered by the type of agreement selected. In the entity-purchase plan, the partnership pays the premiums. The premiums then are charged to the general partnership operating expenses, although they are not deductible for income tax purposes.

In the cross-purchase plan each partner pays the premiums on the policies he or she owns on the lives of the other partners. Although the insurance company could bill each partner separately, the usual practice is for the insurer to bill the partnership at the partnership address. The partnership then pays the premiums and debits each partner's drawing account.

If one of the partners, because of youth and lack of earning power, is unable to meet the premiums due to an older or rated partner, the premiums could be pooled. Each partner would contribute a share of the total premiums in proportion to ownership of the partnership. Or the total premiums could be divided by the number of partners. If the older or rated partner still pays more in premiums than the premium amount on the lives of the partners he or she normally should have insured, then at death the estate could be reimbursed for the excess premiums paid.

An additional consideration is expense. It is not an absolute necessity that the purchase price be 100-percent funded with life insurance in those cases when the premiums for full funding would be oppressive. Even a partially funded buyout plan offers tremendous advantages to the partners, because a substantial down payment is better than nothing.

Because the size of the premium may sell or unsell an otherwise acceptable buy-sell proposal, you should study carefully the prospect's ability to pay premiums. Partial insurance coverages are certainly acceptable. As the business progresses and the financial position of the partners is strengthened, additional insurance can be purchased until the desired level is reached.

Naturally, term insurance also can be used to advantage when premium money is short. As the partners and the partnership improve their working-capital position, portions of this term coverage can be converted to a permanent form.

VALUATION OF PARTNERSHIP INTERESTS

The valuation clause is one of the cornerstones of a partnership purchase agreement, because it puts a price tag on each partnership share or sets forth a method for determining that price.

Advantages of a Valuation Clause

The well-conceived valuation clause accomplishes several things:

1. *It removes the need to haggle.* The partners set the price or the price formula. Surviving partners, therefore, cannot take advantage of the spouse and family. The spouse, further, cannot hold out for what the partner said the business was worth a week before his or her death. If either party feels cheated by the price, then it is not solely the doing of the other party.

2. *It aids all partners in their individual estate and retirement planning.* The partners know the value of their interests and the manner of payment, whether they die or voluntarily withdraw from the partnership. In planning their estates, the partners are able to gauge the size of their estates and determine the impact of the estate costs and taxes.

3. *A carefully drafted agreement may set the value of the partnership share for estate tax purposes.* The Internal Revenue Service may accept the value set forth in the purchase agreement as the value for determination of the federal estate tax, even though at the time of death it might fall considerably short of the "true" value of the business interest.

Methods of Valuation

Various methods commonly are used to determine the value of partnership interests in purchase agreements. Listed below are some of the more popular ones, in random order.

The Agreed Dollar Value

In the *agreed dollar value* method, the parties to the agreement agree that a specific dollar amount represents the value of the business. Actually, this in itself is not a valuation method, but merely a way of expressing the value arrived at in some other fashion. The value may be just an "educated guess," or it may be a way of expressing a value determined by one of the other methods, listed below.

Regardless of the science, or lack of it, in arriving at an agreed dollar value for the business, the assumption is that the parties to the agreement are able to value their business best, and in the end will be satisfied with their results.

It is a common practice, when the agreed dollar method is used, to make provision for the mandatory revaluation of the business value, generally once a year. When a partner dies or withdraws after the time for revaluation has

ILL 5.4 ▪ *Factors for Capitalizing Earnings of Groups or Industries*

Very Narrow Profit Variation	Moderately Narrow Profit Variation	Moderately Wide Profit Variation	Very Wide Profit Variation
10 Times Average Earnings	9 Times Average Earnings	7 Times Average Earnings	6 Times Average Earnings
Cosmetics	Amusement	Advertising	Automobiles
Food	Beverages	Agricultural Impts.	Automobile Accessories
Tobacco	Chemical	Aviation	Construction Machinery
Utility	Container	Boots and Shoes	Non-Ferrous Met.
	Drug	Coal	R.R. Equipment
	Meat Packing	Computers and Data Processing	Steel
	Oil	Elec. Equipment	
	Paper & Paper Prod.	Fast Foods	
	Retail Trade	Financial	
	Television	Household Prod.	
	Textile	Leather	
		Office Equipment	
		Printing	
		Publishing	
		Radio	
		Railroad	
		Rubber	
		Shipping	
		Ship Building	

passed—and if the partners have failed to revalue—most agreements provide for the establishment of a new value either by formula or by a board of arbitrators selected by the interested parties.

Book Value

Book value is simply the excess of the assets over the liabilities of the business, as reflected by the balance sheet of the business. The term *book value* is synonymous with "net worth" and "partners' equity." However, as a measure of the value of a business, it is misleading. The book value neglects not only the goodwill of the business, but also the fact that the physical assets may have been depreciated substantially and their balance sheet values bear no relation to their market value.

Book Value Adjusted to Reflect Goodwill

In this method the book value is adjusted to reflect not only the market value of the tangible assets but also the goodwill of the firm. Goodwill is an intangible asset that generally includes such things as the reputation of the owners, the continued influx of new business and the likelihood that satisfied customers will return. It is common accounting practice to leave goodwill off a balance sheet. Yet not taking this valuation asset into account usually results in seriously understating the value of the company as a going concern.

Capitalization of Earnings

In this method of valuation, the average net partnership earnings—normally a five-year average is employed—are capitalized by a factor set forth in the buy-sell agreement.

The capitalization factor (the multiplier) will depend upon the type of industry. On the following page are some widely accepted factors for various industries.

If a business does not fit into one of the industrial classifications in Ill. 5.4, select the classification that is closest.

If the earnings for the past five years are felt to be abnormal, the average earnings for that period that best represent the future earnings potential for the business may be used. If other figures are not obtainable, the partners might be asked to estimate the degree of abnormality in the last five-year earnings and adjust them accordingly.

■ TAX CONSIDERATIONS IN PARTNERSHIP PURCHASE AGREEMENTS

Income tax considerations under the buy-sell agreement are minimal due to the stepped-up basis of the partnership interest at date of death. Because the estate tax valuation (as generally established by a properly drawn buy-sell agreement) sets both the adjusted basis and the amount realized upon sale of the partnership interest, no gain or loss is realized.

Taxation of Premium Payments

Insurance premiums are not deductible whether they are paid by the individual partners or by the partnership, because the premium payers are directly or indirectly beneficiaries of the policies. In this, life insurance resembles other methods of saving money to meet future purchase obligations of the savers.

Taxation of Policy Proceeds

The policy proceeds received by either the other partners or the partnership are not includable in their gross income and subject to income tax. Of course, this is the same treatment that applies to policy proceeds received by individual beneficiaries in nonbusiness situations. This rule follows from the basic concept that insurance is indemnification for a loss—here the loss of a valued partner.

The income tax exemption for life insurance death proceeds sometimes is lost in business situations because the policy was transferred for a valuable consideration (i.e., sold) during the insured's lifetime. When a "transfer for value" has occurred, the income tax exemption is limited to the consideration paid for the policy plus the subsequent premiums paid by the transferee. Transfers to certain transferees are not subject to the transfer-for-value rule: the insured, a partner of the insured, a partnership in which the insured is a partner, a corporation in which the insured is an officer or shareholder, and anyone whose basis in the policy is determined by reference to the seller's basis. Whenever a transfer for value has occurred, it is possible to wipe the slate clean and restore the full income tax exemption by making a later transfer to someone in the exempt group of transferees.

Estate Taxation of Policy Proceeds

A policy owned by the insured's partnership or a co-partner should not be included in the insured's gross estate if the proceeds are not payable to the insured's estate and the insured holds no incidents of ownership in the policy. The term "incidents of ownership" includes the right: to change beneficiaries, to cancel or surrender the policy, to borrow against the policy or pledge it as collateral, and to assign the policy or revoke an assignment. It also includes a reversionary interest that gives the insured or his or her estate any of the above rights in the event a beneficiary predeceases the insured. Of course, the value of the insured's partnership interest will be includable.

Income Tax Treatment of Buy-Sell Payments

The value of a deceased partner's interest in the partnership may be allocable to three factors:

1. Unrealized receivables

2. Goodwill

3. All other property

The income taxability of the funds received by the heirs for the deceased partner's interest depends on which one of the three types of interest is being purchased and the type of buy-sell arrangement—whether it is an entity plan or a cross-purchase agreement. For simplicity purposes, it may be appropriate to examine the tax treatment afforded the three interests under each of the buy-sell agreement approaches separately.

The Entity Plan

Under an entity plan arrangement, the tax treatment given the three interests is:

Type of Interest	Tax Treatment of Payment Received	Tax Treatment of Payment Made
Partnership interest other than goodwill and unrealized receivables	Capital gains treatment	Not deductible
Unrealized partnership receivables	Ordinary income tax treatment	Deductible to the partnership
Goodwill	May be given capital gains or ordinary income tax treatment, as elected by the partners, provided the deceased partner was a general partner and capital is not a material income-producing factor in the partnership.	Deductible to the partnership if payment treated as ordinary income. Not deductible if payment treated as payment for a capital asset.

Under the entity plan approach, if the partnership qualifies for the ordinary income tax treatment of goodwill and so elects, the portion of the payment to the deceased partner's estate or heirs will be taxable as ordinary income, and the partnership will receive a tax deduction for the goodwill purchased. In addition, the partnership receives an income tax deduction for the value of the unrealized receivables purchased. Ordinary income payments in the liquidation of a deceased partner's interest are income in respect of a decedent (IRD) and do not receive a new basis because of the death of the partner.

The Cross-Purchase Agreement

The taxability of payments received for the deceased partner's interest under the cross-purchase agreement is fundamentally the same as under the entity plan, with one difference: payments for goodwill. Although the partnership—when purchasing the deceased partner's interest under an entity plan—may elect to treat the payment for goodwill as ordinary income and, thereby, obtain a tax deduction, the surviving partners under a cross-purchase agreement do not enjoy the same latitude.

Under a cross-purchase agreement, payments for goodwill must be treated as part of the capital transaction. As a result, the payment to the estate or heirs made under a cross-purchase agreement receives capital gains treatment, and the partners forgo a tax deduction. Furthermore, although the tax treatment given the estate or heirs for the purchase of unrealized receivables is ordinary income, regardless of whether the partnership or the individual partners make the purchase, the individual partners receive no tax deduction for their payment for the unrealized receivables.

The tax treatment given the three partnership interests under a cross-purchase agreement is as follows:

Type of Interest	Tax Treatment of Payment Received	Tax Treatment of Payment Made
Partnership interest other than goodwill and unrealized receivables	Capital gains treatment	Not deductible to the partners
Unrealized partnership receivables	Ordinary income tax treatment	Not deductible to the partners
Goodwill	Capital gains treatment	Not deductible to the partners

THE PROFESSIONAL PARTNERSHIP

Up to this point, we have concentrated on the commercial partnership. Now let's devote some time to studying the professional partnership.

The factors that distinguish a "professional" partnership from a "commercial" partnership have little to do with the professional qualifications of the partners. Instead, the difference lies primarily in two key characteristics:

1. *Nature of assets.* In a commercial partnership, inventory and equipment are just as important for the generation of income as are the management skills of the partners. In a professional partnership, however, it is the skill and talents of the partners which, almost exclusively, leads to income. In a medical or dental partnership, for instance, the chief "assets" of the partnership are the professional skills and earning power of the partners. In this respect, it is difficult to value a professional partnership with any degree of accuracy.

2. *Restriction of sale.* A professional partnership cannot be sold to just anyone. Interested sons or daughters cannot step into the shoes of a father who is a doctor, unless they too possess medical degrees. In short, the sale of a professional partnership is restricted to another qualified practitioner.

SUMMARY

The tools to enable the partnership to survive the death or disability of a partner are what the insurance professional brings to the business marketplace. Given the large number of partnerships in the United States, this represents a sizable opportunity to be of service to this important market.

In our chapter on partnerships, we have examined different partnerships and partnership structures. We found that, despite the real differences among7 the various types, partnerships share certain important characteristics that make the need for life insurance and the services of the insurance professional critical. Among these important characteristics are: the lack of a specific legal life, the pass-through of income and expenses to the partners, joint and several liability and the dissolution of the partnership upon the death of a partner.

Because of these partnership characteristics, the survivors of a deceased partner—both surviving partners and surviving family members—face significant financial and professional problems. For the surviving family, the dissolution of the partnership often means the cessation of income coupled with the substantial costs of estate transfer. For the surviving partners it means not only the loss of income and the depletion of assets, but also the end of a business career.

We further examined the alternatives available upon the death of a partner: liquidation of the partnership, family retention of the deceased partner's interest (and reorganization) and purchase of the interest by the surviving partners. In each case, life insurance is key in facilitating implementation of the chosen alternative.

The types of partnership agreements—entity plan and cross-purchase agreements—were discussed and the advantages and disadvantages of each approach were examined as were their income and estate tax considerations. The importance of a valuation clause in the partnership agreement was discussed, and several methods of valuing the partnership interest were presented. Regardless of the method chosen for disposition of the deceased partner's interest, life insurance plays a role of unsurpassed importance.

■ THREE SAMPLE BUY-SELL AGREEMENTS

Following are three sample buy-sell agreements. The first one is of the cross-purchase type and the second is of the entity-purchase type. Both agreements make provision for both the lifetime withdrawal and the death of a partner. The third sample agreement provides for purchase of the partnership from a disabled partner. Read these agreements carefully to familiarize yourself with the content of a partnership buy-sell agreement. Again we emphasize that these agreements are only representative of the actual agreements the client's counsel will prepare for the client's particular situation.

ILL 5.5 ■ *Sample Partnership Cross-Purchase Agreement*

CAUTION: This is a specimen agreement. The actual agreement used in any particular case must be prepared by a qualified attorney.

Agreement made this _____ day of _____, 20___, by and between _____ and _____ (hereinafter called "partners").

WITNESSETH:

Whereas, _____, _____ and _____ are doing business under the firm name and style of _____ (hereinafter called the "partnership"), and

Whereas, the interest of each partner in the partnership is as follows:

　　　_____ . . . . . _____%;

　　　_____ . . . . . _____%; and

Whereas, the partners mutually desire that upon the death of one, the business shall be continued by the survivor without interruption, liquidation, or the taking in of a new partner, and the deceased partner's estate shall receive the full value of his (her) interest in the partnership; and mutually desire that in the event a partner withdraws from the firm during life, the remaining partners shall have the opportunity to continue the business as aforesaid; and

Whereas, the partners mutually desire to use life insurance to help achieve these objectives;

Now, therefore, in consideration of the mutual agreements and covenants contained herein and for other valuable consideration, receipt of which is hereby acknowledged, it is mutually agreed and covenanted by the partners, for themselves, their heirs, assigns and legal representatives, and by the partnership, for itself as an entity, its successors and assigns, as follows:

Article 1. No partner shall during his (her) lifetime assign, encumber or otherwise dispose of his (her) interest or any part thereof in the partnership, except:

If a partner should desire to dispose voluntarily of his (her) interest during his (her) lifetime, then he (she) shall first offer in writing to sell his (her) interest to the other partners at the price determined in accordance with the provisions of Article 2 below. Each of such buying partners shall have the right to purchase such portion of the interest as his (her) own interest in the partnership at such date shall bear to the total partnership interest excluding the interest of the selling partner, provided, however, that if any such other partner does not purchase his (her) full proportionate share of the interest being sold, then the balance may be purchased by the other partners equally. If the interest is not purchased by the other partners within 60 days of the receipt of the offer to them, then the selling partner may sell it to any other person but shall not sell it without first offering it to the other partners in accordance with the method established above at the price and on the terms offered to such other person if the price is less than the price established by Article 2.

> A provision such as this, restricting the lifetime transfer of the partnership interests is necessary in the value set if the buy-sell agreement is to be accepted as the true fair market value for federal estate tax purposes.

Article 2. Upon the death of any partner the partnership shall be continued by surviving partners who shall purchase and the executor or administrator (hereinafter called the "legal representative") of the deceased partner shall sell his (her) entire interest in the partnership, for the price and upon the conditions stipulated in Article 3.

ILL 5.5 ▪ *Sample Partnership Cross-Purchase Agreement (Cont.)*

> Here is a key provision in the agreement. Under this provision, the decedent's estate must sell, and the survivors must buy. This binding agreement to sell and the corresponding obligation to buy is usually preferable to the various "option" type agreements that could be used. Too, certain "option" type agreements may not effectively establish a value for federal estate tax purposes.

Article 3. It is agreed that the current fair value of all the assets of the partnership, including goodwill, is $_____ and that, therefore, the value of each partner's interest is as follows:

    _____   . . . . . $ _____

    _____   . . . . . $ _____

The partners agree to redetermine these values within 60 days following the end of each fiscal year, such redetermined values to be endorsed on Schedule A attached hereto and made a part of this agreement. If the partners fail to make such a redetermination of values for a particular year, the last previously stipulated values shall control, except that if the partners fail to make such a redetermination within the 24 months immediately preceding the death of a partner, then the values shall be agreed upon by the legal representative of the deceased partner on the one hand and the remaining partners on the other. If they do not agree to a valuation within 90 days after the death of the partner, the value of the deceased partner's interest shall be determined by arbitration as follows: The remaining partner on the one hand and the representative of the deceased partner on the other shall each name one arbitrator; if the two arbitrators cannot agree upon the values, then the two arbitrators shall appoint a third arbitrator and the decision of the majority shall be binding upon all parties. In determining values by arbitration, an amount for the addition to the good will of the partnership by the deceased of not less than $_____ shall be used.

> This provision utilizes the fixed price method and sets the current value of the partnership. It also provides for an annual redetermination of the value, and provides for arbitration in the event the partners fail to follow the revaluation clause. Some attorneys may prefer to have the last stated value control in all instances, but it is felt that this can lead to inequities if there has been no revaluation for a prolonged period of time.
>
> Under this valuation clause, the amount of good will be considered a part of the capital transaction. As such, it will not be taxable income to the deceased partner's successors, nor will it be deductible by the partnership as a business expense.
>
> The fixed price method, coupled with a revaluation provision, has many advantages. Among them are the following:
>
> - **The price that is arrived at initially, and upon subsequent reviews, as a result of head-to-head negotiations probably will be as "fair" as possible.**
>
> - **Such a price provision does not involve complex formulas, and is free of standards and terms that, because of possible ambiguity, could lead to controversy.**
>
> - **It is a flexible method that may be adjusted periodically to reflect the changing fortunes of the business.**

ILL 5.5 ■ *Sample Partnership Cross-Purchase Agreement (Cont.)*

- The parties to the agreement are able to readily determine what price will be paid for their interest and plan their estates accordingly.

- Finally, since the purchase price is a known dollar amount, it is possible at all times to keep the buy-sell agreement "funded" with adequate amounts of life insurance.

An alternate method of valuing the business at the partner's death is the use of some kind of "formula" approach. Under this method, the specific price to be paid for the business is not stated in the agreement. Rather, it is agreed that the value will be determined at the time of the partner's death under an agreed upon, stated formula. Some of the more common formulas used are (1) the actual book value at the time of death; (2) some method of capitalization of earnings; and (3) average book value over a stated period of time. Each of these methods has strengths and weaknesses. The important thing is to have a method set out in the agreement that appeals to all parties as a fair method of establishing the purchase price.

Article 4. The partners are the applicants, owners and beneficiaries of the following life insurance policies issued by _____ Insurance Company.

Policy No. _____ insuring the life of _____ in the amount of $_____, owned by and payable to _____.

Policy No._____ insuring the life of _____ in the amount of $_____, owned by and payable to _____.

Each partner hereby authorizes the partnership to pay the premiums on the policies owned by him (her) and made subject to this agreement as such premiums become due and to charge his (her) account therefor. In case any premium is not paid within 20 days after its due date, the insured shall be entitled to pay such premium as agent of the owner, and the owner agrees to reimburse him (her) promptly for any such payment. Each partner, further, agrees that he (she) will not exercise any of the rights of any policy he (she) obtains the written consent of the insured. Notwithstanding any other provision of this agreement, the partner-owner may at his (her) election, exercise any dividend options or rights as provided by the policy.

Since this is a cross-purchase agreement, each partner owns the policy of life insurance on the other partner. The partnership is not a party to the agreement, but is authorized to make the premium payments simply as a matter of convenience and to facilitate their payment.

Article 5. Each partner shall have the right to purchase any additional insurance on the life of any of the partners; such additional policies shall be listed in Schedule B attached hereto and made a part of this agreement, along with any substitution or withdrawal of life insurance policies subject to this agreement. In the event the partners decide to purchase any additional insurance, each partner hereby agrees to cooperate fully by performing all the requisites of the life insurer which are necessary conditions precedent to the issuance of life insurance policies.

If, in the annual redetermination of value, it is found that the value of the partnership has increased, it may be desirable to purchase additional insurance in order to keep pace with the increase in purchase price.

ILL 5.5 ▪ Sample Partnership Cross-Purchase Agreement (Cont.)

Article 6. Upon the death of a partner, the surviving partners shall proceed immediately to collect the proceeds of the policies on the deceased partner's life which are subject to this agreement. Upon the collection of all such proceeds and the qualification of a legal representative of the deceased partner's estate, the surviving partners shall pay to the legal representative an amount equal to such proceeds, which amount shall constitute payment on account, or in full, as the case may be, for the decedent's interest in the partnership.

Except as hereinafter provided, should the amount paid to the legal representative by the surviving partners under the preceding paragraph be less than the price to be paid for the decedent's partnership interest, the surviving partners (unless they forthwith pay the balance in cash) shall concurrently execute and deliver to the legal representative a series of notes in the amount of $_____ each (except as the note last falling due may be for a lesser remaining balance), which notes shall aggregate the unpaid balance due the decedent's estate for his (her) partnership interest. The first note shall be due _____ months after its execution date, and the remaining notes shall be due at intervals of _____ months thereafter, with interest at the rate of_____% per annum, the interest on each note being payable at its maturity. Each note shall provide that in the event of default in payment of principal, all notes subsequently due shall become due and payable immediately. Each note shall be subject to prepayment in whole or in part at any time. Provided, however, that the legal representative shall have the option to demand in cash an amount at least equal to _____% of the agreed purchase price. Upon failure of the surviving partners to comply with such demand, then this agreement may be terminated at the option of the legal representative.

Upon receipt of an amount equal to the proceeds of insurance subject to this agreement on the life of the deceased partner and any notes required to be delivered to the legal representative of his (her) estate (or cash in lieu of such notes), the legal representative shall execute and deliver to the surviving partners such instruments as are necessary or proper to transfer full and complete title to the deceased's interest in the partnership to the surviving partners; provided, however, that the legal representative shall have a lien upon the assets formerly belonging to the partnership for any unpaid balance. The sale shall take effect as of the close of business on the day of death of the deceased partner.

Upon the consummation of the purchase of the deceased partner's interest pursuant to the foregoing provisions of this Article, the surviving partners shall save harmless and indemnify the estate of the deceased partner against all liabilities of the partnership, which such surviving partners assume and agree to pay. The surviving partners shall be entitled to all the profits of the business, and shall bear all the losses, from the day after the day of death of the deceased partner.

> **This provision sets forth the procedure to follow in the event the insurance proceeds are not equal to the amount of the purchase price.**
>
> **In this connection, it should be noted that while ideally the insurance will cover the entire amount of this purchase price, this is not absolutely essential to the success of the plan. The insured plan can be successful even if the insurance provides only a substantial down payment towards the purchase price.**

Article 7. (a) The surviving partner shall have an option, exercisable within the period of _____ months from the date of death of a partner, to purchase from his (her) estate any or all of the policies owned by the deceased upon the survivor's life subject to this agreement on paying for each a price equal to the amount of (1) the interpolated terminal reserve value as of the date of the transaction, less any indebtedness against such policies, plus (2) the proportionate part of the gross premium last paid before the date of the transaction which covers a period extending beyond the date of the transaction, and plus (3) any accrued dividend on the policy as of the date of the transaction. Any such policy not acquired by the survivor within the above option period may be surrendered to the insurance company by the deceased partner's estate for its cash surrender value, or may be held or disposed of in any lawful manner which the estate deems advisable.

ILL 5.5 ■ *Sample Partnership Cross-Purchase Agreement (Cont.)*

(b) In the event of the termination of this agreement from any cause other than the death of a partner, each partner shall have an option exercisable within 30 days after such termination, to purchase any or all policies on his (her) own life subject to this agreement on paying for each a price calculated on the basis prescribed in the preceding paragraph.

> **This provision sets out a definite procedure under which a surviving partner may purchase the insurance policy on his or her own life in the event of the other partner's death, or in the event the agreement is terminated for some reason other than the death of a partner. In this regard, it should be noted that such a purchase and sale may be made without concern that the policy proceeds would subsequently be taxed under the transfer-for-value rule.**

Article 8. No insurance company which has issued or shall issue a policy or policies subject to this agreement shall be under any obligation with respect to the performance of the terms and conditions of this agreement. Any such company shall be bound only by the terms of the policy or policies which it has issued or shall hereafter issue and shall have no liability except as set forth in its policies.

Article 9. This agreement may be altered or amended in whole or in part at any time by filing with this agreement a written instrument setting forth such changes signed by the partners.

Article 10. This agreement shall terminate upon the occurrence of any one of the following events:

(a) The written agreement of the partnership and the partners to that effect;
(b) By the election in writing of a partner if at any time there should be no insurance subject to this agreement on the life of a particular partner, a party hereto, or if such insurance made subject to this agreement is impaired in value so that it would not provide at any time proceeds at least equal to _____% of the face amount of such insurance.
(c) The bankruptcy of any partner;
(d) The bankruptcy, receivership or dissolution of the partnership;
(e) The cessation of the partnership business; or
(f) If all the parties to this agreement die within a period of 30 days.

Article 11. In the event the terms of this agreement conflict with the partnership agreement of the partners, the terms of this agreement shall prevail.

Article 12. This agreement shall be governed by the laws of the State of _____.

Article 13. The partners, the partnership and the personal representative of any deceased partner shall make, execute and deliver any documents necessary or desirable to carry out this agreement.

IN WITNESS WHEREOF, the partners have executed this agreement the day and year first above written.

_____
Partner

_____
Partner

ILL 5.5 ▪ *Sample Partnership Cross-Purchase Agreement (Cont.)*

SCHEDULE A

It is agreed by the partners that the value of each partner's interest in the partnership shown is as follows:

Name of Partner	Value of Interest	For Fiscal Year Ending	Signature of Partners
_____	_____	_____	_____

SCHEDULE B

The following changes have been made in the life insurance policies held subject to the terms of the foregoing agreement.

ILL 5.6 ▪ *Sample Partnership Entity Agreement*

CAUTION: This is a specimen agreement. The actual agreement used in any particular case must be prepared by a qualified attorney.

Agreement made this _____ day of _____, 20_____, by and between _____ and_____ (hereinafter called "partners" and) _____ (hereinafter called "the partnership").

WITNESSETH:

Whereas, _____ and _____ are co-partners in the practice of _____; and

Whereas, the interest of each partner in the partnership is as follows:

_____ ...... _____%;

_____ ...... _____%;

_____ ...... _____%;

_____ ...... _____%; and

Whereas, the partnership and the partner mutually desire that upon death of a partner the partnership shall be continued by the survivors without interruption or liquidation an the deceased partner's estate shall receive the full value of his (her) interest in the partnership; and mutually desire that in the event of the withdrawal from the partnership of a partner during his (her) lifetime, the remaining partners shall have the opportunity to continue the partnership without interruption or liquidation; and

Whereas, the partnership and the partners mutually desire that life insurance be used as a means of providing all or a substantial part of the funds with which to achieve the aforesaid objective;

Now, therefore, in consideration of the mutual agreements and covenants contained herein and for other valuable consideration, receipt of which is hereby acknowledged, it is mutually agreed and covenanted by the partners, for themselves, their heirs, assigns and legal representatives and by the partnership, for itself as an entity, its successors and assigns as follows:

Article 1. No partner shall during his (her) lifetime assign, encumber or otherwise dispose of his (her) interest or any part thereof in the partnership except if a partner should desire to dispose voluntarily of his (her) interest during his (her) lifetime, then he (she) shall first offer in writing to sell his (her) interest to the partnership at the price determined in accordance with the provisions of Article 2 below; provided, however, that such price shall be paid in cash, fully, on the date of sale, and that the selling partner shall not participate in future profits of the partnership. If the interest is not purchased by the partnership within_____ days of receipt of the offer to it, then the selling partner may sell it to nay other person but shall not sell it without first offering it to the partnership in accordance with the method established at the price and on the terms offered to such other person if the price is less than the price established by Article 2.

> **A provision such as this, restricting the lifetime transfer of the partnership interests is necessary if the value set in the buy-sell agreement is to be accepted as the true fair market value for federal estate tax purposes.**

ILL 5.6 ▪ *Sample Partnership Entity Agreement (Cont.)*

Article 2. Upon the death of any partner, the partnership shall be continued by the surviving partners and the partnership shall purchase and the executor or administrator (hereafter called the "legal representative") of the deceased partner shall sell his (her) entire interest in the partnership, for the price and upon the condition stipulated in Article 3.

> **Here is a key provision in the agreement. Under this provision, the decedent's estate must sell, and the survivors must buy. This binding agreement to sell and the corresponding obligation to buy seems preferable to the various "option" type agreements that could be used. Too, the "option" type agreements may not effectively establish a value for federal estate tax purposes.**

Article 3. It is agreed that the current far value of all the assets of the partnership, including goodwill, is $_____ and that, therefore, the value of each partner's interest is as follows:

_____	...... $_____
_____	...... $_____
_____	...... $_____
_____	...... $_____
_____	...... $_____
_____	...... $_____

The partners agree to redetermine these values with 60 days following the end of each fiscal year, such redetermined values to be endorsed on Schedule A attached hereto and made a part of this agreement. If the partners fail to make such a redetermination of values for a particular year, the last previously stipulated values shall control, except that if the partners fail to make such a redetermination within the 24 months immediately preceding the death of a partner, then the values shall be agreed upon by the legal representative of the deceased partner on the one hand and the remaining partners on behalf of the partnership on the other. If they do not agree to a valuation within 90 days after the death of the partner, the value of the deceased partner's interest shall be determined by arbitration as follows: The remaining partners on behalf of the partnership on the one hand ad the representative of the deceased partner on the other shall each name one arbitrator; if the two arbitrators cannot agree upon the values, then the two arbitrators shall appoint a third arbitrator and the decision of the majority shall be binding upon all parties. In determining values by arbitration, the life insurance proceeds accruing from the policy on the deceased partner's life in excess of the policy's cash surrender value at the time of death, must not be taken into account; further, an amount for the addition to the goodwill of the partnership by the deceased of not less than $_____ shall be used.

> **This provision sets the current value of the partnership. It also provides for an annual redetermination of the value, and calls for arbitration in the event the partners fail to follow the revaluation clause. Some attorneys may prefer to have the last stated value control in all instances, but it is felt that this can lead to inequities if there has been no revaluation for a prolonged period of time.**
>
> **Under this valuation clause, the amount of goodwill will be considered a art of the capital transaction. As such, it will not be taxable income to the deceased partner's successors, nor will it be deductible by the partnership as a business expense.**

ILL 5.6 ▪ *Sample Partnership Entity Agreement (Cont.)*

The fixed price method, coupled with a revaluation provision, has many advantages. Among them are the following:

- The price that is arrived at initially, and upon subsequent reviews, as result of head-to-head negotiations probably will be as "fair" as possible.

- Such a price provision does not involve complex formulas, and is free of standards and terms that, because of possible ambiguity, could lead to controversy.

- It is a flexible method that may be adjusted periodically to reflect the changing fortunes of the business.

- The parties to the agreement are able to readily determine what price will be paid for their interest and plan their estates accordingly.

- Finally, since the purchase price is a known dollar amount, it is possible at all times to keep the buy-sell agreement "funded" with adequate amounts of life insurance.

An alternative method of valuing the business at the partner's death is the use of some kind of "formula" approach. Under this method, the specific price to be paid for the business is not determined at the time of the partner's death under an agreed upon, stated formula. Some of the more common formulas used are (1) the actual book value at the time of death; (2) some method of capitalization of earnings; and (3) average book value over a stated period of time. Each of these methods has strengths and weaknesses. The important thing is to have a method set out i the agreement that appeals to all parties as a fair method of establishing the purchase price.

Article 4. To assure that all or a substantial part of the purchase price for the interest in the partnership of a deceased partner will be available immediately in cash upon his death, the partnership has procured and made subject to this agreement insurance on the lives of the partners as follows:

_____ is insured under Policy No. _____, issued by _____ Insurance Company in the face amount of $_____, and the partnership is the applicant, owner and beneficiary thereof.

_____ is insured under Policy No. _____, issued by _____ Insurance Company in the face amount of $_____, and the partnership is the applicant, owner and beneficiary thereof.

_____ is insured under Policy No. _____, issued by _____ Insurance Company in the face amount of $_____, and the partnership is the applicant, owner and beneficiary thereof.

_____ is insured under Policy No. _____, issued by _____ Insurance Company in the face amount of $_____, and the partnership is the applicant, owner and beneficiary thereof.

ILL 5.6 ▪ *Sample Partnership Entity Agreement (Cont.)*

The partnership agrees to pay all premiums on the insurance policies taken out pursuant to this agreement and shall give proof of payment of premiums to the partners whenever any one of them shall so request such proof. If a premium is not paid within 20 days after its due date, the insured shall have the right to pay such premium. Such payment by the insured shall be considered a loan to the partnership and the insured shall be entitled to recover such loan from the partnership with interest at the rate of _____% per annum. The insurance company is hereby authorized and directed to give the insured, upon his (her) written request, any information about the status of any policy on his (her) life subject to this agreement, but payment of premiums by the partnership shall be accounted for as an ordinary, but nondeductible, business expense.

> **Since this is an entity agreement, the partnership is named the owner and beneficiary of each of the insurance policies. The premiums paid by the partnership, of course, are a nondeductible expense.**

Article 5. The partnership shall have the right to purchase additional insurance on the life of any of the partners; such additional policies shall be listed in Schedule B attached hereto and made a part of this agreement, along with any substitution or withdrawal of life insurance policies subject to this agreement. In the event that the partnership decides to purchase additional insurance, each partner hereby agrees to cooperate fully by performing all the requisites of the life insurer which are necessary conditions precedent to the issuance of life insurance policies.

> **If, the annual revaluation of the partnership, it is found that the value of the partnership has increased, it may be desirable to purchase additional on the partners in order to keep pace with the increase in purchase price.**

Article 6. Upon the death of a partner, the partnership shall proceed immediately to collect the proceeds of the policies on the deceased partner's life payable to its subject to this agreement. Upon the collection of all such proceeds and the qualification of a legal representative of the decedent's estate, the partnership shall pay to the legal representative as much of the proceeds as may be necessary to purchase the interest in the partnership of the deceased partner at the price determined herein, and shall retain any balance as general partnership funds.

Should the amount paid to the legal representative by the partnership under the preceding paragraph be less than the purchase price to be paid for the interest in the partnership of the deceased partner, then concurrently with the payment of such amount the partnership (unless it forthwith pays the balance in cash) shall execute and deliver to the legal representative a series of notes in the amount of $_____ each (except as the note last falling due may be for a lesser remaining balance), which notes shall aggregate the unpaid balance due such deceased partner's estate for his (her) interest in the partnership. The first note shall be due _____ months after its execution date, and the remaining notes shall be due at intervals of _____ months thereafter, with interest at the rate of _____% per annum, the interest on each note being payable at its maturity. Each note shall provide that in the event of default in payment of principal, all notes subsequently due shall become due and payable immediately. Each note shall be subject to prepayment in whole or in part at any time.

Upon receipt of the purchase price in cash, or in cash and notes, as provided above in this Article, in payment for a deceased partner's interest in the partnership, the legal representative shall execute and deliver to the partnership and to the surviving partners such instruments as are necessary and proper to transfer full and complete title to the decedent's entire interest in the partnership to the partnership and the surviving partners, provided, however, that the legal representative shall have a lien upon the assets formerly belonging to the partnership for any unpaid balance. The sale shall take effect as of the close of the business on the day of death of the deceased partner.

ILL 5.6 ▪ *Sample Partnership Entity Agreement (Cont.)*

Upon the consummation of the purchase of a deceased partner's interest pursuant to the foregoing provisions of this Article, the surviving partners, and each of them, shall save harmless and indemnify the estate of the deceased partner against all liabilities of the partnership, which the partnership and the surviving partners, jointly and severally, agree to pay. The surviving partner shall be entitled to all the profits of the business on the day of death of the deceased partner.

> **This provision sets forth the procedure to follow in the event the insurance proceeds are not equal to the amount of the purchase price. In this connection, it should be noted that while ideally the insurance will cover the entire amount of the purchase price, this is absolutely essential to the success of the plan. The insured plan can be successful even if the insurance provides only a substantial down payment toward the purchase price. The life insurance proceeds, if paid by reason of death of the insured partner, will not be taxable income.**

Article 7. In the event of the termination of this agreement, each partner shall have an option, exercisable within 30 days after such termination, to purchase any or all policies on his (her) own life owned by the partnership (1) the interpolated terminal reserve value as of the date of the transaction, less any indebtedness against such policies, plus (2) the proportionate part of the gross premium last paid before the date of the transaction which covers a period extending beyond the date of the transaction, and plus (3) any accrued dividend on the policy as of the date of the transaction.

> **This provision sets out a definite procedure under which a surviving partner may purchase the insurance policy on his or her own life, or in the event the agreement is terminated for some reason other than the death of a partner. In this regard, it should be noted that such a purchase and sale may be made without concern that the policy proceeds would subsequently be taxed under the transfer-for-value rule.**

Article 8. No insurance company which has issued or shall issue a policy or policies subject to this agreement shall be under any obligation with respect to the performance of the terms and conditions of this agreement. Any such company shall be bound only by the terms of the policy or policies which it has issued or shall hereafter issue and shall have no liability except as set forth in its policies.

Article 9. This agreement may be altered or amended in whole or in part at any time, by filing with this agreement a written instrument setting forth such changes signed by the partnership and the partners.

Article 10. This agreement shall terminate upon the occurrence of any of the following events:

(a) The written agreement of the partnership and the partners to that effect;

(b) By the election in writing of a partner if at any time there should be no insurance subject to this agreement on the life of a particular partner, a party hereto, or if such insurance made subject to this agreement is impaired in value so that it would not provide at any time proceeds at least equal to _____% of the face amount of such insurance;

(c) The bankruptcy of any partner;

(d) The bankruptcy, receivership or dissolution of the partnership;

(e) The cessation of the partnership business; or

(f) If all the parties to this agreement die within a period of 30 days.

ILL 5.6 ▪ *Sample Partnership Entity Agreement (Cont.)*

Article 11. In the event the terms of this agreement conflict with the partnership agreement of the partners, the terms of this agreement shall prevail.

Article 12. This agreement shall be governed by the State of _____.

Article 13. The partners, the partnership and the legal representative of any deceased partner shall make, execute and deliver any documents necessary or desirable to carry out this agreement.

IN WITNESS WHEREOF, the parties hereto have executed this agreement the day and year first above written.

_____
Partner

_____
Partner

_____
Partner

_____
Partner

By _____
         Partner

Schedule A

It is agreed by the partners that the value of each partner's interest in the partnership for the purposes of the foregoing agreement, for the fiscal year of the partnership shown is as follows:

Name of Partner	Value of Interest	For Fiscal Year Ending	Signature of Partners
_____	_____	_____	_____

Schedule B

The following changes have been made in the life insurance polices held subject to the terms of the foregoing statement.

ILL 5.7 ▪ *Sample Partnership Disability Purchase Agreement*

CAUTION: This is a specimen agreement. The actual agreement used in any particular case must be prepared by a qualified attorney.

Agreement made this _____ day of _____, 20_____, by and between_____ and _____ (hereinafter called "partners") and _____ (hereinafter called "the partnership").

WITNESSETH:

*Whereas,*_____ and _____ are co-partners in the practice of _____; and

Whereas, the interest of each partner in the partnership is as follows:

    _____ . . . . . _____%;

    _____ . . . . . _____%;

    _____ . . . . . _____%; and

Whereas, the primary purpose of this agreement is to provide (1) that the partnership shall make disability payments to a totally disabled partner for a period not to exceed two years, and (2) that the partnership shall purchase the interest of a disabled partner at a price fixed in this agreement, if the partner remains totally disabled at the end of two years;

Now, therefore, in consideration of the mutual agreements and covenants contained herein and for other valuable consideration, receipt of which is hereby acknowledged, it is mutually agreed and covenanted by the partners, for themselves, their heirs, assigns and legal representatives and by the partnership, for itself as an entity, its successors and assigns as follows:

Article I. Each partner is on the date of this agreement the owner of a policy of disability income insurance described in Schedule A. Each partner hereby authorizes the partnership to pay the premiums on this policy owned by him (her) and to promptly notify him (her) of such payment. In the event that a partner shall become totally disabled within the meaning of said policy of disability income insurance, whether or not the said policy shall then be in effect, then and in that event the disabled partner shall during the period of disability, but for not more than 24 months from the date which said disability commenced, receive each week an amount equal to 40% of the regular salary or drawing account that he (she) received at the commencement of the disability.

> This article provides that upon the disability of a partner, the partnership will continue to pay the disabled partner 40% of his or her regular salary for a period of up to two years. It is contemplated that each partner will supplement this with individually purchased disability income policies adequate to make up the balance of his or her salary. The parties may wish to take possible OASDI benefits into consideration here. The disabled partner will continue to receive a full share of partnership profits for a period of two years.

ILL 5.7 ▪ *Sample Partnership Disability Purchase Agreement (Cont.)*

Because a professional partnership will probably be unable to indefinitely continue even a 40 percent share of a disabled partner's salary or draw, this article provides that at the end of two years of disability the partnership will start to buy out the disabled partner's interest in the business. The two-year period was chosen because morbidity tables show that if an individual is disabled for this long, the chances of recovery are minimal.

At the end of the calendar (fiscal) year of the partnership during which said disabled partner shall have incurred said total disability and also at the end of the next following calendar (fiscal) year an amount equal to 33.33 percent of the net profits of the partnership after the payment of all costs, expenses and salaries paid, including but not limited to, the salary paid to any employee employed to replace the loss of services of the disabled partner, and including all amounts paid as salary or drawing account to both the disabled and the remaining partners during said calendar (fiscal) year.

If the said period of disability shall extend for a period of more than two years, then in that event the partnership shall purchase, and the disabled partner shall sell, the partnership interest of the disabled partner for the purchase price specified in Article 2. The purchase price shall be paid to the selling partner in equal monthly installments over a period of _____ months, the first installment to be paid on the first day of the month in which the said two-year period of disability ends. To secure the payment of such equal monthly installments, the remaining partners on behalf of the partnership shall execute and deliver to the selling partner a series of _____ percent promissory notes to the order of the selling partner. These notes shall allow for the acceleration of the due date of all unpaid notes in the series on default in the payment of any note.

If a disabled partner either dies or ceases to be so totally disabled at some time after such installment payments have commenced but before they have been completed, then such installments shall be spread out further, namely, at the rate of $_____ per month until the balance of said purchase price and interest on the declining balance at the rate of _____ percent per year shall be wholly paid and satisfied.

Article 2. It is agreed that the current fair value of the partnership's capital assets as defined in Section 736(b) of the 1986 Internal Revenue Code, including goodwill, is $_____ and that the fair value of the unrealized receivable is $_____ and that, therefore, the value of each partner's interest is as follows:

_____ . . . . . $ _____

_____ . . . . . $ _____

_____ . . . . . $ _____

The partners agree to redetermine the values within _____ days after the end of each fiscal year, such redetermined values to be endorsed on Schedule B attached hereto and made part of this agreement. If the partners fail to make a redetermination of values for a particular year, the last previously stipulated values shall control, except that if the partners fail to make such a redetermination for two consecutive years, then the value of a partner's interest shall be determined by the independent public accountant regularly retained by the partnership to audit its books. If no such public accountant is available, or if it fails to make such determination of valuation, then the value shall be determined by any other public accountant who may be selected by mutual agreement of the remaining partners and the disabled partner or his (her) representative. In determining a value, the public accountant must use an amount for goodwill of the partnership of not less than $_____.

ILL 5.7 ▪ *Sample Partnership Disability Purchase Agreement (Cont.)*

> This provision utilizes the fixed price method of valuation and sets the current value of the partnership and provides for an annual redetermination of value. It also provides for arbitration in the event the partners fail to follow the revaluation clause. Some attorneys may prefer to have the last stated value control in all instances. While this method may have the advantages of certainty and simplicity, it may lead to inequities if there has been no revaluation for a prolonged period of time. The amount paid for the partnership assets (including goodwill, but excluding unrealized receivables) will be eligible for capital gains treatment. The amount paid for unrealized receivables will be ordinary income to the recipient.

Article 3. The partnership, in order to help fund its obligation under this agreement, has procured and made subject hereto disability on the partners as follows:

(1) _____ is insured under disability income insurance Policy No. _____ issued by the _____ Insurance Company, providing the following amount of monthly income, $_____ and the partnership is the applicant, owner and beneficiary thereof.

(2) _____ is insured under disability income insurance Policy No. _____ issued by the _____ Insurance Company, providing the following amount of monthly income, $_____ and the partnership is the applicant, owner and beneficiary thereof.

(3) _____ is insured under disability income insurance Policy No. _____ issued by the _____ Insurance Company, providing the following amount of monthly income, $_____ and the partnership is the applicant, owner and beneficiary thereof.

The partnership agrees to pay all premiums on the insurance policies taken out pursuant to this agreement and shall give proof of payment of premiums to the partners whenever any of them shall so request such proof. If a premium s not paid within 20 days after its due date, the insured shall have the right to pay such premium and be reimbursed therefore by the partnership. The partnership shall have the right to purchase additional disability income insurance on any of the partners; such additional policies shall be listed in Schedule C attached hereto and made art of this agreement, along with any substitution or withdrawal of disability income insurance policies subject to this agreement. In the event that the partnership decides to purchase additional insurance, each partner hereby agrees to cooperate fully by performing all the requisites of the insurer which are necessary conditions precedent to the issuance of disability income insurance policies. Payment of premiums by the partnership shall be accounted for as an ordinary nondeductible business expense.

> **To fund the purchase of the disabled partner's interest, the partnership purchased disability income policies on each of the partners. Of course, the premiums paid by the partnership on these policies, as well as the policies owned by the individual partners, are a nondeductible expense.**

Article 4. This agreement shall terminate upon the occurrence of any one of the following events:

(a) the written agreement of the partnership and the partners to that effect;
(b) the bankruptcy of any partner;
(c) the bankruptcy, receivership or dissolution of the partnership;
(d) the cessation of the partnership business; or
(e) if all the parties to this agreement die within a period of 30 days.

ILL 5.7 ▪ *Sample Partnership Disability Purchase Agreement (Cont.)*

Article 5. No Insurance company that has issued or shall issue a policy or policies subject to this agreement shall be under any obligation with respect to the performance of the terms and conditions of this agreement. Any such company shall be bound only by the terms of the policy or policies which it has issued or shall hereafter issue and shall have no liability except as set forth in its policies.

Article 6. This agreement may be altered or amended in whole or in part at ay time by filing with this agreement a written instrument setting forth such changes signed by the partners.

Article 7. This agreement shall be governed by the law of the State of _____.

Article 8. The partners, the partnership, the disabled partner or the personal representative of any deceased partner shall make, execute and deliver any documents necessary or desirable to carry out this agreement. In Witness Whereof the parties hereto have executed this agreement at _____ in the County of _____, State of, _____, on the day and year above written.

```
                            _____
                                 Partnership
                    By_____
                                  Partner
                            _____
                                  Partner
                            _____
                                  Partner
```

Schedule A

Schedule of disability income policies owned personally by partners.

Name of Company	Policy Number	Monthly Income	Signature of Partners
_____	_____	_____	_____

Schedule B

It is agreed by the partners that the value of each partner's interest in the partnership for the purposes of the foregoing agreement, for the calendar (fiscal) year of the partnership shown is as follows:

Name of Partner	Value of Interest	For Year Ending	Signature of Partners
_____	_____	_____	_____

Schedule C

Schedule of disability income policies owned by the partnership.

Name of Company	Policy Number	Monthly Income	Signature of Partners
_____	_____	_____	_____

CHAPTER 5 QUESTIONS FOR REVIEW

1. A limited partner

   A. agrees to contribute a stipulated amount of capital

   B. does not take part in the active management and operation of the firm

   C. is liable for company debts only to the extent of his or her capital investment

   D. all of the above

2. All the following are true about a general partnership, EXCEPT

   A. the partnership can be created by a voluntary, oral agreement of the parties

   B. the partnership files a tax return and pays income taxes

   C. the assets of the business are owned by the partners

   D. the partners are liable for all debts of the firm even to the extent of their personal assets

3. Which of the following is a reason that may force a partnership liquidation, even though the intent of the surviving partner is to reorganize and continue the business?

   A. There is a lack of liquidity needed to pay debts

   B. The surviving partner cannot obtain the consent of the deceased partner's heirs to continue the business

   C. The surviving partner cannot work with the relatives of the former partner

   D. All of the above

4. Sale of the business by the deceased partner's family to the surviving partners may be the best choice when

   A. there is more than adequate liquidity and profit in the business to fund the purchase

   B. the deceased partner's children are actively involved in the business

   C. heirs have no knowledge about or skill in the business

   D. None of the above

5. A partnership owned equally by three partners is worth $210,000. They enter into an insured cross-purchase buy-sell agreement. How much life insurance would Partner A own on the lives of Partners B and C?

   A. $35,000 on each

   B. $70,000 on each

   C. $210,000 on each

   D. None of the above

6

The Corporation

The third major business organization form is the corporation. Focusing on the close corporation, this chapter discusses the corporate structure and market, as well as tax advantages, of incorporation. We will also look at the three alternatives facing survivors at the death of a corporate shareholder: liquidation, family retention and sale.

In this chapter, we will discuss the types of corporations and the factors concerning a shareholder's death that encourage other shareholders in a closely held corporation either to liquidate the business or to have their families retain their stock interests in it. We'll also look at the problems these decisions create and the planning and positive steps that must be taken today for either choice. Then we will look at the sale of the business—the third choice—and the insured buy-sell agreement.

■ OPPORTUNITIES IN THE CORPORATE MARKETS

The corporation has become an increasingly popular business form in this country. Especially when dealing with closely held corporations, which are privately owned by a small group, you, as an insurance professional, should be aware of the wealth of opportunities this market offers. These include:

1. *Market size.* According to the 1999 *Statistical Abstract* of the United States, there were a total of 4.6 million corporations in this country as of the end of 1996, up from 3.7 million just six years earlier. Ill. 6.1 breaks down the corporations by industry.

2. *Market demographics.* Contrary to popular belief, the majority of corporations are small businesses, very often run like proprietorships and partnerships, with fewer than 20 employees. The key shareholders are also

ILL 6.1 ■ *Corporations by Industry*

Industry	1984	1990	1996
Agriculture, Forestry, Fishing	81,000	126,000	159,000
Mining	26,000	39,000	36,000
Construction	272,000	407,000	471,000
Manufacturing	243,000	301,000	326,000
Transportation, public utilities	111,000	160,000	206,000
Wholesale/retail trade	796,000	1,023,000	1,142,000
Finance, Insurance, Real Estate	493,000	609,000	723,000
Services	671,000	1,029,000	1,557,000

Number of Corporations

Statistical Abstract of the United States, 1999

the managers; minor shareholders may be spouses or children. In short, these businesses are approachable.

3. *Need awareness.* Incorporation is a conscious business decision, based on the owners' awareness of the tax and other advantages incorporation may bring. Many of today's corporations started out as proprietorships and partnerships; at a certain point, they elected to incorporate. The point is that they understand the need to maximize tax advantages and minimize personal liability. In addition, they recognize the value of working with an insurance professional to protect the business and their families.

4. *Market resources.* Company for company, corporations are the most financially stable and prosperous of the various business forms. Perhaps it is because of their awareness of the need for sound business structure and management; but whatever the reason, total assets held by corporations in this country total more than *$28 trillion.* Of greater interest, the average asset size per corporation comes to more than $6 million.

The bottom line is that corporations, as a viable market for your services, offer need, resources and approachability, which make them ideal prospects.

INTRODUCTION TO THE CORPORATE FORM

Since the beginning of the industrial age in the United States, there has been a definite trend toward the corporate form of doing business. The trend continues. The need for specialization of talents, wider ownership of the business organization and increased capital needs caused by today's high-tech, fast-paced business environment lead many business owners to select incorporation over the proprietorship or partnership forms.

Why Businesses Incorporate

Today, there are two primary reasons why business owners incorporate:

1. *To obtain tax advantages available only to corporations.* This partially reflects corporate income tax rates; however, under current law, the direct income tax advantages of incorporation are minor when compared to taxation at the individual level. More significant, however, are the tax advantages of tax-deductible "fringe" benefits for owners (medical coverage and other insurance plans, pension, etc.), which can be adopted by the board of directors and which are not always available for owners of unincorporated businesses.

2. *To reduce the individual and group liability of the owners.* In contrast to sole proprietorships and partnerships, the legal and financial liability of stockholders in a corporation is limited, very often to no more than the corporation's assets. In most cases, personal assets are protected.

To understand how these advantages work for owners of corporations, let's look at the structure of this business form and how a corporation is formed.

Structure of the Corporation

The most significant characteristic distinguishing the corporation from the sole proprietorship or partnership is that the corporation is regarded as a *separate legal entity*. Once incorporated, a business has a life of its own. It does not end upon the death of an owner. In fact, shareholders who manage and run the business are viewed legally as employees of the corporation.

In essence, a corporation is treated as a "person" under the law. Separate from its owners, a corporation can borrow money, must pay taxes (at special corporate rates) and can buy and sell assets and other businesses. It can even sue and be sued.

Forming a Corporation

The corporation is more complex than either the sole proprietorship or partnership. It must be formally founded under incorporation papers and exists only by authority of the corporation laws of the state in which it is organized. All states require that articles of incorporation be filed, generally with the secretary of state.

These articles of incorporation identify the name of the corporation and the names of the incorporators and the members of the board of directors. They also outline the business purpose of the corporation, that is, the activities it was organized to undertake.

In addition to the formal filing and approval of the articles of incorporation (also sometimes referred to as the company's charter), the process of incorporation normally involves a precise procedure of organizational meetings, as well as times for regular meetings of the board of directors.

Upon incorporation, stock is also issued, in a manner that complies with state and federal securities laws. In closely held corporations, owners contribute assets and, in turn, receive proportionate shares of stocks to reflect their equity interest in the corporation. Each share gives its owner a proportionate voting right in the company, but these rights are limited to electing directors, who in turn select the officers of the company.

Tax accounts with state and federal taxing authorities must be established, and a multitude of important business decisions and tax elections must be made when the corporation is organized.

Types of Corporations

Corporations can be classified as *publicly traded*, *closely held C corporations* or *closely held Subchapter S corporations*.

The Publicly Traded Corporation

Publicly traded corporations have a broad base of investors, possibly numbering in the hundreds of thousands, also known as *stockholders* or *shareholders*. Shares in these corporations are publicly traded on the financial exchanges, such as the New York Stock Exchange or the American Stock Exchange.

While shareholders have a right to vote on the board of directors and other issues at the annual meeting, there is rarely any connection between the shareholders and the active managers of the corporation. Shareholders invest in the corporation's stocks to seek appreciation of the stock's value over time and(or) to receive dividends on their shares.

The Closely Held C Corporations

Closely held C corporations are by far the most popular type of corporation. They are closely held in that their stock is not traded publicly. In fact, it is generally closely held by the managers and the families of those who actively run the business. There may be only a hundred or a thousand shares, owned by a handful of people, all connected in some way to the business. The stock rarely pays dividends or has any market value outside the corporation. It is more a reflection of ownership share in the corporation.

The Closely Held S Corporation

An *S corporation* is similar to other closely held corporations, except that its owners are taxed more like partners in a partnership than shareholders in a corporation. All income in an S corporation passes directly through to the owners. The professional corporation can be either a regular or an S corporation, depending on the needs of the professionals. It is mentioned here because incorporated professionals have unique problems, which require unique solutions from insurance professionals.

■ TAX ADVANTAGES OF INCORPORATION

Corporations are taxed independently from their stockholders. Historically, especially because corporations generally have been taxed at a lower rate than individuals, incorporating served as a direct means of sheltering income and reducing taxes. Under current law, however, the direct tax benefit savings of incorporation are marginal at best.

For instance, under current law, the corporate tax rate is 15 percent on the first $50,000 of corporate taxable income, and 25 percent on the next $25,000 of taxable income ($50,000 to $75,000 of taxable income). Corporate taxable income between $75,000 and $100,000 is taxed at 34 percent and income between $100,000 and $335,000 is taxed at 39 percent. Rates vary from that amount as shown in Ill. 6.2.

Individuals, on the other hand, are subject to a progressive income tax that ranges from 15 percent to 39.6 percent, including surcharge. Naturally, corporations may take advantage of any difference between the corporate tax bracket and that of the major shareholders. When the major shareholders' tax brackets are less than the corporation's bracket, the board of directors may raise salaries or pay bonuses. They also may decide to pay dividends, although dividends will result in double taxation, once at the corporate level and once at the individual level. On the other hand, if the shareholders' brackets begin to exceed the corporation's highest bracket, the profit may be retained in the business. However, the ability of a small, closely held corporation to retain earnings and not pay dividends is limited by the accumulated earnings provisions of the Internal Revenue Code. These provisions assess a penalty tax on earnings of a corporation that have been unreasonably retained beyond a certain minimum allowable retention.

Deductible Salaries

The federal income tax might be reduced further by paying reasonable salaries to working family members, thus spreading the income at lower brackets through the family. Also, if the owner's spouse and children help in the business, placing them on salary gets money out of the corporation on a deductible (expense), rather than a nondeductible (dividend) basis.

Rental Income

It is possible for office-shareholders, or members of their families, to rent buildings or other property to the corporation and receive reasonable rentals. Furthermore, if the rented property is owned by a low-bracket individual—the widowed mother of the shareholders, for instance—the overall effect can be not only to lower taxes in the family group, but to give the shareholders a deductible way of providing for a relative in need.

ILL 6.2 ■ *Federal Tax on Corporate Income*

Taxable Corporate Income			
From (Col. 1)	To	Tax on Col. 1	Rate on Excess
$ 0	$ 50,000	$ 0	15%
50,000	75,000	7,500	25%
75,000	100,000	13,750	34%
100,000	335,000	22,250	39%
335,000	10,000,000	113,900	34%
10,000,000	15,000,000	3,400,000	35%
15,000,000	18,333,333	5,150,000	38%
18,333,333		6,416,667	35%

The lower corporate tax brackets are phased out for income subject to the 35 percent rate. This phaseout is achieved by imposing an additional 3 percent surcharge on taxable income between $15,000,000 and $18,333,333.

Fringe Benefits

Incorporation opens up the whole area of fringe benefits to shareholder-employees. Neither proprietors nor partners are employees, and so they or their unincorporated businesses are barred from deducting fringe benefits provided for them. (An exception to this general rule is the proprietor's or partner's right to elect to be an owner-employee under the Self-Employed Individual's Retirement Law—HR-10 or Keogh Plan).

Fringe benefits provided by corporations to shareholder-employees, on the other hand, can be many and varied. Among these are Social Security taxes paid by the employer, hospitalization and medical care reimbursement plans, salary continuation plans, group life insurance, qualified deferred compensation plans, stock purchase and stock option plans and the corporation's payment of the shareholder-employees' business expenses.

Although payments for these benefits may be regarded as a disadvantage from the corporation's viewpoint, the officers and employees of the corporation usually will want the benefits. Payment of the benefits from corporate dollars reduces the need for the officers and employees to provide the benefits for themselves from their personal income.

Death of an Owner

In a closely held corporation, the key shareholders and company officers are generally one and the same. As a result, they face many of the same problems as unincorporated businesses upon the death of an owner.

Keep in mind, also, that stock in a closely held corporation, unlike shares in a publicly traded corporation, is generally not marketable. It can be sold; however, odds are that there will not be a ready and waiting buyer for it.

Legally, of course, a corporation has an unlimited life and can survive the death of one or more shareholder-employees. However, keep in mind that, as with any other small business, the owners are the business. If one of them dies, the company may face serious problems.

In this situation, the heirs and other remaining shareholders face three alternatives. They can:

1. liquidate the business and distribute assets;

2. arrange for heirs to assume an active management interest in the business; or

3. arrange for the corporation itself or other shareholders to purchase the shares of the deceased shareholder.

■ LIQUIDATION

Any number of close corporations simply will disappear at the death of a major shareholder. The assets will be put up for sale, the debts paid, the corporation terminated and the proceeds distributed among the shareholders. In short, it will be liquidated.

Factors Favoring Liquidation

There are factors present in many corporations that may favor the liquidation of the business and the end to the company at the death of a major shareholder.

No Successor Management

The human life value is still the most important factor in the success of any business. In many corporations, there is only one shareholder, except for a few shares held by a few others to qualify the corporation. The death of this person alone forces the liquidation of the business. This is especially true in corporations in which the skills, knowledge, personality and contacts of the key shareholder are responsible for the success of the enterprise. Even in businesses in which there is a considerable investment in fixed assets and other tangible property, it might be advisable to liquidate the business if no provision has been made for competent successor management.

Insufficient Estate Liquidity

The cash needs of the estate (debts, probate and attorney's fees, estate and inheritance taxes, etc.) may require the liquidation of the corporation. The corporate owner generally has a negligible estate outside the business because most of the corporate owner's spare cash was reinvested in the business. If the corporation, in turn, has little cash, it might be best to liquidate the corporation, rather than risk operation of the business after the owner's death with insufficient working capital.

The legal representative may be forced to sell some or all of the deceased's stock for an entirely different reason. The principal asset of a typical close corporation stockholder is the business interest. Also typical is the lack of liquidity in the stockholder's estate. If other property in the estate is insufficient to pay debts, death taxes, and the expenses of funeral and administration, some portion of the stock will have to be sold to raise money for estate settlement costs. If the stock must be sold at a sacrifice price—not an unlikely occurrence—further losses result.

Although estate taxes may have a devastating effect on any closely held business interest, it is important to be familiar with the special closely held business provisions of the Internal Revenue Code. These provisions are discussed in Chapter 4.

Requisites of an Orderly Liquidation

The close corporation shareholder, having determined the need to liquidate, next must determine the time to dispose of the business. Does the owner dispose of the business now, or does the owner have his or her executor liquidate it at death? If the owner does not plan to dispose of his or her business right now—at this minute—then the owner must plan to have the executor liquidate it at death. This plan includes: (a) a suitable will; and (b) a sufficient life insurance program.

A Suitable Will

The corporate owner's attorney should draft the owner's will to give the owner's executor authority to continue the business until the executor can dispose of it in the most advantageous way possible. This will also would free the executor from any personal liability during the course of this continuation.

More specifically, the executor should have power to:

1. liquidate the interest at either public or private sale and to determine the selling price and the terms of the sale. The executor may dispose of all or part of the interest;

2. retain the business interest for any period that the executor determines as appropriate. The executor, thereby, is not obliged to dispose of the business in a distress sale soon after the shareholder's death, but may continue the business until the executor can liquidate the corporation by the most profitable means;

3. borrow money on the security of the business assets in order to pay the estate obligations, while awaiting the proper time to liquidate the business interest; and

4. select some other way to deal with the business interest, such as a complete redemption of shares by the corporation, or participation in a consolidation or merger with another corporation.

Despite the will provisions discussed above, a liquidation of a business—whether it be a proprietorship, partnership or corporation—generally means that the seller will receive less than the "going" value for the enterprise. As we learned before, the business goodwill will bring nothing. Further, there is bound to be a startling shrinkage in the value received for the tangible assets of the business. The fixed assets and inventory may bring only one-half their original value and, depending upon the nature of the business, the accounts receivable may be difficult or impossible to collect. Obviously, there should be a way to offset this decline in value.

Life Insurance

The second planning tool that is necessary for an orderly liquidation of a closely held corporation is adequate life insurance. As an insurance professional, your role is to work with business owner prospects and clients to help them determine the value of the business and attempt to peg its liquidation value. Also, it is important to meet with all involved shareholders to discuss and work out the details, including the provision that adequate life insurance is placed on the owners' lives.

The Role of Life Insurance

Life insurance is the ingredient that will make the liquidation a positive, successful event at the owner's death, rather than a disaster. Ideally, the proceeds will:

1. offset the diminished value of the business. Asset shrinkage will result despite all attempts at an orderly liquidation. Life insurance can help the shareholder's family replace the income that was lost due to the death and the liquidation sale at bargain prices;

2. pay estate settlement costs and debts; and

3. make possible the retention of the business until the most advantageous disposition can be arranged. Life insurance funds can be used to keep the corporation afloat until a fair sale can be made.

Ownership and Beneficiary Provisions

When it is possible that the business will be liquidated immediately at the death of the corporate owner, it would seem best that the new life insurance should not be purchased by the corporation. The corporate owner or spouse could purchase the policy. If the owner's present income is not adequate to pay the premiums, the corporation could increase his or her compensation. The beneficiary could be the owner's spouse, the owner's estate or perhaps a trustee. If the owner's spouse were named beneficiary, the spouse would have to understand that he or she would have to make some of the insurance proceeds available to the executor for payment of the estate costs, debts and taxes.

■ CASE STUDY: MR. BARNETT

Mr. Barnett is a 90-percent shareholder of the Barnett Plating Co., Inc., a small job-plating company that specializes in chrome, zinc and cadmium plating of nuts, bolts, screws and like items. He is age 53 and has operated this business for 23 years.

His only child, a daughter, is married and living in another state. There is no employee willing or competent to take over the business. Barnett's brother owns the remaining 10 percent of the shares. He has his own business and doesn't want to run this one.

Furthermore, few of his competitors would want to purchase his shop, because the trend is toward larger, more productive operations. Barnett realizes that at his death the business would have to be liquidated.

To aid his executor in this task, he has made the necessary provisions in his will for the orderly liquidation of his corporation. However, he is well aware of the job the executor will face in liquidating his business. Looking realistically at his business values, here is the picture Barnett draws of the business asset value before and after his death—assuming an orderly liquidation is possible.

	Before Death	After Death
Equipment	$145,000	$119,000
Inventory of chemicals and metals	13,000	10,000
Other assets	32,000	25,000
Accounts receivable	112,000	112,000
	$302,000	$266,000
Total debt	50,000	50,000
	$252,000	$216,000

Mr. Barnett has a $30,000 mortgage on a home worth $95,000. He also owns $50,000 of life insurance and $7,500 of miscellaneous marketable securities. These were purchased with his retirement in mind. He also has autos and other personal property worth $10,000.

Providing his executor could get $216,000 for his business at death, Mr. Barnett's estate would look like this:

Assets		Liabilities	
Home	$ 95,000	Funeral bill	$ 5,000
Personal property	10,000	Administration ex.	15,100
Securities	7,500	Mortgage	30,000
Life insurance	50,000	Other debts	5,000
Business interest	216,000	Inheritance tax (etc.)	3,500
	$378,500		$58,600

(There is no estate tax.)

His Needs and Desires

Unless Mr. Barnett wants his executor to spend nearly all of his life insurance proceeds to meet the costs of settling his estate, he has to find an additional $58,600 in estate funds. Where should this money come from? Barnett draws these conclusions from the above facts:

1. He does not want his executor to invade his present life insurance for estate liquidity. His wife must have some basis for her continuing income, because his executor may realize a substantially smaller amount than that estimated from the liquidation of the business, and her Social Security benefit is a number of years away.

2. Actually, he must boost the income provisions he has made for his wife after his death. His income last year—salary and bonus—was $45,000. He realizes that his wife's income after his demise cannot be less than two-thirds of this sum.

The Solution

Mr. Barnett solves his estate income problem by purchasing $150,000 of additional life insurance. The insurance owned by him is made payable to his wife. Barnett asks his wife to earmark $59,000 of the insurance proceeds to pay estate costs and debts, including the home mortgage. He then tells her to consider the balance of the insurance proceeds as offsetting the shrunken value of the business that probably will result from a liquidation. With the $216,000 that Mrs. Barnett might expect to receive from the orderly liquidation of the business, she would have, with the insurance, the present value of $307,000 that could be invested for income, or to which settlement options could be applied. The amount, invested at a reasonable rate of return, will provide her with at least a minimal income.

■ FAMILY RETENTION OF INCORPORATED BUSINESS

The reasons a family retains the interest of a corporate shareholder at death do not vary greatly from the reasons we discussed before under the proprietorship and partnership headings. Generally, the decision of a corporate shareholder to plan family retention of the corporate interest is based on six factors:

1. *The family's stock ownership.* The family presently owns all or a majority of the stock of the corporation. If the family's interest in the corporation is a minority one, the interest of the shareholder should not, in most cases, be retained.

2. *Competent successor management.* There is competent successor management available, preferably within the family.

3. *Customers will accept a successor.* The customers will accept a successor to the present majority shareholder-business operator. Some incorporated

businesses are one-person operations that rely on the personality of the owner and not the name and reputation of the firm. If this is the case, the business might best be terminated at the death of the present owner, rather than risk an almost certain failure by a successor.

4. *An assured line of corporate credit.* The corporate credit line is not dependent upon the presence of the shareholder in the business.

5. *Compatibility with other owner-employees.* As with a partnership, there is always the potential for conflict when an heir of one of the owners attempts to step into the business.

6. *Sufficient estate liquidity.* Will allow the heirs to retain the interest, rather than be forced to sell it to raise cash to settle the estate.

Requirements for Successful Family Retention

As with the choice of liquidation, family retention of a shareholder's interest depends on a carefully crafted will and adequate life insurance to provide liquidity and operating cash to make the transition work.

Provisions in the Will

The shareholders must give their executors the power necessary to deal with the various contingencies that may arise during the period of estate administration. The normal rule of law is that, unless there is a will provision to the contrary, executors are required to act under the direction and supervision of the probate court having jurisdiction over the estate. The executors are personally responsible to that court for the action they take with the corporate shares that form a part of the decedent's estate.

If the decedent has left no instructions to the contrary, the primary concern of the probate court judge (and the executor) is to conserve the assets of the estate, to protect the interests of the heirs, and to convert the estate into conservative and less hazardous investments—not to save the business, perpetuate it for the estate owner's business successors or preserve the fruits of the business owner's years of toil and labor. Of course, the court may not in every case exercise its powers to inquire into the management affairs of the firm in the interest of the heirs, but many court decisions remind us that the possibility of such court action is ever present.

For this reason, major shareholders should see that their wills give their executors the discretionary powers needed to retain the business. These include:

- the power to retain the stock interest indefinitely and absolve the executor from responsibility;

- the power to vote the stock and otherwise manage or participate in the management of the business as needed; and

- the power to borrow money for any purpose advantageous to the estate, including the payment of death costs and taxes.

The Key Is Life Insurance

The primary reason attempts at family retention of a shareholder's interest fail is lack of liquidity. Few closely held corporations pay dividends on their stock. Owners depend on salaries from the corporation, based on their own hands-on management of the business.

When a shareholder dies, the family's income may dwindle. Even when successor management is ready to step in, there will be an adjustment period when the company's income dips. Also, the deceased owner's estate will need immediate cash to settle final expenses and administration costs.

These funds can be raised by selling off personal assets, selling or liquidating business assets or by providing adequate life insurance to offset these costs. The latter is both the easiest and most cost-effective option.

Personal estate liquidity can be created or improved through life insurance. The shareholder's death will create a need for cash within a relatively short period of time—for administration costs, estate debts and estate taxes. The absence of liquidity or the inability of the estate to raise the cash through a sale or pledging of estate assets may result in the executor selling the business interest rather than retaining it.

Estate liquidity also plays a part in the distribution of the estate assets and the future estate income. In most families, not all the family members will participate in the business after the shareholder's death—the spouse and one or more of the children may not be part of the business. While nonliquid assets—other than the stock in the family corporation—can be passed to the spouse and other nonbusiness-connected members of the family, it does little good if these assets fail to earn income. Assets, such as the family home, the summer cottage or undeveloped land, for instance, cannot be expected to satisfy a spouse's need for income or convince other members of the family that they have received "equal" inheritances.

Naturally, here again is a situation in which liquid assets (life insurance proceeds, marketable securities and cash) could ease a critical family situation. The best choice, whenever possible, is life insurance.

The major shareholder should have a substantial block of life insurance. It is the only way to provide for the liquidity his or her estate will need with one premium payment.

SALE OF THE DECEASED'S INTERESTS

In many close corporations, it is not advantageous for an heir to retain the shares, nor is it necessary to liquidate the corporation. In many situations, a sale of the deceased's interest is best for all. Such a sale can be looked at from two points of view: (1) the surviving shareholder's; and (2) the estate's.

Shareholder's Point of View

The surviving shareholder's point of view can be viewed in terms of:

1. relative needs of the heirs versus the needs of the corporation (dividends versus retained earnings);

2. competency of heirs to participate in the business;

3. danger of heir or estate selling to outsiders; and

4. dealing with the estate's personal representative.

Dividends Versus Retained Earnings

After the shareholder's death, heirs not directly involved in the business may expect to receive dividends on their inherited shares. This is especially the case with heirs of a minority shareholder. During the minority shareholder's lifetime, he or she supported dependents through a salary. The loss of this salary after the shareholder's death is barely compensated for by the dividends on the stock interest—if such dividends are paid at all.

Usually the surviving shareholders have little interest in paying corporate dividends. The main reason payment of dividends is avoided is that dividends are taxed twice, once at the corporate level and once at the individual level. The surviving shareholders still have their incomes, and possibly are in high income tax brackets and do not need or desire extra income. Their goal is to retain earnings and plow them back into the corporation for improvements or expansion.

Competency of Heirs as Successors

The heirs that inherit the stock of a majority shareholder also inherit the right to direct and control the future of the corporation. Whether they will, in fact, do an effective job is one factor that will aid in determining whether the interest should be held or sold.

The best person to determine the answer to this question is the majority shareholder during his or her life. The majority shareholder must decide whether or not family members are capable of managing the business and satisfying the other shareholders with their capabilities. If the majority shareholder has some doubt as to their success, he or she probably should plan instead for the sale of his or her interest at death.

Danger of Heir Selling to Outsiders

In the minds of the surviving shareholders, a menace equal to having incompetent heirs in the business is the possibility that the heirs or the estate of the decedent may sell the shares to outsiders. There is no law that says the heirs must retain their shares. In fact, the probate court might order a sale of stock held by the estate to pay estate debts and costs of administration.

Logically, the surviving shareholders or the corporation would wish to be the buyers of such shares. To be able to buy such shares and give the heirs a fair price, the surviving shareholders or the corporation need to be able to raise the cash and to meet the terms of the heirs. A buy-sell agreement is the best way to accomplish these objectives.

Dealing with the Estate's Personal Representative

In the absence of a buy-sell agreement, the surviving shareholders must negotiate with the personal representative for the purchase of the decedent's stock. Of course, the personal representative is obligated by law to get as much as possible for the estate assets. Also, because the personal representative could be held personally liable for any negligence in his or her handling of the estate, he or she may have an inflated idea of the stock value and, as a result, be difficult to deal with in the purchase of the stock interest. As you will see later in this chapter, a buy-sell agreement will insure the sale at a price agreed upon by all parties.

Estate's Point of View

Thus far, we have considered the problems that come with the death of a shareholder largely from the viewpoint of the surviving shareholder. Generally, it is good sales psychology to approach the business continuation with the assumption that the prospect is going to be the surviving shareholder. It is much easier for the prospect to see his or her associate dead and the associate's widow or widower coming into the business. The prospect does not easily visualize himself or herself as the deceased and his or her own spouse as the widow or widower.

However, the fact remains that the prospect may be the first to die. The problems that death brings are not confined to the surviving members of the firm. They exist with equal force and perplexity for the surviving spouse and the estate of the deceased member. Therefore, the position of the heirs must be examined.

The Loss of Income Problem

Loss of income following the death of a shareholder in a close corporation may be the biggest problem the surviving spouse and family will face. Substantially all the decedent's capital is tied up in the corporation, thus leaving only his or her compensation for services during his or her lifetime to support the family. Thus, when the shareholder dies, the income is cut off. As was mentioned earlier in this chapter, there then arises the conflict of interests between the corporation and the heirs. The corporation does not wish to pay out the dividends the heirs need, nor does the corporation wish to pay salaries to incompetent heirs. The heirs' income situation seems futile unless there are assets in the estate available to create income. However, liquid assets in the estate of a close corporation shareholder are often scarce.

Estate Liquidity

The estate, because of the nature of close corporations, may be highly illiquid. That is, there might not be enough easily sold assets in the estate. In the case of a close corporation shareholder, his or her estate probably will consist of shares of stock, a personal residence and other personal effects—all of which are either not easily sold or not readily sold by the heirs.

Inevitably, the surviving spouse and the family must do one of three things to create income:

1. assert their rights as successors and take part in the business so as to earn compensation;

2. remain inactive and hope the other shareholders will give out sufficient dividends; or

3. sell out.

INSURED BUY-SELL AGREEMENT

In the final analysis there is only one safe, simple and sure method of avoiding the hazards involved in the sale of the deceased shareholder's interest. That method involves an agreement under which the surviving shareholders buy and the estate sells the deceased's stock, for a previously agreed and fair price. Such a plan involves two simple steps:

1. the execution of a binding buy-sell agreement between the shareholders, providing that the interest of any member of the firm who dies shall be sold to and will be purchased by the surviving shareholders, under a cross-purchase agreement, or by the firm, as a stock redemption, at a value agreed upon by the parties and stipulated in the agreement; and

2. the establishment of some sort of a funding mechanism that automatically will provide sufficient cash upon the death of any firm member to ensure the prompt execution of the agreement and to guarantee that the surviving parties will have the money with which to carry out their obligations under it.

Life Insurance Advantages for the Surviving Shareholders

Life insurance is the only funding method that will be sure to furnish the required cash to the surviving associates, in full and automatically with the death of a shareholder, regardless of whether death occurs tonight, a year from tonight, or many years from now. Only life insurance can guarantee that the same death that puts the agreement into effect will provide the cash with which to carry out its terms and make the contemplated purchase of the deceased's interest.

Here indeed is the perfect solution to the problem of close corporation management continuity. Any other plan is in large part makeshift or a substitute, because no other plan carries with it equal assurance as to its ultimate completion and the achievement of its objectives.

Buy-Sell Plan Design

The buy-sell plan is simple. Under it, the shareholders agree among themselves and enter into a contract to purchase the interest of any member who dies; each shareholder contracts for the sale of his or her interest to the surviving shareholders or to the corporation upon his or her death. The arrangement is a definite and binding executory contract to buy and sell. A price or method of determining the purchase price is set out in the agreement. Then, to avoid the difficulties inherent in securing the funds with which to make such a purchase, each shareholder's life is insured in an amount equal to the value of his or her interest. At the death of a shareholder, the surviving associates get the business interest of the deceased using the insurance proceeds, and the estate gets the insurance money.

The advantages of the plan are many. They are summarized on the following pages from the viewpoints of the surviving shareholders, the estate of the deceased, and the firm prior to the time that a shareholder dies.

Here we will review the advantages of the business insurance plan for the survivors, either when they arrange to buy a deceased shareholder's stock themselves or when the corporation itself buys the stock.

Prevents Undesired Management Changes

As regards management changes, the plan:

1. prevents the automatic introduction of new, perhaps unwanted management interests;

2. eliminates the danger of forced reorganization of the firm along the lines suitable to heirs who have acquired a majority interest, or suitable to a probate court representing such heirs;

3. eliminates any possibility of a forced revision of management policies in order to meet the objectives of a minority interest heir;

4. eliminates the necessity of taking the surviving spouse or other heirs into the active management of the corporation;

5. eliminates squabbling over the salary or income to be paid heirs who may assume the deceased stockholder's interest; and

6. permits current problems to be met without explanation to persons unfamiliar with the business or interested solely in the estate of the deceased shareholder.

Prevents a Loss of Business Momentum

As regards business momentum, the plan:

7. provides for immediate and automatic transfer of the deceased's interest to the survivors and for the unbroken continuation of business activity. Uncertainty as to the manner and the extent of the readjustment of business policies is avoided;

8. avoids a destruction of business morale through a contest for management control. It prevents any disturbance of the present balance of power, except as agreed to by the parties in advance; and

9. should soothe creditors, who might otherwise become nervous, wondering what the ultimate effects of the person's death would be on the future of the corporation. In particular, employees are not affected by confusion as to their personal future with the corporation, and since service of the business continues as before, corporate goodwill is preserved.

Guarantees the Sale and the Price

As regards the sale and price of the business, the plan:

10. makes certain that the surviving shareholders or the business will have the opportunity to buy the deceased's stock interest. They have a guaranteed contract to buy.

11. makes sure that the heirs will sell. There is a binding contract to sell; and

12. makes reasonably certain that the price will be fair. The shareholders, with full knowledge of the facts, set the sale price during their lifetimes.

Provides the Cash with Which to Buy

As regards providing cash, the plan:

13. with life insurance as a funding vehicle, automatically produces the money when it is needed;

14. does not require that the surviving shareholders mortgage corporate assets or raid the surplus and capital of the corporation to purchase the decedent's stock. Shareholders are not forced to secure a loan at the very moment when credit may be most difficult to obtain, nor are they forced to pay out other corporate cash that is certain to be needed to get the corporation through the period of readjustment following the death of an active shareholder;

15. avoids the need for shareholders to use personal credit sources to raise the required purchase money; and

16. avoids making the heirs of the decedent indirect owners of the corporation, as would occur with a plan that called for a partial payment of the purchase price and a pledge of stock or corporate assets for the balance due. Such a partial payment plan leads at best to future confusion and uncertainty.

The Plan Is Effective and Economical

As regards effectiveness and economy, the plan:

17. assures that surviving shareholders in the business can purchase a deceased shareholder's interest by making a yearly deposit of a fraction of the legal rate of interest on the purchase price. The premiums are paid and the proceeds automatically wipe out the purchaser's obligation to the decedent's estate;

18. obviously will bring an enormous appreciation if a shareholder dies within a decade. Even though all the parties live many years, the purchase price still is discounted by the difference between the premiums paid and the proceeds applied to the purchase;

19. provides the funding medium for an eventual buy-out of a shareholder's business interest at retirement—through accumulating cash values when permanent life insurance is used. Also, funds are available for emergencies or other contingencies; and

20. assures complete and immediate ownership of the business by the survivors when a shareholder dies.

Life Insurance Advantages for the Estate of the Deceased

Now we will look at the advantages of the business insurance plan for the estate and heirs of a deceased shareholder.

Keeps the Surviving Spouse out of the Business

As regards the surviving spouse, the plan:

1. makes it unnecessary for the widow or widower, inheriting a majority stock interest, to step into full control of the business and attempt to assume active management responsibilities. On the other hand, the surviving spouse who inherits a minority interest need not worry about his or her lack of a voice in management, or find that his or her principal source of future income is tied up in a business that pays a very slight return;

2. wipes out the possibility of friction between the surviving spouse and the deceased's family on one hand and the surviving shareholders on the other. If their relations have been cordial and friendly in the past, they will continue to be cordial;

3. avoids the necessity of the widow or widower becoming an employee of the corporation in an effort to supplement income and secure sufficient funds to maintain the family; and

4. protects the surviving spouse against the embarrassment of pleading with the surviving shareholders for money. The surviving spouse is in no way reliant upon them and they are in no way responsible to the surviving spouse.

Guarantees a Full and Fair Cash Price

As regards a full and fair cash price, the plan:

5. gives the estate and the surviving spouse the full fair value of the deceased's stock interest, at once and in cash; and

6. eliminates the need for the surviving spouse or the estate to sell out for a down payment for their shares and a mortgage on the stock. Such a partial payment plan subjects the estate to the hazards of business loss without the opportunity to share in the profits.

Facilitates Settlement of the Estate

As regards settlement of the estate, the plan:

7. avoids any need to hire outsiders to investigate and appraise the corporation's business condition to determine the value of shares or to make sure that the surviving spouse or the estate is getting a fair price for the stock;

8. provides an immediate and certain cash market for the heir's stock;

9. makes possible more prompt and efficient administration of the estate's affairs, saving probate costs and expenses; and

10. protects the family because the executor or administrator is certain to have cash on hand to make temporary support allowances to them.

Protects the Family Against Loss

As regards protecting the family, the plan:

11. avoids the danger of estate depreciation through a forced liquidation of stock, which is the estate's principal asset. The estate is assured of receiving full value for the stock;

12. avoids placing the financial future of the family at the mercy of the surviving shareholders' ability to carry on the business successfully; and

13. immediately converts a nonliquid asset of uncertain value into cash and permits the prompt reinvestment of these sale proceeds into safe and conservative securities.

Life Insurance Advantages While All Shareholders Are Alive

We now will look at some significant advantages of the business insurance plan, both to the business itself and the shareholders, while all of them are alive.

Insures Business Stability

As regards insuring the business's stability, the plan:

1. guarantees the continuity of the corporation and the present management; and

2. can be arranged to provide an old-age retirement fund for the shareholders. The plan can provide for the purchase of a shareholder's stock when the shareholder reaches retirement age.

Provides Business Credit

As regards providing business credit, the plan:

3. supplies collateral for bank and supplier credit; and

4. creates a source of emergency credit to meet sudden and unexpected needs.

Helps Stabilize the Corporation's Bank Credit

As regards stabilizing the corporation's bank credit, the plan:

5. protects the bank against loss because of the interruption of the corporate activities and possible changes in personnel caused by the death of a corporate officer; and

6. shows the banker that the corporation is conscious of the importance of good management in business success.

Income Tax Considerations

Now we will turn to the income tax consequences of an insured buy-sell agreement.

Premium Payments

Premium payments made by a corporation or a shareholder to purchase policies to fund buy-sell agreements are not deductible as a business expense. Whenever the policy owner is directly or indirectly the beneficiary of the policy, he or she may not deduct the premiums paid by the policyowner.

When the corporation pays insurance premiums for a shareholder on policies owned by the shareholder, the premiums will be income to the shareholder. However, the corporation may not always get a deduction for the premiums it pays in the shareholder's behalf if the payments are deemed a form of corporate dividend and not deductible compensation. While the Internal Revenue Service requires income tax withholding on the premiums, and thus clearly indicates that the premiums are compensation, you should be aware of the consequences should the premium payments be determined to be dividends. This could result if the shareholder is an employee and the premium payments, when combined with the shareholder's other compensation, are unreasonable and thereby non-deductible. Dividend treatment of the premium payments also could occur if the corporation and the shareholder-employee show no evidence that they intended the premium payments to be deductible compensation rather than a dividend.

Life Insurance Proceeds

Generally, insurance proceeds received by a corporation or a surviving shareholder are not taxable income to the recipient.

The transfer-for-value rule causes no problems if the insurance was transferred to the corporation and if the insured is a shareholder or an officer of the corporation. However, the rule will cause problems if the policy is transferred among co-shareholders, thus making proceeds from such transferred policies taxable.

Receipt of Purchase Price by the Estate

The tax law specifically provides that when *all* of a shareholder's stock is redeemed by the corporation, the purchase price will be treated as capital gain, and not as a dividend to the estate, for purposes of the income tax.

To determine the amount of taxable gain in a redemption, the estate or heirs of a decedent-shareholder must determine the excess of the redemption price over the redeemed stock's cost basis. The cost basis in the stock is "stepped up" to its date-of-death or alternate valuation date value. Since the stock usually is sold by the estate or heirs at death or shortly thereafter, little or no gain results for income tax purposes, because the decedent's basis in the stock would equal the fair market value. Most agreements use a fair market value type of valuation for their stock, whether it be a stated amount or a formula valuation clause.

The Family Corporation

Ordinarily, a partial redemption will not concern your prospects because they usually desire a complete redemption at death. But a partial redemption and its potential attendant dividend treatment of the distribution can be a problem in the family corporation because of the family attribution rules.

Under the family attribution rules, a shareholder is treated as owning the stock of the corporation that is owned directly or indirectly by his or her spouse, children, grandchildren or parents, or owned by an estate or trust of which he or she is a beneficiary. The stock owned by these individuals named is *attributed* to the shareholder. Thus, what otherwise would be a complete redemption is treated as a partial redemption because of the attribution rules attributing the stock of the aforementioned family members to him or her.

As an example, suppose a father dies owning 1,000 shares of the XYZ Corporation. His adult son, an heir under his will, owns the remaining 500 shares. The corporation seeks to redeem the father's 1,000 shares from the estate. Such a redemption would not be a complete termination of the decedent's interest in the corporation because the son's stock would be attributed to his father and thus to the estate, causing the estate to own all the outstanding shares of stock.

Avoiding Attribution in Family Corporation

There are ways of avoiding family attribution in the family corporation situation. First, one can redeem all the shares owned by the family or others whose stock is subject to attribution. Also, the family can make a timely waiver of the family attribution rules. This method is used often when the surviving spouse becomes a shareholder in the family corporation and there is a desire to redeem those shares. The corporation will redeem the shares and the surviving spouse simultaneously will file a statement with the IRS that he or she has no interest, office or employment in the corporation and will not acquire such within ten years following the redemption. The tax law permits an entity, such as an estate, trust, or corporation, to waive the family attribution rules, under the same conditions as an individual, if the beneficiaries or shareholders join in the waiver. The entity and beneficiaries will be liable if any of them acquire an interest within the 10-year period. This provision applies only to attribution from one family member to another, not to entities and their beneficiaries. There is more to this waiver method than our brief explanation entails, so its use should be supervised by proper legal counsel. When used effectively, the waiver permits the surviving spouse to elect capital gain treatment for the redeemed shares, while the children carry on as majority shareholders.

Another way to avoid the dividend treatment for a partial redemption is to elect a Section 303 redemption. This redemption, as mentioned above, will be discussed specifically in a later chapter. Briefly, it allows you to redeem stock in an amount equal to administrative costs, funeral costs and death taxes and still have capital gains treatment.

A final way to avoid attribution is to use a cross-purchase agreement instead of a stock redemption agreement to effect the sale of stock. Because no corporate funds are used, there is no problem.

Estate Tax Considerations

The stock purchase agreement, be it cross-purchase or stock redemption, will set the value of the business interest for estate tax purposes. This value will be included in the deceased shareholder's estate. Normally, the insurance proceeds funding the buy-sell agreement will not be included because the decedent-shareholder does not have incidents of ownership in the policies. In the cross-purchase situation, the other shareholders are the owners and beneficiaries; in the stock redemption situation, the corporation is the owner and the beneficiary. Of course, the cash value of any policies the decedent-shareholder owned on the surviving shareholders will be includable in his or her estate.

■ SUMMARY

In this chapter, you have learned about the types of corporations and the ways to treat an owner's shares at death. Most of all, you have learned about the key role life insurance plays whether the choice is liquidation, retention or sale of the stockholder's shares. Furthermore, this chapter has shown you that a buy-sell agreement funded by life insurance is the best way to effect such a sale. The next chapter explains the buy-sell agreement in more detail and breaks it down into the cross-purchase plan, stock redemption plan and a hybrid plan called the *wait-and-see* buy-sell.

■ CHAPTER 6 QUESTIONS FOR REVIEW

1. All the following statements are true EXCEPT

   A. the insurance proceeds funding a buy-sell agreement in a close corporation are not includable in the deceased shareholder's estate

   B. the best method of avoiding the hazards involved in the sale of the deceased shareholder's interest is the insured buy-sell agreement

   C. premium payments made by a corporation or a shareholder to purchase policies to fund a buy-sell agreement are deductible as a business expense

   D. when the corporation pays insurance premiums for a shareholder, the premiums will be treated as income to the insured

2. The single most significant characteristic of a corporation is

   A. it files a return and pays taxes at the individual level, just like a person

   B. as a separate legal entity, it is immune from liability of any kind

   C. as a separate legal entity, it has a life of its own and does not end upon the death of an owner

   D. all of the above

3. Under a planned liquidation, the executor of the will of the corporate owner should be given the power to

   A. borrow money on the security of the business assets to pay estate obligations

   B. liquidate the interest at either public or private sale

   C. retain the business interest for any period that the executor deems necessary

   D. all of the above

4. Stock in a closely held corporation

   A. is generally held by a number of investors, possibly numbering in the thousands

   B. is often listed and sold through stock exchanges

   C. gives shareholders specific rights within the corporation

   D. all of the above

5. Why is life insurance considered to be the best method for providing funds for a planned liquidation?

   A. Proceeds provide instant estate liquidity.

   B. Proceeds provide instant replacement income.

   C. Proceeds buy time for the heirs to allow them to sell the business at the best possible time and under the best possible circumstances.

   D. All of the above

7

Other Forms of Incorporation

The corporate form we are accustomed to is known as the C corporation. However, it is only one of the corporate forms. In this chapter, we will look at two corporate variations, the S corporation and the professional, or personal service corporation, along with their unique characteristics. A newer type of business organization, the limited liability company, also is discussed.

The standard corporate form, known as the C corporation, is the most widely used in this country. However, there are exceptions to this corporate structure. Because these exceptions apply strictly to closely held businesses, an understanding of them is important to you as an insurance professional.

The first of these exceptions is the S corporation, whereby income is passed through the business directly to the owners. There it is taxed at their individual rates with no corporate tax involved. The second is the professional, or personal service, corporation, which has a unique tax structure, special restrictions on ownership and limitations on business transfer. A third exception, and one that is rapidly gaining in popularity, is the limited liability company, which can be taxed as a partnership but also provides many of the benefits of the corporate structure without some of the burdensome requirements of the S corporation.

■ ■ ■ ■ ■

■ INTRODUCTION TO THE S CORPORATION

The basic difference between S corporations and other corporations is in how they are taxed. This section will describe the S corporation, the requirements for electing it, its taxation and how business insurance and S corporations work together.

The 1958 amendments to the Internal Revenue Code added Subchapter S, which provided, among other things, that a corporation meeting certain conditions could elect to be taxed substantially like a partnership. Thus corporate profits would be taxed only once, instead of twice, as in a regular corporation.

Other than the change in its tax status, the electing corporation (popularly known as an "S corporation") would retain virtually all the characteristics and advantages of a regular corporation. This opened the corporate door to many business owners who formerly had hesitated to incorporate because of the double income tax. Now they could enjoy the tax advantages of their present form of business organization, yet at the same time gain the many advantages inherent in the corporate form of business organization.

■ WHAT IS AN S CORPORATION?

An S corporation (also known as a Subchapter S corporation) is a business that, because it meets certain specific requirements, is not subject to regular corporate income tax. Instead, all corporate income, losses, deductions and credits are passed directly through to the shareholders in proportion to their interest in the business. Income is taxable in the year earned, whether it is distributed or not.

In this respect, the S corporation is taxed as if it were a partnership. However, the company retains all the characteristics and advantages of the corporate form, including limited liability for its shareholders.

Requirements for S Corporation Status

The election to be taxed under the special provisions of Subchapter S is available only to corporations. Thus, to be eligible to make the election, the unincorporated business owner first must qualify as a bona fide corporation.

A corporation that intends to seek the advantages of Subchapter S, and thus avoid the corporate income tax, must elect this status in accordance with the regulations prescribed by the Secretary of the Treasury. The election must be filed in writing, and it must be consented to by all stockholders. In addition, the corporation must meet the following requirements:

1. *The corporation must have no more than 75 stockholders.* If the stock is owned jointly, each co-owner is considered to be a separate stockholder, unless the co-owners are husband and wife. If husband and wife own the stock jointly, or as community property, they count as one stockholder in meeting the above test.

2. *The corporation must issue only one class of stock.* Differences in voting rights among shares of common stock, however, will not violate this requirement.

3. *The corporation must be owned by stockholders who are either individuals, certain trusts or estates, or certain charitable organizations or qualified retirement plans.* If any of the outstanding stock is held by a corporation, a partnership as an entity, or most trusts, the corporation will fail to qualify.

4. *The corporation must be a domestic corporation.* As defined in the Internal Revenue Code, a domestic corporation is one "created or organized in the United States or under the law of the United States or any State or Territory."

5. *The corporation must have no shareholders who are nonresident aliens.*

When to Elect

The stockholders can elect to be taxed as an S corporation at any time during the year preceding the corporation's taxable year in which they want the election to take effect, or during the first 75 days of the taxable year. Thus, a corporation on a calendar-year basis could make the election between January 1st of the preceding year and March 15th of its current taxable year.

Termination

Once the S election is made, it continues indefinitely, unless terminated voluntarily or by violation of the restrictions. Once terminated, it cannot be made again for five years. A new stockholder cannot terminate the election by refusing to consent unless he or she is a majority shareholder.

The S election will be terminated if the corporation's passive investment income exceeds 25 percent of its gross receipts in each of three consecutive years, and the corporation has accumulated earnings and profits from its years as a C corporation ("regular" corporation), if applicable, at the end of each of the three tax years. Each year the S corporation's passive investment income exceeds 25 percent of its gross receipts, a tax at the highest corporate rate will be levied against the lesser of excess net passive income or the corporation's taxable income. An S corporation with no earnings and profits left over from C corporate years may have unlimited passive investment income. "Passive investment income" includes rents, royalties, dividends, annuities, interest and gain from sale or exchanges of stock or securities.

■ TAXATION OF SHAREHOLDERS

The most significant tax aspect of an S corporation is elimination of the double income tax. However, there are other tax considerations that should be examined. Below is a survey of some of these additional tax factors. They are evaluated to the extent they affect a partnership, an ordinary corporation and an S corporation.

The tax law provides that, like a partnership, an S corporation is a *conduit*, meaning that all income, losses, deductions and credits are passed to the shareholders. Each item is treated as if it were received from the original source, not the corporation.

Some items subject to the pass-through rules are as follows:

1. *Capital gains and losses.* Gains or losses from sales or exchanges of capital assets pass through to the shareholders as capital gains or losses. For certain S corporations, however, that made an S selection before 1987, capital gain results in a tax on the corporation itself. The nontaxable pass-through of long-term capital gain cannot exceed $25,000 if the corporation has not been an S corporation for at least the last three years, and if: (1) the net capital gain exceeds 50 percent of the corporation's taxable income; and (2) the corporation's taxable income is more than $25,000. The corporation will pay the regular corporate tax and any minimum tax on capital gains that cannot be passed through. When this happens, the net capital gain passing through to the shareholders is reduced by the taxes imposed on the corporation. If the tax on net capital gain applies, it will equal the lesser of: (1) 35 percent of the amount by which net capital gain exceeds $25,000; (2) the tax that would have been imposed on the corporation's taxable income if it had not elected S corporation status or; (3) 35 percent of the net capital gain attributable to certain property which may have been acquired from a previous C corporation in a tax-free transaction.

2. *Section 1231 gains and losses.* The gains and losses on certain property used in a trade or business are passed through separately and are aggregated with the shareholders' other Section 1231 gains and losses.

3. *Charitable contributions.* The corporate 10 percent limitation does not apply to contributions by the corporation. As in the case of partnerships, contributions pass through to the shareholders, at which level they are subject to the individual limitations on deductibility.

4. *Tax-exempt interest.* Tax-exempt interest passes through to the shareholders as such and increases each shareholder's basis. Subsequent distributions by a corporation will not result in taxation of the tax-exempt income.

5. *Foreign taxes.* Foreign taxes paid by the corporation pass through as such to the shareholder, who claim such taxes either as deductions or credits (subject to applicable limitations).

6. *Credits.* As with partnerships, items involved in the determination of credits, such as the basis of Section 38 property for purposes of computing the amount of qualified investment eligible for the investment tax credit, pass through to the S corporation's shareholders.

7. *Depletion.* The rules governing depletion with regard to partnership interests in minerals apply to depletion of properties of an S corporation.

8. *Foreign income and loss.* Domestic losses and foreign losses pass through separately. If a corporation had foreign losses and domestic income, or

vice versa, each would pass through separately to shareholders without aggregation at the corporate level.

9. *Other items.* Limitations on the used property investment tax credit, the expensing of certain depreciable business assets and the amortization of reforestation expenditures apply at both the corporate level and shareholder level, as in the case of partnerships. Exclusions of income from discharge of indebtedness are determined at the shareholder level. The election to capitalize intangible costs by a shareholder who does not actively participate in the management of the corporation is the same as the election by a limited partner (i.e., 10-year amortization).

Each shareholder's pro rata share of the items is taken into account in the taxable year. In the case of the death of a shareholder, the shareholder's portion of Subchapter S items is taken into account on the shareholder's final income tax return. Items from the portion of the corporation's taxable year after the shareholder's death are taken into account by the estate or other person acquiring the stock.

Taxation of Distributions

In general, because all earnings pass directly through to shareholders in the years in which they are earned, there is no accumulation of earnings. As a result, S corporations with accumulated earnings and profits are assured of tax-free treatment with respect to distributions, regardless of when made.

For distributions of appreciated property other than those that would result in the complete liquidation of the S corporation, the corporation must recognize gain as if the property had been sold to the shareholder at its fair market value. As with any other gain in an S corporation, it passes through to the shareholders. This rule prevents assets from being distributed tax free and later sold without the shareholder recognizing income at the time of the sale as a result of the stepped-up fair market value basis.

Net Operating Losses

If a partnership sustains a net operating loss, the partners may use their proportionate share of this loss to offset their gross income. Stockholders whose corporations suffer a similar loss cannot do this. The corporation, being a separate legal and taxable entity, applies its own net operating loss against its own income.

If an S corporation suffers a net operating loss during its taxable year, each stockholder may deduct from gross income his or her pro rata share of the loss (with certain limitations).

If a stockholder's pro rata portion of the corporation's net operating loss exceeds adjusted basis in his or her stock plus adjusted basis of indebtedness of the S corporation to the shareholder, the excess may be carried forward until there is basis in stock or debt.

Basis for Sale of Interest

In a partnership, periodic adjustments are made to the basis of the individual partner's interest. An increase in basis occurs as the result of an undistributed share of partnership income. On the other hand, partnership distributions and losses reduce the basis.

In an ordinary corporation, the basis for each stockholder's stock ordinarily remains constant. Thus, if the original basis for a share of stock was $50, and the stock was sold at $60, there would be a gain of $10. Conversely, if the stock was sold at $40, there would be a loss of $10.

The basis for stock in an S corporation fluctuates in a fashion similar to that of a partnership. It is increased by corporate earnings that are taxed to the stockholders. A later distribution of such earnings to the stockholders reduces their basis. The stockholders' pro rata shares of the corporate net operating loss also reduces their basis, but never below zero.

The following items increase a stockholder's basis in his or her stock:

- the corporation's items of income (including tax-exempt income) passed through to the shareholder;

- the corporation's nonseparately computed income; and

- the excess of the deductions for depletion over the basis of the property subject to depletion.

The following items decrease a stockholder's basis in his or her stock:

- nontaxable return of capital distributions;

- items of loss and deduction separately stated and passed through to the shareholder;

- nonseparately computed loss;

- any expense of the corporation not deductible in computing its taxable income and not properly chargeable to capital account; and

- the amount of the shareholder's deduction for depletion with respect to oil and gas wells.

For example, a shareholder of an S corporation has 100 shares with an original basis of $100 per share, or $10,000 for the 100 shares. Later on, the stockholder has a pro rata portion of $3,000 undistributed earnings for which he has been taxed. His basis then would be $130 per share or $13,000 for his 100 shares. If he were to sell all his shares at that time for $14,000, his gain would be $1,000 ($14,000 less his adjusted basis of $13,000). If he did not sell and the following year the corporation suffered a net operating loss, $3,000 of which is his pro rata share, the basis for his 100 shares would again be $10,000 ($13,000 less the $3,000 net operating loss).

Accumulated Earnings Tax

The accumulated earnings tax has no application to S corporations. This is because earnings are taxed each year to the owners, regardless of whether they are distributed.

Fringe Benefits for Shareholders

One of the advantages of the corporate form is fringe benefits for shareholder employees.

Unfortunately, some of the tax advantages of certain fringe benefits are lost to majority shareholders (and many minority shareholders) of S corporations. In fact, important distinctions exist between the treatment of employee-shareholders in the conventional corporation as compared to the S corporation.

Essential fringe benefits for the employee shareholder of a C corporation include company-provided medical insurance, disability protection and group term life insurance that are deductible to the corporation, without being treated as taxable income to the employee.

In an S corporation, however, an employee-shareholder's benefits are deductible by the corporation only to the extent that they are treated as compensation to the shareholder. Therefore, the value of these benefits will be included in the employee's gross income. This rule applies to employees who own more than 2 percent of company stock.

As a result, the incentive for providing company-sponsored benefit packages is not as strong in the S corporation as it is with C corporations. Nonetheless, these corporations should not be ignored. They still have needs for your services and products. In fact, they face virtually the same problems as proprietorships, partnerships and C corporations.

ADVANTAGES AND DISADVANTAGES OF S CORPORATIONS

We can return now to the considerations involved in making the S corporation election.

Advantages

If a corporation has an accumulated earnings tax problem, a Subchapter S election is one solution. The accumulated earnings tax does not apply to an S corporation because earnings are taxed each year to the stockholders, whether distributed or not.

When the personal holding company tax is a problem, a Subchapter S election may help if the personal holding company income in question is derived from personal service contracts that fail to meet the IRS criteria. Subchapter S can also be a solution if the problem stems from investment income, because an S corporation with no earnings and profits from regular corporate years may have unlimited investment income.

If an S corporation suffers a net operating loss during its taxable year, each stockholder may deduct from gross income his or her pro rata share of the loss.

Capital gains and losses pass through to the shareholder without tax at the corporate level, just like other corporate income.

Disadvantages

With the Subchapter S election, the corporation cannot accumulate funds to be taxed at the corporate rate, which is a main reason for incorporation.

Generally speaking, many corporations no longer need to elect Subchapter S. With the accumulated earnings credit of $250,000 ($150,000 for certain service corporations), the accumulated earnings tax (which an S corporation avoids) may not be a serious problem for many corporations.

S CORPORATION BUY-SELL AGREEMENTS

Perhaps the best way to approach S corporation owners is with a discussion of buy-sell plans—how to handle the purchase of shares upon a stockholder's death. Many of the considerations listed for the regular corporate buy-sell agreements apply. These considerations were discussed previously. However, with respect to the desirability of a stock redemption agreement as opposed to a cross-purchase agreement, there can be no manipulation of tax brackets because in a Sub S situation all the corporate income passes through to the shareholders.

Generally speaking, an S corporation that goes the stock redemption route needs an insured plan even more than other corporations. Otherwise, the accumulation of funds in the corporation to fund the agreement will be currently taxed to the stockholders at their highest individual tax rate. Furthermore, if Sub S stock is left to several heirs at death, this could increase the number of shareholders beyond the limit of 75.

One important fact should be reiterated: the S corporation receives life insurance proceeds tax free, and these proceeds retain their tax-exempt character when distributed to the shareholders.

KEY-EXECUTIVE INSURANCE

An S corporation's purchase of key-executive insurance has interesting tax consequences for the shareholders. The corporation, of course, is denied a deduction because it is the beneficiary. Thus, premium payments are taxed to the shareholders and the basis of each shareholder's stock is increased. If the corporation surrenders the policy, or it matures during the insured's life, any gain (proceeds minus net premiums) is taxed as ordinary income to the shareholder.

When the insured dies while the policy is in force, the insurance proceeds are received income tax-free by the corporation and will increase the shareholders' basis for their stock. Upon subsequent distribution, the proceeds will maintain their tax-free status and reduce the shareholders' basis.

■ SECTION 1244 STOCK

Section 1244 is an attractive election for owners of small business corporations and often is used in conjunction with S corporations. Section 1244 allows the individual to treat loss on a sale, exchange, or worthlessness of stock as an ordinary rather than a capital loss. This is advantageous, of course, because ordinary losses are fully deductible, whereas capital losses are restricted in their deductibility. However, there are limitations.

A sale or exchange of Section 1244 stock resulting in gain is treated the same as any other gain on a capital asset. It will be recalled that corporate stock is treated as a capital asset so that any loss upon the disposition of the stock is a capital loss.

Limitations apply to the amount of the loss that may be deducted in the taxable year in which the loss is sustained. Thus, if a shareholder owns stock in a corporation that fails and he sustains a $50,000 capital loss, he will use $3,000 of the loss to offset $3,000 of ordinary income.

Under Section 1244, the shareholder could deduct the full $50,000 in the taxable year in which the loss occurred. If he or she were married and filing a joint return, up to $100,000 of ordinary loss could be deducted.

Amount of Loss Deductible

The deductible loss on Section 1244 stock in a given taxable year may not exceed $50,000, or $100,000 for a married individual filing jointly. If the loss is not fully absorbed in the taxable year in which it was incurred, it is treated as a net operating loss subject to the carryback-carryover period. Thus, if an unmarried shareholder disposes of Section 1244 stock at a loss of $100,000, he or she may deduct $50,000 in the year of disposition and carryback or carryover, as the case may be, the remaining $50,000.

■ THE PROFESSIONAL (PERSONAL SERVICE) CORPORATION

Historically, certain groups designated as professionals were not permitted by law to incorporate. While that prohibition is no longer in force, there are a number of restrictions on incorporation for professionals. As an insurance professional working in the business insurance market, you should be aware of the unique characteristics and restrictions placed on the professional or personal service corporation. The primary distinctions between these and C corporations are in the areas of eligibility to incorporate, transference of stock and taxation.

■ WHAT IS A PROFESSIONAL CORPORATION?

In general, anyone who must obtain a license from the state to practice his or her profession is considered a professional. Each state licenses a different set of occupations.

Eligibility

The following is a general list highlighting the *best* prospects to be found in the professional market.

Physicians	Actuaries
Surgeons	Psychiatrists
Attorneys	Podiatrists
Accountants	Radiologists
Dentists	Pathologists
Optometrists	Ophthalmologists
Engineers	Pharmacists
Architects	Psychologists
Chiropractors	Social Workers
Osteopaths	Marriage Counselors
Veterinarians	Chiropodists

Generally, the stockholders in a professional corporation must practice the same specialty. For example, suppose a psychiatrist is interested in incorporating, but the professional corporation law in his state requires two or more incorporators. The only other doctor he knows who is interested in incorporating is a general surgeon. Can they incorporate? The answer is probably no; the doctors practice two entirely different medical specialties.

The general corporation acts in many states specify a minimum number of officers and(or) directors in every corporation. Many times it is three directors and two officers.

There are also restrictions on transfers in that nonprofessionals cannot own or buy the stock of a professional corporation. Because the market is restricted, this poses a whole new set of transfer problems for corporate owners upon death, which strengthens the need for an advance plan for disposition of the business.

Taxation of Professional Corporations

Professional, personal service corporations cannot use the corporate tax rate for retained earnings. Instead, they are taxed at a flat 35 percent rate, which can dramatically impact a decision to accumulate cash within the corporation. This problem with accumulation also points to the importance of life insurance to fund any purchase agreement.

EMPLOYEE BENEFITS FOR PROFESSIONALS

The most significant advantages of incorporation stem from the fact that incorporated professionals can participate in employee benefit plans because they cease to be nonemployee partners or proprietors and become shareholder-employees. The broadest benefits are available to those professionals also who use the general or C corporate form. Benefits are more restrictive for professionals who use S corporations because of the "conduit" or income pass-through nature of S corporations.

Group Life Insurance

An incorporated professional can exclude from gross income the cost of up to $50,000 of group term life insurance purchased on his or her life by the corporation. The corporation may deduct the premiums as a business expense. Because the unincorporated professional could not deduct the premiums, he or she is able to secure up to $50,000 of life insurance protection on a tax-deductible basis through incorporation.

Medical Expense Reimbursement Plan

The incorporated professional can participate in a medical expense reimbursement plan that pays for any medical expenses incurred by the professional, his or her spouse and all dependents. The corporation is permitted a business expense deduction for any health insurance premium that it pays for medical expense reimbursement. The employee is not taxed on the employer's premiums or the benefits as income. This has obvious advantages over the limited deductions available for medical expenses and health insurance premiums on an individual's income tax return (e.g., the requirement that such expenses exceed 7.5 percent of adjusted gross income). In effect, the medical expense plan converts a nondeductible expense of the employee into a deductible corporate expense without creating taxable income for the individual.

If the medical reimbursement plan is a self-insured plan that discriminates in favor of highly compensated individuals, however, there are different tax implications. Specifically, amounts paid to such highly compensated individuals under self-insured medical expense reimbursement plans or under the self-insured part of a partly insured medical reimbursement plan are taxable to him or her if the plan discriminates in favor or such individuals.

Disability Income Plan

A corporation may install a "wage continuation plan" that will provide employees, including professionals, with income during a period of disability due to sickness or injury. The amounts paid by the corporation are deductible as a business expense whether they represent health insurance premiums or direct compensation payments. The premiums are excludable from the employee's gross income, but benefits will be fully taxable except in cases of total and permanent disability, in which case they may or may not be. The unincorporated professional cannot deduct disability insurance premiums, although disability benefits may be fully excluded from gross income.

Salary Continuation and Deferred Compensation

The corporation and the professional employee may enter into a nonqualified salary continuation and deferred compensation agreement whereby the corporation promises to pay a certain amount at the retirement, death or disability of the professional. If the corporation funds its obligations by investing in life insurance, the death proceeds will be received income tax-free by the corporation. The corporation owns the life insurance policies, pays the premium and serves as beneficiary. A salary continuation plan uses corporate dollars to pay the life insurance premiums. The employee defers income in a deferred compensation plan. Both plans provide the employee with a high rate of return on money accrued for eventual payout to the employee at retirement. Both plans also can be designed to provide significant preretirement death benefits for the employees.

Split-Dollar

A corporation may enter into a split-dollar arrangement with selected employees to provide indemnification to the corporation and to the employee's family in the event of the employee's death. A split-dollar plan is not available for self-employed individuals.

S Corporation Election

The incorporated professional may elect Subchapter S tax treatment in cases for which this is warranted. Generally speaking, this permits the corporation to retain the tax characteristics of a partnership while giving the professional the nontax advantages of corporate status.

TAX PROBLEMS OF INCORPORATION

Before we paint too rosy a picture, however, let us hasten to add that there is also a possible downside to incorporating a professional practice: tax *problems*.

Allocation of Income and Deductions

The IRS may ignore the corporate status of a personal service corporation for tax purposes if:

1. substantially all of the services are performed by employee-owners or related parties for or on behalf of another corporation, partnership or entity; and

2. the principal purpose of the corporation is tax avoidance or evasion. The IRS can allocate income, deductions, credits and exclusions between the corporation and its owners to prevent such tax avoidance or evasion.

Accumulated Earnings Tax

The accumulated earnings tax is the curse of many closely held corporations—professional and nonprofessional alike. The professional corporation, in addition to its customary tax on corporate profits, could be subject to this additional tax if the corporate surplus already has reached $150,000 and further retention of earnings is considered beyond the "reasonable needs" or the "reasonably anticipated needs" of the corporation. Additional profits retained in the current and subsequent years could be subject to the accumulated earnings tax. The tax rate is 39.6 percent of "accumulated taxable income," which is income in excess of the accumulated earnings credit of $150,000 ($250,000 for corporations other than personal service corporations).

The tax is imposed primarily on one-person and other closely controlled corporations in which it is possible for a small group of stockholders to dictate dividend paying policy so as to avoid tax liability on their personal incomes. Of all types of incorporated businesses, the professional corporation may have the most difficult time justifying the reasonableness of earnings accumulations. Normally, it does not own any inventory or much real and personal property. Furthermore, state statutes usually prohibit expansion into another business. As noted earlier, cash values of life insurance policies purchased for legitimate business purposes usually are immune from the accumulated earnings tax.

Personal Holding Company Tax

The personal holding company tax is imposed upon certain undistributed income of corporations that are deemed to be personal holding companies. The tax rate on such income is 39.6 percent in addition to the regular tax on corporate income.

A personal holding company is a corporation that meets both of the following tests:

1. at least 60 percent of its adjusted ordinary gross income is *personal holding company income*; and

2. at some time during the last half of the taxable year, five or fewer individuals directly or indirectly owned more than 50 percent in value of its outstanding stock.

Personal holding company income consists of: (1) income from investments (e.g., dividends, interest and royalties); and (2) income from personal service contracts in which the corporation does not have the right to select the individual who will perform the services, and in which the individual chosen by the client or specified in the contract directly or indirectly owns 25 percent or more of the corporation's stock.

Professional corporations have always had a special fear of the personal holding company tax by reason of their "personal service" nature. This problem has been particularly acute for the incorporated sole practitioner, because the practitioner is the only one who can perform the services. The risk in this situation is that the practitioner's fee is considered personal holding company income, which is subject to the 39.6 percent personal holding company tax in addition to the regular tax on corporate income, unless it is distributed by the corporation as salaries, dividends or as expenses.

The IRS finally cleared up this problem in a way favorable to professional corporations. The IRS has ruled that, in a one-person medical corporation, the establishment of a physician-patient relationship did not result in a personal service contract because (1) there was no specific designation of the employee to perform the services, in that either patient or physician could unilaterally terminate the relationship, and (2) the services of the physician were not so unique as to preclude substitution.

Thus, all contracts with hospitals or other organizations for whom services are performed should be in the name of the corporation. The corporation should designate the individual professionals who will perform the services. The corporation should not contract away this right or indicate that the patient or client has the right to designate the employee who is to perform the services.

Of course, professional corporations that make substantial investments still can run afoul of the personal holding company tax. Investment income must be kept below 60 percent of adjusted ordinary gross income in all events to avoid the tax. But below the 60 percent limit, incorporated professionals now can safely retain earnings in their corporation and use the earnings to fund employee benefit plans, buy-sell agreements and so on.

Reasonable Compensation

There are potential problems with "reasonable compensation." For example, suppose a physician's corporation leases out space in its medical building. If the corporation pays out all of its income in the form of salary, the IRS may claim that part of the salary represents a nondeductible dividend rather than deductible compensation. What is reasonable in a given case is a question to be determined under the particular circumstances. Generally, the following factors are weighed in deciding the "reasonableness" issue: (1) qualifications of the employees; (2) the nature of the work performed; (3) the size and complexity of the business; (4) the relation of salary paid to the gross and net income of the corporation; (5) rates of compensation for similar positions in other similar professions; and (6) the compensation paid to the employee in prior years.

It also is clear that the reasonableness test applies to all forms of compensation, not just salary. Thus, employer contributions to a qualified pension plan on behalf of a professional have been held unreasonable in relation to the services rendered during the taxable year.

State Corporate Income Tax

The states levy their own form of income tax on corporations. This is a tax that partnerships, of course, are exempt from paying. The various state statutes will need to be consulted for specific state rates.

BUYOUT AGREEMENTS IN PROFESSIONAL CORPORATIONS

In a professional corporation, a stock buyout agreement is an absolute necessity because of restrictions on a transfer of professional corporation stock imposed by state law.

In many states, the professional corporation statutes limit stock transfers to other members of the same profession. Some states permit the estate of a deceased stockholder to hold the professional corporation shares, but only for a reasonable period of estate administration. Other states permit nonprofessionals to own the shares, but they cannot vote these shares.

The statutes in some states take an additional step. To provide for orderly transfer of professional corporation stock at the death of a stockholder, these statutes require that the shares be redeemed by the corporation at their book value, in the absence of a buyout provision in the articles of incorporation, the bylaws or a separate agreement. This can have the beneficial side effect of justifying the accumulation of earnings, through insurance or otherwise, to fund the required buyout.

If a stock redemption agreement is used, it may as well do some double duty, as long as it's there to satisfy state law. Thus, if the redemption occurs at the professional's death, his or her estate acquires cash to pay taxes, debts and expenses, while simply doing what's required by law anyway.

Corporate buy-sell agreements have a unique advantage over partnership buy-sell agreements. When properly arranged, a stock redemption agreement can qualify the distribution for capital gains treatment. In a partnership buy-sell agreement, however, the distribution will be ordinary income to the extent attributable to unrealized receivables, which are often substantial in a professional partnership. However, because of the *stepped-up* basis rules, there usually will be no gain or loss.

THE LIMITED LIABILITY COMPANY

The *limited liability company (LLC)* is a unique form of business ownership that combines the best of two worlds: the tax advantages of a partnership and the legal safeguards of a corporation. Before LLCs, only subchapter S corporations permitted the consolidation of these two characteristics and, then, only at the cost of accepting the restrictive S corporation requirements. For example, S corporations limit the number of shareholders to 75 and do not allow corporate or foreign ownership. Such requirements do not apply in the case of limited liability companies.

The applicability of the limited liability company to many business situations has become so widespread that most states have adopted enabling legislation to permit the formation of LLCs. States that have not yet done so will often recognize LLCs that are organized in another state. An LLC is generally formed by filing articles of incorporation with the state in which it is to be organized. Registration as a foreign limited liability company is required if the LLC conducts business or owns property in a jurisdiction other than that in which it is organized.

Limited liability company statutes contain provisions governing such items as the conduct of the entity, the relationships of the members, member liability to third parties, distributions to members, management rights and dissolutions. Many LLC statutes resemble those of the Uniform Liability Partnership Act adopted in the particular state.

Equity participants in the LLC are referred to a *members*. Members may be natural persons, corporations, partnerships, trusts, estates, other LLCs or similar business entities. Most state statutes require at least two members for a LLC.

A LLC is a hybrid business entity that may be taxed as a partnership while providing limited liability protection for all of its members. For tax purposes, an LLC is a pass-through entity. Thus, like a partnership, its income and losses are taxed only at the member level. However, although a LLC receives partnership treatment for tax purposes, its members are protected by the corporate benefit of limited liability. Like the shareholders of a corporation, members of a LLC have limited liability for the LLC's debts and claims against the LLC; no member is saddled with the personal liability of a general partner.

Classification of LLCs

Because LLCs possess qualities of both corporations and partnerships, and because state statutes vary, the IRS has decided to treat them on a state-by-state basis for purposes of taxation. This means that instead of issuing one set of rules to be applied nationwide, taxing authorities will examine each state's LLC act to determine whether an entity should be taxed as a corporation or a partnership. The LLC enabling legislation for most states does not definitively settle this question.

The central objective of using the LLC form of business entity is to provide the protection of the corporation, but also to enjoy the classification as a partnership for tax purposes in order to avoid the double taxation inherent in the normal corporate tax structure. However, a LLC will not automatically achieve partnership taxability status. The individual LLC must be carefully designed because the IRS has held that a business organization with associates and a profit motive will be taxed as a corporation if it possesses three or more of the four primary corporate characteristics:

1. continuity of life;

2. centralization of management;

3. limited liability; and

4. free transferability of interests.

Thus, for a LLC to secure partnership classification, it must be lacking at least two of the above four corporate characteristics.

Continuity of Life

An organization lacks continuity of life if the death, insanity, bankruptcy, retirement, resignation or expulsion of any member causes a dissolution of the organization. Generally, state LLC statutes provide that upon dissolution, for whatever cause, the LLC may be continued by:

1. unanimous consent of the members;

2. consent of a majority of the remaining members; or

3. consent of a majority of the remaining members entitled to receive a majority of the LLC's capital upon dissolution.

Most LLCs incorporate some combination of these options into the articles of organization.

Many times the LLC articles of organization or the state LLC statute itself will provide for automatic dissolution upon the expiration of a period of years. Generally 30 years is the specified time period. Even when such a provision exists, the LLC will have continuity of life as long as no member has the power to dissolve the organization. When the period expires, the LLC can be continued by renewing the articles of organization transferring the entity's assets to a related organization. Statutes that require the consent of all members in order to transfer ownership rights lack the free transferability characteristic.

Centralization of Management

An organization has centralized management when any person or group of persons that does not include all members of the entity has continuing exclusive authority to make the management decisions necessary to conduct the business for which the organization was formed. The key concept is that of representative management: If a group of persons has management authority that resembles the powers and functions of a board of directors of a corporation, centralized management will be found to exist. For a LLC, centralize management exists if members without management authority own substantially all of the membership interests.

The IRS has ruled that a LLC lacked the corporate characteristic of centralized management where management powers were reserved to all members in proportion to their interests in the LLC. This makes the LLC similar to a general partnership whose partners can all be held accountable for the act of one partner. Partnership principles make it impossible for centralized management to exist because of the agency relationship that permits partners to bind each other without notice. As a result, if LLC managers with authority to act on behalf of the LLC are equated to general partners, then even the appointment of managers would not necessarily result in centralized management.

Limited Liability

A business entity has the corporate characteristic of limited liability if, under local law, no member is held personally liable for the debts of, or claims against, the organization. Most state statutes automatically provide for limited liability.

Free Transferability of Interests

An organization has the corporate characteristic of free transferability of interests if each of it members or those members owning substantially all of the interest in the organization have the power, without the consent of other members, to substitute for themselves in the same organization a person who is not a member of the organization. For this power to exist, the member must be able, without the consent of other members, to confer upon his or her substitute all attributes of his or her interest in the organization.

Taxation of LLCs

One of the most significant advantages of the LLC is that, like partnerships, income may flow through untaxed to the individual owners. The owners do not avoid personal taxes, but they can avoid corporate taxes. Corporate shareholders, on the other hand, are caught in a web of double taxation. First, corporations face a tax on corporate income at higher maximum rates. Second, if dividends are paid out, the owners are taxed again. Although S corporations avoid double taxation, they do not enjoy all the advantages of partnership when it comes to juggling income and deductions. For example, the 10 percent owner of an S corporation generally must pay taxes on 10 percent of any corporate income. Partnership members, on the other hand, are free to allocate income and tax liability in any manner they choose. Moreover, partnerships may change the allocations of profit or loss on a year-to-year basis to fit their individual tax needs. The LLC structure can offer comparable flexibility.

Summary of the Advantages of LLCs

Limited liability is certainly one of the attractive benefits of a LLC. With LLCs only the company assets are at risk. The member-owner's personal assets remain outside of the reach of any claimants in a business-related lawsuit. In a partnership, only the assets of limited partners are shielded from liability. However, to enjoy this protection, limited partners are restricted from active participation in the partnership. By contrast, although the assets of general partners are fully at risk, they face no restrictions on participation. LLCs are designed to protect all members while imposing no limits on their business participation.

Limited liability companies have other advantages over the S corporation form of organization. One such advantage is freedom from numerous restrictions imposed on an S corporation. Unlike the S corporation, a LLC may have more than 75 members, and interests may be held by corporations, partnerships, nonresident aliens, trusts, pension plans and charitable organizations. In addition, because a LLC is not restricted by the single class of stock requirement, it may make special allocation to its members.

Because a LLC can be taxed as a partnership, it also has an advantage over an S corporation in the area of deductible losses. The amount of deductible losses allowed by an S corporation shareholder is limited to the sum of the shareholder's basis in his or her stock and any loans from the shareholder to the corporation. In contrast, LLC members may deduct losses using the more favorable rules available for partnership interests. Under those rules, a partner can deduct losses in an amount up to the sum of his or her basis in the partnership interest, the individual's allocable share of partnership income, and the proper allocable share of partnership debt.

The most obvious reason to consider the LLC form of organization is the limited liability protection afforded all LLC members. Limited partnerships are required to have at least one general partner who manages the business and has unlimited liability. With a LLC, however, no member need sacrifice management authority in return for limited liability. In an effort to circumvent the general partner problem, many limited partnerships have an S corporation as the general partner. Using an S corporation as a general partner effectively provides limited liability to all partners; however, this structure is more cumbersome than that of an LLC and does not provide adequate pass-through taxation to the S corporation shareholders. Moreover, limited partnerships formed with a corporate general partner must satisfy minimum net worth and profit allocation requirements that do not apply to LLCs.

Converting to a LLC

A limited or general partnership may be converted into a LLC on a tax-free basis. The IRS has sometimes permitted the tax-free merger of a limited partnership into an LLC where: (1) all of the partnership assets and liabilities were transferred to the LLC and all partners became member of the LLC; (2) all partners became members of the LLC; and (3) the conversion did not change any of the partners' shares of the partnership liabilities.

The limited liability company appears to have many advantage for smaller business entities, which helps to explain its increasing popularity, combining, as it does, many of the most favorable benefits of both the corporate and partnership form of organization.

SUMMARY

As you can see, the business insurance sales for an S corporation and a professional corporation and a limited liability company generally parallel those for a regular corporation. What you should take with you from this unit is the factual background, so that if differences do arise, you are able to recognize them and deal with them comfortably. Watch out especially for the different tax treatment of S, professional corporations and limited liability companies. Also, be sure to obtain the advice of competent legal counsel when preparing plans for these, in fact, all, corporations.

CHAPTER 7 QUESTIONS FOR REVIEW

1. Income to an S corporation

    A. is taxed at the standard corporate rate

    B. is tax-exempt up to the first $50,000, after which it is taxed at the standard corporate rate

    C. is taxed to shareholders at their individual rates

    D. is taxed at the Subchapter S corporate rate

2. Requirements for election of S corporation status include

    A. no fewer than 75 stockholders

    B. no more than one class of stock

    C. at least 25 percent of income be passive investment income

    D. none of the above

3. Which one of the following statements about a limited liability company is incorrect?

    A. It is always taxed as a partnership.

    B. It may be taxed as either a partnership or a corporation.

    C. Its participants are known as "members."

    D. It may be converted from a partnership.

4. In a professional corporation, a stock buyout agreement is important because of

    A. the stepped-up basis rules in a corporation

    B. restrictions on transfer of professional corporation stock

    C. the corporation operating without the need for a written agreement

    D. none of the above

5. Which of the following would be eligible to form a professional corporation?

    A. A group of psychiatrists

    B. An accountant and an attorney

    C. An ophthalmologist and an optometrist, who are, respectively, father and son

    D. All of the above

8

The Corporation—Cross-Purchase or Stock Redemption

This chapter takes the sales solution a step further than Chapter 6 and discusses the buy-sell agreement in more detail. Also covered are the factors to be considered in choosing a cross-purchase versus a stock redemptionbuy-sell agreement, and an alternative to the more traditional cross-purchase or stock redemption agreement—the "wait-and-see" buy-sell agreement.

Finally, this chapter outlines what clauses should be contained in a buy-sell agreement and gives some samples of the specific types of buy-sell agreements.

■ THE AGREEMENT

A properly written agreement that sets out the rights and obligations of the parties is essential in cases in which life insurance will fund the purchase of a deceased shareholder's stock. The written agreement makes certain that the insurance proceeds will be used as the parties intended. For this purpose, it is advisable that this instrument be drawn up by an attorney.

A typical buy-sell agreement creates an immediate and binding contract between the parties. This contract commits stockholders and their estates to sell their shares to either the other stockholders (cross-purchase agreement) or to the corporation itself (stock redemption plan).

Key elements of the effective corporate buy-sell agreement are the provisions within the agreement itself and the availability of funding to carry out the agreement to the benefit and satisfaction of all parties.

As an insurance professional, your job is to explain to your clients the workings of a typical agreement funded by life or disability insurance, depending on the plan under consideration. Offer to assist your clients' attorney in any way possible with information and recommendations. Your primary role, however, is to help guarantee that the funding is present to carry out the agreement by putting the life insurance in force.

Parties to the Contract

As you are aware from our treatment of partnerships in prior chapters, there are two types of buy-sell agreements: the entity-purchase agreement and the cross-purchase agreement. In the entity-purchase plan, the business organization purchases the interest of the deceased shareholder; in the cross-purchase plan the surviving associates purchase his or her interest on a proportionate basis.

In the corporate setting, the entity-purchase plan is called a "stock redemption" plan, because the corporation redeems its outstanding shares when it fulfills its obligation to purchase at a shareholder's death. It is also worthwhile to consider purchase of the business interest by a key employee, who may not currently be a shareholder.

Life Insurance Ownership Provisions

The applicant, owner and beneficiary of each policy vary, depending upon the type of buy-sell plan to be used. Under a stock redemption plan (whereby the corporation purchases the deceased stockholder's shares), the insurance is owned and paid for by the corporation itself. This places full control and ownership with the company. Under a cross-purchase plan, on the other hand, the policies on each shareholder should be purchased and maintained by the other shareholders.

If the plan is to be administered by an independent trustee, the insurance policies and the stock involved in the plan normally will be deposited with the trustee. This ensures prompt execution of the agreement at the death of one of the shareholders. The application for the insurance may be made by the shareholders involved in the plan or by the corporation itself, depending upon the type of plan involved and other arrangements regarding control of the policy and premium payments.

The beneficiaries of the life insurance proceeds are the parties who are obliged to purchase the interest of the deceased shareholder.

Type of Policy

The type of insurance policies used depend on the needs and wishes of the parties. However, whenever possible, permanent, cash value insurance is almost always preferable. There are several reasons for this. First and foremost, permanent, cash value insurance reduces the possibility of the policy lapsing without value in later years, when death is most likely to occur. Also, the policy builds up cash value for other uses, if needed, including lifetime buy out at retirement or disability. Finally, the cost for permanent coverage is more stable than that for term, which rises dramatically in cost as the insured grows older. A cash value contract may also be kept in force during any lean years of the business cycle by providing funds to pay premiums in the form of a policy loan.

In short, use your own discretion. Depending on the specific situation, you may recommend a traditional whole life policy, an interest-sensitive plan, universal life, variable universal life, or joint mortality contracts, such as a joint first-to-die or a joint survivorship policy.

When arranging the coverage, consider that shareholders may wish to retire at age 65. With this in mind, you may want to recommend some form of limited pay policy, with regularly scheduled premiums ending at age 65 or with high cash values.

Finally, in a pinch, if the cash is not available to fund permanent policies, term insurance can be used. However, it should be provided with your clients' understanding that this is a temporary, stop-gap solution, and the coverage should be converted as soon as possible.

Using Existing Insurance

Most corporate owners are reluctant to use existing personally-owned life insurance for buy-sell purposes. These policies were purchased for another purpose (retirement, education or savings, for example), and the shareholders do not desire to disturb their previous plans.

However, in many cases the contemplated buy-sell plan may be part of a reorganization of insurance coverages within the corporate setting. Can insurance policies owned by individual shareholders on the lives of other shareholders be transferred to the corporation? Can life insurance policies owned by the corporation be transferred to individual shareholders to complete the contemplated buy-sell plans? Should they be?

The answer to the first question is that ownership of existing life insurance policies certainly may be changed to finance a buy-sell agreement. Determining whether existing life insurance should be transferred requires an understanding of the possible tax consequences of policy transfer—especially the transfer-for-value rule.

The general rule is that, when an insurance policy is transferred for a valuable consideration, the insurance proceeds paid at the insured's death will be taxed to the purchaser of the policy as ordinary income, to the extent that the proceeds exceeded the cost of acquisition and the premiums subsequently paid by the purchaser. That having been said, there are exceptions. If the new owner is the insured, a partner of the insured, a partnership in which the insured is a partner, *or a corporation in which the insured is an officer or shareholder,* the transfer-for-value rule does not apply.

Therefore, insurance policies owned by the shareholders may be transferred to the corporation for stock redemption purposes. However, the law does not except the transfer of an insurance policy to another shareholder, unless of course the shareholder and the insured are the same person. This rule would preclude the use of a cross-purchase agreement if insurance policies had to be transferred to other shareholders to implement the plan.

Life insurance provides the ideal source of funds for retiring a deceased shareholder's interest, but it is not the only source of funds. The buy-sell plan still can be carried through with the use of a special sinking fund, the use of the cash value of the policies on the lives of the insurable shareholders or perhaps the purchase of his or her shares today.

The Beneficiary

The beneficiaries of the life insurance proceeds should be the parties who are obliged to purchase the interest of the deceased shareholder. Thus, when the purchase is to be made by the surviving shareholders individually, they will be named beneficiaries of the insurance, subject to the terms of the cross-purchase agreement.

When a stock redemption agreement is used, the corporation will be the beneficiary of the policies. An alternative is to name a trustee, but trusteed stock redemption agreements are less commonly used than trusteed cross-purchase agreements.

The corporation should never be named the beneficiary under a cross-purchase agreement when the surviving shareholders are to purchase the shares of the deceased shareholder. Insurance proceeds paid to the corporation, and used to pay for the shares the shareholders individually are obligated to buy, would constitute taxable dividends to the surviving shareholders and would not be deductible by the corporation.

A safe and satisfactory procedure in a buy-sell case is to use a trustee. The trustee is named the beneficiary of the insurance policies and then deals with them in the manner set forth in the trust agreement.

The trustee acts as an impartial party in completing the details of the business insurance plan. The trustee:

- collects the money from the insurance company;

- takes the necessary steps to determine the value of the interest of the deceased shareholder as set out in the agreement;

- applies the insurance proceeds toward purchase of that interest;

- sees that the proceeds are turned over to the estate of the deceased shareholder after proper arrangements by the surviving associates (or by the firm if the corporation buys the stock) for payment of any excess of value over the proceeds; and

- delivers the stock to the purchasers.

Thus, the execution of the business insurance plan is placed in the hands of a responsible third party capable of insisting upon enforcement of the terms of the agreement in the interests of all parties concerned.

Who Should Pay the Premiums?

The problem of premium payment, like that of ownership, turns upon the particular details of the case under consideration. Different plans for payment of premiums may be adopted, such as:

- payment by the corporation itself;

- payment by each shareholder on the policy on his or her own life;

- payment by each shareholder on the policy insuring his or her co-shareholder (or each stockholder's share of the premiums on policies insuring the co-shareholders); or

- payment from a pool to which the parties contribute.

Payment by the Corporation. When the corporation itself is to purchase the stock of a deceased shareholder under a stock redemption agreement, the corporation should own the policies and pay all premiums.

Even though a trustee has possession of the policy and is designated beneficiary of the death proceeds, the policy remains an asset of the corporation prior to the insured's death, as well as at the time of death.

When a cross-purchase agreement is used, the shareholders may, as a convenience, authorize the corporation to draw the premium checks and charge them to the salary accounts of the respective shareholders.

Payment by the Shareholder on His or Her Own Policy. Probably few plans have been set up under which each shareholder has paid the premiums on the insurance on his or her own life. Such an agreement is wrong in principle because it obligates each shareholder to finance the purchase price for the stock he or she already owns, rather than having such price provided by the purchaser of that stock. This arrangement, obviously, would call for full reimbursement of premiums paid by the deceased and could present a serious financial problem upon the death of an older shareholder who was a large stockholder. Such an arrangement should be discouraged.

Payment by the Surviving Shareholders. In the cross-purchase plan, the individual shareholders pay the premiums on the policies they own on the lives of their co-shareholders. There is no problem of reimbursement to the premium payer. However, the deceased shareholder will own policies on the lives of the surviving shareholders. The agreement customarily provides the survivors with the option, for a limited period of time, of acquiring their policies upon payment of the cash values, plus any unearned portion of the last premium paid. This should work out equitably for all parties concerned.

Payment by Contributions to a "Pool." If there is a wide difference in the ages of the shareholders, or if one of the shareholders is rated, younger shareholders under a cross-purchase agreement may object to the higher premium they are obligated to pay on the older or rated shareholder. The younger shareholder may even find that it is impossible to pay such a premium. In such cases, it may be desirable or necessary to resort to a plan for "pooling" the premiums. Two pooling plans are possible:

1. All shareholders contribute a proportion of the total of all premiums equal to their stock interest in the corporation.

2. All shareholders contribute on the basis of the number of shareholders, with premiums on all policies added together and divided by the number of shareholders. Each shareholder then pays a proportionate share.

Under either plan, reimbursement to the estate of the decedent should reflect the proportionate premium contributions made by the deceased on any policies on his or her own life. In other words, if the deceased stockholder paid some of the premiums of the insurance on his or her life due to a pooling arrangement, the sums paid the decedent's estate for the decedent's stock interest should include the proportionate part of the premiums paid.

Adjustment of Premium Amounts. When the insurance premiums for the insurance to fund the full purchase price would be too great, the corporation or the shareholders could buy insurance coverages equal to a percentage of the corporate values. It is not an absolute necessity that the insurance provide 100 percent coverage. The plan holds tremendous advantages even when the insurance provides only a substantial down payment on the purchase price fixed under the agreement.

Adjustment of Insurance Face Value. In many cases, the insurance proceeds paid at death will differ in amount from the value of the deceased's interest in the firm as established by the method set out in the business purchase agreement. Provisions should be included in the agreement covering disposal of any excess of insurance proceeds over the value of the interest purchased and providing for payment of any excess of value over available insurance money.

When the insurance money exceeds the value of the deceased's interest, often it is provided that the insurance benefit constitutes a minimum price for the interests of the parties and that the full amount of the insurance be paid to the estate of the deceased, even though it exceeds the actual value of that interest as determined at the time of death. Such arrangements protect the family by guaranteeing application of the full insurance proceeds to their benefit and by establishing a minimum value regardless of temporary business conditions at the time of death.

When the actual value of the deceased's interest as provided in the agreement exceeds the insurance proceeds, the agreement should indicate the manner in which the surviving shareholders are to settle this difference. Usually, this excess will be payable by the survivors over a period of time, and they will be required to give a series of notes (bearing interest) covering the amount involved. The length of time that may be allowed the survivors for payment of this difference is, of course, a matter of agreement among the parties involved, and no definite rule can be stipulated. Each case should be judged on its own circumstances.

THE "WAIT-AND-SEE" BUY-SELL AGREEMENT

As you can see, there are many factors involved in deciding who should purchase the deceased shareholder's stock. Sometimes, the best solution to this problem is to make the decision after the shareholder is dead, through the use of a *wait-and-see* buy-sell agreement.

A wait-and-see buy-sell typically gives a corporation the option to buy any amount of the deceased's shares within a certain time period after the date of death. Thus, if it is decided that a stock redemption would be favorable, the corporation could exercise its option and purchase *all* the stock from the deceased's estate.

If the corporation exercises the option to purchase less than all the shares, then the surviving shareholders have the option to purchase shares of stock in amounts agreed upon among themselves.

If there are shares left in the estate after the surviving shareholders have exercised their options, then the corporation would be *required* to buy back all the remaining shares. This buy-back is mandatory to protect the estate by guaranteeing a buyer at the prearranged price.

The insurance funding of the agreement can take place in one of two ways:

1. the shareholders could purchase the policies and, if a redemption were chosen, they could loan the proceeds to the corporation; or

2. the corporation could purchase the policies and, if a cross-purchase were chosen, it could loan the proceeds to the shareholders.

SOME FINAL THOUGHTS

Because of the sound business reasons related to buy-sell agreements, many corporations already have them in place. However, the mere fact that an agreement was executed at some time does not mean that the firm's needs are adequately met. If you find that an agreement is in effect, you should obtain additional information. When was the agreement executed? Where will the funds come from to make the agreement work? Even if life insurance was purchased at the time the agreement was established, such factors as inflation, increases in value and other changes in the firm may mean that additional amounts of insurance are needed. In fact, the sale made to bring the funding of the agreement in line with present business values is often much easier than the initial sale to establish the funding for the agreement.

The completion of your study of the corporation should mark the beginning of your approach to the corporate insurance market. Life insurance is an effective answer for corporate shareholders. The corporate owner who visualizes his or her child running the business in the next generation needs life insurance to make a redemption an effective planning tool for meeting estate costs and taxes at his or her death. Likewise, the corporate owner who will liquidate the business someday will need life insurance—if only to offset the estate losses that liquidation certainly brings. Then, too, life insurance provides the funding required in those corporations for which there are shareholders ready, able and willing to carry on the enterprise. Life insurance gives the stock purchase agreement its muscle, so that a shareholder may never have to wonder whether the money will be there to purchase the stock of a deceased associate.

As a life insurance agent or financial planner, you are in a position to make these and other points to corporate shareholders. You will be rewarded for your efforts. New corporations are being formed every day. Furthermore, as the economy grows, so do corporate enterprises. These offer new and challenging sales opportunities to financial planners and life insurance professionals. Be sure that you get your share of the market.

ILL 8.1 ▪ *Cross-Purchase Or Stock Redemption—Decisional Factors*

As discussed, the two basic types of business continuation arrangements are cross-purchase plans and stock redemption plans. The distinguishing factor of a cross-purchase plan is that the individual stockholders agree among themselves to purchase the stock of a deceased stockholder. The distinguishing factor of a stock redemption plan is that the corporation agrees to purchase or redeem the stock of the deceased stockholder. The fundamental differences between the two plans must be applied to your client's particular circumstances. Weighing the following factors will facilitate a decision as to which of the two methods best meets the need:

	Stock Redemption	v.	**Cross-Purchase**
How Arranged	The *corporation* contracts with the stockholders to purchase the stock of any deceased stockholder at an agreed-upon price or according to an agreed-upon formula. The corporation is applicant, owner, premium payer and beneficiary of a policy on the life of each stockholder in an amount needed to purchase the stock.		Stockholders agree among themselves that the survivor(s) will purchase the stock of a deceased stockholder at an agreed-upon price or according to an agreed-upon formula. Each stockholder is applicant, owner, premium payer and beneficiary of the policy (ies) on the life (lives) of other stockholder(s).
Number of Stockholders	When there are more than three stockholders, a stock redemption arrangement may be called for, because only one insurance policy per stockholder is required. This can result in a cost savings for two reasons: (1) larger policies often result in a lower premium per thousand dollars of coverage; and (2) each policy has a built-in "premium adjustment factor," an annual charge for paperwork. Obviously, a one-million-dollar policy will cost less per year than ten $100,000 policies. Also, a corporate premium payer and owner would lead to administrative simplicity and less chance of lapse.		When there are two or three stockholders, the group is usually small enough to minimize administrative problems. The formula for the number of policies needed is $N \times (N-1)$, with N being the number of stockholders.

ILL 8.1 ▪ Cross-Purchase Or Stock Redemption—Decisional Factors (Cont.)

	Stock Redemption	v.	**Cross-Purchase**
Amount of Insurance needed	Slightly larger insurance amounts would have to be carried because when the first owner dies and the corporation receives the proceeds, the value of the corporation's assets jumps and therefore the cost to purchase a given interest increases. (This can be avoided by proper working of the agreement itself.) It also may be possible to offset the value of the proceeds by proving the value of the business is reduced by loss of the key individual's services.		No comparable problem. The net worth of the corporation is unaffected by the receipt by an individual stockholder of life insurance proceeds.
Differences in Ages	Each stockholder pays premiums in proportion to ownership interest. If, because of differences in age, the premiums are unequal (assume the premium on A's life is $1,000 and the premium on B's life is $2,000.) and A and B both own 50 percent of the stock, B might feel the impact of the premiums is inequitable because he or she actually is contributing $500 toward the cost of the policy on his or her own life. (If this were a cross-purchase agreement, the cost would be only $1,000.)		The youngest stockholder has a heavy burden—he or she must pay premiums on the life of the older stockholder and is usually in the weakest financial position to pay these premiums. A split-dollar arrangement between the corporation and the employee may provide a more equitable answer.
Differences in Ownership Interests	Because the corporation is premium payer, there is a "pooling effect" in the payment premiums. The stockholders bear this cost in direct relation to their stockholdings. This works to the disadvantage of stockholders with larger holdings and to the advantage of those with smaller holdings. (If stockholder R owns 80 percent of the corporation, R would be contributing 80 percent of the premium cost to purchase the costockholder's 20 percent of the business.)		Each stockholder pays for what he or she may receive.

ILL 8.1 ■ *Cross-Purchase Or Stock Redemption—Decisional Factors (Cont.)*

	Stock Redemption	v.	**Cross-Purchase**
Certainty of Performance	The corporation can't bind itself absolutely to but its own stock. (Most states require that sufficient surplus funds be available and the redemption not be in fraud of creditors. Naturally, funding life insurance alleviates, but does not eliminate, the problem.		Individuals can bind themselves absolutely to fulfill an agreement.
Creditors' Rights	Because the policies are corporate assets, they are subject to claims of business creditors. Corporate creditors may make claims against policy cash values and proceeds of corporate-owned life insurance.		The corporation is freed from claims of its creditors because the life insurance is owned by individual stockholders on the lives of co-stockholders. Individual stockholders' creditors can reach cash values and proceeds of policies owned by a stockholder on the lives of others.
Ratio of Stockholdings	If the ratio of stock held by each stockholder previous to the redemption is desired to be retained after the redemption, this method is recommended. Surviving stockholders' percentages of stock ownership are increased pro rata by amount of stock redeemed, based on their previous ownership percentages.		If it is desirable to change the ratio of ownership, a cross-purchase is called for because the agreement can specify and effect whatever new ratio of ownership is desired by the parties involved. This would be achieved by varying the amount of stock to be purchased from the decedent's estate.

ILL 8.1 ▪ *Cross-Purchase Or Stock Redemption—Decisional Factors (Cont.)*

	Stock Redemption	v.	**Cross-Purchase**
Possible State Law Restrictions	A corporation may be restricted from purchasing its own shares absent sufficient surplus. Local law and corporate charter and bylaws must be examined. This problem (that the purchase by a corporation of its own stock is normally prohibited by state law except out of its own surplus) can be alleviated by a provision in the stock purchase agreement to the effect that the surviving stockholders will cause the corporation to take such actions as it can to create a surplus; for example, the stockholders might vote to create a surplus by revaluing corporate assets or, alternatively, to recapitalize and reduce the par value of the corporation's stock (thereby creating paid-in surplus—assuming it is not necessary to make the purchase out of earned surplus).		A cross-purchase arrangement is indicated if corporate law may create problems.
Deductibility and Taxation of Premiums	No deduction is allowed to the corporation for premium payments, which are not considered constructive dividends to stockholders unless the purchase discharges a primary, unconditional and personal obligation of the surviving stockholders.		Stockholders receive no deduction. If the corporation gives the employees bonuses that are reasonable, these may be deductible by the corporation (and income to the employees) and used by the employees to purchase insurance on the lives of the other stockholders.
Income Taxation of Insurance Proceeds	The corporation will receive life insurance proceeds income tax free.		Stockholder-beneficiaries will receive life insurance proceeds income tax free.

ILL 8.1 ▪ *Cross-Purchase Or Stock Redemption—Decisional Factors (Cont.)*

	Stock Redemption	v.	**Cross-Purchase**
Alternative Minimum Tax	Life insurance proceeds are a preference item, subject to AMT calculations. If other factors indicate that a redemption plan is preferred, slightly larger insurance amounts could be purchased to compensate. (Note that beginning in tax years after 1997, a small-corporation AMT exemption applies for corporations with average annual gross receipts not exceeding $5 million.)		Life insurance proceeds are not subject to individual AMT calculations.
Comparative Tax Rates	This is indicated if the corporate tax rate is lower than the individual tax rate, because the after-tax cost to pay premiums would be correspondingly lower.		When individuals pay premiums, only after-tax dollars are available. If the individuals are in higher personal tax brackets than the corporation, a cross-purchase is not indicated. If the individuals are in a lower personal income tax bracket, and because life insurance premiums are not deductible by the corporation, the cost of funding by the cross-purchase method would be less. (Even if the salaries of the stockholders have to be increased to provide money for premium payments, as long as they are still in a lower tax bracket than the corporation, this method would be indicated.)

ILL 8.1 ▪ *Cross-Purchase Or Stock Redemption—Decisional Factors (Cont.)*

	Stock Redemption	v.	**Cross-Purchase**
Unreasonable Accumulation of Surplus	Until the total cash accumulated by the corporation—including cash value of these policies—reaches $250,000 ($150,000 for personal service corporations in the fields of health, law, engineering, architecture, accounting, actuarial science, performing arts and consulting) there will be no adverse tax consequences in most cases. Life insurance funding of a stock redemption type agreement per se does not give rise to unreasonable accumulations problems. The key issue is: Does the accumulation have a business rather than a stockholder-oriented purpose?		There is no similar problem because corporate funds are not used.
Survivor's Cost Basis	*Cost Basis* is important because this is subtracted from the amount realized in a sale, and the result becomes the taxable gain (or loss). Under a corporate redemption, although the value of a stockholder's stock interest increases, his or her cost basis remains the same—even after the corporation redeems the decedent's stock. So if a surviving stockholder were to sell his or her share of the business later, the surviving stockholder would have to pay increased taxes because of increased gain. This is because, under stock retirement plans, the surviving stockholder's cost basis is his or her original investment (plus any subsequent paid-in capital) and is not increased by the insurance proceeds—because they were paid, not by the stockholder, but by the corporation.		A survivor receives an increase in "cost basis" for the shares he or she purchased from a decedent stockholder's estate. In the event of a sale during life, his or her taxable gain and, therefore, the tax he or she would have to pay on that sale, is reduced. If there is a strong possibility that the stockholder will sell stock during his or her lifetime, a cross-purchase agreement is indicated. If the survivor does not sell his or her stock and owns it at death, that stock together with all other appreciated assets would receive a stepped-up basis. (This is also true in the case of a stock redemption.)

ILL 8.1 ▪ *Cross-Purchase Or Stock Redemption—Decisional Factors (Cont.)*

	Stock Redemption	**v.**	**Cross-Purchase**
Seller's Cost Basis	The seller (this may be the stockholder-employee or his or her estate or beneficiary) uses cost (more technically, "adjusted basis") as the starting point for ascertaining gain or loss on a sale. The estate or heirs of a decedent will take the federal estate tax value of the stock as their basis for computing gain or loss on a subsequent sale.		Same a stock redemption.
Transfer-for-Value Problems	The corporation continues to own the policies at the death of the stockholder, so that no transfer is necessary at death. This eliminates the possibility of a transfer-for-value problem. Existing policies can be safely transferred to the corporation to initiate the plan.		When each stockholder owns a policy on the lives of co-stockholders and there are more than two stockholders, the possibility of a transfer-for-value problem exists. When one stockholder dies, his or her estate usually will wish to transfer (sell) the policies he or she owned on the other stockholders to the survivors. Because transfer to a co-stockholder of the insured is not an exception to the transfer-for-value rule, a serious income tax problem could result with respect to the death proceeds of any of the transfer policies. The decedent stockholder's estate can sell such policies only to the respective insureds or to the corporation if the insured is an officer or stockholder.
Change of Nature of Agreement	If the agreement is originally of the stock redemption type, a later transfer of life insurance policies to parties other than the enshrouds will generate a transfer-for-value problem.		A cross-purchase plan is recommended if there is a possibility that the nature of the agreement will change in the future. If life insurance policies are transferred to a corporation in which the insured is an officer or stockholder, the proceeds will retain their income tax-free status.

ILL 8.1 ▪ *Cross-Purchase Or Stock Redemption—Decisional Factors (Cont.)*

	Stock Redemption	v.	**Cross-Purchase**
Constructive Ownership Problems of Family Corporations	In almost any family-owned corporation, any close relationship between stockholders may invoke the constructive ownership problem. For example: If a son is an estate beneficiary, the estate, though not actual owner, still would be considered constructive owner of all remaining outstanding shares by virtue of the son's shares being "attributed" to the estate. Thus, the purchase of the shares, not being a complete redemption that terminates the estate's interest in the corporation, would not qualify for treatment as a capital exchange for stock. The result is that the transaction would be considered a dividend distribution, and all the proceeds would constitute ordinary income to the estate.		There is no similar problem because no redemption of stock is involved. Constructive ownership (attribution) problems are avoided.
Estate Taxation of Insurance Proceeds	Assuming the corporation is the beneficiary of the entire proceeds, the proceeds will be considered in valuing stock interest of a decedent-stockholder but will not be separately includible in the insured's estate as life insurance. If the estate is bound to sell and the price agreed upon was arrived at in an arm's length bona fide negotiation, the agreed price will control for federal estate tax purposes.		Because each stockholder owns a policy on the lives of co-stockholders, the cash values of the policies on the lives of surviving stockholders will be includible in the estate of a decedent stockholder. Proceeds of any policies on the life of the decedent owned by his or her co-stockholders will not be includible in his or her estate.

■ SUMMARY

There is no simple answer to the question of which approach to the purchase of a shareholder's interest at death—cross-purchase or stock redemption—is the most appropriate. Often, the proper choice depends on the situation that exists at the time of the shareholder's death, possibly many years after the agreement is drawn up and funded.

This chapter closely looks at issues surrounding the decision to purchase a deceased stockholder's interest by the corporation and by the surviving shareholders, as well as introduces an additional approach. That approach is one that permits all the parties in interest—the corporation and the other shareholders—to wait until the death of the shareholder before deciding on which to buyout method to employ. Called the wait-and-see buy-sell agreement, it avoids locking the corporation or its shareholders into a buyout option that may be less advantageous at the time of death. Despite the somewhat less-settled nature of the wait-and-see approach, the role of life insurance does not change. It remains vital to the facilitation of the terms of the agreement.

This chapter also discussed various particularly important provisions of the buy-sell agreement and the life insurance funding it. Issues including the most desirable policy type to use, its ownership and beneficiary provisions as well as the appropriate premium payor were examined.

The chapter concludes with a summary of the decisional factors in selecting of a buy-sell agreement method and annotated samples of stock-purchase agreements. The annotations highlight why particular provisions are important.

■ SAMPLE STOCK PURCHASE AGREEMENTS

The three stock purchase agreements presented here do not attempt to meet all the criteria set forth in the preceding general outline. They merely attempt to illustrate forms of agreements used by corporate shareholders. Again, these agreements are presented here to acquaint you with the main provisions of customary agreements, and you are encouraged to study them carefully.

ILL 8.2 ■ *Sample Cross-Purchase Agreement*

CAUTION: This is a specimen agreement. The actual agreement used in any particular case must be prepared by a qualified attorney.

AGREEMENT by and between _____ and _____ (hereinafter called the *Shareholders*).

WITNESSETH:

Whereas, the Shareholders own the capital stock of the _____ Company, a corporation with its principal place of business at _____ (hereinafter referred to as the Company), owning _____ shares and _____ owning _____ shares of stock of the Company, and

Whereas, the Shareholders believe that it is to their mutual best interests to provide for continuity and harmony in management and the policies of the Company, and

Whereas, the purposes of this agreement are to provide for the purchase by the other Shareholders of one Shareholder's stock in the event of his (her) death, or in the event he (she) desires to dispose of any of his (her) stock during his (her) lifetime, and to provide the funds necessary to carry out such purchases.

Now, therefore, in consideration of the mutual agreements and covenants contained herein and for other valuable consideration, receipt of which is hereby acknowledged, it is mutually agreed and covenanted by and between the parties to this agreement as follows:

ARTICLE 1.

Restriction on Sale of Stock—Neither Shareholder shall, during their joint lives, assign, encumber or dispose of any portion of their respective stock interests in the Company, by sale or otherwise, unless he (she) first gives written notice to that effect to the other Shareholder. The other Shareholder shall have the right to purchase such stock at any time within 30 days after such notice at the price and under the mode of payment determined by Articles 4 and 5. If the offered stock is not purchased within the above period, the offering Shareholder may dispose of his (her) shares in any lawful manner, except that he (she) shall not sell any shares to any other person without giving the other Shareholder the right to purchase them at the price and on the terms offered by such other person. Upon the consummation of purchase, the selling Shareholder shall deliver the certificates to the purchasers.

> A provision restricting the lifetime transfer of a stockholder's interest is necessary if the buy-sell agreement is to be accepted by the government as the true fair market value for federal estate tax purposes.

ARTICLE 2.

Sale of Stock at Death—Upon the death of a Shareholder, the survivor shall purchase and the estate of the decedent shall sell the stock interest now owned or hereafter acquired by the Shareholder who is first to die. The purchase or sale price and the mode of payment for such stock shall be determined in accordance with the provisions of Articles 5 and 6 of this agreement.

> Here is a key provision in the agreement. Under this provision, the estate must sell, and the surviving stockholders must buy. This binding agreement to sell and the corresponding obligation to buy seems preferable to the various "option" type agreements that could be used. Too, the "option" type agreements may not effectively establish a value for estate tax purposes.

ILL 8.2 ▪ *Sample Cross-Purchase Agreement (Cont.)*

ARTICLE 3.

The Insurance Policies—In order to assure that all or a substantial part of the purchase price for the shares of the deceased Shareholder will be available immediately in cash upon his (her) death, the Shareholders have procured insurance upon each other's lives as follows:

_____ is insured under life insurance policy No. _____ issued by the _____ Insurance Company in the face amount of $_____, and _____ is the applicant, owner and beneficiary thereof.

_____ is insured under life insurance policy No. _____ issued by the _____ Insurance Company in the face amount of $_____, and _____ is the applicant, owner and beneficiary thereof.

Each Shareholder hereby authorizes the Company to pay the premiums on the policies owned by him (her) and made subject to this agreement as such premiums become due and to charge his (her) salary or other account therefor. In case any premium is not paid within 20 days after its due date, the insured shall be entitled to pay such premium as agent of the owner, and the owner agrees to reimburse him (her) promptly for any such payment. The insurance company is hereby authorized and directed to give the insured, upon his (her) written request, any information about the status of any policy on his (her) life subject to this agreement.

Each Shareholder shall retain possession of the policies procured by him (her) on the life of the other Shareholder. He (She) may not, however, exercise any of the policy rights without first having given the insured thereunder thirty days written notice of the contemplated exercise, unless he (she) has obtained from the insured a written waiver of such notice. Notwithstanding any other provision of this agreement, any dividends payable upon the policies prior to maturity by the death of the insured shall be paid to the owner in cash or disposed of as such owner may choose to direct. This agreement shall extend to and include all additional life insurance policies issued pursuant to this agreement, such additional policies to be listed in Schedule B attached hereto and made a part hereof.

> **Since this is a cross-purchase type plan, each shareholder is named the owner of the life insurance policy on the other shareholder's life. Although the corporation is authorized to make the premium payments on behalf of the shareholders, the corporation is not a party to the agreement, and this provision simply facilitates premium payments.**
>
> **Since, when the business is revalued annually, it may be found that the purchase price has increased substantially, this article also includes authorization for additional policies to be purchased and made a part of the agreement.**

ARTICLE 4.

Transfer of Deceased Shareholder's Stock—Upon the death of a Shareholder, the surviving Shareholder shall proceed immediately to collect the proceeds of the policies on the deceased Shareholder's life which are subject to this agreement. Upon collection of all such proceeds and the qualification of a Legal Representative of the decedent's estate, the surviving Shareholder shall pay to the Legal Representative an amount equal to such proceeds, which amount shall constitute payment on account, or in full, as the case may be, for the stock of the deceased Shareholder.

If the purchase price set forth in Article 5 exceeds the proceeds of life insurance, the balance of the purchase price shall be paid in _____ consecutive (monthly) (quarterly) (semiannual) (annual) payments beginning _____ months after the date of the decedent's death.

ILL 8.2 ▪ *Sample Cross-Purchase Agreement (Cont.)*

The unpaid balance of the purchase price shall be evidenced by a series of negotiable promissory notes made by the surviving Shareholder to the order of the estate of the deceased with interest at _____ percent per annum. Said notes shall provide for the acceleration of the due date of all unpaid notes in the series on default in the payment of any note or interest thereon and shall give the maker thereof the option of prepayment in whole or in part at any time. All of the stock of the decedent covered by this agreement shall be pledged with the decedent's estate as security for the payment of said notes, provided, however, that the surviving Shareholder shall be entitled to exercise all rights of ownership in such stock prior to default in the payment of any note or interest thereon.

> Since the purchase price and the insurance coverage may not precisely keep pace with each other at all times, it is important that provision be made for payment of any balance of the purchase price in excess of the life insurance proceeds. The exact terms of any notes to be executed also should be included in the buy-sell agreement.
>
> In this connection, it should be noted that while ideally the full value of the business should be covered by life insurance, this is not an absolute necessity. This plan of purchase can be successful even where the life insurance provides only a substantial down payment toward the purchase price.

ARTICLE 5.

The Shareholders agree that the present value of their stock is $_____ per share. Within 60 days after the end of each fiscal (calendar) year, or as soon thereafter as possible, the Shareholders, acting unanimously, shall redetermine the value per share of their stock and shall indicate such value by endorsement with their signatures upon Schedule A attached hereto and made a part hereof. If the Shareholders fail to redetermine the price agreed upon within 24 months following the end of the fiscal (calendar) year, the value of a deceased Shareholder's stock shall be agreed upon by the representative of the decedent and the surviving Shareholder. If the representative of the decedent and the surviving Shareholder do not agree upon the value within _____ days after the death of a Shareholder, the value of the deceased Shareholder's stock shall be determined by arbitration as follows: the surviving Shareholder shall name one arbitrator and the representative of the estate shall name one arbitrator. If the two arbitrators do not agree upon the value of the stock of the deceased Shareholder within _____ days of their appointment, they shall appoint a third arbitrator and the decision of the majority shall be binding.

For the purpose of this agreement the price at which the stock shall be sold and purchased during the life of a Shareholder shall be the same as the price established immediately above.

> This provision utilizes the fixed price method of valuation and sets forth the current value of the corporate stock. It also provides for an annual redetermination of value. The importance of performing this revaluation should be impressed upon all of the stockholders. Too often, this provision is either forgotten or ignored, and disputes over the value of the business subsequently develop. Since this is the case, a clause is included in the agreement that provides for arbitration if the parties have not revalued the business within a certain period prior to the death of a stockholder. Some attorneys may prefer to have the last value stated control in any event. While this has advantages of simplicity and certainty, it can lead to inequities if a long period of time has passed since the last valuation.

ILL 8.2 ■ *Sample Cross-Purchase Agreement (Cont.)*

The fixed price method, coupled with a revaluation provision, has many advantages. Among them are the following:

- The price that is arrived at initially, and upon subsequent reviews, as a result of head-to-head negotiations probably will be as "fair" as possible.

- Such a price provision does not involve complex formulas and is free of standards and terms that, because of possible ambiguity, could lead to controversy.

- It is a flexible method that may be adjusted periodically to reflect the changing fortunes of the business.

- The parties to the agreement are able to readily determine what price will be paid for their interest and plan their estates accordingly.

- Finally, since the purchase price is a known dollar amount, it is possible at all times to keep the buy-sell agreement "funded" with adequate amounts of life insurance.

An alternative method of valuing the business at the proprietor's death is the use of some kind of "formula" approach. Under this method, the specific price to be paid for the business is not stated in the agreement. Rather, it is agreed that the value will be determined at the time of the proprietor's death under an agreed upon, stated formula. Some of the more common formulas used are (1) the actual book value at the time of death; (2) some method of capitalization of earnings; and (3) average book value over a stated period of time. Each of these methods has strengths and weaknesses. The important thing is to have a method set out in the agreement that appeals to all parties as a fair method of establishing the purchase price.

ARTICLE 6.

Disposition of Insurance Policies on Death or Termination—The surviving Shareholder shall have an option exercisable within a period of _____ months from the date of death of the deceased Shareholder, to purchase from his (her) estate any or all of the policies owned by the deceased upon the survivor's life subject to this agreement on paying for each a price equal to the amount of (1) the cash surrender value thereof, if any, calculated on a prorated basis to the date of the transaction exclusive of any dividend, dividend accumulations, cash value of any paid-up insurance additions or policy loans, plus (2) the pro rata portion of any premium paid prior to such date which covers a period extending beyond the date of the transaction, and less (3) any policy loan plus interest then due. Any such policy not acquired by the survivor within the above option period may be surrendered to the insurance company by the deceased Shareholder's estate for its cash surrender value, or it may be held or disposed of in any lawful manner which the estate deems advisable.

In the event of the termination of this agreement from any cause other than the death of a Shareholder, each Shareholder shall have an option, exercisable within 30 days after such termination, to purchase any or all policies on his own life subject to this agreement on paying for each a price calculated on the basis prescribed in the preceding paragraph.

ILL 8.2 ▪ *Sample Cross-Purchase Agreement (Cont.)*

A provision such as this that sets a definite procedure under which the stockholders are allowed to purchase the policies on their own lives from the estate of a deceased stockholder, or in the event the agreement is terminated for some other reason should be included.

ARTICLE 7.

Endorsement of Stock Certificates—Upon the execution of this agreement, the above designated stock certificates shall be surrendered to the Company for the affixation of the following endorsement thereon, to wit:

"This certificate is transferable only upon compliance with provisions of certain Agreement dated_____, 19____by and between _____, and _____, a copy of which is on file in the office of the Secretary of the _____ Company."

Following endorsement of the certificates as above provided, such certificates shall be returned to the Shareholder. Any stock issued to a Shareholder subsequent to the date of this agreement shall carry the same endorsement.

Endorsement of the stock certificates is necessary to give any prospective purchaser of a shareholder's interest notice of the restrictions on the transfer of the stock. When an endorsement such as this is on the certificate, any transfer made in violation of the terms in the stock redemption agreement will be invalid.

ARTICLE 8.

Termination of Agreement—The agreement shall terminate on:

(a) the written agreement of the Shareholders;
(b) the dissolution, bankruptcy or insolvency of the Company;
(c) the death of both Shareholders simultaneously or within a period of____days; or
(d) the transfer of the stock of a deceased Shareholder to the surviving Shareholder, or by the sale by a Shareholder during his (her) life of all of his (her) stock to someone other than the other Shareholder as herein provided.

ARTICLE 9.

Agreement to Be Bound by Contract—The executor, administrator or personal representative of a deceased Shareholder shall execute and deliver any documents or legal instruments necessary or desirable to carry out the provisions of this agreement. The agreement shall be binding upon the Shareholders, their heirs, legal representatives, successors or assigns.

ARTICLE 10.

Amendment or Alteration—The agreement may be amended or altered in any provision and such change shall become effective when reduced to writing and signed by the Shareholders who are parties hereto.

ILL 8.2 ■ *Sample Cross-Purchase Agreement (Cont.)*

ARTICLE 11.

Liability of Insurers—Notwithstanding the provisions of this agreement, a life insurance company that has issued a policy of life insurance subject to the provisions of this agreement is hereby authorized to act in accordance with the terms of such policies as if this agreement did not exist. The payment or other performance of its contractual obligations by any such insurance company in accordance with the terms of any such policy shall completely discharge such company from all claims, suits and demands of all persons.

In Witness Whereof the parties hereto have executed this agreement by subscribing their names at_____, County of_____, State of_____, on this_____day of_____, 20_____.

_____

_____

SCHEDULE A

The undersigned mutually agree on this_____day of_____, 20___, that for the purposes of this Stock Purchase Agreement each share of the Company has a value of $_____.

_____

_____

SCHEDULE B

Schedule of life insurance policies subject to Stock-Purchase Agreement:

Name of Company	Policy Number	Face Amount	Signature of Shareholders
_____	_____	_____	_____

ILL 8.3 ■ *Sample Stock Redemption Agreement*

CAUTION: This is a specimen agreement. The actual agreement used in any particular case must be prepared by a qualified attorney.

AGREEMENT made this _____ day of _____, 20_____, by and between _____, _____ and _____ (hereinafter referred to as *Shareholders*), and the _____ Company, Incorporated (hereinafter referred to as the *Company*), created and existing under the laws of the State of _____.

WITNESSETH:

Whereas, _____, _____, and _____ are the sole Shareholders of the Company, _____ owning _____ % of the stock hereof, _____ owning _____ % and _____ owning _____ %; and

Whereas, the parties to this agreement believe that it is to their mutual best interests to provide for continuity and harmony in management and the policies of the Company; and

Whereas, the purposes of this agreement are (1) to provide for the purchase by the company of the shares of any Shareholder in the event of his (her) death, (2) to provide for the purchase of the shares of a Shareholder who during his (her) lifetime desires to dispose of any of his (her) stock, and (3) to provide the funds necessary to carry out such purchases;

Now, therefore, in consideration of the mutual agreements and covenants contained herein and for other valuable consideration, receipt of which is hereby acknowledged, it is mutually agreed and covenanted by and between the parties to this agreement as follows:

ARTICLE 1.

Disposal of Stock During Lifetime—During his (her) lifetime, no Shareholder shall transfer, encumber or dispose of any portion or all of his (her) stock interest in the Company except that if a Stockholder should desire to dispose of any of his (her) stock in the Company during his (her) lifetime, he (she) shall first offer such stock to the Company at a price determined in accordance with the provisions of Article 2. Any shares not purchased by the Company within 30 days after receipt of such offer in writing shall be offered at the same price to other Shareholders, each of whom shall have the right to purchase such portion of the remaining stock offered for sale as the number of shares owned by all the other Shareholders excluding the selling Shareholder. Provided, however, that if any Shareholder does not purchase his (her) full proportionate share of the stock, the balance of the stock may be purchased by the other Shareholders equally. If the stock is not purchased by the remaining Shareholder within 30 days of the receipt of the offer to them, the Shareholder desiring to sell may sell it to any other person but shall not sell it without giving the Company and the remaining Shareholders the right to purchase such remaining stock at the price and on the terms offered to such other person.

A provision restricting the lifetime transfer of a stockholder's interest is necessary if the buy-sell agreement is to be accepted by the government as the true fair market value for federal estate tax purposes.

ILL 8.3 ■ *Sample Stock Redemption Agreement (Cont.)*

ARTICLE 2.

Unless and until changed as hereinafter provided, the value of each share of stock of the Company held by each Shareholder shall be $_____. This price has been agreed upon by the Shareholders and the Company as representing the fair value of the interest of each Shareholder, including his (her) interest in the goodwill of the corporation. The respective Shareholders hereby mutually agree to sell the stock standing in their names and subject to this agreement at the value herein stipulated, or at the value stipulated in any proper amendment of this agreement. The Shareholders and the Company agree to redetermine the value of the Company and their respective interests therein within 60 days following the end of each fiscal year. The value so agreed upon shall be endorsed on Schedule A attached hereto and made a part of this agreement. If the Shareholders and the Company fail to make a redetermination of value for a particular year, the last previously stipulated value shall control, except that if Shareholders and the Company have not so redetermined the value within the 24 months immediately preceding the death of a Shareholder, then the value of the Shareholder's interest shall be agreed upon by the representative of the deceased Shareholder and the Company through its surviving Shareholders. If they do not agree upon a valuation within 120 days after the death of a Shareholder, the value of the deceased Shareholder's interest shall be determined by arbitration as follows: The Company through the surviving Shareholders and the representatives of the estate of the deceased Shareholder shall each name one arbitrator; if the two arbitrators cannot agree upon a value within 30 days, they shall appoint a third arbitrator and the decision of the majority shall be binding upon all parties. In any determination of value made after the death of a Shareholder, the value of the insurance proceeds in excess of the policy's cash surrender value at the time of the decedent's death must not be taken into account.

> **This provision utilizes the fixed price method of valuation and sets forth the current value of the corporate stock. It also provides for an annual redetermination of value. The importance of performing this revaluation should be impressed upon all of the stockholders. Too often, this provision is either forgotten or ignored, and disputes over the value of the stock subsequently develop. Since this is the case, a clause is included in the agreement that provides for arbitration if the parties have not revalued the business within a certain period prior to the death of a stockholder. Some attorneys may prefer to have the last value stated control in any event. While this has advantages of simplicity and certainty, it can lead to inequities if a long period of time has passed since the last valuation.**
>
> **The fixed price method, coupled with a revaluation provision, has many advantages. Among them are the following:**
>
> - **The price that is arrived at initially, and upon subsequent reviews, as a result of head-to-head negotiations probably will be as "fair" as possible.**
>
> - **Such a price provision does not involve complex formulas and is free of standards and terms that, because of possible ambiguity, could lead to controversy.**
>
> - **It is a flexible method that may be adjusted periodically to reflect the changing fortunes of the business.**
>
> - **The parties to the agreement are able to readily determine what price will be paid for their interest and plan their estates accordingly.**

ILL 8.3 ▪ *Sample Stock Redemption Agreement (Cont.)*

- Finally, since the purchase price is a known dollar amount, it is possible at all times to keep the buy-sell agreement "funded" with adequate amounts of life insurance.

An alternative method of valuing the business at the stockholder's death is the use of some kind of "formula" approach. Under this method, the specific price to be paid for the business is not stated in the agreement. Rather, it is agreed that the value will be determined at the time of the stockholder's death under an agreed upon, stated formula. Some of the more common formulas used are (1) the actual book value at the time of death; (2) some method of capitalization of earnings; and (3) average book value over a stated period of time. Each of these methods has strengths and weaknesses. The important thing is to have a method set out in the agreement that appeals to all parties as a fair method of establishing the purchase price.

ARTICLE 3.

Upon the Death of a Shareholder—Upon the death of any Shareholder, the Company shall purchase, and the estate of the decedent shall sell, all of the decedent's stock in the Company now owned or hereafter acquired. The purchase price of such stock shall be computed in accordance with the provisions of Article 2 of this Agreement.

If the purchase price exceeds the proceeds of the life insurance, the balance of the purchase price shall be paid in _____ consecutive annual payments beginning _____ months after the date of the Shareholder's death. Such unpaid balance of the purchase price shall be evidenced by a series of negotiable promissory notes executed by the Company to the order of the estate of the deceased with interest at _____% per annum. Such notes shall provide for the acceleration of the due date of all unpaid notes in the series on default in the payment of any note or interest thereon and shall provide that upon the default in the payment of interest or principal, all notes shall become due and payable immediately and shall give the Company the option of prepayment in whole or in part at any time. Provided, however, that the Legal Representative shall have the option to demand in cash an amount at least equal to _____% of the agreed purchase price. Upon failure of the surviving Shareholder to comply with such demand, then this agreement may be terminated at the option of the Legal Representative.

Here is a key provision in the agreement. Under this provision, the estate must sell, and the corporation must buy. This binding agreement to sell and the corresponding obligation to buy seems preferable to the various "option" type agreements that could be used. Too, the "option" type agreements may not effectively establish a value for estate tax purposes.

Since the purchase price and the insurance coverage may not precisely keep pace with each other at all times, it is important that provision be made for payment of any balance of the purchase price in excess of the life insurance proceeds. The exact terms of any notes to be executed should also be included in the buy-sell agreement.

In this connection, it should be noted that while ideally the full value of the business should be covered by life insurance, this is not an absolute necessity. This plan of purchase can be successful even where the life insurance provides only a substantial down payment toward the purchase price.

ILL 8.3 ▪ *Sample Stock Redemption Agreement (Cont.)*

ARTICLE 4.

The Insurance Policies—The Company, in order to help fund its obligations under this agreement, has procured and made subject hereto insurance on the lives of the Shareholders as follows:

(1) _____ is insured under life insurance policy No. _____ issued by the _____ Insurance Company in the face amount of $_____ and the Company is the applicant, owner and beneficiary thereof.

(2) _____ is insured under the insurance policy No. _____ issued by the _____ Insurance Company in the face amount of $_____ and the Company is the applicant, owner and beneficiary thereof.

(3) _____ is insured under the insurance policy No. _____ issued by the _____ Insurance Company in the face amount of $_____ and the Company is the applicant, owner and beneficiary thereof.

The Company agrees to pay premiums on the insurance policies taken out pursuant to this agreement and shall give proof of payment of premiums to the Shareholders whenever any one of them shall so request such proof. If the premium is not paid within _____ days after its due date, the insured shall have the right to pay such premium and be promptly reimbursed therefor by the Company. The Company shall have the right to purchase additional insurance on the lives of any or all of its Shareholders; such additional policies shall be listed in Schedule B, attached hereto and made a part of this agreement, along with any substitution or withdrawal of life insurance policies subject to this agreement. In the event that the Company decides to purchase additional life insurance on any Shareholder, each Shareholder hereby agrees to cooperate fully by performing all the requirements of the life insurer which are necessary conditions to the issuance of life insurance policies. The Company shall be the sole owner of the policies issued to it, and it may apply any dividends toward the payment of premiums. Upon the joint agreement of the Shareholders, other policies may be substituted for any policies made subject to this agreement or any policies subject hereto may be withdrawn. The Shareholders agree, however, that if at any time there should be no insurance subject to this agreement on the life of a particular Shareholder a party hereto, or if such insurance made subject to this agreement is impaired in value so that it would not provide at any time proceeds, at least equal to _____% of the face amount of such insurance, such Shareholder may at that time elect to declare this agreement terminated by giving written notice to that effect to the other Shareholders. Any addition, substitution or withdrawal of policies shall be endorsed on Schedule B, attached hereto and signed by the Shareholders.

> **Since this is an entity type plan, the corporation is named the owner of the life insurance policies on each shareholder's life. The corporation is also the beneficiary under the policies. The premiums paid by the corporation are, of course, a nondeductible expense.**
>
> **When the business is revalued annually, it may be found that the purchase price has increased substantially. Thus, in order to keep pace with this increase in value, this article also includes authorization for the corporation to purchase additional policies on the shareholders' lives.**

ILL 8.3 ▪ *Sample Stock Redemption Agreement (Cont.)*

ARTICLE 5.

Purchase of Nonmatured Policies by the Insured—If any Shareholder withdraws from the Company during his (her) lifetime or if this agreement terminates before the death of a Shareholder, then such Shareholder shall have the right to purchase the policy or policies on his (her) life owned by the Company by paying an amount equal to the (cash surrender value) (aggregate or net premiums paid) as of the date of transfer, less any existing indebtedness charged against the policy or policies. This right shall lapse if not exercised within _____ days after such withdrawal or termination.

> **A provision such as this that sets a definite procedure under which the stockholders are allowed to purchase the policies on their own lives from the corporation in the event the agreement is terminated for any reason during the shareholder's lifetime should be included.**

ARTICLE 6.

Endorsement of Stock Certificates—The Shareholders agree to endorse the certificates of stock held by them as follows:

"The sale or transfer of this certificate is subject to an agreement between the _____ Company, Inc., and _____, _____ and _____, its Shareholders, dated the _____ day of 20_____. A copy of this agreement is on file in the office of the Secretary of said Company."

> **Endorsement of the stock certificates is necessary in order to give any prospective purchaser of a shareholder's interest notice of the restrictions on the transfer of the stock. When an endorsement such as this is on the certificate, any transfer made in violation of the terms in the stock redemption agreement will be invalid.**

ARTICLE 7.

Execution of the Agreement—A duly authorized officer of the Company and the executor or administrator of the deceased Shareholder shall make, execute and deliver any documents necessary to carry out this agreement. This agreement shall be binding upon the Company and the Shareholders, their heirs, legal representatives, successors and assigns.

ARTICLE 8.

Amendment of Agreement—This agreement may be altered, amended or terminated by a writing signed by the Company and all Shareholders.

ARTICLE 9.

Termination of the Agreement—This agreement shall terminate on the occurrence of any of the following events:

(a) the written agreement of the Shareholders to that effect.
(b) the exercise of a Shareholder's election to terminate this agreement pursuant to Article 4, or the exercise of a similar option by the Legal Representative pursuant to Article 3.
(c) bankruptcy, receivership or dissolution of the Company.

ILL 8.3 ▪ *Sample Stock Redemption Agreement (Cont.)*

(d) death of two or more Shareholders simultaneously or within a period of 30 days.
(e) when there remains only one Shareholder a party to the agreement.

ARTICLE 10.

Liability of Insurer—No insurance company that has issued or shall issue a policy or policies subject to this agreement shall be under any obligation with respect to the performance of the terms and conditions of this agreement. Any such company shall be bound only by the terms of the policy or policies that it has issued or shall hereafter issue and shall have no liability except as set forth in its policies.

ARTICLE 11.

State Law Governing—This agreement shall be subject to and governed by the law of the State of_____, irrespective of the fact that one or more of the parties now is or may become a resident of a different state.

ARTICLE 12.

Effect of Bar Against Stock Redemption—If the Company is unable to make any purchase required of it hereunder because of the provisions of the applicable statutes or of its charter or by-laws, the company agrees to take such action as may be necessary to permit it to make such purchases, and the Shareholders who are parties to this agreement agree that they will also take such action as may be necessary for the Company to make such purchases.

In Witness Whereof the parties hereunto have executed this agreement at _____, in the County of _____, State of, _____, on this day of _____, 20____.

_____ Company, Inc.

By _____

_____
Shareholder

_____
Shareholder

_____
Shareholder

Schedule A

The undersigned mutually agree on this _____ day of _____, _____, that for purposes of this Stock Redemption Agreement, each share of the Company has a value of $_____.

_____

_____

ILL 8.3 ▪ *Sample Stock Redemption Agreement (Cont.)*

Schedule B

Schedule Of Life Policies Subject to Stock Redemption Agreement:

Name of Company	Policy Number	Face Amount	Signature of Shareholders
_____	_____	_____	_____

ILL 8.4 ▪ *Sample "Wait-and-See" Buy-Sell Agreement*

CAUTION: This is a specimen agreement. The actual agreement used in any particular case must be prepared by a qualified attorney.

AGREEMENT made this _____ day of _____, 20 _____, by and between _____, _____ and _____ (hereinafter referred to as "Shareholders"), and the _____ Company, Incorporated (hereinafter referred to as the "Company"), created and existing under the laws of the State of _____

WITNESSETH:

Whereas, _____ and _____ are the sole Shareholders of the Company; and

Whereas, the parties to this agreement believe that it is to their mutual best interests to provide for continuity and harmony in management and the policies of the Company; and

Whereas, the purposes of this agreement are (1) to provide for the purchase by the company or, in the alternative, the remaining Shareholders of the shares of any Shareholder in the event of his (her) death, (2) to provide for the purchase of the shares of a Shareholder who during his (her) lifetime desires to dispose of any of his (her) stock, and (3) to provide the funds necessary to carry out such purchases;

Now, Therefore, in consideration of the mutual agreements and covenants contained herein and for other valuable consideration, receipt of which is hereby acknowledged, it is mutually agreed and covenanted by and between the parties to this agreement as follows:

ARTICLE 1.

Disposal of Stock During Lifetime—During his (her) lifetime, no Shareholder shall transfer, encumber or dispose of any portion or all of his (her) stock interest in the Company except that if a Shareholder should desire to dispose of any of his (her) stock in the Company during his (her) lifetime, he (she) shall first offer such stock to the Company at a price determined in accordance with the provisions of Article 2. Any shares not purchased by the Company within 30 days after receipt of such offer in writing shall be offered at the same price to other Shareholders, each of whom shall have the right to purchase such portion of the remaining stock offered for sale as the number of shares owned by all the other Shareholders excluding the selling Shareholder. Provided, however, that if any Shareholder does not purchase his (her) full proportionate share of the stock, the balance of the stock may be purchased by the other Shareholders equally. If the stock is not purchased by the remaining Shareholders within 30 days of the receipt of the offer to them, the Shareholder desiring to sell may sell it to any other person but shall not sell it without giving the Company and the remaining Shareholders the right to purchase such remaining stock at the price and on the terms offered to such other person.

> **A provision restricting the lifetime transfer of a stockholder's interest is necessary if the buy-sell agreement is to be accepted by the government at the true fair market value for federal estate tax purposes.**

ILL 8.4 ▪ Sample "Wait-and-See" Buy-Sell Agreement (Cont.)

ARTICLE 2

Unless and until charged as hereinafter provided, the value of each share of stock of the Company held by each Shareholder shall be $_____. This price has been agreed upon by the Shareholders and the Company as representing the fair value of the interest of each Shareholder, including his (her) interest in the goodwill of the corporation. The respective Shareholders hereby mutually agree to sell the stock standing in their names and subject to this agreement at the value herein stipulated, or at the value stipulated in any proper amendment of this agreement. The Shareholders and the Company agree to redetermine the value of the Company and their respective interests therein within 60 days following the end of each fiscal year. The value so agreed upon shall be endorsed on Schedule A attached hereto and made a part of this agreement. If the Shareholders and the Company fail to make a redetermination of value for a particular year, the last previously stipulated value shall control, except that if Shareholders and the Company have not so redetermined the value within the 24 months immediately preceding the death of the Shareholder, then the value of the Shareholder's interest shall be agreed upon by representative of the deceased Shareholder and the Company through its surviving Shareholders. If they do not agree upon a valuation within 120 days after the death of a Shareholder, the value of the deceased Shareholder's interest shall be determined by arbitration as follows: The Company through the surviving Shareholders and the representatives of the estate of the deceased Shareholder shall each name one arbitrator; if the two arbitrators cannot agree upon the a value within 30 days, they shall appoint a third arbitrator and the decision of the majority shall be binding upon all parties. In any determination of value made after the death of a Shareholder, the value of the insurance proceeds in excess of the policy's cash surrender value at the time of the decedent's death must not be taken into account.

> **This provision utilizes the fixed price method of valuation and sets forth the current value of the corporate stock. It also provides for an annual redetermination of value. The importance of performing this revaluation should be impressed upon all of the stockholders. Too often, this provision is either forgotten or ignored, and disputes over the value of the stock subsequently develop. Since this is the case, a clause is included in the agreement that provides for arbitration if the parties have not revalued the business within a certain period prior to the death of a stockholder. Some attorneys may prefer to have the last value stated control in any event. While this has advantages of simplicity and certainty, it can lead to inequities if a long period of time has passed since the last valuation.**
>
> **The fixed price method, coupled with a revaluation provision, has many advantages. Among them are the following:**
>
> - **The price that is arrived at initially, and upon subsequent reviews, as a result of head-to-head negotiations probably will be as "fair" as possible.**
>
> - **Such a price provision does not involve complex formulas and is free of standards and terms that, because of possible ambiguity, could lend to controversy.**
>
> - **It is a flexible method that may be adjusted periodically to reflect the changing fortunes of the business.**
>
> - **The parties to the agreement are able to readily determine what price will be paid for their interest and plan their estates accordingly.**

ILL 8.4 ■ *Sample "Wait-and-See" Buy-Sell Agreement (Cont.)*

- Finally, since the purchase price is a known dollar amount, it is possible at all times to keep the buy-sell agreement "funded" with adequate amounts of life insurance.

An alternative method of valuing the business at the stockholder's death is the use of some kind of "formula" approach. Under this method, the specific price to be paid for the business is not stated in the agreement. Rather, it is agreed that the value will be determined at the time of the stockholder's death under an agreed upon, stated formula. Some of the more common formulas used are (1) the actual book value at the time of death; (2) some method of capitalization of earnings; and (3) average book value over a stated period of time. Each of these methods has strengths and weaknesses. The important thing is to have a method set out in the agreement that appeals to all parties as a fair method of establishing the purchase price.

ARTICLE 3.

Upon the Death of a Shareholder—Upon the death of a Shareholder (hereinafter referred to as Deceased Shareholder) all of the shares owned by such Shareholder at his (her) death shall be sold by the executor or administrator for the value provided in Article 2 of this agreement, under the other terms herein provided, and in the following order of purchase:

(A) The Company shall have the option to purchase, and the estate of the decedent shall sell any or all of the Deceased Shareholder's shares. The Company has _____ days after the Deceased Shareholder's death to exercise such option to purchase the shares.

(B) If the Company does not exercise its option to purchase all of the Deceased Shareholder's shares pursuant to Section (A) of this Article, then the remaining Shareholders shall have the right equally to purchase, and the estate of the decedent shall sell any shares not purchased by the Company.

(C) Any shares not purchased by the remaining Shareholders must be purchased by the Company.

If the purchase price exceeds the proceeds of the life insurance, whether owned by the Company or the Shareholders, the balance of the purchase price shall be paid in _____ consecutive annual payments beginning _____ months after the date of the Shareholder's death. Such unpaid balance of the purchase price shall be evidenced by a series of negotiable promissory notes executed by the Company or Shareholders, as appropriate, to the order of the estate of the deceased with interest at_____% per annum. Such notes shall provide for the acceleration of the due date of all unpaid notes in the series on default in the payment of any note or interest thereon and shall provide that upon the default in the payment of interest or principal, all notes shall become due and payable immediately and shall give the Company or Shareholders the option of prepayment in whole or in part at any time. Provided, however, that the Legal Representative shall have the option to demand in cash an amount at least equal to _____% of the agreed purchase price. Upon the failure of the Company or the Shareholders to comply with such demand, then this agreement may be terminated at the option of the Legal Representative.

This is the key provision to the "wait-and-see" buy-sell. This provision allows the company and the shareholders through the use of the options to select either a redemption or a cross-purchase, while still ensuring that all the stock will be eventually purchased from the decedent's estate. It also ensures that the estate will sell.

ILL 8.4 ■ *Sample "Wait-and-See" Buy-Sell Agreement (Cont.)*

The first step in which the company could redeem only a portion of the stock would not be considered a partial redemption under the logic of *Zenz v. Quinlivan,* 213 F.2d 914 (1954). In *Zenz,* the taxpayer sold her entire interest in her corporation first by a direct sale of some stock to a purchaser and then by a retirement of the rest of the stock to the corporation. The court allowed capital gains treatment for the entire transaction: "Since the intent of the taxpayer was to bring about a complete liquidation of her holdings... the conclusion is inevitable that the distribution of the earnings and profits by the corporation in payment for said stock was not made... as to make the distribution and cancellation or redemption thereof essentially equivalent to the distribution of a taxable dividend."

Since the purchase price and the insurance coverage may not precisely keep pace with each other at all times, it is important that provision be made for payment of any balance of the purchase price in excess of the life insurance proceeds. The exact terms of any notes to be executed should also be included in the buy-sell agreement.

In this connection, it should be noted that while ideally the full value of the business should be covered by life insurance, this is not an absolute necessity. This plan of purchase can be successful even where the life insurance provides only a substantial down payment toward the purchase price.

ARTICLE 4.
(Company as Owner of Policies)

The Insurance Policies—The Company, in order to help fund its obligations under this agreement, has procured and made subject hereto insurance on the lives of the Shareholders as follows:

(1) _____ is insured under life insurance policy No. _____ issued by the _____ Insurance Company in the face amount of $_____, and the Company is the applicant, owner and beneficiary thereof.

(2) _____ is insured under life insurance policy No. _____ issued by the _____ Insurance Company in the face amount of $_____, and the Company is the applicant, owner and beneficiary thereof.

(3) _____ is insured under life insurance policy No. _____ issued by the _____ Insurance Company in the face amount of $_____, and the Company is the applicant, owner and beneficiary thereof.

The Company agrees to pay premiums on the insurance policies taken out pursuant to this agreement and shall give proof of payment of premiums to the Shareholders whenever any one of them shall so request such proof. If the premium is not paid within _____ days after its due date, the insured shall have the right to pay such premium and be promptly reimbursed therefor by the Company. The Company shall have the right to purchase additional insurance on the lives of any or all of its Shareholders; such additional policies shall be listed in Schedule B, attached hereto and made a part of this agreement, along with any substitution or withdrawal of life insurance policies subject to this agreement. In the event that the Company decides to purchase additional life insurance on any Shareholder, each Shareholder hereby agrees to cooperate fully by performing all the requirements of the life insurer which are necessary.conditions to the issuance of life insurance policies.

ILL 8.4 ■ Sample "Wait-and-See" Buy-Sell Agreement (Cont.)

The Company shall be the sole owner of the policies issued to it, and it may apply any dividends toward the payment of premiums. Upon the joint agreement of the Shareholders, other policies may be substituted for any policies made subject to this agreement or any policies subject hereto may be withdrawn. The Shareholders agree, however, that if at any time there should be no insurance subject to this agreement on the life of a particular Shareholder a party hereto, or if such insurance made subject to this agreement on the life of a particular Shareholder a party hereto, or if such insurance made subject to this agreement is impaired in value so that it would not provide at any time proceeds, at least equal to _____% of the face amount of such insurance, such Shareholder may at that time elect to declare this agreement terminated by giving written notice to that effect to other Shareholders. Any addition, substitution or withdrawal of policies shall be endorsed on Schedule B, attached hereto and signed by the Shareholders.

ALTERNATIVE ARTICLE 4
(Shareholders as Owners of Policies)

The Insurance Policies—The Shareholders, in order to help fund their obligations under this agreement, have procured and made subject hereto insurance on the lives of each other.

(1)_____ is insured under life insurance policy No. _____ issued by the _____ Company in the face amount of $_____, and _____ is the applicant, owner and beneficiary thereof.

. . .

(n)_____ is insured under Life insurance policy No. _____ issued by the _____ Company in the face amount of $_____, and _____ is the applicant, owner and beneficiary thereof.

The Shareholders agree to pay premiums on the insurance policies taken out pursuant to this agreement and shall give proof of payment of premiums to any other Shareholder whenever any one of them shall so request such proof. If the premium is not paid within _____ days after its due date, the insured shall have the right to pay such premium and be promptly reimbursed therefor by the appropriate Shareholder. The Shareholders shall have the right to purchase additional insurance on the lives of any or all of the Shareholders; such additional policies shall be listed in Schedule B, attached hereto and made a part of this agreement. In the event that the Shareholders decide to purchase additional life insurance on any Shareholder, each Shareholder hereby agrees to cooperate fully by performing all the requirements of the life insurer that are necessary conditions to the issuance of life insurance policies. The Shareholders shall be the sole owner of the policies issued to them, and they may apply any dividends toward the payment of premiums. Upon the joint agreement of the Shareholders, other policies subject hereto may be withdrawn. The Shareholders agree, however, that if at any time there should be no insurance subject to this agreement on the life of a particular Shareholder a party hereto, or if any such insurance made subject to this agreement is impaired in value so that it would not provide at any time proceeds, at least equal to _____% of the face amount of such insurance, such Shareholder may at that time elect to declare this agreement terminated by giving written notice to that effect to the other Shareholders. Any addition, substitution or withdrawal of policies shall be endorsed on Schedule B, attached hereto and signed by the Shareholder.

ILL 8.4 ■ Sample "Wait-and-See" Buy-Sell Agreement (Cont.)

ARTICLE 5.

Purchase of Nonmatured Policies by the Insured—If any Shareholder withdraws from the Company during his (her) lifetime or if this agreement terminates before the death of a Shareholder, then such Shareholder shall have the right to purchase the policy or policies on his (her) life owned by the Company or the other Shareholders by paying an amount equal to the (cash surrender value) (aggregate or net premiums paid) as of the date of transfer, less any existing indebtedness charged against the policy or policies. This right shall lapse if not exercised within _____ days after such withdrawal or termination.

ARTICLE 6.

Endorsement of Stock Certificates—The shareholders agree to endorse the certificates of stock held by them as follows:

"The sale or transfer of this certificate is subject to an agreement between the _____ Company, Inc., and _____ and _____, its Shareholders, dated the _____ day of, _____. A copy of this agreement is on file in the office of the Secretary of said Company."

> **Endorsement of the stock certificate is necessary in order to give any prospective purchaser of a shareholder's notice of the restrictions on the transfer of the stock. When an endorsement such as this is on the certificate, any transfer made in violation of the terms in the stock redemption agreement will be invalid.**

ARTICLE 7.

Execution of the Agreement—A duly authorized officer of the Company, if the agreement is carried out under Article 3, Section (A) or (C), and the executor or administrator of the Deceased Shareholder shall make, execute and deliver any documents necessary to carry out this agreement. If the agreement is carried out under Article 3, Section (B), the purchasing Shareholder(s) and the executor or administrator of the Deceased Shareholder shall be binding upon the Company and the Shareholders, their heirs, legal representatives, successors and assigns.

ARTICLE 8.

Amendment of Agreement—This agreement may be altered, amended or terminated by a writing signed by the Company and all the Shareholders.

ARTICLE 9.

Termination of Agreement—This agreement shall terminate on the occurrence of any of the following events:

(a) The written agreement of the Shareholders to that effect.

(b) The exercise of a Shareholder's election to terminate this agreement pursuant to Article 4, or the exercise of a similar option by the Legal Representative pursuant to Article 3.

(c) Bankruptcy, receivership or dissolution of the Company.

(d) Death of two or more Shareholders simultaneously or within a period of 30 days.

(e) When there remains only one Shareholder a party to the agreement.

ILL 8.4 ▪ Sample "Wait-and-See" Buy-Sell Agreement (Cont.)

ARTICLE 10.

Liability of Insurer—No insurance company which has issued or shall issue a policy or policies subject to this agreement shall be under any obligation with respect to the performance of the terms and conditions of this agreement. Any such company shall be bound only by the terms of the policy or policies which it has issued or shall hereafter issue and shall have no liability except as set forth in its policies.

ARTICLE 11.

State Law Governing—This agreement shall be subject to and governed by the law of the State of _____, irrespective of the fact that one or more of the parties now is or may become a resident of a different state.

ARTICLE 12.

Effect of Bar Against Stock Redemption—If the Company is unable to make any purchase required of it hereunder because of the provisions of the applicable statutes or of its charter or by-laws, the company agrees to take such action as may be necessary to permit it to make such purchases, and the Shareholders who are parties to this agreement agree that they will also take such action as may be necessary for the Company to make such purchases.

In Witness Whereof the parties hereunto have executed this agreement at _____, in the County of _____, State of _____, on this day of _____, 20____.

_____ Company, Inc.

By _____

_____
Shareholder

_____
Shareholder

_____
Shareholder

SCHEDULE A

The undersigned mutually agree on this _____ day of _____, 20_____, that for purposes of this Buy-Sell Agreement, each share of the Company has a value of $_____.

_____

SCHEDULE B

Schedule of life insurance policies subject to Buy-Sell Agreement:

Name of Company	Policy Number	Face Amount	Signature of Shareholders
_____	_____	_____	_____

CHAPTER 8 QUESTIONS FOR REVIEW

1. Cash value life insurance is generally the product of choice to fund a corporate buy-sell agreement because

   A. it provides lifelong protection

   B. costs do not increase in later years, when death is most likely to occur

   C. it builds up a fund that can be used to purchase a shareholder's stock at retirement

   D. all of the above

2. When existing coverage is used to fund a buy-sell agreement, the transfer-for-value rule could make the proceeds taxable as income to the purchaser if the purchaser is

   A. another shareholder

   B. a corporation in which the insured is an officer or shareholder

   C. the insured

   D. all of the above

3. Under a cross-purchase agreement involving shareholders of significantly different ages, the premium burden can be disproportionate for the younger shareholder. A possible solution may be

   A. for the corporation to pay the cost of the premiums, then charge them to the salary accounts of the owners

   B. for all shareholders to contribute to a pool on the basis of their stock interest in the business

   C. for all shareholders to contribute a proportionate share to a pool on the basis of the number of shareholders

   D. all of the above

4. Under the "wait-and-see" buy-sell agreement

   A. other shareholders may buy a deceased owner's shares if they wish

   B. the corporation has the option to purchase any amount of the deceased's shares within a specified period of time

   C. the corporation is obligated to purchase any shares not purchased by other stockholders

   D. all of the above

5. Under a cross-purchase agreement, which of the following beneficiary designations would result in taxable dividends to the shareholders?

   A. Shareholders themselves

   B. Trust

   C. Corporation

   D. Spouses of the shareholders

9

Section 303 Redemptions

This chapter covers the use of life insurance to fund a Section 303 redemption of corporate stock, including an examination of tax consequences and limitations. Section 303 redemptions involve partial redemptions of stock designed to fulfill the liquidity needs of surviving family members. Having covered the use of life insurance to fund complete stock redemptions through buy-sell agreements in a close corporation, we now turn to another use of life insurance for funding a more limited kind of redemption. This chapter will describe a Section 303 redemption, its tax consequences, its uses and its limitations.

INTRODUCTION TO SECTION 303

The two biggest problems estates of corporate business owners face are immediate liquidity and taxes. Section 303 of the Internal Revenue Code helps solve that problem. It enables the corporation to purchase, or redeem, *part* of a deceased stockholder's shares in the business under favorable tax conditions. Specifically, a corporation can make a partial redemption of stock equal to the funeral bill, administration costs, and estate, inheritance, legacy and succession taxes (including interest) imposed because of the deceased shareholder's death, without subjecting the estate or other person selling the stock to ordinary income tax on the distribution from the corporation.

Instead, the redemption is treated as a capital transaction. Any profit from the redemption is taxable as a capital gain at a maximum tax rate of 20 percent. Because basis in the stock being redeemed is stepped-up to the stock value at the date of death or alternate valuation date, however, there is little likelihood of gain that must be recognized for income tax purposes. If, on the other hand, the distribution from the corporation were determined to be a dividend, no basis could be taken into consideration. As a result, the entire amount distributed by the corporation, rather than the gain over basis, would be taxable.

In other words, there is little or no gain to tax because the stock takes a stepped-up basis to its fair market value at death (or alternate valuation date). This contrasts favorably with a lifetime sale of the stock, in which the seller's basis generally is limited to his or her cost. It contrasts even more favorably with the tax treatment of dividends, in which the shareholder's basis generally is ignored (i.e., the entire distribution from the corporation is taxed as ordinary income).

The purpose of the law was to provide liquidity for the otherwise "locked in" shareholder and thus perpetuate the family corporation. The Section 303 redemption's main advantage is that the shareholder's general estate need not be stripped of cash or liquid assets before this redemption can be employed. Instead, the corporation can distribute the cash needed for taxes and expenses, leaving the shareholder's savings and personally owned life insurance available for other purposes. Without a Section 303 redemption, a partial stock redemption would be treated as a dividend, rather than a capital transaction.

A Section 303 redemption can be used even if the estate has sufficient liquidity, the redemption proceeds are not used to pay death taxes and costs, and(or) the corporation distributes an illiquid asset in exchange for the stock.

QUALIFIED STOCK FOR REDEMPTION

The stock to be redeemed by the corporation must have been includable in the deceased shareholder's gross estate and, generally, must have been owned directly by him or her. Stock transferred to a revocable trust, subject to a general power of appointment, or which the decedent gave away, retaining the right to receive dividends, could also qualify under Section 303.

If stock held jointly is acquired by right of survivorship, and only part of the value of such stock is included in the decedent's gross estate, only this portion of the stock is eligible for Section 303. The portion attributed to the surviving co-owner is not.

The Percentage Test

The amount of stock in the estate must meet certain percentage requirements to qualify. The value of all the stock of the corporation included in the decedent's gross estate must be more than 35 percent of the adjusted gross estate, that is, after *allowable* deductions for funeral and administration expenses, debts, casualty losses and thefts. This 35 percent test is applied before the marital share is taken off. For example, assume a decedent had a $1,000,000 estate with $80,000 worth of costs and $300,000 of closely held stock:

Gross Estate	$1,000,000
Costs	− 80,000
Adjusted Gross Estate	920,000
Marital Deduction	(not relevant)
Remaining Deductions	(not relevant)
Taxable Estate	(not relevant)
	× .35
	$ 322,000

This estate would not be eligible for Section 303, because the $300,000 of stock is less than $322,000, which is 35 percent of the adjusted gross estate.

There is no requirement that redemption proceeds actually be used to pay death taxes and costs. Similarly, the estate or heir could redeem *less* than the maximum that would qualify under Section 303, if desired. If the shareholder redeems *more* than the amount eligible for Section 303 treatment, the excess generally will be treated as dividend income.

The stock of two or more corporations can be combined for purposes of meeting the 35 percent test, if 20 percent or more of the value of all the outstanding stock of each corporation is includable in the decedent's gross estate.

There are few limits on the identity of the redeeming shareholder. In the vast majority of cases, the redeeming shareholder is the executor of the estate, who needs the cash proceeds from the redemption to secure liquidity for estate settlement. However, the regulations make it clear that anybody "who acquired the stock . . . [from the decedent], including the heir, legatee, or donee of the decedent, a surviving joint tenant, surviving spouse, appointee, or taker in default of appointment, or a trustee of a trust created by the decedent" can take advantage of Section 303.

Time for Redemption

The redemption of stock under Section 303 must be made within three years and 90 days after the federal estate tax return is filed. If a timely petition for redetermination of the estate tax is filed with the Tax Court, then the time limit can be extended to 60 days after that court's decision becomes final. When the estate is eligible for and elects the deferred estate tax payment option under Section 6166, the law allows a deferral period of five years for the first installment and permits a subsequent period of up to 10 years of equal annual payments for the remainder of the tax.

TAX CONSEQUENCES

If all requirements and limitations are met, the seller of the shares will not be subject to ordinary income tax on the distribution from the corporation. Instead the seller will receive capital gains, if there are any, on the sale. For the purposes of figuring gain, the executor's or the estate's basis is the fair market value at the date of death or at the alternate valuation date. Thus, the seller will realize gain only if the redemption price exceeds this basis, which will happen only if the stock has appreciated in value since the time of death (or the alternate valuation date).

Section 304 (Redemptions through Related Corporations)

A Section 303 redemption may be available in certain cases for which, superficially, it would not appear to be. This is due to the special rules created by Section 304, which apply to the "redemption through a related corporation." Specifically, if an estate controls two corporations and it sells the stock of one corporation to the other, the sale will be treated as a redemption of the stock of the corporation that bought the stock. The stock received by the corporation acquiring the stock will be treated as a contribution to the capital of the acquiring corporation. Then Section 303 is applied to determine whether the transaction is treated as a sale or a dividend. This is the so-called brother-sister corporation case, in which the two corporations are under common control (i.e., by the executor of a deceased shareholder's estate). Code Section 304 also applies to the "parent-subsidiary" situation, where one corporation (the subsidiary) acquires from a shareholder of another corporation (the parent) stock in the other corporation, and the acquiring corporation is controlled by this latter corporation. In this case, the transaction is treated as if the parent corporation redeemed its own stock.

"Control," for Section 304 purposes, means ownership of stock possessing at least 50 percent of the total combined voting power of all stock entitled to vote, *or* at least 50 percent of the total value of all classes of stock.

Brother-Sister Corporations

A revenue ruling illustrates how the Sections 303/304 opportunity is available in brother-sister corporation situations. The executor owned 40 percent of the stock of X Corporation and 50 percent of the stock of Y Corporation. The deceased shareholder's children owned the balance of the stock in both corporations. The Y stock met the percentage test for Section 303 eligibility, but the X stock did not. So, instead of redeeming the X stock directly and recognizing dividend income, the X stock was sold to Y Corporation. Because of the attribution rules, the estate was deemed to own all of the stock of both X and Y, and was therefore in control of both. Further, Y's purchase of the X stock was considered a redemption through a related corporation (i.e., treated as if Y redeemed its own stock) and, as such, qualified for capital gains treatment.

The following case study demonstrates some of the Sections 303/304 planning possibilities in a brother-sister, common control situation.

■ CASE STUDY: ACME MFG., INC. AND ZEPHYR DISTRIBUTORS, INC.

Suppose there are two corporations, which we'll call Acme Mfg., Inc. and Zephyr Distributors, Inc. Acme has a total value of $6,666,666, and the estate of our deceased shareholder owns 18 percent, or $1,200,000, of the Acme stock. Zephyr has a total value of $800,000, and the estate of our deceased shareholder owns 80 percent, or $640,000, of the Zephyr stock. Based on these facts, the estate tax picture looks as follows:

Acme stock	$1,200,000
Zephyr stock	640,000
Other assets	300,000
Gross estate	2,140,000
Less: expenses*	140,000
Adjusted gross estate	$2,000,000

*Assume that the decedent had no debts or losses, and that all expenses are funeral and administration expenses.

The Acme stock qualifies for Section 303, because $1,200,000 is more than 35 percent of $2,000,000. However, the Zephyr stock does not qualify for Section 303 because $640,000 is less than 35 percent of $2,000,000. Also, note that Acme and Zephyr cannot be combined in order to satisfy the 35 percent test because the estate does not own 20 percent or more of *both* corporations; it only owns 20 percent or more of Zephyr.

Let's continue with the example:

Adjusted gross estate	$2,000,000
Less: marital deduction*	1,000,000
Taxable estate	1,000,000
Tentative estate tax	345,800
Less: unified credit 2000	220,550
Federal estate tax due**	125,250
Plus: expenses	140,000
Maximum §303 amount	$265,250

*Assume that the decedent's estate plan calls for use of the split estate concept rather than use of the unlimited martial deduction.

**Assume that the decedent died in Florida, which levies only a credit estate tax. Thus, the state death tax will equal exactly the maximum federal credit allowed therefor, and we can use the $125,250 figure for the combined federal and state death taxes.

It is reasonable to ask why the executor wouldn't just redeem $265,250 worth of Acme stock under Section 303. While that could certainly be done, it would dilute the estate's ownership percentage substantially in Acme from 18 percent to about 14 percent. [($1,200,000 - $265,250) / $6,666,666 = .14)]

Using Section 304, Acme can purchase the stock of Zephyr rather than redeem its own stock, and the transaction will be treated as if Acme redeemed it s own stock. The transaction could be diagrammed as follows:

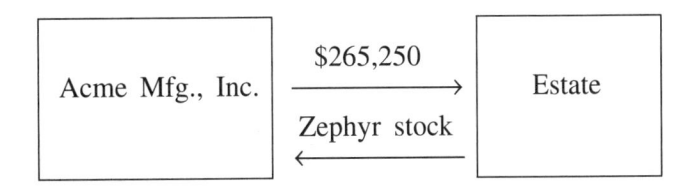

```
┌─────────────────┐    $265,250      ┌──────────┐
│                 │ ───────────────> │          │
│ Acme Mfg., Inc. │                  │  Estate  │
│                 │   Zephyr stock   │          │
│                 │ <─────────────── │          │
└─────────────────┘                  └──────────┘
```

The result, from the perspective of corporate control, is that the estate continues to own 18 percent of Acme, and the estate's direct control over Zephyr is reduced to about 47 percent [($640,000 - $265,250)/$800,000 = .47]. However, the estate continues to control somewhat more of Zephyr through the estate's stake in Acme, which now owns a portion of Zephyr.

Note that the policy used to fund the redemption will not be affected by use of the Section 304 technique. Acme would be the owner, beneficiary and premium payer of a policy on the life of the shareholder. At his or her death, Acme could use the proceeds to redeem its own stock from the estate or to buy the Zephyr stock in the transaction just described.

Parent-Subsidiary Corporations

Consider a parent-subsidiary situation in which the stock of the parent would qualify for Section 303 in a deceased shareholder's estate. The parties have several options: (1) the parent could redeem its stock from the estate in a conventional Section 303 transaction; (2) the parent could purchase stock of the subsidiary from the estate under the Section 303 shelter; or (3) the subsidiary could purchase stock of the parent and qualify for Section 303 pursuant to Section 304(a)(2).

Further, the Tax Court has concluded that the Sections 303/304 redemption that occurs when a subsidiary buys stock of its parent corporation from a stockholder of the latter is not treated as a taxable cash dividend from the subsidiary to the parent followed by the parent's redemption of its own stock with such cash.

CASE STUDY: FOUR CORPORATIONS

Let's examine a case study of four corporations, Apple, Orange, Pear and Pineapple. Each corporation is owned equally by the same six shareholders, as follows:

Corporation	Total Value	Value of Each Shareholder's Interest
Apple, Inc.	$ 900,000	$150,000
Orange, Inc.	1,500,000	250,000
Pear, Inc.	3,000,000	500,000
Pineapple, Inc.	1,200,000	200,000

None of the shareholders can satisfy the 35-percent-of-the-adjusted-gross-estate test with respect to any of the stock, nor the 20 percent test for two or more corporations. On the surface, then, it appears that the Section 303 opportunity is not available.

But, let's assume that three of the shareholders form a personal holding company, Cornucopia, which thereby has 50 percent control of Apple, Orange, Pear and Pineapple. With respect to each of the three shareholders, their Cornucopia stock could satisfy the 35 percent test. Here's the estate situation of one of the shareholders:

Cornucopia stock	$1,100,000*
Other assets	1,000,000
Gross estate	2,100,000
Less: expenses**	100,000
Adjusted gross estate	2,000,000
	× .35
	$ 700,000

*The value of the Cornucopia stock consists of the combined values of the shareholder's interests in the other four corporations ($150,000 + $250,000 + $500,000 + $200,000 = $1,100,000).

**Assume that the decedent has no debts or losses and that all expenses are funeral and administration expenses.

Because $1,100,000 exceeds 35 percent of the adjusted gross estate, Section 303 is now available. Unfortunately, Cornucopia owns nothing but stock and has no cash with which to fund a Section 303 redemption. The subsidiaries—one or more of which may be cash-rich, perhaps due to insurance proceeds pouring into the corporation at the shareholder's death—come to the rescue. For example, Orange, Inc. could buy Cornucopia stock from the estate, and secure Section 303 treatment through the operation of the Section 304 parent-subsidiary rules. In effect, Section 304 says that this purchase is treated as a redemption by Cornucopia of its own stock and, as a result, the Cornucopia stock qualifies for Section 303. Incidentally, there is nothing magic about Orange, Inc.; any or all of the other corporations could be used to accomplish the Section 303 redemption.

Section 303 and Generation-Skipping Transfers

Section 303 is available with respect to stock subject to the generation-skipping transfer tax, where the generation-skipping transfer occurs at or after the death of the deemed transferor. In such a case, the trust involved in the generation-skipping transfer and the deemed transferor's estate will be treated separately for purposes of Section 303 qualification. Thus, stock in the trust will qualify under Section 303 if it comprises more than 35 percent of the amount of the generation-skipping transfer, but of course only to the extent of the generation-skipping transfer tax. The time limitation for the redemption is to be measured from the date of the generation-skipping transfer rather than the date of death, if the dates are different. The three-year, 90-day rule apparently applies, because the deferred payment election is not available for the generation-skipping transfer tax.

■ LIFE INSURANCE TO ASSURE A SECTION 303 REDEMPTION

Life insurance owned by the corporation on the lives of the shareholders solves a number of the problems that face a corporation contemplating the use of a Section 303 redemption at the death of a shareholder:

1. Life insurance provides cash for a quick redemption. The parties can be assured that the redemption will be completed within the statutory period—generally three years and 90 days after the estate tax return is filed.

2. Furthermore, there is no need to deplete the corporation's cash account or mortgage its assets, if the insurance purchased is sufficient.

3. The reasonableness of the annual retained earnings will continue to be a problem in many closely held corporations. When life insurance is purchased, however, there would be a smaller amount of earnings accumulated, as represented by the annual premiums paid, than there would be if the entire amount necessary for a Section 303 redemption had been accumulated.

4. The life insurance proceeds increase the shareholder's equity to the extent that they exceed the cash value as carried on the corporation's balance sheet. The equity increase, in turn, increases the value of the deceased's shares and makes it easier for the estate to meet the 35 percent requirement.

5. The increase in the shareholder's equity caused by the payment of the insurance proceeds also might make possible a redemption that was legally barred under state law because of an impairment of capital. Many states only authorize stock redemptions created from earned surplus (retained earnings), which do not result in an impairment of capital.

6. While the corporation cannot deduct the premiums it pays, it receives the death proceeds income tax free. Even if the corporation has purchased an existing policy to fund the redemption, the purchase will fall under an exception to the transfer-for-value rule and the proceeds will remain income tax exempt.

SECTION 303 REDEMPTION AGREEMENTS

A formal agreement between the corporation and the shareholder requiring the corporation to redeem sufficient shares at the shareholder's death for Section 303 purposes normally is not necessary when the shareholder owns a majority of the shares. When a majority shareholder dies, the executor or heirs succeed to a position of control and therefore are in a position to see that the redemption is carried out.

An agreement, though, would seem advisable. For instance, it guarantees that the shareholder's estate will be able to dispose of an otherwise illiquid asset, and it assures the surviving stockholders that outside, inactive interests will not come into the business at the death of an owner. If a minority shareholder's stock is to be redeemed under Section 303, an agreement lends certainty to the arrangement. In addition, if antagonism exists between the majority and minority interests, a preexisting agreement to redeem a majority shareholder's stock would allay criticism by the surviving minority interests.

Examples of predeath and postdeath resolutions and agreements to carry out Section 303 redemptions appear near the end of this unit.

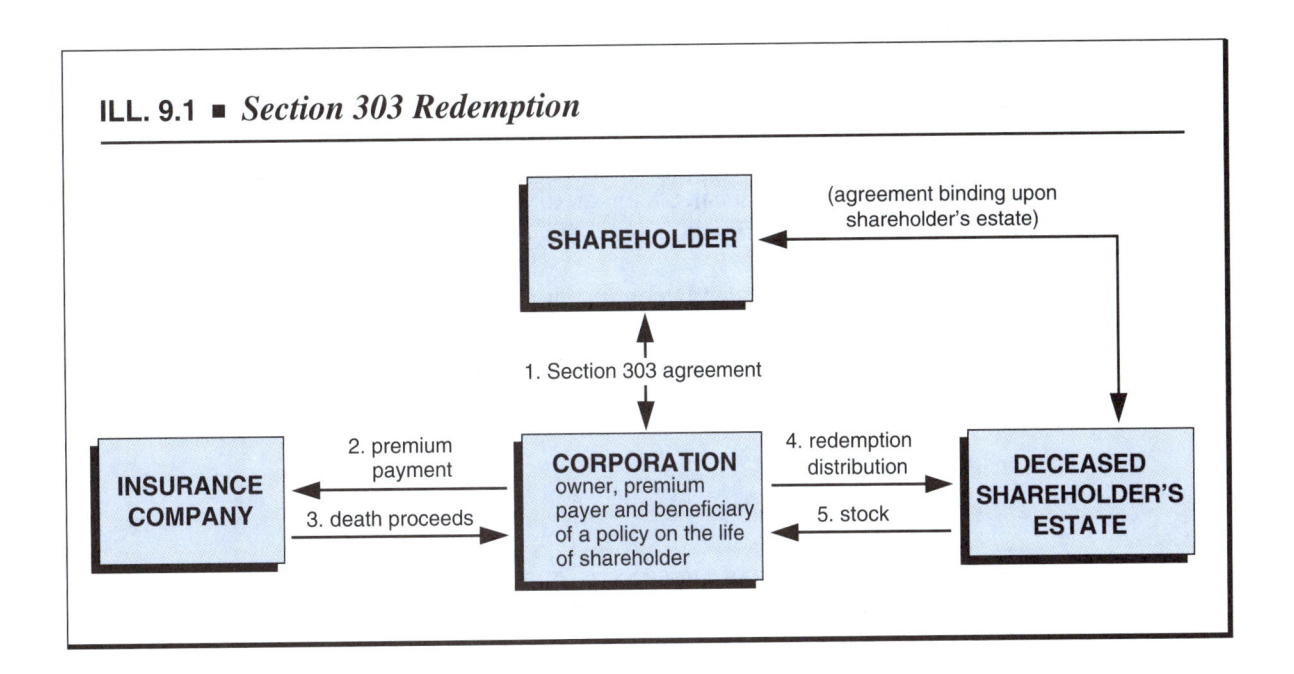

ILL. 9.1 ■ *Section 303 Redemption*

[Diagram showing the flow of a Section 303 Redemption transaction between Shareholder, Corporation, Insurance Company, and Deceased Shareholder's Estate:
- 1. Section 303 agreement (between Shareholder and Corporation)
- Agreement binding upon shareholder's estate
- 2. premium payment (Corporation to Insurance Company)
- 3. death proceeds (Insurance Company to Corporation)
- 4. redemption distribution (Corporation to Deceased Shareholder's Estate)
- 5. stock (Deceased Shareholder's Estate to Corporation)
- Corporation is owner, premium payer and beneficiary of a policy on the life of shareholder]

■ A SUGGESTED SECTION 303 SALES APPROACH

To communicate the benefits of Section 303 to prospects, you should first have a clear understanding of the mechanics of the plan. The graphic illustration on the following page simplifies the Section 303 transaction and can also be used to explain Section 303 to a prospect.

Six Steps

There are six steps to the Section 303 transaction:

1. The shareholder and the corporation enter into a Section 303 agreement obligating the corporation to buy, and the shareholder's estate to sell, the stock.

2. The corporation applies for, owns and names itself beneficiary of a policy on the life of the shareholder.

3. The corporation pays the premiums.

4. At the shareholder's death, the insurance proceeds are paid to the corporation.

5. The executor of the deceased shareholder's estate submits the stock to the corporation for redemption.

6. The corporation distributes cash from the insurance proceeds to the executor in exchange for the stock.

Prospecting

There is no shortage of prospects for insurance-funded Section 303 redemptions. Many small and medium-sized corporations will have shareholders whose estates are eligible. Some good sources of referred leads for Section 303 prospects are bankers, the local Chamber of Commerce, attorneys, accountants, business friends and acquaintances, and business clients.

You may wish to consider becoming an "industry specialist." An agent who has sold and installed a Section 303 plan at ABC Baking Co. already has a foot in the door at XYZ Baking Co. The effect is cumulative. The more successes the agent has in the local baking industry, the more his or her success builds on itself.

Approaching the Prospect

To find out whether your prospect is eligible for Section 303, you will have to gather some facts from him or her directly.

A way to begin, once you have a name, is with a preapproach letter. This will prepare the prospect for your telephone call to set up an appointment:

> Dear Mr./Ms. Prospect:
>
> As a corporate business owner, you are keenly aware of the impact of tax law on your personal and business planning. Indeed, taxes are what motivate many persons to incorporate their businesses in the first place.
>
> Fortunately, some tax laws are beneficial to corporate shareholders. One such law is Section 303 of the Internal Revenue Code, which may give you a one-time chance to get money out of the corporation *income tax free* for the benefit of your survivors.
>
> I can help you determine whether you are eligible and how this opportunity applies specifically in your case. With this in mind, I'll call you in a few days to arrange an appointment.
>
> Sincerely,

We suggest that you mail a suitable preapproach brochure with the above letter—one that explains the problems that death taxes and costs can cause for the estate and heirs of a small business owner.

The telephone conversation a few days later might go like this:

> "Mr./Ms. Prospect, this is Andrew, Insurance Agent from Mutual of El Paso. A few days ago, I sent you a letter and brochure calling to your attention a special opportunity that exists for corporate business owners. I would like to meet with you to explain this in more detail, answer any questions that you have about it, and determine how it applies in your case. Which day next week would be best for you? *(Wait for response.)* Morning or afternoon?"

ILL 9.2 ■ *Proposal for a Section 303 Stock Redemption*

PROPOSAL FOR A Section 303 STOCK REDEMPTION
for

Shareholder: _____

Corporation: _____

**Presented by
Andrew Underwriter, CLU**

Date: _____

Conducting the Interview

The purpose of the interview is to gather the facts necessary to determine eligibility and to develop a proposal. The facts needed are listed below and may be entered on the fact-finding form that appears later in this chapter:

- name, birth date and sex of each stockholder;
- fair market value of the *total* corporate stock;
- percentage ownership interests of each of the shareholders;
- gross estate of each shareholder for federal estate tax purposes;
- debts of each shareholder; and
- manner in which the stock is owned.

From this information, it will be possible to estimate funeral and administration expenses, and the federal and state death taxes.

In a community property state, the last item above is especially important. You must determine whether the stock is community or separate property.

It is also a good idea to get a copy of the corporate financial statements in order to spot possible accumulated earnings tax problems, problems with state capital impairment laws and also possible sources of premium dollars.

> **ILL 9.3** ■ *Section 303 Fact Finder Worksheet*
>
> 1. Name of Corporation: _____
> 2. Name of Shareholder: _____
> 3. Birth Date: _____
> 4. Sex: _____
> 5. Total Value of Corporation: _____
> 6. Percentage Ownership: _____
>   (*Note:* If community property, enter only the shareholder's one-half.)
> 7. Value of Shareholder's Interest: Line 5 times Line 6) _____
> 8. Gross Estate: _____
> 9. Debts: _____
> 10. Funeral & Administration Expenses (estimate): _____
> 11. Adjusted Gross Estate: (Line 8 minus sum of Lines 9 and 10) _____
> 12. 35 percent of Line 11: _____
> 13. Does Line 7 exceed Line 12? If "no," stop here; the shareholder does not qualify for Section 303. If "yes," proceed to Line 14: <u>yes or no</u>
> 14. Federal Estate Taxes: _____
> 15. State Death Taxes: _____
> 16. Sum of Lines 10, 14 and 15. This is the maximum amount of stock that may be redeemed under Section 303: _____

Developing the Proposal

The three-page form reproduced below is a combination fact-finding form, worksheet and sales proposal. It enables you (1) to determine if your prospect is eligible for Section 303; if so, (2) to determine the maximum amount of stock that can qualify under Section 303; and (3) to record the relevant policy information for your prospect. Further, you can accomplish all these tasks during the initial interview, provided you have the means at hand to compute the federal and state death taxes. This form assumes that you are taking a single needs approach in the interview. If you are taking a total or multiple-needs approach, you may wish to use your company's fact-finding form. Any proposal, of course, that illustrates an equity-based product must conform to compliance procedures of the company issuing the product.

Working with Attorneys and Accountants

In Section 303 sales, as in other advanced sales situations, the agent often will be dealing with the client's attorney and(or) accountant. The first step in good attorney-agent or accountant-agent relations lies in their judging the professional competence of one another.

While it may not be fair, the "burden of proof" in professional relationships is on the agent.

Below is a catalog of specific ways in which an agent can establish a professional relationship with attorneys and accountants:

ILL 9.4 ▪ *Life Insurance*

Insured: _____ (shareholder's name) _____

Face Amount: _____ (no less than line 16 on worksheet) _____

Owner: _____ (usually the corporation) _____

Beneficiary: _____ (usually the corporation) _____

Annual Premium: _____

Premium Payer: _____ (usually the corporation) _____

Policy Year	Annual Premium	Annual Cash Value Increase	Annual Expense	Aggregate Premiums	Aggregate Cash Value
1					
2					
3					
4					
5					
10					
20					
30					
Age 65					

1. Recognize the nature of the attorney-client or accountant-client relationship. Attorneys and accountants are subject to strict ethical standards in their dealings with clients.

2. Bring the other appropriate advisers into the planning process as early as possible. This avoids any appearance of usurping their prerogatives and presenting them with an after-the-fact situation.

3. Defer to the attorney or accountant on questions that require legal or financial expertise.

4. Make insurance recommendations that can withstand the tough scrutiny of the other advisers.

5. Provide prompt responses to requests for explanations or more information.

6. *Do not give legal advice or prepare legal documents.* Not only will you alienate the attorney but in many states you would be committing a felony.

7. Join the local estate planning council. This will acquaint you with the attorneys who practice estate planning in your area. Further, it indicates to others your open commitment to professional excellence.

8. Learn the language of law and accounting. An agent must be able to communicate with the other advisers in their own terms.

9. Don't be overly technical in describing insurance products. The actuarial aspects of life insurance are as complex as law or accounting, and an agent cannot expect attorneys and accountants to understand sophisticated insurance concepts unless they are explained in lay terms.

Reviewing the Plan Periodically

The cornerstone of any well-designed Section 303 plan is periodic review. The plan should be reviewed at least every two or three years to ensure that the shareholder's estate still qualifies for Section 303, and that the amounts of insurance are adequate. Often, as the shareholder's assets increase in value, additional purchases of insurance to fund the Section 303 agreement will be necessary.

Looking for Other Sales Opportunities

Your Section 303 activity will turn up many opportunities for related business insurance sales. An alert agent working on a Section 303 plan may discover needs for pension plans or disability income coverage, group life and health insurance, key executive insurance, split-dollar coverage, deferred compensation and, of course, personal insurance.

■ CASE STUDY: MR. BROWN AND ABC ELECTRONICS CORPORATION

Mr. Brown, educated as an electrical engineer, is age 52 and the major shareholder and founder of a successful electrical component manufacturing firm. He began his professional career with one of the nation's largest electronics firms and, after a successful 15 years there, left that firm to found his own business.

The corporation has been a success. In six years the business has expanded to a point at which its asset value is $832,000.

Mr. Brown recently was approached by his life insurance agent, who said that his estate may have a liquidity problem. Previous conversations had revealed that Mr. Brown saw no reason why his family should sell his interest in the corporation at his death—especially now that his eldest son was proving his worth in the business.

In further discussions, the need for additional estate liquidity loomed even larger than it was thought to be in the beginning. The agent indicated that a Section 303 stock redemption might be the answer. Mr. Brown agreed that the following factors would have to be considered:

1. He does not want to invade his present life insurance to provide estate liquidity, because it is needed for basic family income.

2. Most of his personal estate holdings (other than the close corporation stock) are nonliquid, and he prefers that they not be disturbed because of the potential for appreciation.

Mr. Brown and his agent then reviewed the facts given below. The company's balance sheet looked like this:

ABC ELECTRONICS CORPORATION
Balance Sheet December 31, 20 ___

Assets

Cash	$ 22,000
Accounts receivable	285,000
Inventory	235,000
Fixed assets	290,000
Total	$832,000

Liabilities and Stockholders' Equity

Accounts payable	$190,000
Notes payable	285,000
Other accrued liabilities	107,000
Capital stock	235,000
Retained earnings	15,000
	$832,000

Assuming no change in the balance sheet figures as shown, and based on these figures alone, the total funds available for a Section 303 redemption by the corporation would be only the $15,000 of retained earnings. Even though the corporation has $22,000 of cash, state impairment-of-capital laws prevent the use of corporate assets in excess of the amount of retained earnings for a stock purchase by the corporation. More cash would then be required to fund a redemption, as we will see.

Mr. Brown's estimated gross estate amounts to $1,500,000 and, in addition to his business interest, includes mostly real estate. He has personal debts of $70,000 and stock of the corporation presently worth $480,000. (Although the book value of the stock is $250,000—it is shown on the balance sheet as capital stock of $235,000 and retained earnings of $15,000—its current market value is significantly higher.) Estate administration and funeral expenses are estimated to total $60,000. The adjusted gross estate would be $1,370,000 ($1,500,000 − $130,000). His estate would meet the percentage requirement of Section 303, because his business interest is valued at more than 35 percent of his adjusted gross estate.

When the above figures were charted and explained by his life insurance agent, Mr. Brown soon grasped the potential liquidity problem. The maximum allowable stock redemption amount under Section 303 would be $90,000—$60,000 of estimated estate administration and funeral expenses and $30,000 of estimated state death taxes. (The federal estate tax would not be a factor in this case because Mr. Brown's estate is sheltered fully by the deductions for expenses and debts, the marital deduction and the unified credit.) The agent pointed out that the retained earnings of $15,000 could be used for partial funding of the proposed stock redemption.

However, an economical solution to the problem would be for the corporation to purchase at least $90,000 of life insurance (or preferably more to allow for probable increases in estate costs) on the life of Mr. Brown. The premiums would be paid by the corporation and would not be deductible as a business expense. However, the policy proceeds would be payable to the corporation at Mr. Brown's death on an income tax–free basis. Mr. Brown accepted the solution and the sale of a $100,000 policy to fund the stock redemption was finalized.

DISTRIBUTION OF PROPERTY OTHER THAN CASH

The redeeming shareholder does not actually have to receive a liquid asset in exchange for the stock in order to get the Section 303 tax benefits. The stock can be acquired by the corporation in exchange for property or even a promissory note. In either case, the estate's (or heir's) basis in the property will be the fair market value of the stock redeemed.

From the Corporation's Standpoint

The corporation has to be careful not to put itself in a situation in which it realizes a taxable gain from the redemption. If cash is used to carry out the redemption, there is no recognition-of-gain problem. However, taxable gain can occur if appreciated property is used.

Even a corporation that has insurance proceeds or other cash with which to carry out the redemption may wish to distribute noncash property and use the cash for other purposes. But when a corporation distributes appreciated property in kind in exchange for its stock, it would normally recognize gain on the transaction. However, there is a special rule in the law that eliminates this gain to the extent that Section 303 applies to the redemption. When a redemption distribution includes both cash and appreciated property, and exceeds the Section 303 ceiling, the appreciated property is deemed to have been distributed first to minimize or eliminate the corporation's gain on the transaction.

A corporation also will recognize gain if it distributes to a shareholder (1) property subject to a debt that exceeds its basis, or (2) LIFO inventory. There is no exception for Section 303 redemptions here.

If there is a formal, written agreement to implement the Section 303 redemption, it should contain a statement from the deceased shareholder's personal representative (or heir) that the redemption satisfies the Section 303 requirements, so the corporation can be assured that it will not recognize gain on a distribution of appreciated property.

Recapture of depreciation deductions could be involved if the corporation distributes depreciable personal property or depreciable real property that has been depreciated under accelerated methods. In addition, there could be recapture of the investment credit if taken by the corporation for tangible personal property distributed in the redemption. The recapture rules will apply even if the redemption qualifies under Section 303.

If recapture is not a major problem, the corporation could distribute fully depreciated real estate (e.g., the building in which the corporation conducts business). The recipient would take the fair market value of the stock as his or her basis for renewed depreciation deductions. The real estate then could be leased back to the corporation. This could be used as an "inheritance equalization" technique in the family setting. For example, Dad wants Child #1 to take over the business, yet still wants to provide for Child #2 in some way. Dad could leave stock to Child #2, who would exchange it for corporate-owned real estate under Section 303. Child #2 gets an income stream from the lease payments, and Child #1 gets control of the corporation.

■ SUMMARY

When a corporate distribution is considered to be a dividend it is subject to taxation at both the corporate level and the individual level. As a result, close corporations generally avoid paying dividends on their stock, preferring to characterize payments made to their shareholder-employees as compensation.

A partial redemption of stock owned by a stockholder may be consider by the IRS to be a dividend. Internal Revenue Code Section 303, however, provides that the partial redemption of stock of a deceased shareholder in an amount equal to certain final expenses will be treated as a capital transaction rather than as a dividend distribution, provided certain requirements are met. As a result of this IRC provision these partial stock redemptions, often referred to simply as 303 redemptions, are subject to income tax only to the extent that the price received for the stock exceeds its cost basis. Since the cost basis in the redeemed stock is stepped-up to the fair market value on the shareholder's date of death or alternate valuation date, it is possible that the transaction will result in no income tax liability. So, being able to dispose of stock by way of a 303 redemption can be an extremely valuable right for the family owning a corporation.

This chapter discussed the timing and requirements for the use of the 303 redemption, including that the stock must have been owned directly by the deceased shareholder and that it must constitute more than 35 percent of his or her adjusted gross estate. The use of corporate-owned life insurance on the life of the shareholders to fund the stock redemption was then examined. Corporate-owned life insurance used to fund the 303 redemption assures the availability of cash when required, and its proceeds are received income tax free.

The steps involved in the Section 303 transaction were addressed, and a suggested approach to prospects for life insurance to fund the redemption was offered. Guidelines for the agent's working with the prospect's advisors were given. A discussion of the problems and opportunities in the corporation's distribution of noncash property in exchange for the redeemed stock concluded the chapter.

> **ILL 9.5** ■ *Pre-Death Minutes and Resolution of Board of Directors*
>
> **CAUTION: This is a specimen resolution. The actual resolution used in any particular case must be prepared by a qualified attorney.**
>
> The President reported that John Doe, a shareholder of the Corporation, had discussed with him a redemption of part or all of the stock owned by John Doe. This redemption would occur after John Doe's death and would keep control of the corporation with the surviving shareholders. The redemption price would be the value of the stock as finally determined for federal estate tax purposes. The President recommended the adoption of an agreement between John Doe and the Corporation in order to bind the personal representative of John Doe's estate to submit the stock for redemption after John Doe's death.
>
> After discussion, the following resolution was unanimously adopted:
>
> RESOLVED, that the President is authorized to enter into an agreement with John Doe for the redemption of part or all of the stock owned by John Doe, if so requested by the executor. This redemption shall occur after John Doe's death. The redemption price shall be the value of such stock as finally determined for federal estate tax purposes.

■ SAMPLE AGREEMENTS AND RESOLUTIONS

Reproduced in this unit is the documentation for two different situations: (1) the agreement is entered into while the shareholder is still alive, and (2) the agreement is entered into after the shareholder's death. In each case, there is a sample resolution of the board of directors and a specimen agreement.

Note that there are different agreements for common-law and community property states for both the predeath and postdeath situations. Also included is a board resolution authorizing the purchase of key-executive insurance, which could be useful in "camouflaging" the purpose of the insurance when a potential accumulated earnings tax problem exists.

A separate Section 303 redemption agreement will not be necessary when there is an overall buy-sell agreement.

Caution: The drafting and execution of Section 303 agreements should be undertaken only by attorneys. The sample agreements in this chapter are illustrative only.

ILL 9.6 ■ *Pre-Death Section 303 Stock Redemption Agreement*

CAUTION: This is a specimen agreement. The acutal agreement used in any particular case must be prepared by a qualified attorney.

(Common-Law States)

THIS AGREEMENT is made by and between _____ (hereinafter called the *Corporation*) and _____ (hereinafter called the *Shareholder*).

RECITALS:

A. The Shareholder is the owner of _____ shares of the outstanding capital stock of the Corporation (hereinafter called *Stock*).

B. The parties believe it to be in the best interest of the Corporation that, if necessary, the Corporation purchase shares of Stock to meet the death taxes and expenses of the Shareholder upon his (her) death, as provided in Internal Revenue Code Section 303, rather than force the sale of such stock to outside, inactive interests.

THERFORE IT IS AGREED:

1. INSURANCE

The Corporation shall apply for, and name itself as owner and beneficiary of, a policy of insurance on the life of the Shareholder in the face amount of $_____.

(a) *Additional Insurance*—The Corporation shall have the right to take out additional insurance on the life of the Shareholder whenever, in its opinion, additional insurance may be necessary or useful in helping it carry out its obligations under this agreement.

(b) *Premiums*—The Corporation shall pay all the premiums on insurance policies taken out pursuant to this agreement.

> **If an accumulated earnings tax problem is anticipated, the agreement should not refer to the insurance, and the above provision should be eliminated.**

2. DEATH OF SHAREHOLDER

(a) *Purchase of Stock*—In the event of the death of the Shareholder, his(her) personal representative shall have the option to require the Corporation to purchase any part or all of the stock upon the following terms:

(i) The purchase price of each share of Stock shall be its value in the shareholder's estate as finally determined for federal estate tax purposes.

(ii) The maximum number of shares that can be required to be purchased shall be those having an aggregate value equal to the sum of the estate, inheritance, legacy and succession taxes (including any interest collected as a part of such taxes) imposed because of the Shareholder's death, plus the amount of funeral and administration expenses allowable as deductions to the Shareholder's estate under Internal Revenue Code Section 2053.

(b) *Option Mechanics*—Such option shall be exercised by the personal representative's delivery to the Secretary of the Corporation written notice setting forth the number of shares to be purchased and the price for each. Within 30 days following receipt of such notice, the Corporation shall deliver payment in full and in cash to the personal representative who shall immediately on receipt of such payment, assign and deliver the purchased shares to such Secretary for cancelation.

ILL 9.6 ▪ *Pre-Death Section 303 Stock Redemption Agreement (Cont.)*

(c) Limitations—Notwithstanding subsections (a) and (b) of this Paragraph 2, such option shall be exercisable, and the subject shares shall be purchased and paid for in full by the Corporation, within the following periods:

(i) The periods set forth in Paragraphs (A) and (B) of Internal Revenue Code Section 303(b)(1), or comparable provision of the Internal Revenue Code then in effect; or

(ii) If the election under Internal Revenue Code Section 6166 is made, the period set forth in Paragraph (C) of Internal Revenue Code Section 303(b)(1).

3. INSUFFICIENT SURPLUS

If at the time the Corporation is required to purchase Stock hereunder its surplus is insufficient for such purpose, then the entire available surplus shall be used to purchase part of such Stock, and the Corporation shall promptly take all reasonable action to create additional surplus through recapitalization of its Stock or otherwise, and the Corporation shall purchase so much of the balance of such Stock as is possible.

4. PURCHASE OF POLICIES BY SHAREHOLDER

In the event of any termination of this agreement, then the Shareholder shall have the right to purchase from the Corporation any and all policies of insurance listed on Exhibit "A."

(a) *Methods of Purchase*—Such right shall be exercisable only be a written notice of intent delivered to the Secretary of the Corporation any and all policies of insurance listed on Exhibit "A."

(b) *Purchase Price*—The purchase price of each policy of insurance shall be its interpolated terminal reserve, increased by nay unearned premium, dividend credits and accrued dividends, and decreased by the amount of any loans against the policy. However, in the event the policy is then paid up, the purchase price of each policy shall be the replacement cost of a comparable contract.

> **The conservative draftsman may wish to eliminate Paragraph 4, for two reasons. First, it refers to the insurance policies, which may be a bad idea from an accumulated earnings tax standpoint. Second, the IRS ruled in Rev. Rul. 79-46, 1979-1 C.B. 303, that the insured's right to purchase a policy for its cash value was an incident of ownership. This position was later rejected by the Tax Court in *Estate of John Smith v. Comm'r*, 73 T.C. 307 (1979). However, the IRS abruptly dropped its appeal in the *Smith* case, and acquiesced in the Tax Court decision, I.R.B. 1981-13,6.**

5. AMENDMENT OF AGREEMENT

This agreement may be altered, amended or terminated by a writing signed by the corporation and the Shareholder.

6. APPLICABLE LAW

This agreement is executed in and is to be construed under and governed by the laws of the State of _____.

ILL 9.6 ▪ *Pre-Death Section 303 Stock Redemption Agreement (Cont.)*

7. BINDING EFFECT

This agreement shall be binding on the Corporation and its successors by consolidation, merger or otherwise, and on the Shareholder, his (her) personal representative and heirs.

IN WITNESS WHEREOF, the parties have signed their names hereto this _____ day of _____, _____.

_____
(Corporation)

By:_____

_____
(Shareholder)

ILL 9.7 ■ *Pre-Death Section 303 Stock Redemption Agreement*

CAUTION: This is a specimen agreement. The actual agreement used in any particular case must be prepared by a qualified attorney.

(Community Property States)

THIS AGREEMENT is made by and between _____ (hereinafter called the "Corporation") and _____ (hereinafter called the "Shareholder").

RECITALS:

A. The shareholder is the owner of an undivided community property interest in _____ shares of the outstanding capital stock of the Corporation (hereinafter called "Stock").

B. The parties believe it to be in the best interest of the Corporation that, if necessary, the Corporation purchase shares of Stock to meet the death taxes and expenses of the Shareholder upon his (her) death, as provided in Internal Revenue Code Section 303, rather than force the sale of such stock to outside, inactive interests.

THEREFORE IT IS AGREED:

1. INSURANCE

The Corporation shall apply for, and name itself as owner and beneficiary of, a policy of insurance on the life of the Shareholder in the face amount of $_____.

(a) *Additional Insurance*—The Corporation shall have the right to take out additional insurance on the life of the Shareholder whenever, in its opinion, additional insurance may be necessary or useful in helping it carry out its obligations under this agreement.

(b) *Premiums*—The corporation shall pay all premiums on insurance policies taken out pursuant to this agreement.

> **If an accumulated earnings tax problem is anticipated, the agreement should not refer to the insurance, and the above provision should be eliminated.**

2. DEATH OF SHAREHOLDER

(a) *Purchase of Stock*—In the event of the death of the Shareholder, his (her) personal representative shall have the option to require the Corporation to purchase any part or all of the deceased shareholder's interest in the Stock upon the following terms:

(i) The purchase price of each share of Stock shall be its value in the Shareholder's estate as finally determined for federal estate tax purposes.

(ii) The maximum number of shares which can be required to be purchased shall be those having an aggregate value equal to the sum of the estate, inheritance, legacy and succession taxes (including any interest collected as a part of such taxes) imposed because of the Shareholder's death, plus the amount of funeral and administration expenses allowable as deductions to the Shareholder's estate under Internal Revenue Code Section 2053.

ILL 9.7 ▪ *Pre-Death Section 303 Stock Redemption Agreement (Cont.)*

(b) *Option Mechanics*—Such option shall be exercised by the personal representative's delivery to the Secretary of the Corporation written notice setting forth the number of shares to be purchased and the price for each. Within 30 days following receipt of such notice, the Corporation shall deliver payment in full and in cash to the personal representative who shall immediately on receipt of such payment, assign and deliver the purchased shares to such Secretary for cancelation.

(c) *Limitations*—Notwithstanding subsections (a) and (b) of this Paragraph 2, such option shall be exercisable, and the subject shares shall be purchased and paid for in full by the Corporation, within the following periods:

(i) The periods set forth in Paragraphs (A) and (B) of Internal Revenue Code Section 303(b)(1), or comparable provision of the Internal Revenue Code then in effect; or

(ii) If the election under Internal Revenue Code Section 6166 is made, the period set forth in Paragraph (C) of Internal Revenue Code Section 303(b)(1).

3. INSUFFICIENT SURPLUS

If at the time the Corporation is required to purchase Stock hereunder, its surplus is insufficient for such purpose, then the entire available surplus shall be used to purchase part of such Stock, and the Corporation shall promptly take all reasonable action to create additional surplus through capitalization of its Stock or otherwise, and the Corporation shall purchase so much of the balance of such Stock as is possible.

4. PURCHASE OF POLICIES BY SHAREHOLDER

In the event of any termination of this agreement, then the Shareholder shall have the right to purchase from the Corporation any and all policies of insurance listed on Exhibit "A".

- *Method of Purchase*—Such right shall be exercisable only by a written notice of intent delivered to the Secretary of the Corporation within the 180 days following the date of such termination.
- *Purchase Price*—The purchase price of each policy of insurance shall be its interpolated terminal reserve, increased by any unearned premium, dividend credits and accrued dividends and decreased by the amount of any loans against the policy. However, in the event the policy is then paid up, the purchase price of each policy shall be the replacement cost of a comparable contract.

> **The conservative draftsman may wish to eliminate Paragraph 4, for two reasons. First, it refers to the insurance policies that may be a bad idea from an accumulated earnings tax standpoint. Second, the IRS ruled in Rev. 79-46, 1979-1, C.B. 303, that the insured's right to purchase a policy for its cash value was an incident of ownership. This position was later rejected by the Tax Court in *Estate of John Smith v. Comm'r*, 73 T.C. 307 (1979). However, the IRS abruptly dropped its appeal in the *Smith* case, and acquiesced in the Tax Court decision, I.R.B. 1981-13, 6.**

5. AMENDMENT OF AGREEMENT

This agreement may be altered, amended or terminated by a writing signed by the Corporation and the Shareholder.

6. APPLICABLE LAW

This agreement is executed in and is construed under and governed by the laws of the State of _____.

ILL 9.7 ▪ *Pre-Death Section 303 Stock Redemption Agreement (Cont.)*

7. BINDING EFFECT

This agreement shall be binding on the Corporation and its successors by consolidation, merger or otherwise, and on the Shareholder, his(her) personal representative and heirs.

IN WITNESS WHEREOF, the parties have signed their names hereto this _____ day of _____.

_____
(Corporation)

By:_____

_____
(Shareholder)

Spouse's Consent

I, the undersigned spouse of _____, hereby consent to and ratify the foregoing agreement this _____ day of _____, _____.

_____
(Spouse)

ILL 9.8 ▪ *Post-Death Minutes and Resolution of Board of Directors*

CAUTION: This is a specimen resolution. The actual resolution used in any particular case must be prepared by a qualified attorney.

The President reported that the XYZ Trust Co. of _____, _____, as Personal Representative of the Estate of John Doe, had discussed with him a redemption of part of the stock of the corporation owned by the late John Doe, and offered 1,000 shares for redemption in exchange for the principal sum of $250,000. The President further reported that this sum is equal to the estate tax value of the 1,000 shares to be redeemed.

After discussion, the following resolution was unanimously adopted:

RESOLVED, that the President is authorized to enter into an agreement with XYZ Trust Co., as Personal Representative of the Estate of John Doe, for the redemption of 1,000 shares of common stock of this corporation in exchange for the principal sum of $250,000.

This resolution and the two agreements that follow assume that $250,000 is the federal estate tax value of the 1,000 shares to be redeemed under Section 303.

ILL 9.9 ▪ *Post-Death Section 303 Stock Redemption Agreement*

CAUTION: This is a specimen agreement. The actual agreement used in any particular case must be prepared by a qualified attorney.

(Common-Law States)

AGREEMENT made this _____ day of _____ 20____, by and between ABC Corp., an Indiana corporation with its principal office at _____ in the city of _____, ("ABC") and XYZ Trust Co. of _____ _____, as Personal Representative of the Estate of John Doe ("Executor").

1. ABC agrees to purchase and Executor agrees to sell 1,000 shares of ABC's common stock in exchange for the principal sum of $250,000, such exchange to occur on the same day as the signing of this agreement.

2. ABC represents and warrants that it has full legal authority to enter into and to perform this contract.

3. Executor represents and warrants that it has full legal authority to sell the shares covered by this agreement, free and clear of all liens, claims, equities and encumbrances.

4. This agreement shall bind the parties hereto and their successors and assigns.

IN WITNESS WHEREOF, the parties hereto have signed their names on the date and year first above written.

ABC CORP.

By _____

XYZ TRUST CO.

By _____

We have assumed here that there are insurance proceeds to fund the corporation's obligation under the agreement. If the corporation wishes to distribute appreciated property in kind, it should require a representation and warranty from the executor that the redemption distribution will qualify under Section 303. If Section 303 were not available, the corporation would recognize gain on such a distribution.

ILL 9.10 ■ *Post-Death Section 303 Stock Redemption Agreement*

CAUTION: This is a specimen agreement. The actual agreement used in any particular case must be prepared by a qualified attorney.

(Community Property States)

AGREEMENT made this _____ day of _____, 20____, by and between ABC Corp., an Indiana corporation with its principal office at _____ in the city of _____, (*ABC*) and XYZ Trust Co. of _____, as Personal Representative of the Estate of John Doe (*Executor*).

1. ABC agrees to purchase and Executor agrees to sell 500 shares of ABC's common stock in exchange for the principal sum of $125,000, such exchange to occur on the same day as the signing of this agreement.

2. ABC represents and warrants that it has full legal authority to enter into and to perform this contract.

3. Executor represents and warrants that it has full legal authority to sell the shares covered by this agreement, free and clear of all liens, claims, equities and encumbrances.

4. This agreement shall bind the parties hereto and their successors and assigns.

IN WITNESS WHEREOF, the parties hereto have signed their names on the date and year first above written.

ABC CORP.

By _____

XYZ TRUST CO.

By _____

SPOUSE'S CONSENT

I, the undersigned spouse of the deceased, John Doe, hereby consent to and ratify the foregoing agreement this _____ day of _____, 20____.

_____
(Spouse)

> We have assumed here that there are insurance proceeds to fund the corporation's obligation under the agreement. If the corporation wishes to distribute appreciated property in kind, it should require a representation and warranty from the executor that the redemption distribution will qualify under Section 303. If Section 303 were not available, the corporation would recognize gain on such a distribution.

ILL 9.11 ▪ *Board Resolution Authorizing*

CAUTION: This is a specimen resolution. The actual resolution used in any particular case must be prepared by a qualified attorney.

Key-Executive Insurance

When the accumulated earnings tax poses a potential threat, it may be desirable to characterize the life insurance destined to fund a Section 303 redemption as key-executive insurance. The following board of directors pre-death resolution should be used in such cases.

WHEREAS, _____ is now and for many years has been the President of the Corporation, and by reason of his unusual ability as its chief executive officer, it has consistently earned profits for the stockholders well above the average for the industry; and

WHEREAS, the termination of the services of said _____ by reason of his death would result in the loss of his managerial skill, experience and profit-making ability to the Corporation; and

WHEREAS, the Corporation desires to make secure its financial position in the event of the death of the said _____ and to indemnify itself against losses to its earning power which his death would occasion:

THEREFORE, IT IS HEREBY RESOLVED, that the (corporate officer) be authorized and instructed to take such action and execute such papers as may be necessary to secure a policy or policies of life insurance _____ on the life of _____ having a total face value of $_____ with the Corporation to be named beneficiary of such policy or policies and to be the owner of same; the policies so obtained shall be of the _____ type. The Treasurer is hereby instructed to pay all premiums on such policy or policies as they come due.

CHAPTER 9 QUESTIONS FOR REVIEW

1. For a stockholder's estate to be eligible for a Section 303 redemption of shares, the stock must constitute what percentage of the estate?

   A. 20 percent

   B. 35 percent

   C. 50 percent

   D. 80 percent

2. Advantages of a Section 303 redemption of stock include

   A. liquidity for the deceased shareholder's estate

   B. ordinary income tax treatment on any gain

   C. opportunity by the corporation to redeem the deceased shareholder's entire stock holding on a favorable tax basis

   D. none of the above

3. Expenses used to calculate the amount that can be redeemed under a Section 303 redemption include

   A. funeral bills

   B. estate and inheritance taxes

   C. estate administration costs

   D. all of the above

4. The advantages of using life insurance for a Section 303 redemption include

   A. inflation of the corporation's retained earnings position

   B. reduction of the impaired capital problem that might otherwise prevent the redemption

   C. reduction of each shareholder's equity value in the corporation, reducing estate tax-consequences

   D. all of the above

5. Premiums on a policy to fund a Section 303 redemption plan should be paid by

   A. the insured shareholder

   B. the corporation

   C. other stockholders

   D. an irrevocable trust

10

Key-Executive Life Insurance

K ey-executive life insurance can be important in protecting a business against the loss of key people. The mechanics of such a plan, its tax consequences and its effect on valuation of stock are examined in this chapter.

■ HUMAN VALUES IN BUSINESS

The primary function of life insurance is to offset the economic loss that comes with the death of an individual—to compensate for the human value that disappears with death. We are aware from our other insurance field experiences how life insurance acts to indemnify a family against the loss of an income-earning parent. The key-executive experience is similar. In this case, however, it is the business that stands to be indemnified against loss.

Businesspeople accept without question the wisdom of insuring the firm against the loss of its property values. They take care to insure the physical assets against loss from fire, tornados and other hazards. Yet, protection against the loss of human life values, which is provided by life insurance on the key people, may be a far more vital need.

In the first place, the probability of loss is considerably greater. It has been estimated that the chance of death of a key executive at age 45 is 14 times greater than the chance of a fire loss. It increases to 17 times at age 50, and to 23 times at age 55.

Moreover, a fire loss may never occur, but death someday is inevitable. While the great majority of buildings never burn, and the bulk of insured goods is never damaged by fire, about one out of every three individuals dies in the working period of life with a consequent loss to his or her business.

Furthermore, the average fire loss probably does not exceed 10 percent of the property value insured, while the death loss is always complete.

In the second place, the loss of a key executive through death is likely to be a far more permanent business loss. The plant that is destroyed by fire can be rebuilt. Moreover, the new building probably will be an improvement over the old one—more efficient, sounder, representing the latest in engineering developments, and thereby, more useful and valuable than the old.

Can the same be said for the new manager? The executive who died may have had a talent or ability that is tremendously difficult or impossible to replace. In most cases, it is possible to replace it. However, until the new person becomes familiar with the duties and problems of the job, he or she will be less useful to the business.

What Life Insurance Provides the Business

Life insurance cannot replace the mind that has been lost to the business when death strikes. But life insurance indemnifies the business for the cash value of the services that will be lost, so far as those human life values can be measured.

Simply, life insurance can provide the business with cash:

- to keep the business running;

- to assure creditors that their loans are safe;

- to assure customers that the business will continue operations;

- to cover the mistakes that the deceased's successor will make until he or she learns the things the deceased knew from experience;

- to cover the losses involved in a less capable successor's mistaken decisions;

- to cover the special expenses of finding, securing and training a new person to take the deceased's place; and

- to be made available for many uses that cannot be determined in advance because they depend upon the particular circumstances of that particular business at that particular time.

The key executive is a valuable business asset, vitally important to the continued welfare of the firm. Without insurance to offset the loss resulting from a key person's death, there may be a very serious interruption of the flow of business profits. The business has to carry life insurance only on this key executive, payable to the firm, to indemnify itself for the loss when it occurs. Aided by the insurance proceeds, the business may continue without serious loss. Thus, the business protects itself against financial reverses that will result to the firm from the loss of the key executive through death. Today, the business can be made aware of the importance of this key person to its success. And, today the business can act to protect its management assets with key-executive life insurance.

More than a Million Prospects

Every business has at least one key executive or employee who makes a profound contribution toward the operation and the success of the business. This employee's sudden death would mean losses to the firm. This employee can be either one of the owners or a key worker in a key position.

Business Owners as Key Executives

Active business owners are often a company's most valuable executives. When a close corporation or a partnership is organized, it is usually the combined talents of the organizers who are instrumental in making the business a success.

If one of them were to die, the work of the team would be disrupted. The death of a business owner or co-owner can have various other side effects on the company, such as:

1. the restriction of financial assistance from banks and other creditors who may be concerned about the company's future;

2. the slowing down of the business due to customers' concern about the future of its services and products;

3. the loss of customers who utilized the company's services or products only because of their relationship with the deceased executive; and

4. the loss of other key executives to the competition because of their fears for their future in the company.

It is easy to see that a business could suffer serious financial blows unless provisions are made to offset such monetary losses that result from the death of a key executive. Therefore, a company should insure the life of every active owner in the firm to protect itself and the surviving owners against such damages.

Nonowners as Key Executives

A company usually has one or more nonowner key executives whose expertise is vital to the company's overall success. The death of such a vital employee likely would be reflected in reduced profits for the business.

The death of a nonowner-executive, besides possibly reducing profits, also could result in additional costs:

1. for finding and attracting adequate replacement personnel;

2. of training the new person to take over certain duties; or

3. from the inexperience and mistakes of the replacement until he or she attains the skill of the deceased person.

MECHANICS OF THE PLAN

There is no particular form of agreement or special contract needed by the business to carry key executive life insurance on a key owner or employee. The insurance contract is purchased to indemnify the firm and speaks for itself. However, the board of directors should authorize the maintenance of the insurance and the payment of premiums.

Insurable Interest

A corporation or other business has an insurable interest in the life of any executive or employee, actively associated with the firm, whose death would cause it tangible loss. Likewise, a corporation has an insurable interest in the life of a shareholder who owns a large portion of the corporate stock, and whose skill and experience are relied on to a great extent to continue the business successfully.

Among the specific executives it is possible for a corporation to insure are its secretary and treasurer, a vice president, the president, its general manager and its active manager. Moreover, in several states there are statutes that permit corporations to insure the life of an officer or shareholder of the firm.

Applicant, Premium Payer, Owner and Beneficiary

The applicant for key executive life insurance is the business. The application is signed by an officer of the business other than the insured. The key executive also may be asked to sign to acknowledge or to affirm the personal data that appears on the application.

The premiums should be paid by the applicant—the business. The business will own the policy and possess all incidents of ownership. The business will be the beneficiary, because it is purchasing the policy for its own benefit.

The Type of Policy

The type of policy should be one that best suits the needs of the firm. However, cash value permanent life insurance is often used in key-executive situations. Permanent policies can be attractive because when the executive retires and the company ceases premium payments, funds accumulated in the contract may be used to provide an additional benefit to the insured individual plus a method for the employer to recapture the cost of the insurance.

Waiver of Premium

The key-executive life insurance policy may include a waiver of premium provision, which would relieve the firm of premium payments during a period of total and perhaps permanent disability.

It would be advantageous to the firm to retain the insurance policy on the executive's life after he or she becomes disabled, because if the key person recovers enough to return to work, the likelihood is that the key executive will have lost his or her insurability.

Moreover, during the period of disability, the money formerly paid out in insurance premiums could be directed toward the payment of "sick pay" to the insured key executive. Because "sick pay" is deductible by an employer, if reasonable in amount, the payment to the disabled key executive could be considerably greater than the amount of the waived insurance premiums, without the business assuming a larger outlay. For example, if the annual premium outlay had been $5,000, a sick pay benefit of as much as $7,500 a year could be paid by the employer at an approximate net outlay of only $5,000. In fact, if the employer considers also the increase in cash values during the period of disability, all cost to the employer would be eliminated. A similar justification could be made for the payment of an early retirement benefit, should disability prevent the key executive from ever returning to work.

Guaranteed Insurability Option

Another rider that may be offered as part of a key-executive life insurance policy is the guaranteed insurability option. This option would allow additional insurance to be purchased at various future dates without a new medical examination or other evidence of insurability. Such a rider would insure the employer's ability to buy additional coverage later as the key executive becomes more valuable to the business.

Termination of Key Executive

The majority of court decisions support the general rule that the firm has a legal right to continue to pay premiums on a key-executive policy after the executive's termination and to receive the proceeds upon his or her death. The question of insurable interest arises only at the beginning (when the insurance policy is purchased) despite the later termination of the insured's employment.

Many insurance companies offer a change of insured provision. This provision allows the employer to select another executive to insure subject to normal underwriting. The best advice is either to use a change of insured provision or to sell the policy to the insured on termination of employment of the key executive. When the insurance policy is transferred to the terminated executive, the business is in a position to purchase a policy on the life of the insured's successor.

Rights of the Insured in Key-Executive Insurance

The insured key executive has no rights in the policy itself. By a separate agreement, though, the insured could be granted the right to purchase his or her own policy. Also by separate agreement, the key individual could be given the right to purchase the policy owned by the firm in event of termination of employment.

Determining the Amount of Insurance

The key executive's employer often has a difficult time arriving at the amount of insurance it should purchase on the employee's life. The employer is dealing with human life values, not property values, so no set formula or rule can be used. The determination of insurance amounts in a buy-sell insurance case, for instance, is much more precise because the assessment of the insurance amounts is determined largely, again, by the property values. In many key-executive insurance cases, however, the amount of insurance will be established in more or less arbitrary fashion. Nevertheless, there are a few points that might be considered in reaching a reasonable figure.

1. *How much would it cost to replace the person in question?* A new person will have to be hired to take his or her place at death. Will the new individual demand more salary? Would the new individual likely do the job as well? How long would it probably take to train the new person to reach the proficiency level of this key employee? How much, then, could the company be expected to spend in finding and training a capable successor?

2. *How much is this person worth to the firm in net profits?* The executive is making a definite contribution to the firm's success and is accountable for some proportion of its profits. In many cases, it may not be difficult to apportion the profits that can be credited to his or her efforts; for example, in the case of a good salesperson, whose sales records provide a definite "yardstick." In other cases, it might be difficult to relate the executive's performance to profits.

3. *How much would it cost the business if this executive died today?* The answer to this question turns on how difficult it would be to replace the special talents of the key individual. Would the company itself collapse without this person? Would a special project have to be abandoned or a department closed if this executive died?

4. *What proportion of the company's actual loss is it willing to insure?* The company's desire to insure completely against the loss of the key individual may be limited by working-capital considerations.

A Special Method

A number of alternatives are available for determining the human life value of the key executive. One method is similar to the approach commonly used to determine the value of a breadwinner to his or her family:

1. Estimate the person's average annual earnings over his or her working life.

2. Deduct the federal and state income tax and the cost of maintaining himself or herself.

3. Determine the person's life expectancy or the number of years to retirement, whichever is shorter.

4. Select a reasonable rate of interest at which future earnings will be discounted.

5. Multiply 1. minus 2. by the present value of $1 per annum for the period determined in 3., discounted at the rate of interest selected in 4. The product is the human life value.

For example, a key executive, age 55, has at least ten years of active service remaining with her employer. The company estimates that its loss of earnings if she died today would amount to $20,000 annually. Over a 10-year period the loss would be $200,000. If we discount the value of $20,000 annually for ten years, using a 5 percent discount table, we arrive at the present value of the key executives's services, namely, $154,440. This figure could be used as the face amount for life insurance to replace the financial loss to the company. If there were other people in the company capable of taking up the slack caused by the executive's demise, then the amount of key-executive life insurance could be reduced accordingly.

Home office life underwriters often have additional guidelines for key person coverage. Frequently, the amount they will issue is limited to 5 or 10 times the executive's compensation.

■ CASE STUDY: THREE KEY EMPLOYEES

As noted, it is difficult to measure accurately the value of a key employee's contribution to an enterprise. However, an objective method can be used to arrive at a ballpark figure. Assume that a corporation employs three key employees whose contributions are approximately equivalent. Assume further that it would take five years for a replacement to acquire the key employee's managerial expertise. Finally, assume that 8 percent is a reasonable rate on the shareholder's equity, which is $200,000. The value of the key employee can be computed as follows:

Annual net earnings (five-year average)		$220,000
Less: Estimated replacement salaries for key employees' routine duties	$130,000	
Earnings on net worth of $200,000 at 8%	16,000	
		146,000
Annual earnings attributable to managerial expertise		74,000
Portion attributable to key employee (a)		24,667
Value of key employee (replacement needs five years to acquire managerial expertise)		$123,335

By purchasing three $125,000 key-executive insurance policies, the corporation could indemnify itself for the loss of the key employees' services during the five-year replacement period.

TAXATION OF KEY-EXECUTIVE LIFE INSURANCE

An important aspect of the sale of key-executive life insurance is its tax treatment. There are important elements to consider for both the business and the employee.

From the Corporation's Standpoint

In establishing taxable income, only certain types of business expenditures are allowed as a deduction from the gross income of the corporation. Accordingly, deductibility is a primary issue.

Deductibility of Premiums

Generally, key-executive life insurance premiums are not deductible as a business expense. If the firm is the beneficiary of such insurance, it "is directly or indirectly a beneficiary, under the policy," and therefore, the Internal Revenue Code does not permit a deduction. The primary reason for this nondeductibility is that the premiums are considered to be in the nature of a capital investment rather than a business expense.

Specifically, as long as the business has a beneficial interest in the policy, no deduction is allowed. The key word here is beneficial interest. Beneficial interest may be defined as the right to change the beneficiary, to surrender the policy for cash or to make policy loans.

Increase in Cash Values

Annual increases in the cash values of key-executive insurance policies may be subject to federal income taxation. Under the rules of the alternative minimum tax, 75 percent of the difference between the annual premium paid and the increase in the policy cash value (if any) becomes a tax preference item. (See previous discussion on corporate AMT).

Taxation of Proceeds

Life insurance proceeds received upon the death of a key executive are not subject to federal income tax. The Internal Revenue Code states: "Except as otherwise provided . . . gross income does not include amounts received (whether in a single sum or otherwise) under a life insurance contract, if such amounts are paid by reason of the death of the insured." The rule applies to sole proprietors, partnerships and corporations as beneficiaries.

There are two exceptions to the general rule. First, when such proceeds are received in installments, the interest element in the installments is taxable. Second, when a policy has been transferred to a corporation under circumstances that make the transfer-for-value rule applicable, the gain realized by the corporation on the policy will be taxable.

Key Person Policy Loan Interest Deduction

There is a general rule of nondeductibility of policy loan interest. However, the Code provides a limited policy loan interest deduction for indebtedness on company-owned life insurance covering a key person.

Under the key person exception to the general rule prohibiting the policy loan interest deduction, policy loan interest under a life insurance policy covering a key person is deductible to the extent that the indebtedness does not exceed $50,000. This limited exception is further limited by the definition of key person and the amount of interest that may be deducted.

For purposes of the policy loan interest deduction, a *key person* is defined as an officer or 20 percent owner of the company. The number of employees who can be treated as key persons is limited to the greater of:

- five individuals; or

- the lesser of:

    - 5 percent of the total officers and employees; or

    - 20 individuals.

Generally, all members of a controlled group are treated as a single taxpayer for purposes of determining a 20 percent owner and for applying the $50,000 limit.

There is also an interest limitation that may affect deductibility. Interest in excess of the *applicable rate of interest* cannot be deducted. The applicable rate of interest for any month is Moody's Corporate Bond Yield Average—Monthly Average Corporates published by Moody's Investor Service.

Transfer-for-Value Rule. Let us assume that the corporation did not purchase a new policy on the key executive, but had transferred to it an existing policy on the key executive. Would the death proceeds of the transferred insurance policy escape income taxation?

The Internal Revenue Code provides that when there is a transfer for value of a life insurance policy, the proceeds in the hands of the transferee shall be subject to income tax as ordinary income after deducting (a) the amount paid for the policy and (b) subsequent premiums paid. Exempt from this rule, however, are the following transferees: the insured, a partner of the insured, a partnership in which the insured is a partner and a corporation in which the insured is a shareholder or officer.

Note that the favored group of transferees does not include co-stockholders of the insured. It is also important to remember that, when the key executive is merely a valuable employee and not an officer or shareholder, the proceeds are taxable under the main provisions of the transfer-for-value rule.

Death proceeds received by a corporation from a transferred insurance policy will escape taxation so long as the key executive is an officer or shareholder of the corporation at the time of transfer. Note that employee or director status alone is insufficient.

Death Proceeds Received in Installments. If a corporation receives the death proceeds of life insurance in installments, the interest portion of the installment payments is taxable income to the corporation. Installments, as used here, include payments under a fixed-amount option, a fixed-period option or an annuity income option.

The interest portion of each payment is determined by prorating the original amount of death proceeds held by the insurance company over the period the payments are expected to be made, excluding the amount determined by such proration. Thus, if $100,000 of death proceeds are payable to the corporation over a fixed period of 10 years, $10,000 will be excluded each year and the balance of the payments received each year will be taxable income to the corporation-payee.

Corporate Distribution of Proceeds. Once life insurance proceeds are received by the corporation, they lose their insurance identity. Upon distribution thereafter, they are taxable to stockholders the same as any corporate dividends. This is also true when a trustee, as beneficiary, receives the proceeds for distribution to the stockholders, provided the trustee acts in behalf of the corporation.

Directly naming stockholders as beneficiaries of a corporation-owned policy does not alter the situation. The Internal Revenue Service has ruled that proceeds of such a policy are taxable as dividends because the result is the same as if the proceeds had been received tax free by the corporation and then distributed to the stockholders as dividends.

Key-Executive Insurance in an S Corporation

An S corporation derives the same advantages from key-executive life insurance as a regular corporation. The S corporation cannot deduct its premium payments. Such payments also will result indirectly in a higher basis of the stock. The proceeds retain their tax-free character when distributed to the shareholders.

Taxability of Proceeds Received During the Insured's Life

A corporation occupies the same tax position as an individual taxpayer when receiving the proceeds of a life insurance policy surrendered or matured during the lifetime of the insured.

Surrender or Maturity—Loss

When a corporation surrenders a policy, or a corporation-owned endowment policy matures, for less than the premium cost, a deductible loss seldom arises. The portion of the premium not credited toward the policy reserve represents the cost of insurance protection for which value has been received. The balance of the premiums—the portion credited toward the policy reserve—comprises the policy's basis for loss purposes. Thus, a deductible loss can arise only when the premiums credited toward the reserve exceed the cash value—only on surrender in a very early policy year. Usually there is no loss.

Surrender or Maturity—Gain

However, if an insurance policy is surrendered or matures during the insured's lifetime, there is a gain for income tax purposes if the cash surrender value received exceeds the aggregate net premiums and other consideration paid. Premiums paid for disability and accidental death provisions of the policy are not counted as part of the aggregate net premiums. Any gain realized on surrender of a policy is taxable as ordinary income.

If the corporation elects to receive the matured or surrendered policy's cash values in installments, in lieu of a lump sum, and such option is exercised not later than 60 days after the lump sum became payable, no part of the lump sum is includable in the corporation's gross income as being constructively received. Instead, the installments are taxed as an annuity, based on the cost of the policy. The portion of each installment payment received that is equal to the ratio that the net premiums or other consideration bears to the aggregate amount of the installments to be received is excluded. Only the balance of each installment payment received is taxable income to the corporation-payee.

For example, Ms. A is an executive of the ABC Corporation. She is retiring from the corporation. The corporation has had a $100,000 key-executive life insurance policy on Ms. A for 30 years. It desires to use the cash values of this policy to fund a 10-year retirement pension for A. The corporation paid $41,884 in premiums for this policy over 30 years. It expects to receive $61,000 from the insurance company on a 10-year-only option, with which it can then pay Ms. A. By relating the premiums paid to the aggregate amount to be received, $41,884/$61,000, it is evident that 68 percent of each installment will be tax-free to the corporation, and the balance will be taxable income.

Accumulated Earnings Tax

The purpose of this special tax is to place an additional tax on any corporation that prevents the imposition of income tax upon its shareholders through retention of earnings beyond the "reasonably anticipated needs" of the corporation.

Because life insurance proceeds payable to a corporation are not part of the corporation's taxable income, they do not enter its accumulated taxable income. However, the excess of the proceeds over the premiums paid will be considered earnings and profits which, if accumulated, would begin to apply toward the $250,000 credit (or $150,000 credit for professional corporations).

The question is whether the tax may apply to income retained by a corporation for the purpose of paying premiums on key-executive insurance. The answer is quite straightforward.

The premiums paid each year will be taken into account in determining a corporation's accumulated taxable income. When this sum exceeds $250,000 (or $150,000 in a professional corporation), the premium paid for the year will be subject to the accumulated earnings tax unless the corporation can prove that the premium was paid for the reasonable needs of the business.

The purchase of key-executive insurance should not, generally, incur any accumulated earnings tax liability if there exists a genuine need for the protection being carried by the corporation, and if the policies are of types and in amounts that are reasonable and proper in the light of the insured's worth to the business.

So as not to trigger a claim of unreasonable accumulation of earnings by the Internal Revenue Service, the corporate owners should keep in mind the following requirements for key-executive life insurance:

1. The insured key individual actually is a vital employee of the corporation, whose death would result in a loss to the corporation.

2. There is a valid reason for the corporation to own the insurance: to indemnify itself against loss of the key person by death.

3. The insurance amount bears a reasonable relation to his or her value to the corporation.

4. The type of policy is in keeping with the indemnification objective. The use of policies possessing a substantial investment element might indicate an effort to use corporate income to build accumulated earnings for purposes other than the reasonably anticipated needs of the business.

5. The directors of the corporation adopt a resolution authorizing the purchase of the policy and the payment of the premiums. The resolution also states the reasons for the purchase of the policy. The courts have been prone to recognize the judgment of the board of directors with regard to the business need for the insurance.

From the Key Executive's Standpoint

When considering the tax consequences of a key-executive insurance policy, it is important to keep in mind that the arrangement also must be to the advantage of the key executive.

Premiums as Taxable Income to the Insured

If the key-executive insurance policy is purchased in the recommended manner—with the corporation as the owner and beneficiary—the insurance premiums paid by the corporation will not be taxed as additional income to the insured employee. The insurance premiums are taxable income to the insured employee only when: (1) the employee has the right to name the beneficiary; or (2) the proceeds of the policy directly benefit the employee, his or her dependents, or the employee's estate.

So, in the classic key-executive insurance situation, the key executive is not taxed on the premiums paid by the corporation because the corporation is the owner and beneficiary of the policy.

Sale to the Key Employee

If the corporation owns a policy on an employee's life and sells the policy to the employee for less than its value, the employee realizes a taxable gain to the extent that the cash surrender value exceeds any payments made by the employee. If the policy is paid up, it appears the employee's gain would equal the excess of the policy's replacement value over the bargain price.

Basically, the "value" of the policy in excess of the purchase price is treated as additional compensation to the employee. Presumably, the employer could deduct this amount upon proper proof of intent to compensate.

Estate Taxation of Key-Executive Insurance Proceeds

In key-executive life insurance, the firm possesses all incidents of ownership and is the beneficiary. The proceeds are not paid to the key executive's estate, nor does he or she possess any incidents of ownership in the policy. The proceeds therefore are not includable in the key executive's estate.

Key Executive with "Incidents of Ownership." In the typical corporate key-executive life insurance arrangement, the corporation possesses all incidents of ownership in the policy, and the insured none. If the insured executive does possess direct incidents of ownership in the policy the proceeds will be includable in his or her estate. Even if the insured executive does not directly possess any incidents of ownership in the policy, the corporation's ownership may be attributable to the insured (with resulting estate tax liability) if he or she is the sole, or a controlling, stockholder.

To avoid possible future taxation problems, the insurance agent probably will want to encourage prospects to arrange key-executive insurance policies along standard lines whenever possible, thus making it clear that all incidents of ownership rest in the corporation.

In any case, if a decedent is the sole or controlling stockholder of a corporation owning insurance on his or her life, the corporation's incidents of ownership will be attributed to the insured stockholder, except to the extent the proceeds are payable to the corporation, or to a third party for a valid business purpose. The payment of the proceeds to a creditor of the corporation serves a valid business purpose, and the incidents are not attributed. Whether payable to the corporation or to a third party for the benefit of the corporation, however, the proceeds would be taken into account in determining the value of a deceased owner's stock in the corporation.

EFFECT OF KEY-EXECUTIVE INSURANCE ON VALUATION OF STOCK

Unless a buy-sell agreement has pegged the value of the stock, an estate tax problem may arise in connection with key-executive policies that are carried on the life of a key executive who is also a stockholder in the beneficiary corporation.

Life insurance proceeds paid to a corporation under a key-executive policy are treated as corporation assets to be considered, along with other assets and all other relevant factors, in valuing the corporation's stock in the insured's estate for death tax purposes. The full value of the proceeds is included in establishing the value of the corporation's stock, not just the cash values immediately preceding the insured's death. The insurance proceeds are added to the other assets, so the sum becomes one of the factors in valuing the corporation's stock.

However, because the policy cash values are already carried on the corporate balance sheet as an asset, the insurance proceeds increase the asset value only to the extent they exceed the cash values.

In any case, insurance proceeds payable to or for the benefit of the corporation effectively increase the net worth of the corporation and the value of the insured's stock in the corporation.

Next comes the question of the loss the corporation may sustain as a result of the key executive's death. It could be that this loss is enough to offset the increase in asset value created by the receipt of the insurance proceeds. On the other hand, if the corporation fails to prove it has suffered a loss by the death of the insured, the entire face amount, less any cash value, will be included in the corporate assets for the purpose of determining the value of the stock.

The adoption of a resolution by the board of directors authorizing the purchase and payment of premiums, and stating the purpose of the purchase, is perhaps the most acceptable way of establishing the fact of loss upon the death of the key individual.

AN UNDERSOLD MARKET

The market for key-executive insurance remains today a relatively undersold one. Often life insurance on a key employee is sold because a lender demanded that the key executive be insured as a condition to granting a loan, not because an insurance agent recommended it.

Most businesses have at least one key person whose death would cause a tangible loss to the business. This loss may be measured or estimated. The business should buy as much life insurance as it can to cover the possible loss. Furthermore, key-executive life insurance certainly will be helpful when the business owners face their banker.

While life insurance can be a source of credit itself, its chief function is to lend additional character to a projected loan and assure the lender that the loan

> **ILL 10.1** ■ *Sample Preapproach Letter*
>
> Dear _____:
>
> In every business there are certain key assets that must be protected against loss. For example, a business building is protected against fire; office equipment is protected against theft. But what about the most important asset—what about key people?
>
> Regardless of the size of a business, its key executives and managers are responsible for its success. They are the "brains behind the business." And their loss can be far more damaging than any fire or theft.
>
> Nothing can replace the mind that has been lost to a business when death strikes. But there is a way—through life insurance—to indemnify the business for the cash value of the services that are lost, at least so far as human life values are measurable.
>
> Please take a few moments to look over the brochure I've enclosed. I think you'll find it interesting. I will call you next week to arrange an appointment. I have some ideas I'd like to share with you.
>
> Sincerely,

will be repaid even if the key owner is not alive to do so. Life insurance also can stabilize an existing credit line or loan, so that the owner's successors will not find the business's credit cut off at a key executive's death.

And for the key executive concerned about providing financial stability for his or her family upon death, adequate amounts of additional life insurance can help offset the sometimes devastating effects of taxation on the estate, above and beyond the "normal" estate shrinkage that can be expected.

This is the key-executive insurance story. If told with conviction, it can lead to many significant sales for the insurance professional and to business stability for clients. Ill. 10.1 is a sample preapproach letter to be used in conjunction with an appropriate brochure or modified to permit the agent to discuss the topic without using a brochure.

■ SUMMARY

Life insurance can help indemnify a business upon the loss of a key executive in precisely the same way that life insurance can indemnify a family upon the loss of its breadwinner. Although the financial losses sustained by the corporate and family beneficiaries are different, both may avoid financial ruin through life insurance.

In this chapter we discussed key-executive life insurance and examined its benefits to the business. It was noted that, although the probability of a key executive's death is many times greater at most ages than the probability of property loss, it remains an undersold need.

We discussed the possible effects on the business of the loss of a key person and saw that they include the loss of financing, the decrease in business and the possible loss of other executives who may be concerned about the future of the business without the key executive. Each of these negative effects may be compensated for by life insurance on the key executive. In addition, the loss of a key executive often increases the company's costs as it recruits, selects and trains a replacement for the departed individual.

There are various policy riders and provisions that can be of substantial value in life insurance policies that insure key executives, including waiver of premium and guaranteed insurability option riders as well as a change of insured provision. These riders add value to the key executive policy and facilitate various corporate objectives. Determining the amount of key-executive life insurance that is appropriate is considerably more art than science, but several factors may be used to establish an amount. In addition, many life insurance companies employ a rule of thumb that limits key-executive life insurance amounts they will issue to some multiple of the individual's salary. That multiple varies with insurers but is often 5 to 10 times compensation.

The chapter concludes with a discussion of the tax treatment of key-executive life insurance, including the non-deductibility of premiums, the limited tax deductibility of policy loan interest on policies covering key persons, the income tax free receipt of death benefits and the subjecting of cash value increases to the alternative minimum tax.

RESOLUTION OF BOARD OF DIRECTORS

As stated earlier, the purchase of key-executive life insurance and the payment of premiums should be approved by the board of directors, although no special agreement is necessary. Reproduced on the following page is a sample resolution of the board of directors authorizing the purchase of insurance on the life of a key employee.

ILL 10.2 ▪ *Resolution*

CAUTION: This is a specimen resolution. The actual resolution used in any particular case must be prepared by a qualified attorney.

WHEREAS, _____ is now and for many years has been the President of the Corporation, and by reason of his unusual ability as its chief executive officer, it has consistently earned profits for the stockholders well above the average for the industry; and

WHEREAS, the termination of the services of said _____ by reason of his death would result in the loss of his managerial skill, experience and profit making ability to the Corporation; and

WHEREAS, the Corporation desire to make secure its financial position in the event of the death of the said _____ and to indemnify itself against losses to its earning power which his death would occasion;

THEREFORE, IT IS HEREBY RESOLVED, that the __(corporate officer)__ be authorized and instructed to take such action and execute such papers as may be necessary to secure a policy or policies of life insurance on the life of _____ having a total face value of $_____ with the Corporation to be named beneficiary of such policy or policies and to be the owner of same; the policies so obtained shall be of the _____ type. The Treasurer is hereby instructed to pay all premiums on such policy or policies as they come due.

CHAPTER 10 QUESTIONS FOR REVIEW

1. The primary purpose of key-executive insurance is to
   A. provide a business with a retirement plan
   B. indemnify the heirs upon the death of a key employee
   C. indemnify the business upon the death of a key employee
   D. supplement an employee's salary

2. Under a key-executive insurance plan
   A. death benefits are included in the key executive's gross estate
   B. premiums are deductible
   C. death proceeds are received income tax free
   D. all of the above

3. Waiver of premium is recommended in a key-executive insurance plan because
   A. the insurance coverage will be maintained at no cost to the company while the employee is disabled
   B. money presently allocated for premiums can be used to provide "sick pay" for the disabled employee
   C. the company is relieved of the burden of premiums during the employee's disability
   D. all of the above

4. If an existing policy is used for key-executive insurance, death benefit proceeds would be treated as taxable income
   A. in all cases
   B. never
   C. if the policy is transferred to a co-stockholder
   D. if the policy is transferred to a partner of the insured

5. If $120,000 of proceeds under a key-executive plan are received by a corporation in three equal, annual installments of $43,000, how much is received tax free each year?
   A. None
   B. $3,000
   C. $40,000
   D. $43,000

11

Nonqualified Deferred Compensation Plans

D eferred compensation—how it works and what its tax consequences will be (for both the employee and the employer)—are examined in this chapter. Special attention is paid to the question of deferred compensation for majority shareholders and the provisions of a deferred compensation agreement (with several sample agreements presented).

In today's highly competitive business environment, one of the key elements of a company's ongoing success is its ability to retain and adequately reward key personnel. However, when it comes to providing qualified fringe benefits, including profit-sharing and pension plans, many federal tax provisions prevent what is known as discrimination: special perks for officers, executives and other high salaried owner-employees.

DEFERRED COMPENSATION PLANS

There is a way to provide adequate retirement and other benefits for a key person in this high-salary group. That is through a *nonqualified deferred compensation plan*—a contractual arrangement to pay benefits in the future. Because life insurance provides an excellent means of assuring that the funds will be available in the future to pay the benefits promised by these plans, the promotion and sale of deferred compensation is a natural activity for the insurance professional. While the nonqualified deferred compensation plans discussed in this chapter and the salary continuation plans discussed in the following chapter are sophisticated sales, the basic concepts are relatively simple.

How Deferred Compensation Works

There are numerous variations of deferred compensation. However, under a basic arrangement, the employee agrees to either a reduction in current salary or deferral of a raise. In return, the employer commits to a series of payments to the employee at retirement, with the amount, frequency and duration of payments determined at the time the agreement is set up.

There may also be ancillary benefits in the form of payments to the employee's surviving spouse or other beneficiary in the event of death prior to or after retirement, and for payments to the employee in the event of disability.

The arrangement generally has a two-fold objective: on the part of the employer, to attract and retain key employees; on the part of the employee, to receive additional compensation at retirement.

A Nonqualified Plan

Salary continuation and deferred compensation plans are not subject to most of the requirements of the Employee Retirement Income and Security Act of 1974 (ERISA). Payments into a plan are not income tax-deductible. A number of unique tax benefits can be realized when life insurance is used as the funding mechanism for such plans. However, the ultimate recipient of the benefit pays ordinary income tax on the funds received. A qualified plan, in contrast, is subject to all of the requirements of ERISA. Nonqualified plans are, by definition, more flexible than qualified plans. The state of the art in salary continuation and deferred compensation plans has evolved to the extent that such plans are exceptionally flexible and are virtually always custom designed to the needs of the purchasing entity.

Uses of Deferred Compensation

Deferred compensation may be recommended to:

1. *Substitute for a formal pension plan.* The employer has complete freedom of action in the selection of the employees to participate. Because no government approval is required, the plan can be discriminatory. Further, it can be tailored to fit the funds available and may be continued or terminated at will. Also, the employees not included in the plan never need know of its existence.

2. *Supplement a qualified pension plan.* Regulations affecting pension and profit-sharing plans operate to limit benefits that can be paid to the executive class of employees. Further, the executive may have been employed by the organization late in life and may be either ineligible for the formal plan, or because of service requirements, eligible for only a reduced pension.

3. *Supplement a qualified profit-sharing plan.* In some plans, when the profit-sharing contributions are projected to retirement, it is evident that an adequate benefit will not be provided. In other plans, the key employee entered the plan late in life so that the plan will not develop

benefits for the person commensurate with those projected for the firm's younger employees.

4. *Aid in recruiting new key executives.* In many cases, deferred compensation can give the new key employees a greater fringe benefit program than what they left behind.

5. *Retain valuable key personnel.* An important employee can be deterred from leaving his or her present employment, if leaving means the loss of substantial deferred compensation benefits.

6. *Retain key employees to run the business for the family.* When business owners desire to see their families continue to own a business, deferred compensation can hold the key people and keep the business alive, until the owners' minor or inexperienced children can take over.

7. *Make executive compensation more meaningful.* Because of the graduated tax structure, much of a pay raise or bonus to a key executive is taken by taxes. Deferral of such a raise or bonus to a future date—until after retirement, for example—will allow the executive to keep far more after taxes because a retiree may be in a lower tax bracket.

8. *Substitute for stock or an ownership interest.* Deferred compensation for key employees is to be preferred to a minority stock interest in many close corporations, especially if few or no dividends are paid.

Why Nonqualified Deferred Compensation?

The popularity of nonqualified deferred compensation plans has grown considerably in recent years as congressional limitations of qualified plans have become more complex and more restrictive.

Changes in the law providing for tougher nondiscrimination rules and more stringent vesting provisions have made qualified plans more expensive both in meeting new actuarial requirements and coping with increases in administrative costs. Caps on salaries for the purposes of computing qualified plan benefits have had adverse effects on providing retirement income for highly compensated employees.

Therefore, employers are turning more and more to nonqualified plans to provide logical solutions for executive pay deferred benefits. Among these types of plans are *top hat*, *SERPs*, *excess benefit* and *executive bonus plans*.

Top Hat Plans

A *top hat plan* is maintained by an employer primarily to provide deferred compensation for a select group of management or highly compensated employees. Under a top hat plan, executives forgo receipt of currently earned compensation, such as a portion of salary, commissions, or bonuses, and direct these funds to be paid out at retirement. These plans are typically set up as defined contribution plans, that is, the amount deferred and investment gain are credited to an account set up for the executive. The executive's benefit is an aggregate

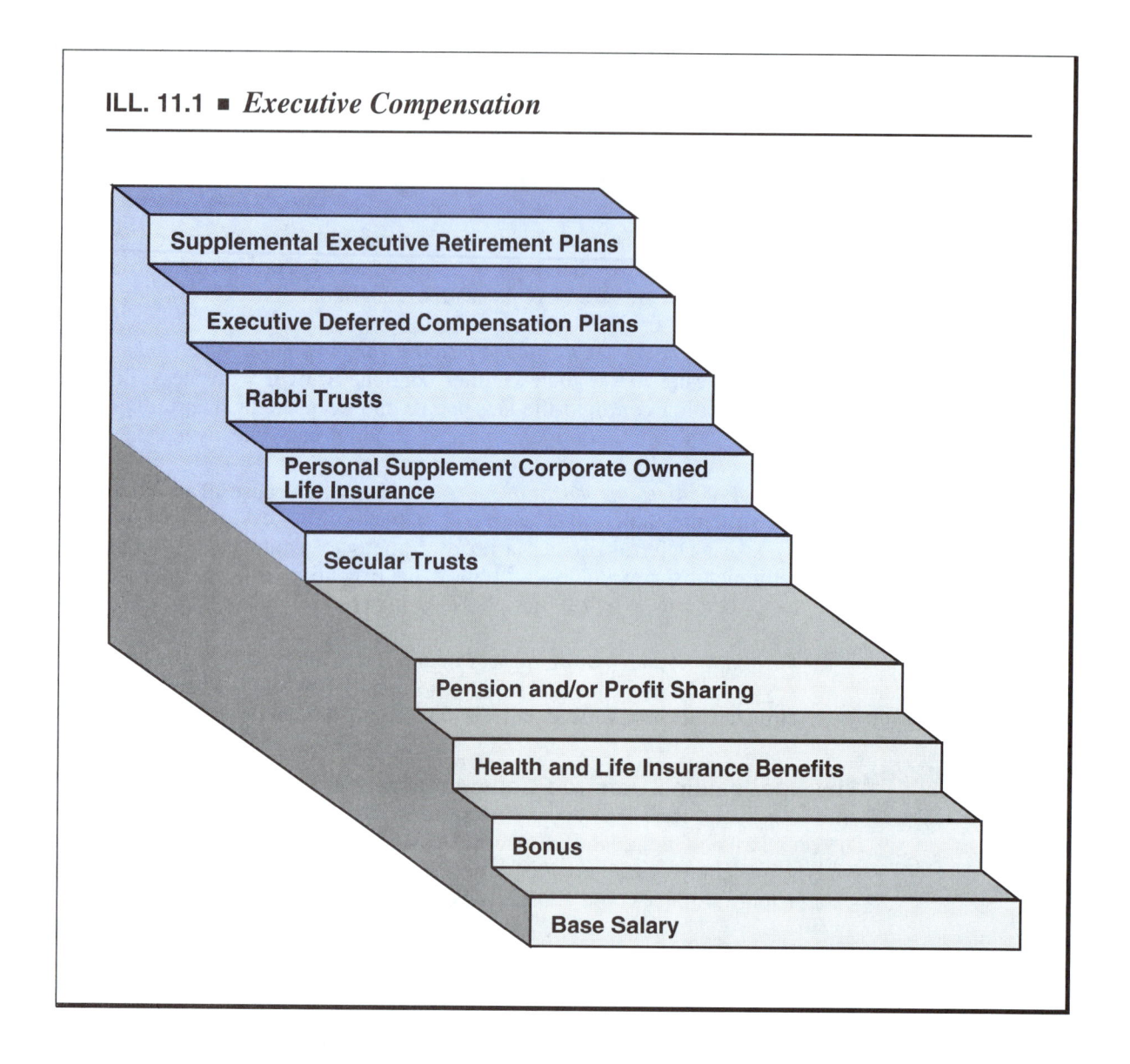

ILL. 11.1 ■ *Executive Compensation*

- Supplemental Executive Retirement Plans
- Executive Deferred Compensation Plans
- Rabbi Trusts
- Personal Supplement Corporate Owned Life Insurance
- Secular Trusts
- Pension and/or Profit Sharing
- Health and Life Insurance Benefits
- Bonus
- Base Salary

amount of all contributions and earnings. The employer may initiate these plans as a perk or at the request of the executive during employment contract negotiations.

The SERP

A supplemental executive retirement plan (SERP) is the most popular type of nonqualified plan. A SERP satisfies the employer objective of bringing executive retirement benefits up to desired levels in an already existing qualified plan. Like the top hat plan, a SERP is maintained by the employer primarily for the purpose of providing deferred compensation (in this case not a deferred salary but rather a deferred benefit) for a select group of management or highly compensated employees.

Candidates for SERPs include employers who want to:

1. cut back benefits under their qualified plan because of increased costs;

2. provide a higher income replacement ratio for executives than they can afford, or desire to provide, for all employees;

3. defeat the dollar cap on compensation that can be considered in determining qualified plan benefits; and

4. recruit, retain and retire key employees.

The Excess Benefit Plan

An excess benefit plan is used for executives who are already "maxed out" under their employer's qualified retirement plan. An excess benefit plan satisfies the employer objective of exceeding the maximum contribution and benefit limits for qualified plans—the so-called Code Section 415 limits.

The Section 415 limits for qualified plans differ depending on whether the qualified plan is a defined benefit plan, a defined contribution plan or a combination plan. The statutory limit for a defined benefit plan is $90,000, indexed annually for inflation. The limit for a defined contribution plan is the lesser of 25 percent of salary or $30,000. The limit for a combination plan is slightly greater than the limit available under either plan. What's more, the combined plan limit is reduced if a plan is deemed a super top heavy plan (as are most small employer plans).

Key Executive Bonus—Section 162 Plans

An *executive bonus plan*, also known as an *insured bonus plan* or *Section 162 plan* from the section of the Internal Revenue Code that governs its taxation, is a nonqualified plan that allows an employer to determine who will participate and how large the benefit will be while obtaining an adequate income tax deduction for the plan contribution. The employer and the employee both benefit from these plans. It should also be kept in mind that in every close corporation, the senior executive wears two hats. He or she is the employer and is also an employee. Clearly, the opportunity is present for the owner of a business to benefit himself or herself alone, or to reward specific key-executives.

The Bonus Plan and the Life Insurance Sale

When a corporation pays a bonus to an employee, the amount is often based on a percentage of profits. However, the corporation is fairly free to use other criteria, such as a percentage of sales or other benchmarks that will not appear unreasonable to the IRS. A written resolution should be passed by the board of directors to authorize the bonus expenditure. The board may include language in the resolution mandating that the additional bonus is specifically designated for the premium payment on individual permanent cash value life insurance. When the bonus is paid to the executive, he or she pays the premium for the policy contract. In some situations, the executive may direct the corporation to pay the premiums for the executive who receives the bonus. In any event, the employee is the owner of the policy, selects the beneficiary, and chooses the appropriate settlement option.

Benefits at Early Termination of Employment

If the executive should leave the company before the retirement date specified in the plan document, provisions may be made either for no distribution whatever or for a partial distribution according to a predetermined schedule.

It is customary for salary continuation plans or SERPs to pay no benefit at all to the executive who leaves the firm before the specified retirement date. Executives who leave the employment of an employer who has established a deferred compensation plan generally receive their total deferrals with modest accumulated interest, such as interest at the prevailing passbook savings account rate. Thus, there is a substantial financial incentive for a participating executive to stay with the company until normal retirement.

Rabbi Trusts and Secular Trusts—Guaranteeing the Funds

The *rabbi trust* derived its name from a trust created in a nonqualified retirement plan by a rabbi concerned that future decision makers in his congregation might not be as kindly disposed to providing for his retirement as the current leaders. He arranged for the plan assets to be placed into a trust with conditions that they could only be used for his retirement. However, in order to avoid the current income taxation on those assets, the trust document left the assets available to the claims of the employer's general creditors. Similar trust arrangements have been upheld by the Internal Revenue Service and offer a planning alternative appropriate in some circumstances.

The increase in mergers and acquisitions of recent years has spawned another trust known as a *secular trust*. Unlike the taxation of the trust corpus of a rabbi trust, all trust assets of a secular trust are currently income taxable to the executive. Such taxation occurs because the opportunity for forfeiture of assets is sufficiently reduced by trust provisions to create current income to the executive. This type of a trust is perceived by some executives to be of value if it is supposed that the income tax rate will increase dramatically in the future or if it is likely that the existing corporation will be merged or sold to unfriendly future owners.

Two Types of Prospects

The motivation to enter into a deferred compensation agreement comes from one of two directions:

1. The agreement may be employer-motivated. Deferred compensation can be offered to an employee by the employer as an inducement to stay with the company.

ILL. 11.2 ■ *Sample Preapproach Letter*

Dear _____:

No doubt about it, the continuing success of any business enterprise is largely dependent on attracting and keeping key employees. And one of the most effective means of assuring this is through the offer of corporate fringe benefits—specifically, a special retirement program for key people.

There is a plan available to businesses like yours that can provide future benefits in return for present services. Commonly known as deferred compensation, it is a systematic retirement program for key executives and top managers, and offers many advantages to employer and employees alike.

Take a few moments to review the brochure I've enclosed; I think you'll find this plan an attractive approach to attracting and retaining key employees. I would like to arrange a meeting with you in order to explain in more detail how a deferred compensation plan can benefit your organization. Why don't I call you next week to set up an appointment?

Sincerely,

---

2. The agreement may be employee-motivated. For example, an employee earning in excess of $75,000 annually may desire some tax relief. The individual may feel that he or she is not saving enough money for retirement. The employee would like to defer a portion of present income and thereby drop to a lower tax bracket. By using the salary reduction approach, highly paid executives can gain substantial tax savings.

Where Prospects Are Found

In general, prospects for deferred compensation plans can be found in corporations, partnerships and proprietorships, as well as nonprofit organizations such as country clubs, trade associations, hospitals and other service and charitable organizations. Moreover, the workers covered by deferred compensation may be employees—such as general managers, engineers or sales managers—or they may be independent contractors—such as hospital- or clinic-associated physicians, manufacturers' representatives or attorneys.

Sample Preapproach Letter

Illustration 11.2 is a sample preapproach letter for your prospects. We recommend that the letter be used in conjunction with a suitable brochure. The same letter can apply to salary continuation discussed in the next chapter.

The Three Elements of a Deferred Compensation Plan

The terms "deferred compensation plan" and "salary continuation plan" are used interchangeably by life insurance salespeople and corporate executives. Deferred compensation plans use employee money and salary continuation plans use employer funds. Both plans have three common elements. We will discuss these three features in this chapter.

The first element is a promise by the employer to pay the employee a stated benefit. The benefit usually is expressed in an amount of retirement income for a fixed period of time—a defined benefit plan—or in terms of what a certain amount of money will purchase at a given age—a defined contribution plan. In addition to a promised retirement benefit, many plans offer a preretirement death benefit if the employee stays with the employer until retirement. It is important to understand that the plan document specifies the package of benefits.

The second element is a wall or barrier that exists between the promised benefits and a fund of cash. The wall or barrier is never breached in plan design. It is inviolate. There is never any connection between the promised benefits and the accumulating fund.

In theory, a nonqualified plan could stop there. Benefits could be paid from the future earnings of the firm or from any of several investment options. The question facing the employer is "What is the least expensive way to provide the promised benefits?" We have seen throughout this course that permanent life insurance has an inevitable gain at death, and that it builds cash values in an income tax-sheltered manner, because the growth of the cash values is not taxed until the cash values ultimately are received through the death benefit or through a retirement income stream. The answer to the employer's question is that permanent life insurance is the least expensive way to create a fund to pay promised preretirement and postretirement benefits.

The fund of money is the third element. Life insurance is also the most financially attractive way to ensure that the cash will be there when it is needed. When competitive insurance products designed for these plans are used, the internal rate of return often is better than can be obtained through stocks, bonds or mutual funds. The death benefit adds to the cash accumulation. In fact, in any moderate size group of employees, it is virtually certain that one or more deaths will occur during the working years. However, life insurance does not fund the plan in the usual sense; instead, it is often referred to as *informal funding*. This distinction between funding in the usual sense and the informal funding of life insurance is important.

No connection exists between the amount of insurance on the participants and their contribution in a deferred compensation plan, or between the contributions made for them by the employer in a salary continuation plan.

Participants are insured, but they do not have any interest in the life insurance policies. The policies are owned by the corporation, the premiums are paid by the corporation and the corporation is the beneficiary. Thus, if a participant should be uninsurable, the necessary insurance simply can be placed on the life of another participant. The law of large numbers will cause the cash accumulating within the fund to be appropriate to the needs of the plan over time.

■ THE DEFERRED COMPENSATION AGREEMENT

We will discuss now the main provisions of typical deferred compensation agreements (see sample agreements at the end of this chapter). A general knowledge of the content of such agreements will enable you to be of genuine service to your deferred compensation prospects and clients.

Although there are other provisions in a deferred compensation agreement, these are the most important:

1. The contract will apply only to that income unearned at the time of the signing of the agreement; that is, only to that income that is expected to be earned in the future and be subject to the agreement.

2. The employer's agreement with the employee is a mere promise to pay sums in the future. The employee has no right to any asset of the employer prior to the events specified in the contract (generally disability, retirement or death). This lack of employee rights to employer assets applies even if the employer has purchased insurance policies or other assets to help meet its obligation to the employee.

3. All payments made to the employee, the employee's spouse or family must flow from the employer. If the employer owns any insurance on the employee's life, none of the incidents of ownership should be transferred to the employee, nor should the spouse or other family member be named beneficiary of the policy.

4. Conditions may or may not be a part of the agreement. These are clauses that condition the payment of the benefits upon the employee either doing or not doing one or more acts—such as not competing with the employer after retirement, not attempting to assign the deferred benefits, or remaining with the employer until retirement age and acting in an advisory capacity afterward.

Life Insurance—An Important Part of the Plan

Life insurance is ideal for ensuring that the promised benefits of a deferred compensation plan will be available when necessary. Few organizations could commit themselves to pay a preretirement death benefit that might total, as our examples indicated, many thousands of dollars. It is obvious that life insurance gives the employer the leverage it needs when it obligates itself to continue benefit payments to the executive's estate or heirs. For a fraction of the sum insured, the employer can receive the insurance proceeds at the executive's death—tax free—to meet its obligations to the executive's family.

Type of Policy

The particular type of policy to suggest depends upon the general financial situation of the corporation and the ages of the prospective insureds. A cash value policy, preferably a whole life, universal life or variable life plan, is recommended, freeing the corporation to make the promised payments out of current earnings or accumulated surplus.

Policy Application and Ownership

The insurance should be applied for by the employer. The employer should be the beneficiary, as well as the owner of all incidents of ownership in the policy.

If an attempt is made to designate the employee's wife as direct beneficiary under the policy, or if the proceeds are made payable to a trustee to be held for the benefit of the insured's family, the premiums paid by the employer likely would be taxed in the current taxable year as additional compensation to the insured.

It is equally important that when an attorney drafts the deferred compensation agreement, there are no provisions giving the employee *any* rights to the insurance policy, either presently or upon retirement. It must be remembered that the deferred compensation agreement has no direct relation to the insurance. In fact, an effective deferred compensation agreement could be carried out regardless of whether there is life insurance, as indicated earlier. The sole purpose of the life insurance is to strengthen the corporation's overall financial picture. And, of course, that means greater peace of mind for the insured key person who realizes that the deferred compensation agreement has set up a substantial future liability in his or her favor.

From the employer's point of view, the use of insurance means that the business will be in a sound financial position when new liabilities are created for amortizing the future cost of paying benefits to a retired employee and offsetting payments that may be made to a widow or widower in those cases in which the spouse is included under the plan.

Handling Policy at Retirement

When the employee reaches retirement age, ownership of the insurance policy should remain vested in the employer. If the policy or any of the incidents of ownership are transferred or assigned to the insured-employee, the fair market value of the policy at the time of transfer would constitute income and be taxable to the employee in the taxable year the transfer was carried out.

The employer may select the cash value method of paying the benefits. Depending upon company practice, the employer may be permitted to elect to receive the maturity or cash surrender values under an income option for a fixed period of years. If the employer is obligated to pay an income to the employee for, let us say, ten years, then the employer may find it a convenient arrangement to elect an income option for a 10-year guaranteed period.

As the employer receives the payments from the insurance company, they could in turn be paid over to the employee. In that manner, the employee would incur income tax liability only to the extent of the amounts actually received in the taxable year of receipt.

In many instances, it would be best for the employer not to disturb the insurance policy. Assume that the employer has sufficient current earnings and profits from which to pay the employee without resorting to the accumulated cash values contained in the insurance policy. The policy could be kept intact so that the employer would receive the entire face amount of the insurance whenever the employee died. Moreover, if it is participating insurance, the employer would receive dividends after the policy becomes paid up. They would be income tax free until they exceed the cost basis of the policy, perhaps offering some assistance in meeting payments being made to the employee.

Proceeds Paid at Death

At the employee's death, the employer, as direct beneficiary, collects the insurance proceeds income tax free. The proceeds thus could serve as an income tax–free addition to the surplus serving as an offset against the employer's possible liability to the surviving spouse under the plan. Under no circumstances, of course, should the spouse have been named direct beneficiary or payee in the policy. The employer always should retain these rights.

The best way is for the insurance proceeds to be paid to the corporation. The employer then pays the surviving spouse directly from the corporation's own funds.

The insured key employee may desire that the payments go directly from the insurance company to his or her spouse. In this case, the employer could arrange with most insurance companies to make payments directly to the surviving spouse—but subject to the corporation's right to rescind the payment order. In this situation, the insurance company is acting as the agent for the employer in making the payments. The employer remains the sole payee.

Resolution of Board of Directors

The execution of a deferred compensation agreement and the purchase of life insurance to fund it informally should be approved by the board of directors. A resolution should be adopted authorizing the purchase of the insurance similar to the sample at the end of this chapter.

THE "INSURED" PLAN IN ACTION

Perhaps it is easier to understand deferred compensation with examples of typical cases. Let us see, therefore, how deferred compensation can be applied. Various types of financing may be used with deferred compensation plans, but life insurance has significant advantages. Also, you will want to keep in mind that such plans may be arranged with either defined or variable benefits.

■ CASE STUDY: DEFERRED COMPENSATION PLAN

Mr. Y, age 50, is the president of the Nut and Bolt Fastener Co., Inc. N&B is a successful medium-sized manufacturer, and Mr. Y is well worth the $100,000 salary and the $20,000 bonus he received last year. His income is what troubles Mr. Y. While he does not want to reduce his total compensation, he wonders whether there is some way for him to rearrange his receipt of income, so as to lower his present income tax.

After a talk with his agent, Mr. Y approaches the controlling shareholders of N&B with this proposition:

"Instead of paying me all my bonus next year and in the following years as current compensation, defer the first $10,000 of any bonus until I retire."

The shareholders and Mr. Y work out the following plan:

1. At age 65, N&B will pay him $10,000 per year for 15 years. If he should die after he retires, but before N&B has completed its payments to him, the $10,000 per year payments will be continued to his wife or other beneficiaries for the remainder of the 15 years.

2. If he should die before he retires, N&B will pay $10,000 per year to his wife or other beneficiaries for 15 years. Thus, she is assured of receiving $150,000 whenever death occurs before retirement.

3. If he becomes disabled before he retires, N&B will pay him an income of $10,000 per year, as long as he is disabled or until his age 65, when it will pay him a retirement income of $10,000 per year for 15 years.

At the time the parties signed the deferred compensation agreement, N&B took the net cost of a $10,000 bonus, if paid today ($6,600 in the 34 percent tax bracket) and purchased a $100,000 life insurance policy on Mr. Y, to ensure that the funds will be available to meet its obligation. N&B is the owner and the beneficiary of the policy, so the policy values are solely its property, and the proceeds are payable only to it.

The Employee's Viewpoint

Mr. Y gains greatly from the deferral of the $10,000 bonus that might otherwise come to him as current compensation. His salary reduction approach to deferred compensation will bring him tremendous tax savings. He has reduced his current income from $120,000 to $110,000.

The Employer's Viewpoint

How does N&B fare if Mr. Y were to die in the 12th year of the agreement? (We assume that insurance dividends were used to purchase paid up additions and that N & B is, and will remain, in the 34 percent tax bracket.)

Insurance ($100,000 + additions)	$185,000
Premiums ($6,600 × 12)	79,200
Gain	105,800
$150,000 payments after tax deduction	99,000
Net contribution to surplus	$ 6,800

Compare this result for N&B had Mr. Y continued to take the deferred $10,000 bonus as current compensation and died in the 12th year:

Bonuses—$10,000 × 12	$120,000
Tax deduction	40,800
Net charge to surplus	$ 79,200

It is evident then that N&B also benefits from this insured compensation plan.

Constructive Receipt Doctrine and Economic Benefit Doctrine

Two income tax concepts are particularly pertinent to deferred compensation: the constructive receipt doctrine and the economic benefit doctrine. The constructive receipt doctrine states that income that is not actually received may be taxed as if it had been, if the individual "constructively" received the income. This happens when the income was set aside for the individual, credited to his account or made available to the individual without any substantial restrictions on the individual's control over the income.

The economic benefit doctrine states that an individual recognizes income if property has been handled in a way that provides a cash-equivalent economic benefit to the individual. You will want to keep these two principles in mind as we discuss the taxation of deferred compensation arrangements.

Fortunately, under the law, a mere unsecured promise to pay income in the future does not constitute constructive receipt, provided the employee does not have access to the compensation that has been deferred. As a result, when properly set up, a deferred compensation plan usually will not result in current taxable income to the employee.

THE QUESTION OF MAJORITY SHAREHOLDERS

What about deferred compensation for an employee who is also the principal shareholder of the corporation? The answer to this question is of great importance to the insurance professional, because it is considerably easier to sell deferred compensation for the principal shareholder than for any other employee. However, the plan should be structured so that benefits will be paid to the principal shareholder at retirement or to the shareholder's family at death, even in the event that the corporation is no longer in existence.

Insurance Premiums

Premiums paid by a corporation on an insurance policy it owns on the life of a shareholder-employee will not be taxed to the employee as a dividend.

The Employer's Deduction

The employer may deduct payments made to an employee, provided that:

1. the payment of the benefits is a "necessary" business expense; and

2. the size of the benefit is "reasonable" in amount.

The first prerequisite can be satisfied in most cases with a binding, written agreement at the time the deferral of income begins. However, in the case of the majority shareholder, how necessary is it for that individual to have a deferred compensation agreement? The majority stock interest permits the shareholder, within the law, to set the corporation's salary schedules both now and in the future.

The second prerequisite may give the majority shareholder even more trouble than the first one. Are the distributions made to this employee reasonable compensation for services rendered and, therefore, deductible; or should they be regarded as dividends flowing to this individual because of his or her stock ownership and, therefore, not deductible by the corporation?

If the corporation has had difficulty during this shareholder-employee's working years justifying the reasonableness of the compensation paid, how much more difficult will this justification be after that individual retires, when the basis for the reasonableness of the deferred benefits will be the total services he or she performed for the corporation during the working years!

Accumulated Earnings

Furthermore, what of the corporation that accumulates reserves to enable it to meet its obligation to the shareholder-employee? Can it argue that these accumulations serve a legitimate business purpose and, therefore, escape the accumulated earnings tax? It would seem that when the employee is the principal shareholder, the corporation generally will find the money to pay the person a deferred benefit, because it does not need to accumulate the funds.

From our discussion, it is apparent that deferred compensation for the principal shareholder-employee is another rather uncertain area of the law and should be explored thoroughly by tax counsel before being effected.

It would seem, though, that from the point of view of the accumulated earnings tax, the corporation would be best advised to use a life insurance policy to fund its deferred compensation obligations, whether the covered employee is the majority shareholder or not. At any time during the employee's lifetime, there would be a smaller amount accumulated as annual premiums paid than with any other method of funding.

In those cases in which the persons are minority shareholders, there appears to be no reason why they cannot be covered by a deferred compensation agreement, providing the amounts are reasonable in the best judgment of the directors and shareholders.

OTHER TAX ISSUES

There are a number of other tax issues that arise concerning deferred compensation plans. Chief among these are the employer's income tax deduction and the tax liability of a surviving spouse or the decedent's estate.

Employer's Income Tax Deduction

The employer-paid premiums for insurance on the employee's life are clearly nondeductible when the employer owns and is the beneficiary of the insurance. The same principle would apply in setting up any other type of reserve. Of course, the employer receives the insurance proceeds free of income tax at the death of the employee. This result is no different than when life insurance is purchased for any other purpose.

The employer must await the time when payments to the employee under a deferred compensation agreement actually are made to deduct such payments. So the tax deduction is not lost, but only postponed and increased.

The "Necessary" and "Reasonable" Tests

To be deductible by the employer, deferred compensation payments made by an employer for majority shareholders also must qualify as ordinary and necessary business expenses and as a reasonable allowance for services actually rendered. These are not difficult tests to meet when the employer and the employee enter into a written arm's length agreement to pay deferred compensation.

The necessity and the reasonableness of the deferred compensation benefits more likely can be issues when, as pointed out before, the employee is also a principal shareholder of the firm. In these cases, the corporation's deduction of a portion or all of the deferred compensation payments may be disallowed as being, in effect, a distribution of dividends.

Payments to Employee's Widow/er

Tax law permits the deduction by the employer of payments made to the surviving spouse of a deceased employee under the terms of a deferred compensation contract.

Tax Liability of Surviving Spouse or Estate

An employee's estate or surviving spouse will have both income tax and estate tax consequences for payments provided under a deferred compensation agreement.

Income Tax

Payments received by an employee's surviving spouse or other beneficiary under a deferred compensation contract are reportable as gross income. This rule applies even though the source of the payments is insurance proceeds received by the employer, and which were excludable as income when received by the employer. The surviving spouse receives these payments because of the deferred compensation contract—not as income excludable as "amounts received under a life insurance contract."

Payments to a surviving spouse under a deferred compensation contract also are known as "income in respect of a decedent." Therefore, the estate tax attributable to these payments creates an income tax deduction for the survivor. This deduction can be applied against the payments as they are received.

Estate Tax

A deferred compensation agreement, evidenced by a contract, which promises benefits beyond the death of the employee, always will be included in the decedent's gross estate and possibly be subject to federal estate tax. The includability of the value of the deferred compensation benefits payable to the decedent's surviving spouse or other beneficiary is based on the fact that the decedent had a contractual right to have his or her employer make these payments.

It is the *present value* of deferred compensation payments payable after the employee's death that is includable in the decedent's gross estate. The Treasury's annuity and life expectancy tables are used to value the present worth of the payments.

Finally, if a deferred compensation plan is noncontractual and the employer may modify or terminate it at any time before the employee's death or retirement, its death benefits may not be subject to estate tax.

SUMMARY

With the conclusion of our study of deferred compensation, it is important that we properly classify deferred compensation among business insurance sales ideas. Deferred compensation is an excellent door opener. But even the most experienced agent probably makes few deferred compensation sales.

There are two possible reasons for this. One is the absence of an immediate tax deduction for amounts set aside by the employer to meet a deferred pay obligation. Perhaps a greater deterrent is the fact that in most sales situations the agent discusses deferred compensation with the majority shareholders of corporations, who generally have little reason to take advantage of it.

The result is that a sales conversation that began with an explanation of the merits of deferred compensation often ends with the shareholder and the agent switching the emphasis to other ideas helpful to the closely held business, namely:

1. a qualified pension or profit-sharing plan;

2. a corporate health and medical care plan;

3. a split-dollar plan;

4. key-executive insurance;

5. group life insurance;

6. estate planning;

7. a Section 303 stock redemption;

8. a buy-sell agreement; or

9. Subchapter S election.

Again, it is important that, as an insurance professional, you maintain a flexible stance in the sales interview. Deferred compensation is an excellent tool for rewarding a valued employee and helping to retain the services of such an individual. But it is just one of a number of great business insurance ideas you will want to discuss with prospects.

ILL 11.3 ■ *Resolution*

CAUTION: This is a specimen resolution. The actual resolution used in any particular case must be prepared by a qualified attorney.

Whereas, a deferred compensation agreement has been executed with _____, Vice-President of this corporation whereby he(she) is entitled to have his (her) salary continued in a reduced amount for ten years, commencing at age _____, should he (she) remain employed until that time and meet certain specified conditions thereafter; and

Whereas, the corporation recognizes the fact that some immediate plans should be formulated in order to place itself in a financial position to be able to meet this future contingency; and

Whereas, it is deemed advisable by the Board of Directors of this corporation that the life of _____, Vice-President of this corporation, be insured for the purpose of protecting this corporation from loss in the event of death and disability of said _____;

> This paragraph should be expanded to detail the precise manner in which the employee is of value to the corporation. This description will vary with each case.

Therefore, Be It Resolved that the _____(officer) _____ be authorized and instructed to take such action and execute such papers as may be necessary to secure a policy or policies of life insurance in the _____(company or companies)_____on the life of _____ having a total face value $_____, with the corporation to be named as beneficiary of such policy or policies and to be the owner of same; the policies so obtained shall be of the _____ type; and

Resolved Further, that said _____ shall not have any rights whatsoever in said policy; that all dividends, accumulations, and other benefits accruing from said policy shall belong and be payable to this corporation; and that this corporation shall undertake to pay the premiums upon such policy as they become due and payable during the life of said _____; and

Resolved Further, that the board of Directors shall have the right to surrender the insurance taken out upon the life of said _____ at any time, and to receive for the benefit of this corporation the cash surrender and other values of the policy.

> **RATIFICATION BY BOARD OF DIRECTORS:** The deferred compensation agreement should be presented to the Board of Directors for vote. If it pertains to an officer of the corporation, the officer should not participate in the vote. If the party is a shareholder, then the agreement should also be presented to the shareholder for ratification.
>
> Such question for ratification might be presented in the following form:

Resolved, that the payments due said _____ or his (her) beneficiaries at the time of his (her) retirement or death, or disability be fixed as provided for in a deferred compensation agreement executed and dated _____.

_____
President

_____
Secretary

ILL 11.4 ■ *Sample Deferred Compensation Agreement*

CAUTION: This is a specimen agreement. The actual agreement used in any particular case must be prepared by a qualified attorney.

Agreement entered into as of the _____ day of _____, _____, between the _____, a domestic corporation having its principal office in _____ (hereinafter referred to as the *Company*) and _____ of _____ (hereinafter referred to as the *Employee*).

Whereas the Employee has rendered the Company many years of valuable service and it is the desire of the Company to have the benefit of his (her) continued loyalty, service and counsel and also to assist him (her) in providing for the Contingencies of disability, death and old age dependency, it hereby is agreed:

1. **DISABILITY BENEFIT**—Should the Employee, before _____ day of _____, _____, while in the employ of the Company, become totally disabled, resulting from bodily injury or disease, which prevents the Employee from engaging for remuneration or profit in any and every occupation or business for which he (she) reasonably is suited by education, training or experience. (The total and irrevocable loss of the sight of both eyes, or the use of both hands, both feet, or one hand and one foot will be regarded as total disability in any event.) The Company (beginning at a date to be determined by the Company but within six months from the date of disability) will commence to pay him (her) _____ ($)_____ per month for the duration of the disability, or until the Employee's age 65, or until the Employee's death, whichever occurs first.

    Many deferred compensation agreements provide for disability income payments, as well as death and retirement benefits.

2. **DEATH BENEFIT**—Should the Employee die before the _____ day of _____, _____, while in the employ of the Company (subject to the provisions of paragraph hereof), the Company (beginning at a date to be determined by the Company but within six months from the date of death) will commence to pay _____ ($)_____ per month for a continuous period of _____ months to _____, otherwise to the Executors, or Administrators of the Employee. The beneficiaries named hereon may be challenged at any time by the Employee, with the agreement of the Company, by written amendment. The benefit shall not be payable for death of the Employee resulting from suicide, whether sane or insane, within two years after signing the agreement.

    At the employee's death, the employer collects the insurance proceeds income tax free. The proceeds thus serve as an income tax-free addition to surplus, which serves as an offset against the employer's liability to the employee's surviving spouse. Under no circumstances, of course, should such survivor be named direct beneficiary or payee of the policy. The employer should always retain these rights.

3. **RETIREMENT BENEFIT**—Should the Employee still be, for purposes of this agreement, in the employ of the Company upon the _____ day of _____, _____, the Company (beginning on a date to be determined by the Company but within six months from such retirement date) will commence to pay him (her) should die after said payments have commenced but before the expiration of said _____ month period, the unpaid balance of the payments due will continue to be paid by the Company to those beneficiaries designated in paragraph 2 above.

ILL 11.4 ▪ *Sample Deferred Compensation Agreement (Cont.)*

> When the employee reaches retirement age, ownership of the insurance policy should remain vested in the employer. If the policy or any of the incidents of ownership are transferred or assigned to the insured-employee, the fair market value of the policy at the time of transfer would constitute income and be taxable to the employee in the taxable year of transfer. Since such an income tax would obviously destroy one of the main purposes of the agreement, no attempt should be made to transfer the policy to the employee.

4. **CONDITIONS**—(a) The provisions of paragraph 3 are conditional upon the continues employment of the employee by the Company (including periods of total disability described in paragraph 1 and subject to the provisions of paragraph 5 hereof) until the _____ day of _____, _____, or his (her) death, whichever is sooner, and upon the further condition that, during the period that retirement payments are made, the Employee shall not engage in business activities that are in competition with the Company without first obtaining written consent of the Company.

   > Revenue Ruling 60-31, eliminated the need for conditions, from a constructive receipt of income standpoint, where the agreement calls for a mere promise to pay.

   > However, there are still obviously good business reasons for inclusion of such conditions. For example, an employer may be hesitant to enter into an agreement whereby the employee could terminate employment, receive the deferred compensation, and then immediately use the funds to finance himself (herself) as a competitor. In such a case, the deferred compensation contract would include a condition that all benefits are lost should the employee terminate prior to age 65.

5. **LEAVE OF ABSENCE**—The Company may, in its sole discretion, permit the Employee to take a leave of absence for a period not to exceed one year. During this time the Employee will be considered to be still in the employ of the Company for purposes of this agreement.

6. **ACCELERATION OF BENEFIT PAYMENTS**—The Company hereby reserves the right to accelerate the payment of any of those sums specified in paragraphs 1, 2 and 3 above without the consent of the Employee or the Employee's estate, beneficiaries, or any other person claiming through or under him (her).

7. **ASSIGNABILITY**—Except to the extent that this provision may be contrary to law, no assignment, pledge, collateralization, or attachment of any benefits under this agreement shall be valid or recognized by the Company.

8. **EMPLOYMENT RIGHTS**—This agreement creates no rights in the Employee to continue in the Company's employ for any specific length of time, nor does it create any other rights in the Employee or obligations on the part of the Company, except those set forth in this agreement.

9. **LAW GOVERNING**—This agreement shall be governed by the laws of the State of _____.

ILL 11.4 ▪ *Sample Deferred Compensation Agreement (Cont.)*

THIS AGREEMENT is solely between the Company and the Employee. Further, the Employee and his (her) beneficiaries shall have recourse only against the Company for enforcement. However, it shall be binding upon the beneficiaries, heirs, executors and administrators of the Employee and upon the successors and assigns of the Company.

EXECUTED as of the day first written above.

COMPANY

By:_____

Title

_____

Employee

ILL 11.5 ▪ *Deferred Compensation For Public Employees*

State and local government employees are permitted to establish nonqualified deferred compensation plans similar to those for employees in the private sector. Reproduced below are a sample salary reduction agreement and a sample joinder agreement for such plans.

CAUTION: This is a specimen agreement. The actual agreement used in any particular case must be prepared by a qualified attorney.

SAMPLE DEFERRED COMPENSATION AGREEMENT
(Salary Reduction)

THIS MASTER AGREEMENT, made this _____ day of, 20_____, by and between __(ORGANIZATION)__ and the Participants who become a party to this agreement by reason of a "Joinder Agreement" signed at this time or at a time in the future.

WITNESSETH:

Whereas, the Participants are valued employees or independently contracted persons of the Organization, and the Organization desires to retain these individuals in its service;

Whereas, it is to the mutual benefit of the parties hereto that said relation continue for an extended number of years so that the Participants shall continue to participate in the operations of the Organization;

Now, Therefore, the parties hereby agree as follows:

Section 1—Definitions

(a) Compensation" shall mean all payments for normal services, rendered by the Participants to the Organization, including but not limited to the gross salary of the individual. These amounts would be before any deductions for Federal or State, F.I.C.A., or pension plan contributions.
(b) Includable Compensation" is the compensation that results after deferred compensation or tax-deferred annuity reduction amounts have been reduced from the original compensation and which will be shown on the IRS Form W-2.
(c) Compensation Reduction" shall mean that amount deferred which results from the Participant's election to reduce his compensation under the Joinder Agreement and which the Participant and Organization mutually agree shall be deferred in accordance with this Agreement.
(d) Participant" shall mean an individual who is eligible to defer compensation and who fulfills the eligibility requirements of this Agreement.
(e) Organization" shall mean _____.
(f) Beneficiary" shall mean the beneficiary or beneficiaries designated in the Joinder Agreement by the Participant.
(g) Normal Retirement" for purposes of this Agreement shall mean a retirement from service with the Organization which becomes effective on the first day of the calendar month after the Participant attains age 65.
(h) Early Retirement" for purposes of this Agreement shall mean a retirement from service with the Organization which is effective prior to age 65, provided the Participant has attained age 55.

ILL 11.5 ■ *Deferred Compensation For Public Employees (Cont.)*

(i) Late Retirement" for purposes of this Agreement shall mean a retirement from service with the Organization which becomes effective after the Participant has attained age 65. (When any Participant is placed on extended service with the Organization after attaining age 65, the amount of compensation deferred by the Participant prior to age 65 plus any amount deferred under compensation reduction subsequent to age 65 under this Agreement will be continued for the period of such extended service.)

(j) Termination of Service" shall mean severance of the Participant's contract or employment with the Organization prior to the Participant's 55th birthday by reason other than death or disability.

(k) Disability" means total and permanent disability which prohibits the Participant from engaging in any substantial gainful activity by reason of any medically determinable physical or mental impairment which can be expected to result in death or to be of long and indefinite duration.

(l) Underutilized Deferrals" means the amount by which the compensation actually included in the participant's income for the previous taxable years exceeded the amount which would have been included in income had the maximum deferral been utilized.

Section 2—Eligibility

Any participant of the Organization who, with the consent of the Organization, irrevocably elects to reduce and defer compensation as specified in Section 3 and as elected through the Joinder Agreement shall be a Participant.

Section 3—Reduction of Compensation

The Organization and Participant agree that the Participant's compensation which would otherwise be receivable during a period of employment subsequent to the effective date of the Joinder Agreement shall be irrevocably reduced and that portion of compensation reduction shall be deferred as specified in this Agreement.

It is further agreed that:

(a) The annual compensation reduction amount will not exceed the lesser of:

—25% of compensation (33a% of includible compensation) or;

—$10,500.

(b) An eligible Participant may utilize a limited "catch-up" provision for any, or all, of the last three taxable years of a Participant immediately preceding the normal retirement age specified in Section 1(g). The maximum that can be deferred in any taxable year through the utilization of both the defined contribution limits and the "catch-up" provision is $15,000. The "catch-up" amount may not exceed the underutilized deferrals. (See Section 1(l) Definitions.)

(c) An eligible person, with respect to participation commencing in the initial year of the plan, for an individual when he or she first becomes eligible to participate, may become a Participant prior to or within 60 days after the plan becomes effective or the employee first becomes eligible, by agreeing to defer compensation not yet earned, but such agreement must be made prior to the beginning of the period in which it is to become effective.

ILL 11.5 ■ *Deferred Compensation For Public Employees (Cont.)*

(d) A Participant shall have the right exercisable within 30 days prior to the beginning of any calendar year to elect to increase or decrease the compensation reduction for the ensuing calendar year by executing another Joinder Agreement.

(e) For purposes of this Agreement, a Participant's failure to file written notice of his (her) elective choice as provided in (d) above shall constitute a waiver by the Participant of his (her) right to elect a different reduction sum for the next succeeding calendar year and an affirmation and ratification to continue the stated compensation reduction as chosen in the prior period.

(f) A Participant may elect to discontinue compensation reductions for any subsequent calendar year following the effective date of his (her) Joinder Agreement; provided, however, the Participant shall notify the Organization of such discontinuance at least 30 days prior to the subsequent calendar year.

Section 4—Coordination with Tax-Deferred Annuity 403(b) Plans

If an individual participates in a tax-deferred annuity 403(b) plan (TDA), these TDA contributions reduce both the $10,500 and the 25% of gross compensation (33a% of includable compensation) limitations explained in Section 3(a)(1)(2) and (b). The maximum combined annual contribution of both TDA and deferred compensation plans shall not exceed the lesser of 25% of compensation of $10,500. The only exception to this normal rule is where the participant is using the "catch-up" provision explained in Section 3(b).

Section 5—Benefits

(a) The following alternative types of benefits shall be available to the Participants under this Agreement:

  (i) *Retirement Benefits*
  The participant must elect the method in which deferred amounts are to be paid no later than 30 days prior to actual retirement. For purposes of this subsection, the definitions of early, normal, or late retirement will be used in determining the actual retirement date. The methods of distribution are found in subsection 5 of this section. Payments will begin not later than 30 days after the retirement date.

  (ii) *Termination Benefits*
  Should the Participant terminate services other than by retirement, disability, or death, the Organization shall make payment to the Participant so qualifying as elected in the Joinder Agreement. These elections include any of those mentioned in paragraph (5) which follows. Such payment(s) will begin not later than 30 days after said termination.

  (iii) *Disability Benefits*
  In the event the Participant shall, prior to his (her) normal retirement date, become totally and permanently disabled as defined in Section 1(k), the Organization shall pay benefits to the Participant so qualifying as elected in the Joinder Agreement. These elections include any of those mentioned in paragraph (5) which follows. Such payment(s) will begin not later than 30 days after receipt of proof of said disability.

  (iv) *Death Benefits*
  In the event the Participant dies prior to his (her) retirement date, the Organization agrees to pay death benefits to the Participant's beneficiary or to the Participant's estate as elected in the Joinder Agreement. These elections include any of those mentioned in paragraph (5) which follows. Such payment(s) will begin not later than 30 days after receipt of proof of death.

ILL 11.5 ▪ *Deferred Compensation For Public Employees (Cont.)*

If the Participant dies after he (she) has begun receiving any benefits to which he (she) is entitled but before the receipt of all payments, the Organization agrees to continue to pay the balance of such payments to the Participant's designated beneficiary, if living, otherwise to the Participant's estate.

    (v) *Joinder Agreement Settlement Options*
        (a) Lump Sum, (b) Life Annuity, (c) 60, 120, 180 or 240 Months Certain and Life, (d) Unit Refund Life Annuity, (e) Installment Refund Life Annuity, (f) Joint and Full Survivor or Two-Thirds to Survivor Annuity, (g) Installments for a designated period or amount, (h) or any other mutually agreeable payout option.

(b) Factors determining the benefits under this agreement are age at the time compensation is deferred; the amounts of reduced compensation deferred; and the age at retirement, termination, disability, or death. To determine these benefits, the participant's age on the birth date nearest the date he (she) elects to defer compensation will be used as the "age at the time compensation is deferred."

The benefits under this Agreement shall be dependent upon that amount which has accumulated in the Organization's general account with respect to the Participant or beneficiary for whom such payments are being determined under the funding media selected

(c) Each Participant shall have the right to designate a beneficiary, including a contingent beneficiary, to receive any benefits which may be payable upon the death of the Participant. The Participant shall have the right to change any beneficiaries designated under this Agreement. Changes of a beneficiary designation are binding only if they have been made in a manner acceptable to the Organization and prior to the payment of the amounts that become due.

(d) The Organization shall have no obligation to set aside, earmark, or entrust any fund, policy, or money with which to pay its obligations under this Agreement. The Participant, and any successor in interest to him (her) shall be and remain simply a general creditor of the Organization with respect to the compensation deferred under this Agreement in the same manner as any other creditor who has a general claim for an unpaid liability. The Organization shall be the sole owner and beneficiary of any assets acquired for its general account under this Agreement. The Organization shall not make any substantial loans or extend substantial credit to a Participant or designated Beneficiary which will be offset by benefits payable under this Agreement.

Section 6—Withdrawal for Hardship

A Participant may request a withdrawal under this Agreement prior to retirement or termination of service, but such a request will not be honored unless great hardship conditions exist. Hardship conditions must be the result of a real emergency beyond the control of a Participant or his (her) beneficiary. Withdrawals must be limited to amounts necessary to meet the hardship. The withdrawal shall be effective upon approval by the Organization and shall be paid in lump sum to the Participant.

Section 7—Amendment or Termination

The Organization reserves the right to amend any provision of this Agreement at any time to the extent that it may deem advisable without the consent of the Participant or any beneficiary.

The Organization reserves the right to terminate this Agreement at any time. Upon termination, the Organization shall pay to each Participant an amount of money which would have been available had the Participant terminated his (her) service at that time. The Organization will make payments in lump sum not later than 30 days after said termination of plan.

ILL 11.5 ■ *Deferred Compensation For Public Employees (Cont.)*

Section 8—Nonassignability Clause

No benefits under this agreement shall be subject in any manner to anticipation, alienation, sale, transfer, assignments, pledge, or encumbrance. Any attempt to do so shall be void. Such benefits shall not be subject to or liable for the debts, contracts, liabilities, engagements, or torts of the Participant or his (her) beneficiary.

Section 9—Headings

Headings and subheadings in the Agreement are inserted for convenience of reference only and constitute no part of this Agreement.

Section 10—Waiver

Notwithstanding any other provision of this Agreement, the Organization shall not be liable to the Participant or any beneficiary hereof for any mistakes in judgment in the making or retaining of any investments, nor for any loss from investing the funds so long as the Organization performs its obligations hereunder in good faith.

Section 11—Types of Investments

The deferred amounts may, at the sole discretion of the Organization, be invested in Lincoln National Life Group Variable Annuity or life insurance products.

Nothing herein shall require the Organization to purchase investments or assets, but in the event the Organization should purchase such investments or assets, it shall not be required to exercise any option, election, or right with respect to such investments or assets, or if it wishes to exercise any option, election, or right under such investments or assets it shall not be required to exercise such option, election, or right in any particular manner.

Section 12—Applicable Law

This Agreement shall be construed under the law of the State of _____ and Section 457 of the Internal Revenue Code of 1986, as amended.

IN WITNESS WHEREOF, the Organization has caused this Agreement to be signed by its duly authorized Officer, and attested by its Secretary on the _____ day of _____, 20____.

ATTEST: ORGANIZATION:

_____   By_____

                                                                 Title_____

ILL 11.6 ■ *Sample Joinder Agreement*

CAUTION: This is a specimen agreement. The actual agreement used in any particular case must be prepared by a qualified attorney.

**Application for Participation and
Beneficiary Designation Under the <u>Organization</u>
Master Deferred Compensation Agreement**

The undersigned hereby agrees to the terms and conditions of the Master Deferred Compensation as such Agreement now exists, and as it may be amended, and applies for participation thereunder effective as of _____.

The undersigned agrees that the Organization's payroll department shall have the irrevocable right to reduce his (her) income by $_____ each pay period. This election to reduce income shall continue until the undersigned makes a subsequent election as provided by the Master Agreement.

The participant hereby elects to have benefit payments described in Section 5 of the Agreement made as follows:

- Lump Sum
- Life Annuity
- 60 Months Certain and Life
- 120 Months Certain and Life
- 180 Months Certain and Life
- 240 Months Certain and Life
- Unit Refund Life Annuity
- Installment Refund Life Annuity
- Joint and Full Survivor
- Joint and Two-Thirds Survivor
- Installments for a Designated Period
- Installments for a Designated Amount
- _____

Termination Benefit_____
above is elected under Section 5(a)(2)

Disability Benefit_____
above is elected under Section 5(a)(3)

Death Benefit_____
above is elected under Section 5(a)(4)

ILL 11.6 ▪ *Sample Joinder Agreement (Cont.)*

The undersigned acknowledged that the Organization is under no obligation to continue the Deferred Compensation Agreement and that being a participant thereunder in no way guarantees his (her) employment. Until further notice, the undersigned requests that any death benefits be payable to:

_____
Name

_____
Address   Relationship

however, if there be no surviving beneficiary then to the Participant's estate.

This application shall become effective as of the effective date above stated without further notice upon receipt by the Organization.

_____
Date   Signature of Participant

The consent of the participant's spouse is required in the event that the designated beneficiary is other than said spouse. (Applies only to community property states.) I hereby consent to the beneficiary designation set forth above.

_____
Date   Signature of Participant's Spouse

Application for Participation and Beneficiary Designation received this _____ day of _____, 20_____.

_____
Organization

By_____

CHAPTER 11 QUESTIONS FOR REVIEW

1. Under a typical deferred compensation agreement, the employee
   A. can demand the payment of the deferred compensation at any time
   B. can borrow deferred amounts, but at a "fair market" rate of return
   C. can have no right to deferred amounts prior to the stipulated event, such as retirement
   D. none of the above

2. The owner and beneficiary of the life insurance policy under a deferred compensation plan is
   A. the employee
   B. the employer
   C. the employee's spouse or other beneficiary designated by the employee
   D. the employee's estate

3. At retirement, payments to the employee are
   A. taxable income to the employee as received
   B. partially tax free
   C. received entirely tax free
   D. taxable in a lump sum in the year of retirement

4. The advantages of an insured deferred compensation to the employee include
   A. an annual tax deduction for premiums
   B. supplemental retirement income
   C. tax-free receipt of payments at retirement
   D. all of the above

5. Which of the following is true about a deferred compensation plan?
   A. The employee's widow will receive taxable income
   B. The employee can exclude $5,000 from taxable income
   C. The employer can deduct no more than $5,000 in payments as a necessary and reasonable business expense
   D. None of the above

12
Salary Continuation Plans

Salary continuation plans are distinguished from the deferred compensation plans covered in the last chapter. Tax aspects of the life insurance informally-funded plan, ERISA, reasonable compensation considerations and the interplay with Social Security each are examined in turn. The chapter concludes with an examination of the salary continuation agreement and a look at the provisions of a sample agreement.

In the previous chapter, we discussed nonqualified deferred compensation. In this chapter, we'll look at another nonqualified benefit available to business officers and executives: *salary continuation plans*.

Under a salary continuation plan, the employer agrees to continue a portion of the executive's salary upon the executive's death, retirement, and(or) disability. This plan is distinguishable from the nonqualified deferred compensation plan whereby the executive either agrees to a salary reduction or to receive, in lieu of a current salary increase, a stipulated number of payments beginning at retirement. The deferred compensation plan is funded with the executive's dollars; the salary continuation plan, with the employer's dollars.

Although salary continuation plans have long been used by employers, the further restrictions on qualified plans by recent tax legislation have made salary continuation agreements much more important and appealing. Because of changes in coverage, participation, integration and funding requirements, qualified benefit plans have become more expensive to establish, administer and maintain. Nonqualified salary continuation plans provide greater flexibility and permit the employer and employee to avoid much of the complexity of qualified plans.

PLAN OVERVIEW AND DESIGN

Under a typical salary continuation arrangement, the employer agrees to pay the employee or his or her assignee continuing payments at retirement, death or disability. This is subject to the condition that the employee continues employment with the employer. Or the plan may require that the employee provide continuing consulting-type services after retirement.

Typically, the plan is unfunded. The use of life insurance to aid the employer in paying obligations does not make the plan "funded" in the usual sense of the word (when specific assets are set aside for and identified with the employee). Instead, the plan is said to be "informally funded." This is an important distinction, because funded plans are not exempt under the stringent requirements of ERISA covering qualified plans, and there would be no advantage to salary continuation plans if they had to meet the numerous ERISA reporting and disclosure requirements.

The decision to vest benefits usually is left up to the employer and employee. If the benefits are vested, there should be no current income consequences to the employee as long as: (1) the employer's promise is unsecured; and (2) the agreement is made before the services are rendered. Moreover, when the plan is funded with life insurance, there will be no income tax consequences as long as the following additional requirements are met: (3) the employee has no interest in the policy; (4) the general creditors of the employer can access the policy's cash value; and (5) the employer is the applicant, owner and premium payer of the policy.

Nonetheless, be aware that for a salary continuation plan to obtain the desired tax advantages for both the employer and the employee, a number of specific requirements must be met. For this reason, it is always a good idea to work closely with your client's other advisors when setting up the plan.

Benefits of a Salary Continuation Plan

Salary continuation plans are popular executive benefits. However, many executives hesitate giving up present benefits for future benefits. This is not to say that salary continuation plans should be avoided. On the contrary, in the right situation with the right client, they have much to offer, especially when supported by life insurance to provide future benefits.

A salary continuation plan is primarily a fringe benefit utilized by an employer to help retain key personnel and to encourage performance. But the plan offers numerous other advantages, including:

1. The employer's unsecured promise to make payments at a future date does not give rise to current taxable income to the participant; the executive is not taxed on the income until it is received—ideally at a time when he or she is in a lower tax bracket.

2. Policy proceeds are not included in the employee's gross estate.

3. The plan is easier to establish than a qualified plan because it avoids the majority of ERISA requirements when it pertains to highly compensated individuals or a select group of management personnel, or when it is defined as an "excess benefit plan" under ERISA. However, there is a minimal reporting and disclosure requirement and a need to name a fiduciary for the plan.

4. The employer receives an income tax deduction when the benefits are actually paid.

5. At the death of the employee, the employer receives death proceeds income tax free to aid in funding any other obligations.

6. The employer can be selective in rewarding key personnel. There is no need to follow the nondiscriminatory rules under the Code that are applied to qualified retirement plans.

7. The employer can provide the employee with a benefit with little or no after-tax cost when the plan is informally funded with life insurance.

An additional advantage to the employer is that the company can retain the services of the employee through "golden handcuffs." In exchange for the future benefits, the employee usually must comply with certain conditions of employment before, and perhaps after, retirement. The conditions are set forth in an agreement with the employer and may include the executive's promise:

1. to remain with the company for a specified number of years;

2. to refrain from becoming employed by, or in any way serving, competing companies after retirement; and

3. to act as business consultant to the company after retirement.

A salary continuation arrangement enables a company to provide substantial retirement benefits exclusively for top management personnel on a selective basis. Such a plan requires no qualification with the IRS. However, certain minimal reporting procedures must be followed.

■ CASE STUDY: SALARY CONTINUATION PLAN

Ms. X, age 45, is a key engineer for Zoom Electronics. Her salary of $72,000 per year only partially reflects her value to Zoom. In addition to her being responsible for several important Zoom products, Mr. Zoom sees Ms. X as a possible interim president if he should die before his own son comes of age. Ms. X has thrown a scare into Zoom on several occasions by saying that she might quit and move to the West Coast. Zoom Electronics currently has no qualified retirement plan.

Encouraged by his insurance agent, Zoom executes a deferred compensation agreement with Ms. X, for the purpose of encouraging Ms. X to stay with Zoom.

The agreement provides that upon X's reaching age 65, Zoom Electronics promises to pay her a retirement income of $5,000 per month ($60,000 per year) for 120 months. Should X die after retirement, but before reaching age 75, the retirement benefits will be continued to her husband or other family member for the remainder of the 10 years.

Should Ms. X die before retirement, Zoom agrees to pay her widower or other family member $5,000 per month for 10 years.

Should Ms. X become disabled, Zoom agrees to pay Ms. X $5,000 per month for as long as she is disabled, or until age 65. At age 65, Ms. X will qualify for the above retirement benefit. As a disabled person, Ms. X also may qualify for her full Social Security benefit.

These payments from Zoom Electronics to Ms. X are conditioned on the following:

1. Ms. X will continue as an employee of Zoom until the occurrence of any of the above events.

2. After retirement from Zoom, Ms. X shall not engage in business activities that are in competition with Zoom without first getting the written permission of the company.

Ms. X further agrees that her beneficiaries shall receive nothing if she should commit suicide within two years after the signing of the agreement. She also recognizes that she cannot assign, pledge or actively anticipate in any way the benefits provided under the agreement.

At the time the parties sign the deferred compensation agreement Zoom Electronics purchases a $600,000 life insurance policy on Ms. X to ensure that funds will be available to meet the retirement and death payments. The company is the owner and beneficiary of the policy, which is for the amount equal to the total payments promised Ms. X ($5,000 × 120 months, or $600,000). As Zoom is the owner and the beneficiary of the policy, the policy values are solely its property and the proceeds are payable only to the company.

The Employee's Viewpoint

Ms. X, of course, is delighted with her agreement. For no additional effort on her part, she and her family have been assured of at least $5,000 per month income should she live to retirement, die or become disabled. Social Security, to the extent that she and(or) her family qualify, will increase the income received. Further, Zoom has taken the steps necessary to ensure that it will be in a position to meet its obligations to X; namely, it has insured X's life for the full amount of the promised payments.

The Employer's Viewpoint

The obvious advantage to Zoom is that it has taken a positive step to hold a key employee without incurring the cost of a comprehensive pension plan. But there's another major advantage to the company; namely, the low actual cost of the plan. Because the company is in the 34 percent federal bracket, when federal and state income taxes are considered, the costs are lowered by almost half. Let's break down the cost of the deferred compensation plan to the company. Zoom has promised Ms. X or her family 120 payments of $5,000 each month after her death or retirement. Because the company can deduct these payments when made as an ordinary and necessary business expense, the actual cost to Zoom is $396,000 over a 10-year period, assuming a 34 percent federal corporate income tax bracket.

The cost of the plan to the company would have been considerably greater had the company chosen not to insure Ms. X. While the life insurance premiums are not deductible by Zoom, the insurance proceeds received at death will be tax free. As a result, the company stands to "gain" in some years and reduce its cost in every year the plan is in effect. Here is an illustration, if Ms. X died after five years, or after 20 years. (The insurance values are approximate and reflect a policy purchased on Ms. X, age 45, with a face amount of $600,000.)

	5 yrs.	20 yrs.
Insurance proceeds	$600,000	$600,000
Premiums (used for illustration only)	100,000	400,000
Insurance gains	$500,000	$200,000
$60,000 payment (over 10 yrs.) after tax	$396,000	$396,000
Gain or reduction in surplus	104,000	(196,000)

The corporation further benefits from the purchase of the waiver of premium rider with the policy. Ms. X's disability before retirement would free the premium payments to help defray the cost of the promised disability benefit.

Our insurance illustration also acts as a comparison between insured deferred compensation and a present cash bonus to the executive. In our illustration, the maximum cost to Zoom of this plan is, $196,000. On the other hand, a present bonus of $60,000 for 10 years would cost the company the same as an uninsured deferred compensation plan—namely $396,000.

In the above illustration, it could be advantageous for the employer to retain the paid-up policy in force after Ms. X's retirement or disability and to pay the promised benefits out of current or retained earnings. Some employers, of course, will choose (generally for "cash" reasons) to convert the policy to an annuity and use its values to pay the promised benefits. Terminating the death benefit, however, will increase the employer's overall cost for the program because it will be forgoing the opportunity to recover some of its costs upon Ms. X's eventual death.

When other corporate assets are adequate to pay the benefits, this cash value funding method should be discouraged. The employer loses the leverage gained while holding the life insurance policy by waiting for the disabled or retired employee to die and collecting the insurance proceeds tax free. Furthermore, by cashing in or converting the policy at the time of disability or retirement, the employer may be subject to income tax to the extent it has shown a profit on the policy.

Identifying and Working with Prospects

To ensure the success of a salary continuation plan, be sure that certain conditions are present in the business. Among these conditions are:

1. Plans should be in force to continue the business beyond the retirement of the key employee. Remember, there must be a business for the benefits to be paid.

2. There must be competent successor management. It would make no sense to set up a salary continuation plan for a company's key personnel only to discover, too late, that the business is unable to keep its commitments.

3. One or more key employees must desire additional retirement income, without incurring additional income taxes currently.

Working with Advisors

As mentioned earlier, a properly set up salary continuation plan requires compliance with a number of requirements. As an insurance professional, you are expected to be knowledgeable about tax matters, although not an expert in the rules and regulations of the Internal Revenue Code. So it is generally recommended that you get an attorney and your home office specialists involved at the early stages of plan discussion.

Another option is to arrange to split the case on a joint-work basis with another producer who has proven his or her expertise with these plans. By working with an established expert, the salesperson who is new to the nonqualified marketplace can learn the nuances of these sophisticated sales while satisfying the requests of other advisors.

Protecting Benefits

A key concern of the executive counting on retirement and other benefits from a salary continuation plan is that the funds will actually be available when promised. Sometimes trusts are used for this purpose. Two such trusts are a rabbi trust and a secular trust.

Rabbi Trusts

Rabbi trusts were used more frequently in nonqualified plans several years ago than they are used today. A rabbi trust is an irrevocable grant or trust that is subject to the claims of the employer's creditors. The nonqualified plan participant is an unsecured general creditor. These trusts commonly are used when the plan participant wishes to protect his or her deferred compensation or salary continuation promised benefits from new management in takeover situations.

As with all funds in nonqualified plans, funds in a rabbi trust must be reachable by creditors of the employer in bankruptcy or insolvency proceedings. Thus, a rabbi trust simply provides a degree of additional protection that some nonqualified plan participants feel is appropriate.

Secular Trusts

Secular trusts are a form of irrevocable trust used to help separate benefits from the company. As opposed to the rabbi trust, funds in the secular trust are not subject to the claims of the employer's general creditors. Typically, the secular trust is used when the employee wants to recognize income currently, possibly due to lower current tax rates, yet still retain the other benefits of a nonqualified retirement plan.

There has been some controversy over the secular trust. The IRS has held such trusts to be grantor trusts, with the grantor being the employee. Therefore, such a trust would not be under ERISA jurisdiction. The Department of Labor has contested this view and has asserted that secular trusts must be governed by ERISA with all of its non-discrimination and other requirements. There is as yet no definitive answer on this question.

In addition, some secular trusts have been disqualified for favored tax treatment because the employer sought to have some restrictive language included. However, the IRS has asserted that the basic concept of the secular trust is not in question and that an arrangement incorporating a simple trust with the employee as grantor is quite acceptable.

TAX ASPECTS OF THE LIFE INSURANCE-FUNDED PLAN

Because the employer's obligation is guaranteed under a salary continuation plan, informal funding with cash value life insurance seems to be the best way of ensuring the employer's ability to meet its obligations. Cash value life insurance provides flexibility and tax leverage for the employer.

Income Taxation of the Employer

Tax-free proceeds and cash value accumulation from the plan's being used as an employee fringe benefit provide substantial tax benefits for an employer.

As for deductibility of premiums, there is no premium deduction for the employer. However, the employer may deduct the payments when made to the employee or beneficiary.

Income Taxation of the Employee

Salary continuation plans are also advantageous to an employee in that he or she receives a contractual promise for future benefits that do not incur current income taxation. Salary continuation plans will not run afoul of the constructive receipt doctrine because the future benefits are subject to substantial restrictions. The common restrictions are the attainment of retirement age and termination of employment by the employee. Also, a requirement to surrender or forfeit a valuable right is a sufficient restriction to avoid the constructive receipt doctrine.

Moreover, even if the employee has absolute, nonforfeitable rights in the plan, the constructive receipt doctrine still will not apply as long as:

1. the plan is entered into before services are rendered; and

2. the employer's promise is unsecured.

The employer can informally fund the plan with life insurance and avoid the constructive receipt doctrine as long as the employee has no incidents of ownership in the policy.

Another factor to be considered is the economic benefit doctrine, which should not be confused with the constructive receipt doctrine. The economic benefit doctrine generally is applied to tax anything of value given by employer to employee.

Income Taxation of Retirement Benefits

When benefits finally are received by the retired employee under the plan, they are taxable as ordinary income, without the use of special averaging or lump-sum provisions. The advantage is that the benefits will be received after retirement when, at least in theory, the employee (or the surviving beneficiary) is typically in a lower tax bracket and will be eligible for double the personal exemption at age 65. Also, such payments usually are spread out over a period of years, thus spreading the tax burden as well.

Note also that payments made by an employer from a salary continuation plan are subject to withholding tax.

Income Taxation of Death Benefits

Death benefits paid by an employer to an employee's beneficiary are taxable as ordinary income when received.

Income Taxation of Severance Benefits

Any severance benefits paid under a salary continuation plan are includable as taxable income. This is true even if they are paid under a life insurance policy.

Estate Taxation of the Plan

In general, the present value of guaranteed survivor's benefits is includable in the deceased employee's gross estate if:

1. the employee was receiving benefits at death; or

2. the employee had contractual rights to future benefits.

The above applies to lifetime benefits. However, a salary continuation plan can be set up to provide death benefits only, in which the employee's beneficiary receives a payment at the employee's death. This can be in either a lump sum or in periodic installments. In either case, provided that the employee does not have the right to change the beneficiary designation or the amount of the payments, the death benefit will not generally be included in the estate of the employee for estate tax purposes. This is because, at death, the employee does not have lifetime rights or benefits under the plan.

The Question of Social Security

Amounts paid under a salary continuation plan are included in the employee's wage base for purposes of Social Security (FICA) and Federal Unemployment (FUTA). The question is when? The law is somewhat unclear whether the amounts are included currently during the employee's working years or later, when they are received at retirement.

Under current law, they will be included in the employee's wage base on either the date the services are performed or the date the employee's rights to the payments become nonforfeitable—whichever is later.

So, they should not be included currently, provided there is a "substantial risk of forfeiture" of the benefits in the future or if the promise is unsecured or unfunded. Generally, most conditions of the plan are not considered a substantial risk of forfeiture. If benefits are vested, of course, there is no risk of forfeiture, and the amounts will be subject to FICA and FUTA taxes prior to receipt of benefits.

Keep in mind, however, that the employee would often want deferred wages to be subject to FICA tax currently, because there is a better chance of his or her income being above the maximum taxable wage base during working years than in retirement. In this situation, FICA tax liability will apply only to contributions for HI (Medicare).

ERISA AND SALARY CONTINUATION PLANS

ERISA imposes strict and burdensome requirements upon many retirement plans. However, a properly designed salary continuation agreement or deferred compensation agreement will be exempt from most of those requirements. Two ERISA exemptions are potentially applicable:

1. the excess benefit plan exemption; and

2. the select group exemption.

The excess benefit plan exemption is available for a plan that is maintained solely to provide certain employees with benefits in excess of the limits for qualified plans. The select group exemption is available for a plan maintained to provide compensation to a select group of management or highly paid employees. To qualify for either of these exemptions, a plan must be unfunded. An employer may use insurance policies for informal funding and still have an unfunded plan for purposes of the exemption. A plan will be unfunded if the following requirements are met:

1. the employer is the named beneficiary on the policies and proceeds will be paid only to the employer;

2. the employer has all ownership rights under the policies;

3. the policies are subject to claims of the employer's creditors;

4. the employee does not have any beneficial ownership interest in the policies nor any preferred claim against them;

5. there is no representation to the employee that the policies will be used to provide benefits;

6. benefits will not be limited or governed by the policies; and

7. the plan does not require or allow employee contributions.

An exempt plan must meet minimal reporting and disclosure requirements. The plan administrator must file a short written notice with the Secretary of Labor within 120 days after the inception of the plan. The notice must state:

1. the employer's name and address;

2. the employer's federal identification number;

3. that the primary purpose of the plan is to provide deferred compensation to a select group;

4. the number of these plans maintained by the employer and the number of participants in each plan; and

5. that the employer will provide plan documents, if any, upon request by the Secretary of Labor.

"Select Group" Defined

Determining the boundaries of the select group exemption is important, because a salary continuation plan could be subject to all ERISA requirements if *one* employee does not fit within the select group. Certain general standards can be surmised:

1. The employees must be key employees and should be identified as such by the employer.

2. The employees must be a highly paid, select minority group determined either by a fixed minimum salary or an average salary of the group versus the average salary of other employees.

Also, to come within the "select group" exemption, the plan must be "unfunded" and be established primarily for the purpose of giving deferred compensation to the select group of employees.

Because the application of the ERISA exemption to salary continuation plans is a highly complex subject in which the slightest error or oversight could invoke all the ERISA requirements, an attorney should be consulted in the drafting of proposed salary continuation plans.

■ REASONABLE COMPENSATION CONSIDERATIONS

Because salary continuation plans involve compensation for the employee's services, it must be decided whether the compensation paid, including the value of the salary continuation plan, is reasonable under the circumstances. If not, the employer will not be allowed a deduction for payments.

There are 21 factors that should be considered. They are:

1. qualifications and training of the employee;
2. scope of duties;
3. size and complexity of business operations;
4. comparable compensation rates in similar enterprises;
5. ratio of compensation to business's net income;
6. salary policy as to other employees;
7. correlation between shareholder-employees compensation and shareholdings;
8. underpayments in previous years;
9. economic conditions;
10. job responsibility;
11. employee's contribution to the business's success;
12. when compensation was determined;
13. number of other qualified employees;
14. employee's previous compensation;
15. corporate dividend history;
16. contingent compensation formulas agreed on prior to the rendering of services and based on equal bargaining relationship between employer and employee;

17. issue of whether compensation was an inducement to keep the employee;

18. compensation paid in accordance with a plan;

19. condition of business after payment of compensation;

20. issue of whether employee's compensation was fixed by board of directors; and

21. results of employee's efforts.

The first nine are the most frequently used criteria in determining reasonableness. Because an advance ruling on reasonableness of compensation is unattainable from the IRS, prospects always should be informed of the possibility of the issue arising, and every effort should be made to assimilate as many of the factors as possible into the employee's overall compensation package.

In valuing a salary continuation plan to determine whether it will be viewed as reasonable compensation, the best bet is to use *any reasonable* valuation method adopted by the employer that gives the lowest value for the benefit.

As a rule, the question of reasonable compensation usually does not come up in cases of publicly held corporations or minority or nonshareholder-employees in close corporations. The most caution should be exercised in cases involving majority shareholders in close corporations.

■ SUMMARY

Salary continuation plans and deferred compensation plans are distinguished by one important factor: whose cash is funding the benefit. While in a deferred compensation plan the employee voluntarily forgoes current income, the salary continuation plan is funded entirely by the employer. The salary continuation plan does not represent cash that the employee could have enjoyed now.

Often used by the employer to attach *golden handcuffs* to valued key employees, the benefits of a salary continuation plan typically are payable only if the employee continues in the service of the employer to a stated age. For example, a typical salary continuation plan would provide the promised benefit if the employee remains in service of the employer to age 65.

While the benefit to the selected employee is the unsecured promise of additional income at retirement, the benefits to the employer are more varied. The primary benefits of salary continuation plans to the employer include the:

- added financial motivation given to selected employees to remain with the employer;

- ability to be selective in including employees in the plan;

- generally greater income tax deduction available to the employer when benefits are paid;

- ability of the employer to recover some or all of the costs for the benefit; and

- plan is exempt from most of the burdensome ERISA requirements that accompany qualified plans.

In general, salary continuation plans are considered to be unfunded. That does not mean that no provision has been made to pay the promised benefit. It means only that specific assets have not been identified and set aside to provide the benefit. Life insurance, when used to assist in providing the promised benefits, causes the plan to be considered informally funded.

Usually, neither the promise of benefits by the employer nor the employer's payment of life insurance premiums will result in current taxation to the employee. Instead, salary continuation funds are subject to income taxation only when received during the employee's lifetime or by a beneficiary upon his or her death. The exception to that general rule occurs when a secular trust is used in connection with the plan.

The use of irrevocable trusts—a secular trust or a rabbi trust—is designed to help ensure that the benefit will be available as promised. A rabbi trust is an irrevocable trust that protects the benefits from a change in management. Because the funds in a rabbi trust are still subject to the company's creditors, the employee has no current income tax liability. A secular trust provides greater protection to the employee, because the funds in the trust are not subject to the company's creditors. In return for that additional protection, however, the employee is required to recognize current income.

The most important requirement for a successful salary continuation plan is the continuity of the business. If the business cannot survive the death, disability or retirement of the employee, no benefit is likely to be paid.

THE SALARY CONTINUATION AGREEMENT

The specimen agreement that follows is designed to create a pure salary continuation agreement. Basically, it is designed to minimize the risk that the employee will be deemed to have received some measurable economic benefit in a plan informally funded with insurance. The specimen is also designed to avoid current income taxation to the employee, even if the employer elects to fund its obligation informally using life insurance contracts.

As an employer fringe benefit plan, the specimen agreement is constructed to favor the employer. Counsel will need to make modifications to the agreement if the corporation agrees to make "concessions" in the terms to the employee under the agreement. Modifications also will need to be made if the employer is other than a corporation, because the specimen agreement speaks in terms of a corporation.

ILL 12.1 ▪ *Sample Corporate Minutes and Resolutions*

CAUTION: This is a specimen resolution. The actual resolution used in any particular case must be prepared by a qualified attorney.

The Chairman discussed the Corporation's need for life insurance protection on its key personnel, namely Messrs. _____ (Name of Key Officers or Employees) _____,
_____.

He explained the importance to the Corporation of obtaining "key-executive insurance" to compensate the Corporation for its economic loss if one of the Corporation's key personnel should prematurely die, and to provide the funds necessary to discover, attract and retain the valuable services and business counsel of these key personnel and to prevent the substantial financial loss the Corporation would suffer if any of these key personnel were to leave, and enter the employment of one of the Corporation's business competitors. The Chairman noted that all the key personnel have indicated their willingness to remain in the employment of the Corporation provided the Corporation would provide each of them certain additional benefits in the event of death, disability or retirement.

The Chairman then discussed a proposed plan whereunder the Corporation would enter a salary continuation plan with each of its key personnel. The Chairman presented a proposed copy of such an agreement with the Corporation's president, _(Name of President)_ , and read the agreement in its entirety. He explained its terms, relevant business and tax considerations, and answered board members' questions about the agreement. The Chairman stated that similar agreements had been prepared for Messrs. _____
_____
_____.

The Chairman noted that these agreements should help relieve these key personnel of anxieties concerning financial security for themselves and their families at retirement, and thereby make them currently more productive. In addition, he noted that the agreements would guarantee the continuing business advice and consultation of these key personnel after their retirement. After considerable general discussion of the board the key personnel present at the meeting were excused. On motion, duly made and seconded, the following resolution was then adopted:

RESOLVED: that the salary continuation agreement between the Corporation and the president, _(Name of President)_ , a copy of which is hereby attached to and made a part of this resolution, is hereby approved and the vice president is expressly authorized and directed to execute said agreement on the Corporation's behalf.

RESOLVED: that in order to fund its obligations under the salary continuation agreement described in the prior resolution, and to insure itself against the financial losses and other expenses which would arise in the event of a pre-retirement death of _(Name of President)_ , the vice president of the Corporation is hereby authorized to enter into a contract of _(Description of life insurance contract)_ life insurance for coverage of $____ insuring the life of _(Name of President)_ .

Resolutions similar to the foregoing should be adopted and added to the minutes at this point for each of the key personnel who will have a salary continuation plan.

ILL 12.2 ▪ *Sample Salary Continuation Agreement*

CAUTION: This is a specimen agreement. The actual agreement used in any particular case must be prepared by a qualified attorney.

This agreement is entered into this _____ day of _____, 20_____, by and between __(Name)__ a domestic Corporation having its principal office in _____ hereinafter called the "Corporation," and __(Name)__, resident of __(Name of City, Town, or County)(Name of State)__ hereinafter called the "Employee."

WITNESSETH:

Whereas, the Employee has been employed by the Corporation for _____ years, and is currently employed by the Corporation in the capacity of __(Title of Employee's Position)__;

Whereas, the Corporation is motivated to retain the valuable services and business counsel of the Employee and to induce the Employee to remain in his executive capacity with the Corporation;

Whereas, the Corporation wishes to retain the Employee in order to prevent the substantial financial loss which the Corporation would incur if the Employee were to leave and were to enter the employment of a competitor;

> **The two preceding provisions were designed to help establish that the agreement is an employer-motivated "inducement-to-stay" deferred fringe benefit arrangement using the corporation's money, and thereby does not involve the elective deferral of any of the employee's current compensation.**

Whereas, The Employee is willing to continue in the employment of the Corporation, provided the Corporation will agree to provide an additional fringe benefit in the form of certain payments in the event of the Employee's retirement, disability, or death;

Whereas, the Employee is considered a highly compensated employee or member of a select management group of the Corporation;

> **One of the important advantages, and therefore important objectives, in designing a salary continuation plan, is that the plan can avoid most of the burdensome requirements imposed by ERISA on qualified plans. This provision helps to establish that the agreement is a so-called top hat employee pension plan; that is, a nonqualified employee pension benefit plan maintained by the corporation primarily for the purpose of providing unfunded deferred compensation to a member of a select group of management or highly compensated individuals. As such, the plan should be exempt from nearly all ERISA regulatory requirements. The "select group" exemption for pension plans maintained primarily for a select group of management or highly compensated employees eliminates all reporting and disclosure requirements under Title I, Part 1 of ERISA, including summary plan descriptions, all participation and vesting requirements under Part 2, all funding requirements under Part 3, all of the termination insurance requirements under Title IV, and probably the fiduciary requirements of Part 4, unless the plan contains a death or disability benefit provision.**

ILL 12.2 ▪ *Sample Salary Continuation Agreement (Cont.)*

> In that case, the fiduciary requirements will probably have to be met. The plan will also probably require a claims procedure. The benefits must be paid: (i) solely from the employer's general assets, or (ii) through life insurance contracts with the premiums thereon being paid directly by the employer out of its general assets, or (iii) both to qualify for the "select group" exemption.

Now, Therefore, the parties agree as follows:

1. CONDITIONS

A. The payment of benefits to the Employee or his designated recipient(s) under this Agreement is conditioned upon the continuous employment of the Employee by the Corporation (including periods of disability and authorized leaves of absence as described in this Agreement) until the _____ day of _____, 20_____, or his death, whichever is sooner, and upon the Employee's compliance with the terms of this Agreement.

B. Payment of benefits is further conditioned upon the Employee rendering such reasonable business consulting and advisory services as the Corporation's board of directors may call upon him to provide, and as his health may permit for a period from his retirement to his death, or until prior disability.

 1. It is understood that such services shall not require the Employee to be active in the Corporation's day-to-day activities, and that the Employee shall perform such services as an independent contractor.

 2. It is further understood that the Employee shall be compensated for such services in an amount to be then agreed upon, and shall be reimbursed for all expenses incurred in performing such services.

C. Payment of benefits is further conditioned upon the Employee not acting in any similar employment capacity for any business enterprise which competes to a substantial degree with the Corporation, nor engaging in any activity involving substantial competition with the Corporation, during his employment with the Corporation, after his retirement from the Corporation or after his prior disability while he is receiving benefits, without the prior written consent of the Corporation.

> This provision provides for the preconditions which the employee must meet in order to qualify for the corporation's payment of the benefits: (1) continuous employment until retirement or death (including periods of disability and authorized leaves of absence); (2) rendering of consulting services to the corporation after retirement; and (3) noncompetition during the life of the agreement. They form the heart of the provisions which help prevent the employee from being in constructive receipt of income under the salary continuation plan.
>
> The performance of consulting services after retirement is a more important condition than may be suspected at first glance. It may help prevent the argument that the employee is in constructive receipt of the benefits at retirement, since the employee must still continue to render services to the employer, even after retirement in order to receive the benefits under the agreement.
>
> The provision provides that the employee will provide these consulting and advisory services as an independent contractor, and not as an employee. This construction is intended to help prevent any reduction of the retired employee's Social Security benefits.

ILL 12.2 ▪ *Sample Salary Continuation Agreement (Cont.)*

Social Security Act Section 203(f)(1) provides that benefits will not be reduced, if the individual:

a. did not receive wages of more than $416.66 for services rendered as an employee (for 1980), or

b. did not render "substantial" self-employment services, in any month.

These limitations apply regardless of the individual's earnings. Therefore, if the individual's consulting services are rendered to the corporation as an employee, and the amount exceeded $416.66 in any month, a reduction in Social Security benefits would occur.

Counsel should note that, even with regard to consulting services provided as an independent contractor, such services must not be "substantial" if Social Security benefits are to remain undiminished. Fortunately, the Social Security regulations provide some guidance as to what constitutes "substantial" services. Although the regulations provide that 45 hours or less of services per month will not normally be considered substantial, 15 hours or less is a safer limit. The reason for this is that the 45-hour provision does not provide a clear safe harbor since the value of the retired employee's services can affect whether the time involved is considered substantial.

This construction should also preserve the retirement exemption from includability for the entire cost of $50,000 of group term life insurance under Section 79. Section 79 and the regulations to it provide that the entire cost of $50,000 of group term life insurance is excludable from gross income if:

a. the employee has reached retirement age (or been disabled), and

b. terminated his (her) services as an employee.

Therefore, if the services are provided as an independent contractor, the retired employee will have terminated his (her) services with the corporation as an employee, and the group term exclusion will be preserved.

This condition that the employee provide consulting services after retirement (and remain with the corporation until retirement) also helps to preserve the $5,000 death benefit exclusion.

There are in certain instances, however, some estate planning implications in utilizing a provision requiring consulting and advisory services in a salary continuation agreement. It may not be possible for a stockholder-employee to do a stock redemption under the "10-year safe harbor rule" of Section 302(b)(3) and thereby avoid Section 318 attribution, if the salary continuation agreement contains such a provision.

ILL 12.2 ■ *Sample Salary Continuation Agreement (Cont.)*

The shareholder-employee will probably not have terminated his (her) "interest in the corporation" as required by the "10-year rule" so long as he (she) is under agreement to provide such services. On the other hand, this construction, making the retired employee an independent contractor, will help prevent a lump-sum distribution to the retired employee from a qualified plan in which he (she) may be a participant from being treated wholly as ordinary income. Normally, such a distribution will be treated as part ordinary income and part capital gain when an employee separates from service with the corporation. However, if the separating employee retained some employee status for the purpose of the consulting services, the distribution would not qualify for this special treatment. Of course, as an independent contractor, the separating employee does not retain such status, and a distribution from a qualified plan should be entitled to the special treatment.

The validity of a covenant not to compete is governed by applicable state law. Therefore, counsel should satisfy himself that the covenant contained in the specimen will be valid under applicable state law if counsel desires to use the specimen language, which is extremely restrictive. An alternative format for this subsection might appear as follows:

C. Payment of benefits is further conditioned upon the Employee's agreement that he will not directly or indirectly compete with the Corporation by acting in a similar capacity for any business enterprise which competes with the Corporation, or engaging in any activity involving substantial competition with the Corporation. This agreement by the Employee not to compete shall be limited to that time period the Employee is in the Corporation's employ and to a _____ year period after the Employee's termination or retirement from employment with the Corporation. It shall also be limited to competition by the Employee within a _____ mile radius of the principal office of the Corporation or any of its subsidiaries.

Of course, any modification of the covenant should also conform with applicable state law. It may be possible to provide for a distribution of the compensation deferred for a "severe financial hardship" (meaning hardship caused by "accident, illness, or any other event which is beyond the control of the participant") without constructive receipt. Under the facts of the letter ruling, a committee was to make the determination whether severe financial hardship actually existed.

ILL 12.2 ▪ *Sample Salary Continuation Agreement (Cont.)*

2. DEATH BENEFIT

A. If the Employee dies during the period of his active employment, or during a disability as defined under Section 3 of this Agreement, a payment shall be made as provided in the attached "Schedule A," made a part hereof. Such payment shall be made by the Corporation to such person(s) as the Employee shall designate in writing prior to his death. The Employee shall have the right to change the designated recipient(s) of these payments by presenting a written amendment to the Corporation prior to his death in a form as provided in "Schedule B," attached hereto and made a part hereof. In the event the Employee shall fail to designate a recipient prior to his death, the payments shall be made to the Employee's surviving spouse, if alive; otherwise to the Personal Representative of the Employee's estate.

B. However, this benefit shall not be payable if the Employee's death results from suicide, whether sane or insane, within two years after the execution of this Agreement.

> **This provision provides for benefit payments in the event of the employee's death during his active employment. It contains a denial of death benefits for reason of the employee's suicide during the first two years of the life of the agreement. The language in this exception parallels the language in the suicide provisions in one carrier's life insurance contracts and is designed to prevent the corporation from having to pay benefits if the contract, which informally funds the agreement, would not be paid by reason of the employee's suicide. Counsel should satisfy himself (herself) that this specimen language adequately parallels that in the actual insurance contract used in the client's situation. Some states may require a different definition of suicide in the insurance contract. Except perhaps for this suicide provision, counsel can exercise considerable latitude in designing the death benefit provision to conform to the corporation's wishes.**
>
> **The draftsman of the specimen considered simply referencing to the life insurance contracts involved for the definition of suicide, but rejected this approach based upon the draftsman's opinion, after researching the case law, that the agreement should disconnect the plan from the informal funding mechanism and make as little mention as possible of any insurance contracts that support the agreement. This construction is designed to help avoid incident of ownership questions, and the application of any rationale similar to that applied in *Goldsmith v. Comm'r*. In these cases, pure deferred compensation plans informally funded with life insurance were held to result in economic benefit to the employee. (It should be noted that the *Goldsmith* case may have been nullified by the Revenue Act of 1978 although the IRS would almost certainly dispute this contention.) Counsel might determine to disagree with this approach and simply incorporate the contract language by reference.**
>
> **This designation by the employee of a recipient of the death benefit under this provision by filing schedule B of the specimen with the corporation does not constitute a completed gift for tax purposes. This is because the employee retains the unrestricted right under the agreement to change the recipient.**

ILL 12.2 ▪ *Sample Salary Continuation Agreement (Cont.)*

3. DISABILITY BENEFIT

If, prior to the retirement of the Employee, such Employee becomes totally and permanently disabled as the result of an injury or a sickness, and such total disability prevents the Employee from performing all of the substantial and material duties of his regular occupation, the Corporation agrees to pay the Employee payments in the sum of $_____ per month for sixty (60) months. If, after this sixty (60)-month period of disability, the Employee is unable to perform all the substantial and material duties of any occupation for which he is reasonably fitted by education, training or experience, and such disability is the result of injury or sickness, the Corporation will continue the monthly payments for the duration of his disability or until age 65, whichever occurs first.

> **This provision provides for disability payments to the employee during the period of his (her) active employment with the corporation. The definition of disability parallels the language contained in the waiver of premium benefit rider contained in GALIC's life insurance contracts. Counsel should satisfy himself, however, that this language does, in fact, adequately parallel the contract language in the actual life insurance policy involved. This specimen provision for payment of the disability benefit contemplates using the premium amount that the corporation would have available, if premium payments were waived under the insurance contract, to make the disability benefit payments to the employee. For example, if the corporation is in a 50 percent tax bracket and is making premium payments of $6,000 per year on a policy on the employee's life, it can afford to make disability payments of $12,000 per year to the employee if he (she) becomes disabled, and the premium is waived under the policy's waiver of premium provision.**
>
> **Of course, in the alternative, a disability income policy could be purchased to cover the corporation's obligation under this provision. A combination of both these methods could also be used, if desired.**

4. SALARY CONTINUATION

If the Employee is still in the employ of the Corporation at retirement under this Agreement, whether or not disabled, the Corporation shall, within 30 days after the Employee's retirement, commence monthly payments as provided in the attached "Schedule C," made a part hereof. In the event the Employee should die after these payments have begun, but before the end of the _____ payment month, the unpaid balance of the payments due shall be continued to be paid by the Corporation to the recipient as designated in Section 2 herein.

> **This provision provides for the payment of benefits to the employee after his (her) retirement from the corporation. The provision also provides for a survivor benefit if the employee should die before a specified number of these retirement payments have been made. Counsel can exercise considerable latitude in designing the salary continuation retirement benefit to conform to the corporation's wishes. Counsel should note that this provision provides that the survivor's benefit shall be paid to the recipient of the death benefit as named in Section 2. If the employee desires to name a different recipient of the survivor's continuation benefit and the death benefit, a modification will need to be made in this provision and schedule B.**

ILL 12.2 ■ *Sample Salary Continuation Agreement (Cont.)*

5. NAMED FIDUCIARY AND CLAIMS PROCEDURE

A. The Named Fiduciary of the plan and for purposes of claims procedure under this Agreement is (Insert Title of Corporate Officer) of the Corporation.

   1. The business address and telephone number of the Named Fiduciary under this Agreement is: (Enter Business Address and Telephone Number): Telephone: (   )   .

   2. The Corporation shall have the right to change the Named Fiduciary of the plan created under this Agreement. The Corporation shall also have the right to change the address and telephone number of the Named Fiduciary. The Corporation shall give the employee written notice of any change of the Named Fiduciary, or any change in the address and telephone number of the Named Fiduciary.

B. Benefits shall be paid in accordance with the provisions of this Agreement. The Employee, or a designated recipient, or any other person claiming through the Employee (hereinafter collectively referred to as the "Claimant") shall make a written request for the benefits provided under this Agreement. This written claim shall be mailed or delivered to the Named Fiduciary.

C. If the claim is denied, either wholly or partially, notice of the decision shall be mailed to the Claimant within a reasonable time period. This time period shall exceed not more than 90 days after the receipt of the claim by the Named Fiduciary.

D. The Named Fiduciary shall provide a written notice to every Claimant who is denied a claim for benefits under this Agreement. The notice shall set forth the following information:

   1. the specific reasons for the denial;

   2. the specific reference to pertinent plan provisions on which the denial is based;

   3. a description of any additional material or information necessary for the Claimant to perfect the claim and an explanation of why such material or information is necessary; and

   4. appropriate information and explanation of the claims procedure under this Agreement to permit the Claimant to submit his claim for review.

   All of this information shall be set forth in the notice in a manner calculated to be understood by the Claimant.

E. The claims procedure under this Agreement shall allow the Claimant a reasonable opportunity to appeal a denied claim and to get a full and fair review of that decision from the Named Fiduciary.

   1. The Claimant shall exercise his (her) right of appeal by submitting a written request for a review of the denied claim to the Named Fiduciary. This written request for review must be submitted to the Named Fiduciary within (not less than) 60 days after receipt by the Claimant of the written notice of denial.

ILL 12.2 ▪ *Sample Salary Continuation Agreement (Cont.)*

    2. The Claimant shall have the following rights under this appeal procedure:

        a. to request a review upon written application to the Named Fiduciary;

        b. to review pertinent documents with regard to the employee benefit plan created under this Agreement;

        c. the right to submit issues and comments in writing;

        d. to request an extension of time to make a written submission of issues and comments; and

        e. to request that a hearing be held to consider Claimant's appeal.

F. The decision on the review of the denied claim shall promptly be named by the Named Fiduciary:

    1. within <u>(not more than 60)</u> days after the receipt of the request for review if no hearing is held; or

    2. within <u>(not more than 120)</u> days after the receipt of the request for review, if an extension of time is necessary in order to hold a hearing.

        a. if an extension of time is necessary in order to hold a hearing, the Named Fiduciary shall give the Claimant written notice of the extension of time and of the hearing. This notice shall be given prior to any extension.

        b. The written notice of extension shall indicate that an extension of time will occur in order to hold a hearing on Claimant's appeal. The notice shall also specify the place, date, and time of that hearing and the Claimant's opportunity to participate in the hearing. It may also include any other information the Named Fiduciary believes may be important or useful to the Claimant in connection with the appeal.

G. The decision to hold a hearing to consider the Claimant's appeal of the denied claim shall be within the sole discretion of the Named Fiduciary, whether or not the Claimant requests such a hearing.

H. The Named Fiduciary's decision on review shall be made in writing and provided to the Claimant within the specified time periods in Paragraph F. This written decision on review shall contain the following information:

    1. the decision(s);

    2. the reasons for the decision(s); and

    3. specific references to the plan provisions of the Agreement on which the decision(s) is/are based.

All of this information shall be written in a manner calculated to be understood by the Claimant.

This specimen provision is intended to comply with ERISA Sections 402 and 503 and DOL Reg. Section 2560.503-1. Since a salary continuation plan is an "employee benefit plan" under ERISA, it must have:

ILL 12.2 ▪ *Sample Salary Continuation Agreement (Cont.)*

(a) a named fiduciary (sometimes referred to as plan administrator); and

(b) a written claims procedure, even though it is a plan primarily for a select group of management or highly compensated employees.

Apparently, only these plans that are not covered by ERISA at all escape these requirements. ERISA Section 402 merely requires that an employee benefit plan, such as a salary continuation plan, have a named fiduciary. This specimen provision provides that a corporate officer, designated by official title (e.g., president, treasurer, secretary), and not by personal name shall be the named fiduciary on the salary continuation plan. Because the committee report and the regulations to ERISA Section 503 use the term plan administrator, counsel may wish the provision to designate the named fiduciary and plan administrator. However, ERISA Section 503 itself uses only the term "named fiduciary." The terms appear to be interchangeable, therefore the draftsman of the specimen believes this "double" designation is unnecessary. Further, the provision provides the "official" mailing address, and telephone number of the named fiduciary and allows the corporation to change these items, but requires it to give written notice of changes to the employee.

ERISA Section 503 generally requires an employee benefit plan to have a written claims procedure that:

(a) provides plan participants written notice of a denial of benefits in an understandable form; and

(b) affords plan participants with an opportunity for a "full and fair" review of a denial of benefits by the named fiduciary.

Counsel may wish to consider the creation of claim forms for the corporation in conjunction with the claims procedure outlined in this specimen procedure, since it requires a written request for benefits. The regulations to ERISA Section 503 explicitly detail this claims procedure requirement. The specimen provision is basically designed to parallel the requirement detailed in the regulations. Counsel should be advised, however, that in some respects the specimen provision goes beyond the requirements of the regulations.

In subparagraph f, there are certain enumerated claimant's rights. The regulations mandate only the first three enumerated rights contained in the specimen. The draftsman has added the last two:

(a) the right to request a hearing, and

(b) the right to request an extension of time in which to make a written submission of issues and comments.

Counsel may wish to keep these two additions in. If counsel determines to eliminate them, the entire specimen provision should be reviewed for consistency and adjusted, if necessary. If additional rights are added by counsel to the basic three, the entire specimen provision should be reviewed for uniformity and integration of the various subparagraphs.

ILL 12.2 ▪ *Sample Salary Continuation Agreement (Cont.)*

The regulation specifies "certain minimum requirements for employee benefit plan procedures pertaining to claims by participants and beneficiaries (claimants) for plan benefits, consideration of such claims, and review of claim denials...." Counsel has leeway to design the claims procedure to fit the client's needs. However, counsel should carefully examine and refer to DOL Reg. Section 2560.503-1 while drafting the claims procedure provision, since the regulations mandate specific requirements (time limits, etc.) to establish a reasonable claims procedure. In general, counsel should be guided by the intent in ERISA Section 503 in designing a claims procedure. Moreover, given the lack of authority of the kinds of requirements that might make the claims procedure unreasonable, it appears wise to keep the claims procedure as close to the regulations as possible, and as simple as the client's circumstances will permit.

6. FUNDING

A. The Corporation's obligations under this Agreement shall be an unfunded and unsecured promise to pay. The Corporation shall not be obligated under any circumstances to fund its obligations under this Agreement. The Corporation may, however, at its sole and exclusive option, elect to fund this Agreement in whole or in part.

B. If the Corporation shall elect to fund this Agreement informally, in whole or in part, the manner of such informal funding, and the continuance or discontinuance of such informal funding shall be the sole and exclusive decision of the Corporation.

C. If the Corporation shall determine to informally fund this Agreement, in whole or in part, by procuring as owner, life insurance for its own benefit on the life of the Employee, the form of such insurance and the amounts shall be the sole and exclusive decision of the Corporation. The Employee hereby agrees to submit to medical examinations, supply such information, and execute such documents as may be required by the insurance company or companies to whom the Corporation may have applied for such insurance if the Corporation shall determine to informally fund this Agreement with life insurance.

This provision is designed to make it clear that the plan is an unfunded nonqualified deferred benefit plan. This is important for several reasons. First, the tax consequences vary for an unfunded plan and a funded plan. The desired tax consequences are those of an unfunded plan. Of course, the use of an insurance contract to "informally fund" a plan does not make it a "funded" plan under Section 83, so long as the employee has no beneficial interest in the policy and the fund remains accessible to the employer's general creditors. Second, the specimen provision affirms compliance with the "select group" ERISA exemption provisions, which require that the plan not only be for a select group but also be "unfunded." Counsel should note that the term "unfunded" may not have the same meaning for income tax and ERISA purposes.

Counsel will note that these provisions specifically deny any obligation of the employer to use insurance to informally fund the plan, even though the use of insurance contracts to informally fund will clearly be contemplated. After researching the case law and the case law trend, it is the draftsman's opinion that a "Chinese Wall" should be constructed separating the agreement from any life insurance that may be purchased to informally fund the plan.

ILL 12.2 ▪ *Sample Salary Continuation Agreement (Cont.)*

A review of the case law strongly suggests to the draftsman of the specimen that the more closely the agreement and any insurance contracts (which are purchased to fund the plan) are interrelated, the more likely it is that adverse tax consequences will occur to the employee under the income tax, or at death under the estate tax. Since absolutely no mention of the insurance contracts is necessary to make the agreement valid or enforceable, it appears wise to simply avoid these risks by clearly and cleanly divorcing the agreement and the informal insurance funding that will be obtained to support it. This means not merely leaving out any mention of specific insurance contracts, which may be purchased to informally fund the plan, but affirmatively denying any obligation of the employer to obtain or maintain such contracts.

Inclusion of mention of the insurance contracts in the agreement appears to be more for the psychological security of the employee in most instances, anyway. While that may be of enough importance to justify inclusion of mention of the specific policies in the agreement, in fact, the employee has and can have no interest in the policies, if the plan is to have the intended results for both the employee and the employer. Therefore, any real security is probably illusory. Counsel must reach his (her) own conclusions on this point, however.

EMPLOYMENT RIGHTS

A. This Agreement shall not be deemed to create a contract of employment between the Corporation and the Employee and shall create no right in the Employee to continue in the Corporation's employ for any specific period of time, or to create any other rights in the Employee or obligations on the part of the Corporation, except as are set forth in this Agreement. Nor shall this Agreement restrict the right of the Corporation to terminate the Employee for cause, or restrict the right of the Employee to terminate his employment.

B. "Cause" as defined in this Agreement shall mean:

1. incompetence

2. insubordination

3. conviction or a plea of nolo contendere in a felony case

4. intoxication

5. drug addiction

> This provision is designed to make it clear that the agreement is not an employment contract, and that the employer retains the right to terminate the employee "for cause," which is defined as incompetence, insubordination, conviction or a plea of nolo contendere in a felony case, intoxication, or drug addiction. Counsel may wish to keep this definition or change it by adding or deleting to it according to the particular situation of his (her) client. The employee can likewise terminate his (her) employment with the employer; however, at the expense of the loss of his (her) benefit.

ILL 12.2 ▪ *Sample Salary Continuation Agreement (Cont.)*

Some employers have permitted some mitigation of this result by providing for a severance benefit, usually under a schedule that increases the amount according to the employee's length of service after the agreement is executed.

8. EMPLOYEE RIGHT TO ASSETS

The rights of the Employee, any designated recipient of the Employee, or any other person claiming through the Employee under this Agreement, shall be solely those of an unsecured general creditor of the Corporation. The Employee, the designated recipient of the Employee, or any other person claiming through the Employee, shall only have the right to receive from the Corporation those payments as specified under this Agreement. The Employee agrees that he, his designated recipient, or any other person claiming through him shall have no rights or interests whatsoever in any asset of the Corporation, including any insurance policies or contracts which the Corporation may possess or obtain to informally fund this Agreement. Any asset used or acquired by the Corporation in connection with the liabilities it has assumed under this Agreement, except as expressly provided, shall not be deemed to be held under any trust for the benefit of the Employee or his recipients. Nor shall it be considered security for the performance of the obligations of the Corporation. It shall be, and remain, a general, unpledged, and unrestricted asset of the Corporation.

> **This provision is designed to make it clear that the employee's rights under the agreement are those of a general, unsecured creditor and that the employee possesses no interest in any assets of the corporation, specifically including insurance policies that may be purchased to informally fund the plan. This provision is necessary for two reasons: (1) for the employee to avoid current income taxation, there must be no constructive receipt or current economic benefit, the employee's promise must be unsecured, and the fund (when the plan is informally funded, as with life insurance) must remain accessible to the employer's general creditors; and (2) the benefits must be paid from the general assets of the corporation, or insurance purchased solely by the employer in order to qualify for the ERISA "select group" plans exemptions as an unfunded deferred compensation plan.**

9. INDEPENDENCE OF BENEFITS

The benefits payable under this Agreement shall be independent of, and in addition to, any other benefits or compensation, whether by salary, or bonus or otherwise, payable under any other employment agreements that now exist or may hereafter exist from time to time between the Corporation and the Employee. This Agreement between the Corporation and the Employee does not involve a reduction in salary or foregoing of an increase in future salary by the Employee. Nor does the Agreement in any way affect or reduce the existing and future compensation and other benefits of the Employee.

> **This provision clarifies that the benefits under the agreement are separate from and in addition to any other benefits provided by the corporation to the employee. It removes any doubt concerning whether or not the agreement is intended to substitute for any other of the employee's current compensation or fringe benefits. This provision should thereby help substantiate that the agreement is an employer-motivated "inducement to stay" agreement using the corporation's money, and not an employee-motivated salary reduction agreement using the employee's money.**

ILL 12.2 ▪ *Sample Salary Continuation Agreement (Cont.)*

10. ACCELERATION OF PAYMENTS

The Corporation reserves the right to accelerate the payment of any benefits payable under this Agreement without the consent of the Employee, his estate, his designated recipients, or any other person claiming through the Employee.

> **This provision gives the corporation the right to accelerate payment of the benefits provided hereunder. The employer may desire to have this flexibility to pay off the obligation for business reasons. The sample provision does not provide for discounting the accelerated payment by some specified interest rate to a present value at the time of accelerated payment. Counsel may or may not wish to consider such an addition to the provision depending upon his (her) client's wishes, and the agreements negotiated between the corporation and the employee.**

11. LEAVES OF ABSENCE

The Corporation may, in its sole discretion, permit the Employee to take a leave of absence for a period not to exceed one year. During such leave, the Employee will still be considered to be in the continuous employment of the Corporation for purposes of this Agreement.

> **This provision permits the corporation to grant leaves of absence to the employee that will not count as a break in "continuous employment" for the purposes of the agreement. The provision specifies one year as the maximum time period for such an authorized leave of absence. This figure can be modified by counsel either up or down, but it would appear wise to keep the maximum time period reasonable, since the agreement contemplates deferred payment of the benefits in return for future services to the corporation. Payment of the benefits is thus subject to a substantial condition that helps prevent a constructive receipt by the employee. If the employee can, in effect, collect the benefits but be absent from the corporation for substantial periods of time, the question may be raised whether those future services really exist and whether the benefits are actually, in fact, payment for services already rendered. If so determined, the employee might be determined to be in constructive receipt of the benefits.**

12. ASSIGNABILITY

Except in so far as this provision may be contrary to applicable law, no sale, transfer, alienation, assignment, pledge, collateralization, or attachment of any benefits under this Agreement shall be valid or recognized by the Corporation.

> **This provision primarily prevents the assignment by the employee of the benefits under the agreement. This prevents the corporation from having to deal with any persons, when paying benefits, other than those outlined under the agreement, and prevents the loss of the psychological incentive to stay with the corporation that might occur if the employee were permitted to transfer his rights under the agreement. Some commentators have taken the position that it is advisable to prohibit in the agreement the employee's assignment of the future payments.**

ILL 12.2 ▪ *Sample Salary Continuation Agreement (Cont.)*

> The theory is that this type of nonassignment provision will help prevent application of the economic benefit theory to the agreement for income tax purposes. Including a nonassignment provision to avoid these potential nontax and tax problems, then, probably would be good practice.

13. AMENDMENT

During the lifetime of the employee, this Agreement may be amended or revoked at any time, in whole or part, by the mutual written agreement of the parties.

> This provision permits the employer and the employee to change the agreement with a written amendment signed by both parties. A right to receive deferred compensation if the plan is amended may put the employee in constructive receipt of deferred amounts. However, the question will probably only come up where the plan may be unilaterally amended by the corporation and a number of employees are included under the same plan instrument.

14. LAW GOVERNING

This agreement shall be governed by the laws of the state of (Name of State.) This agreement is solely between the Corporation and the Employee. Further, the Employee, his designated recipients or other persons claiming through the Employee shall only have recourse against the Corporation for enforcement of the Agreement. However, it shall be binding upon the designated recipients, beneficiaries, heirs, executors and administrators of the Employee and upon the successors and assigns of the Corporation.

> This provision specifies the state whose law will govern the agreement. Although federal tax law considerations are normally paramount in these agreements, the selection of a state's law to govern the agreement is not unimportant. For instance, the validity of the covenant not to compete in the agreement depends upon applicable state law. In a case involving Illinois contract law, the First Circuit affirmed a district court ruling that a covenant not to compete, contained in a deferred compensation agreement, was not invalid. The covenant read:
>
> If, without the prior written consent of the Company, any Participant or former Participant shall engage in any activity in competition with the Company during his employment or within three years after his retirement or termination of employment, his termination in the Plan shall thereupon automatically terminate, and the Company shall have no obligation to make any payments to such Participant or former Participant.
>
> The First Circuit said that, under Illinois law, a covenant not to compete is not illegal per se, but depends upon the reasonableness of the agreement in light of all the facts.

ILL 12.2 ■ *Sample Salary Continuation Agreement (Cont.)*

In some states, the covenant as included in this specimen agreement might not be valid. Since the employer will probably prefer the covenant not to compete that is included in the specimen (it extends for the period the employee is actively employed and receiving benefits under the agreement), counsel will probably desire to include this covenant for the employer, if at all possible. However, counsel will have to review applicable state law to determine whether use of the specimen language is possible without modification. Counsel will therefore probably wish to review the proposed state's contract law for any peculiarities that should recommend, or suggest rejection of, that state as the governing jurisdiction.

_____
(Name of Corporation)

_____
(President)

_____
(Employee)

(Corporate Seal, if any)
Witnessed by:

_____
(Secretary)

SCHEDULE A

It is agreed this _____ day of _____, _____, that the Corporation shall make payment at death to the designated recipient(s) as follows: $_____ per month, beginning within 30 days of death, continuously for a period of _____ months.

SCHEDULE B

DESIGNATION OF SALARY CONTINUATION

AND DEATH BENEFIT RECIPIENT

I, _____, request that the Corporation (mark/change) its record to reflect _____ as the designated recipient(s) of the Salary Continuation Benefit Payable under Provision 4, and the Death Benefit payable under Provision 2 of a Salary Continuation Agreement dated _____, ____, and to make payment of the Salary Continuation Benefit and the Death Benefit to the above designated recipient(s) as provided under the terms of the Agreement. You are instructed to retain the above designated recipient(s) until such time as you receive a new "Designation of Salary Continuation and Death Benefit Recipient" from me which makes a change.

_____
(Date)

_____
(Employee's Signature)

SCHEDULE C

It is agreed this _____ day of _____, 20___, that the Corporation shall make monthly payments of $_____ each to the Employee for a period of _____ months, aggregating cumulative payments of $_____.

CHAPTER 12 QUESTIONS FOR REVIEW

1. Advantages of salary continuation plans for the employee include
   A. deferral of current income
   B. tax-free income at retirement
   C. tax-free benefits for a beneficiary
   D. none of the above

2. When life insurance is used in a salary continuation plan, the plan is said to be
   A. unfunded
   B. informally funded
   C. fully funded
   D. vested

3. Advantages of using a rabbi trust include
   A. immediate access to the funds if the company is liquidated
   B. separation of salary continuation funds from the general funds of the company
   C. protection of the funds from the general creditors of the company
   D. all of the above

4. Advantages of using a secular trust include
   A. current recognition of income to the employee for tax purposes
   B. separation of salary continuation funds from the general funds of the company
   C. protection of the funds from the general creditors of the company
   D. all of the above

5. An entire salary continuation plan could fail to qualify for the ERISA exemption if
   A. the plan is established primarily to benefit a select group of employees
   B. one employee under the plan fails to meet the reasonable compensation requirements
   C. an employee's rights to benefits become vested at a later date
   D. all of the above

13

Split-Dollar Plans

Large or small, every business organization recognizes the need for attracting top-flight new blood to the company and for retaining its existing key personnel. One of the attractive executive benefits that a company can offer is a split-dollar life insurance plan. Simply put, a split-dollar plan is an arrangement that allows an employer and employee to share premium payments toward the purchase of insurance on the employee's life. Business organizations have found the split-dollar plan to be an effective and yet economical way to provide a desired benefit for key employees.

This chapter covers the basic structure of the split-dollar plan, with its various modifications and its beneficial points from the standpoint of both the employer and employee. Included is a discussion concerning income tax and estate tax benefits of the plan. Finally, it covers the uses of split-dollar plans, including a sample agreement.

■ BASIC SPLIT-DOLLAR PLAN

Split-dollar insurance plans enable an employer and any employee of the employer's choosing to share premium payments toward the purchase of insurance on the employee's life. Therefore, the split-dollar policy is a method of buying life insurance rather than a reason for buying it. The employee already has determined the need for the insurance but lacks the entire premium needed to purchase it. The employer has the funds to help finance the purchase of the insurance and has a specific reason for doing so—the desire to attract and hold key employees. Thus, the need is coupled with the combined purchasing power, and a split-dollar plan is the result.

The split-dollar plan is informal in nature; it requires no approval by the Internal Revenue Service. The employer may choose those employees he or she wishes to participate. However, in the case of shareholder-employees, the employer normally will set up a plan that includes employees other than just shareholder-employees to avoid any suggestion that the plan is a disguised dividend.

Premium Contributions

In the basic split-dollar plan, the employer pays that part of the premium equaling the annual increase in the cash value of the policy, and the employee contributes the balance. The employee's contribution may be made directly or by authorized payroll deduction. When the annual increase in the cash value equals or exceeds the net premium (gross premium less dividends in the case of a participating policy), the employer pays all subsequent premiums.

Death Benefits

If the insured employee dies while the plan is in effect, the employee's beneficiary receives that part of the proceeds equal to the difference between the face amount of the policy and its cash surrender value. The employer receives an amount equal to the policy's cash surrender value, which will at least equal, and sometimes exceed, the amount the employer has paid into the plan.

The employee's death benefit decreases each year in direct proportion to the increasing cash surrender value payable to the employer. However, this decrease is gradual. Even after 20 years, the insured's family will receive, in most cases, more than 50 percent of the policy's face amount, depending on the type of policy.

Policy Ownership

Under the basic split-dollar plan, the employer is the applicant and owner of the policy, and the employee's rights are spelled out in a separate, written agreement. (A sample agreement is included at the end of the chapter.) Specifically, the agreement calls for the employer to pay the premiums and the employee to reimburse the employer each year for any excess of premium over the increase in cash value. The agreement also empowers the employee to name a beneficiary and requires the employer as policyowner to designate such person as beneficiary for all proceeds above the cash value. This latter provision is implemented by a beneficiary endorsement made to the policy itself.

Termination Rights

A split-dollar plan may terminate prior to the insured's death for several reasons, including: failure by the employer or employee to make the contribution due toward the premium, termination of the employee's employment or an independent agreement between the parties to terminate the plan.

Without a provision to the contrary, if the basic plan terminates, the employer would be entitled to all existing policy values. However, it is customary to include in the agreement an option permitting the employee to purchase the policy from the employer for an amount equal to its cash value. This option is not considered an incident of ownership for estate tax purposes.

ILL 13.1 ▪ Basic Split-Dollar Plan

Varying Amounts of Contribution
Decreasing Employee Death Benefit
Amount $100,000   Annual Premium $2,264

Age 40 Male   Life Full Paid at 95, Nonparticipating

	Cash Value and Premium Data			Death Benefits		Income Tax Treatment	
	1	2	3	4	5	6	7
Year	Guaranteed Cash Value End of Year	Employer's Contribution (a)	Employee's Contribution (b)	Employer's Death Benefit	Employee's Death Benefit	P.S. 58 Cost of Employee's Death Benefit	Employee's Reportable Income (Col. 6 minus Col. 3)
1	$ 1,200	$ 1,200	$1,064	$ 1,200	$98,800	$ 437	–0–
2	2,700	1,500	764	2,700	97,300	460	–0–
3	4,600	1,900	364	4,600	95,400	484	$ 120
4	6,600	2,000	264	6,000	93,400	508	244
5	8,700	2,100	164	8,700	91,300	534	370
6	10,700	2,000	264	10,700	89,300	563	299
7	12,600	1,900	364	12,600	87,400	593	229
8	14,500	1,900	364	14,500	85,500	626	262
9	16,400	1,900	364	16,400	83,600	660	296
10	18,300	1,900	364	18,300	81,700	697	333
11	20,200	1,900	364	20,200	79,800	736	372
12	22,200	2,000	264	22,200	77,800	776	512
13	24,100	1,900	364	24,100	75,900	819	455
14	26,100	2,000	264	26,100	73,900	864	600
15	28,100	2,000	264	28,100	71,900	911	647
16	30,100	2,000	264	30,100	69,900	960	696
17	32,100	2,000	264	32,100	67,900	1,012	748
18	34,100	2,000	264	34,100	65,900	1,066	802
19	36,100	2,000	264	36,100	63,900	1,122	858
20	38,100	2,000	264	38,100	61,900	1,181	917
21	40,000	1,900	364	40,000	60,000	1,244	880
22	42,000	2,000	264	42,000	58,000	1,307	1,043
23	43,900	1,900	364	43,900	56,100	1,374	1,010
24	45,900	2,000	264	45,900	54,100	1,441	1,177
25	47,800	1,900	364	47,800	52,200	1,513	1,149

(a) The employer's contribution equals the annual increase in the cash value of the policy.

(b) The employee's contribution is the difference between the annual premium and the employer's contributions.

An Illustration

An illustration of a basic split-dollar plan is shown in Ill. 13.1. You will note that the employer's premium contribution is limited to the cash value increase, with the employee making up the difference, if any. Also, the basic plan results in a decreasing death benefit for the employee's designated beneficiary.

ADVANTAGES OF THE SPLIT-DOLLAR PLAN

A split-dollar plan today will help key executives and other key employees overcome the most important financial problem they have: providing adequately for their families' welfare in event of death. Furthermore, a split-dollar plan develops a group of loyal key executives at practically no cost. There are other advantages of a split-dollar plan to the employer and the employee. A summary of the more important ones follows.

Advantages to the Employer

The advantages of a split-dollar plan to the employer are significant.

1. *It is an incentive plan.* The employer can bind a key employee more closely to the business by providing substantial assistance in the purchase of needed life insurance protection. The employer's contributions to the plan depend on the employee remaining with the corporation.

2. *It may be selective.* The plan, being informal, enables the employer to be selective among its employees, thus keeping the plan on a confidential basis.

3. *No IRS approval is required.* The plan can be installed with a minimum of procedural detail and need not be submitted to the Internal Revenue Service for approval.

4. *It creates a business reserve.* Being the owner of the split-dollar policy, the employer also owns its cash value. Thus, the company has a growing and readily available reserve fund to call upon for business needs and emergencies. If the insured employee lives to retirement, the company can use the cash value of the policy to fund a special retirement plan for the employee.

5. *There is no direct cost.* There is no cost to the employer other than the net after-tax loss of earnings if the money were invested elsewhere. When the employee dies, the employer receives back its contributions to the plan free of income tax. If, for any reason, the insured employee leaves the company, the employer can terminate the plan and, under the conventional arrangement, get back every dollar it has invested.

Advantages to the Employee

The advantages to the insured employee are equally as significant:

1. *It provides low-cost insurance.* The employee obtains life insurance protection at the lowest possible cost. Although the employee must report as income the economic benefit received under the plan, the employee nevertheless obtains insurance coverage on a favorable cost basis. In the case of a junior executive, he or she obtains adequate coverage at a time when he or she is least likely to be able to afford it. The highly compensated executive, on the other hand, otherwise might be unable to purchase additional coverage because of the tax impact on top dollars. Split-dollar solves the problem.

2. *It is a hedge against uninsurability.* The split-dollar plan represents a hedge against the employee becoming uninsurable in the future. If a disability should strike and the acquisition of additional insurance becomes impossible, the employee nevertheless will be insured to an extent greater than otherwise might have been possible.

3. *It offers coverage beyond retirement.* The plan may permit the employee to continue coverage after retirement by paying the employer the amount of its contributions. This arrangement enables the employee to acquire a substantial amount of permanent life insurance with premiums based on the employee's age when the policy was issued, rather than on the age when the employee purchases the policy from the employer.

■ VARIATIONS ON BASIC SPLIT-DOLLAR PLANS

The high cost of the plan to the employee in its early years prompted efforts to find alternatives to the basic plan. Today, the basic plan is the exception. The employer and the employee are free to include whatever arrangement they wish for splitting the premium and the proceeds. One of the more common variations is the noncontributory plan, in which the employer pays the entire premium but the proceeds still are split at the employee's death. Another is the level contribution plan, which allows the employee to contribute a level amount over the expected premium-paying period of the policy, rather than high initial amounts and low (or no) later amounts. Another is the level death benefit plan, which gives the employee level death benefit protection at least until retirement age.

In addition to the plans for splitting the premiums and proceeds, there are other terms for describing the structure of the split-dollar arrangement. These terms are: (1) the *collateral assignment method* and (2) the *endorsement method*.

The Collateral Assignment Method

Under the *collateral assignment method*, the employee initially applies for, owns and is the premium-payer on the policy on his or her own life. The employee also names his or her own beneficiary. In a separate agreement, the employer agrees to lend the employee, at a nominal (or no) interest rate, an amount equal to each year's increase in the cash value of the policy, not to exceed the annual premium. In exchange, the employee collaterally assigns the policy to the employer as security for annual loans that are repayable upon termination of employment or the earlier death of the employee. Upon the employee's death, the employer recovers its loans from the proceeds, and the balance is paid to the employee's named beneficiary. Because the employer is only a collateral assignee, however, the cash value is not available to him or her during the employee's lifetime.

It is customary for the employee to sign a loan agreement, together with demand notes evidencing the total increasing indebtedness to the employer. This procedure, of course, creates a valid creditor-debtor relationship, but as just noted, usually no interest is charged, which generally is in keeping with the "employee benefit" aspect of a split-dollar plan.

The collateral assignment split-dollar method evolved primarily because of tax considerations. (The tax treatment of this plan is discussed later.) However, certain nontax factors also are important, and should be noted.

Advantages

One important advantage of the collateral assignment method is the ease with which the employee may take over the policy unencumbered. Because the employee owns the policy and merely has collaterally assigned it to the employer, the employee may recover it simply by paying off the indebtedness. For example, the employee could secure a policy loan, concurrently with a release of assignment, and use the borrowed funds to pay off the split-dollar loan. There would be no sale and transfer of title, as would be the case under an employer-owned plan.

An existing, personally purchased policy also may be put on a split-dollar basis via a collateral assignment to the insured-employee's employer. If this is done with a policy that has been in force for a number of years—at a time when the annual cash value increases equal or exceed the net premium due—the insured would be relieved of any further premiums. In fact, these released premium dollars could be used to purchase new insurance when indicated.

Disadvantages

The principal disadvantage of the collateral assignment method is that the employer's rights in the policy are limited to those of a collateral assignee. Thus, because it does not *own* the policy, the employer cannot view the policy's cash value as a sinking fund available for use in the business.

The Endorsement Split-Dollar Method

Under the *endorsement* method, the employer is the applicant for and the owner of the policy on the employee's life. As the owner, the employer is responsible for paying premiums. However, under a separate split-dollar agreement, the employee agrees to reimburse the employer for the portion of the premiums it contributes, and the employer agrees to let the employee name a beneficiary for his or her portion of the proceeds. The employee's rights are protected by a special endorsement to the policy. Under the endorsement method, the employer typically recovers only an amount of the proceeds equal to its premium payments.

The endorsement method has two advantages for the employer:

1. *The business is able to show the cash value of the policy as a business asset on the firm's balance sheet.* These cash values are available for investment or emergency needs.

2. *The employer benefits by the apparent ease of paying premiums along with other company bills.* Although there is no immediate income tax advantage to the company when a split-dollar premium is paid (because such premiums are not federal income tax deductible), many corporate owner-executives feel that it is preferable for the business to pay the premiums rather than to write a personal check.

The Split Ownership Method

Another method for splitting the various elements of the life insurance policy (premium, death benefits, cash values) in a split dollar plan is the split ownership method.

Under the split-ownership method, the applicant s the insured or other third-party owner, and the original application indicates the policy's special split ownership arrangement. Typically, the special requests section of the application should contain the following language: "policy should be issued as a split ownership/split dollar plan." A special assignment form creating the split ownership is customarily submitted at the time of application.

The applicant (either the insured or a third party) would receive the premium notices and be responsible for submitting premium payments, which would, of course, include the portion paid by the employer. The beneficiary is designated by the insured or, if ownership vests in a third party, in a third party. In the event the policy is owned by a third party, he or she should also be the beneficiary.

The employer's interest in the split ownership/split dollar policy is severely limited. The employer's interest is limited to the:

- right to borrow or withdraw from the policy an amount equal to its interest in the policy, which is equal to the premiums it has paid; and

- right to receive an amount equal to its cumulative premium payments from either the death benefit or surrender proceeds.

Although the split ownership form of split dollar can be used in any situation in which the collateral assignment method would be appropriate, it is especially useful in two situations. Those situations in which the split-ownership arrangements may be especially applicable are those where:

- there are potential transfer for value issues because of third-party ownership; or

- interest-free loans to shareholders or employees are prohibited by state law.

State Law Considerations

It is important that relevant state statute and corporate bylaw provisions be checked to determine whether a corporation may make loans to its employees. Many states have statutes relating to loans to stockholders, directors and officers. Typically, these statutes hold directors who approve such loans liable for corporate debts to the extent any loss occurs as a result of such loans. Some statutes specifically prohibit the practice.

In states imposing personal liability on the directors, the statutes should not be a problem, because the split-dollar loans under the employee-owned plan are fully collateralized. Legal counsel should be sought nevertheless.

Level Death Benefit Plan

A fundamental characteristic of the basic split-dollar plan is that, to the extent premium dollars are provided by the employer, the insured-employee's protection decreases each year. To offset this effect, many insurance companies have developed modifications of the basic plan.

Fifth Dividend Option

In participating policies the so-called *fifth dividend option* enables the insured-employee to have level protection at least up to his or her retirement age. It is an arrangement under which one-year term additions are purchased each year out of current dividends or dividend accumulations. The term additions purchased on each policy anniversary are equal to the cash value of the policy, or such smaller amount as the current dividend and any accumulations will purchase. To the extent that dividends are adequate to purchase term additions, death proceeds will equal the initial face of the policy plus its cash value. After payment of the cash value to the employer (or premiums paid, if greater), the employee's beneficiary will receive the balance, which will approximate the initial face amount. This type of plan is illustrated in Ill. 13.2. The manner in which the premiums are split will be covered later.

As the insured's age and the cash value increase, the amount of the current dividend needed to purchase the term additions likewise increases. For this reason, some agents recommend maintaining the level death benefit longer by accumulating the balance of the dividend and interest after the purchase of term additions. However, because the interest on dividends is reportable and taxable, most agents use maximum paid-up additions. Alternatively, the balance may be used to reduce premium, which results in a lower current premium outlay. In most instances, the level coverage will be maintained at least to age 65, even though premiums are paid on a net basis after purchase of the term additions.

Other Dividend Options

Other dividend options, elected either in conjunction with the fifth dividend option or independently, also will produce an employee death benefit greater than that paid under the basic plan. The paid-up additions option, for example, affords attractive opportunities. If the employer owns the policy and makes the election, the policy will be paid in the same manner as the basic policy (i.e., cash value to employer, amount at risk to employee). The employee's death benefit would be increased to the extent of additions purchased to date of death.

If the employee owns the policy, the employee also owns the dividends and any paid-up additions with them. Using dividends in this manner both increases the amount payable to the employee's beneficiaries and builds a cash fund for use at the employee's own retirement.

Finally, dividends may be accumulated at interest under various arrangements.

Special Policies and Riders

A level employee death benefit also may be maintained by using a special term rider or a specially designated policy that increases the death benefit annually to retirement age in an amount equal to the cash value of the basic policy. These modifications are not dependent upon policy dividends or special dividend options.

First-Year Premium Problem

Under the basic split-dollar plan, in which the employer's contribution is measured by the yearly increase in cash value, the employee is required to make his or her most substantial contribution the first policy year. But each year thereafter, as the policy's cash value increases, the employee's contribution decreases and, under certain types of plans, will be eliminated altogether at some point during the premium-paying period.

Even though the employee is able to acquire life insurance at a very modest overall cost, payment of a substantial first-year premium could present a practical problem. Several methods have been developed, however, to lessen this possible burden.

Level Contribution Plan

The split-dollar illustration shown in Ill. 13.2 uses a leveling technique designed to lessen the first-year premium burden. (This technique also has income tax ramifications, which are covered later.) Under the illustrated arrangement, the employer's contributions are fixed at a level amount until the insured reaches age 65, when, presumably, the plan would terminate. The employer's annual level contribution of $2,026 is arrived at by dividing the cash value of the policy at the insured's 65th year by 25 (the number of years covered by the plan).

It also is possible to level the employee's contribution simply by dividing the employee's total projected contribution by the desired number of years he or she is to participate in the plan. However, it is not possible to level both the employer's and the employee's contribution when a participating policy is used in the manner illustrated, namely, by using balance of dividends to reduce premium. This could be done when premiums are paid on a gross basis, or with a nonparticipating policy.

When contributions are leveled in the manner illustrated, the death benefit payable to the employer equals the greater of the employer's total contributions or the cash value of the policy. Should the plan be terminated for any other reason in the early years, the employer lacks security to the extent of the difference between the cash value and contributions made to date of termination, less any dividend paid in the year of termination. However, as column three of Ill. 13.2 reveals, the amount of this excess is modest and eventually disappears. (When the prior year's dividend is taken into account, there is no "excess" after the sixth policy year.)

As a practical matter, the prospective insured is a questionable candidate for split-dollar if the employer is concerned unduly about contributing these modest amounts in excess of the policy's cash value.

Other Methods

Other methods can be used to lessen the employee's first-year premium burden:

1. *The employer advances a portion or all of the first-year premium.* A repayment schedule is set up wherein the employee contributes not only his or her normal share of the premium but an amortized share of the initial premium borrowed as well. Although the initial loan is not fully covered by cash values, the employer is paid in full in the event the employee dies.

2. *The policy is originally carried as key-executive insurance.* The employer in the first year would be the owner and beneficiary of the policy and would pay the full first-year premium. In the second year, the split-dollar plan is entered into wherein the employee pays for the amount at risk. The first-year premium never is carried by the employee.

3. *The employer pays first and all subsequent premiums.* Under this arrangement, the employer is the owner of the policy and the beneficiary to the extent of premiums it pays or the policy's cash value, whichever is greater. The employee names a beneficiary to the extent of the difference between the face of the policy (and any term additions, if included) and the amount payable to the employer. The employee pays nothing directly for this insurance benefit. However, this insurance will be an "economic benefit" to the employee. The value of it will be charged to the employee as income. Nevertheless, the employee has obtained additional insurance at the lowest possible cost.

4. *The employee pays the P.S. costs.* Under this approach, the only premium paid by the employee each year is an amount that is equal to the P.S. cost for that year. Because the amount of income that the employee must report as a result of his or her split-dollar plan is equal to the P.S. 58 cost (or the alternative insurer's ART rates) less any premium amount contributed by the employee, the employee's paying a portion of the premium equal to the rates means that there will be no income to report. Because both the P.S. 58 and alternative ART rates generally increase each year, they are at their lowest in the first year of coverage. As a result, the first year required employee contribution under this approach tends to be relatively modest—and certainly well below the first-year contribution required under the basic split-dollar plan.

5. *P.S. 58 split-dollar costs can be bonused.* P.S. 58 refers to the table issued by the IRS that lists the cost of the economic benefit referred to above. The employer can bonus the amount of the P.S. 58 cost or can bonus the amount of the P.S. 58 cost and the tax on the bonus. Also, the plan will work without a bonus, with the P.S. 58 costs simply reportable.

Split-Dollar Combined with Other Plans of Insurance

A split-dollar insurance plan can be combined with another insurance need or concept to fulfill a number of functions. For instance, the need of the employee for insurance coverage and the employer for key-executive coverage can be combined in one plan. This could be accomplished simply by adding a rider—paid for by the employer—to a corporate-owned policy. Also, a split-dollar plan can be combined with a deferred compensation plan.

Nothing prevents an employer from using the cash value portion of a split-dollar insurance policy as the funding base for a deferred compensation agreement with the insured employee. In fact, this option is perhaps a better answer for the employee than the conventional deferred compensation plan. In the conventional deferred compensation plan, the employer pays a benefit at the time of the employee's retirement, disability or death. When the employee dies, the payments the employer makes to the employee's spouse or family, after the $5,000 exclusion, will be taxable income to them. Note, however, that this is not the case when the death benefit is arranged under a split-dollar plan.

Under the split-dollar plan, the death benefit qualifies as insurance proceeds to the employee's beneficiaries and, as such, comes to them income tax-free. In other words, the employee avoids income taxation of the death benefit by paying a minimal split-dollar insurance cost during his or her lifetime.

Reverse Split-Dollar Plans

In a reverse split-dollar life insurance plan, the key employee applies for and purchases a life insurance policy on his or her life. A formal agreement is adopted that clearly defines the death benefit to be received by the employer. The employer pays that portion of the premium attributable to the P.S. 58 cost of the coverage received each year. The employee pays the balance of the premium.

ILL 13.2 ■ Split-Dollar Plan (Fifth Dividend Option)

Employer's Contribution Level Age 40 Male — Whole Life — Dividends Purchase One Year Term—Balance Reduce Premiums Amount $100,000 — Annual Premium $2,745

	(1)	(2)	(3)	(4)	(5)	(6)	(7)	(8)	(9)	(10)	(11)	(12)	(13)
Year	Guaranteed Cash Value End of Year	Employers Cumulative Contribution (a)	Total Contribution Exceeding Cash Value	Dividend at End of Previous Year	Cost of Term Insurance	Balance of Dividend	Gross Premium Less Balance of Dividend	Employee's Net Contribution (Col. 7 minus $2,026)	Term Insurance Purchased (b)	Employer's Death Benefit (c)	Employee's Total Death Benefit (d)	P.S. 58 Cost of Employee's Basic Death Benefit ($100,000 less Col. 10)	Reportable Income (Col. 4 plus Col. 12 less $719 (3))
1	$ 889	$ 2,026	$1,137	-0-	-0-	-0-	$2,745	$719	-0-	$ 2,026	$ 97,904	$ 434	-0-
2	2,968	4,052	1,084	278	12	$266	2,479	453	$2,968	4,052	98,916	454	$ 13
3	5,069	6,078	1,009	335	22	313	2,432	406	5,069	6,078	98,991	476	92
4	7,194	8,105	910	392	33	359	2,386	360	7,194	8,104	99,090	500	173
5	9,341	10,130	789	450	47	403	2,342	316	9,341	10,130	99,211	526	257
6	11,507	12,156	649	507	62	445	2,300	274	11,507	12,156	99,351	553	341
7	13,692	14,182	490	565	80	485	2,260	234	13,692	14,182	99,510	582	428
8	15,726	16,208	482	625	100	525	2,220	194	15,726	16,208	99,518	613	519
9	17,775	18,234	459	684	124	560	2,185	159	17,775	18,234	99,541	645	610
10	19,836	20,260	424	744	151	593	2,152	126	19,836	20,260	99,576	680	705
11	21,905	22,286	381	804	182	622	2,123	97	21,905	22,286	99,619	717	802
12	23,982	24,312	330	864	219	645	2,100	74	23,982	24,312	99,670	755	900
13	26,065	26,338	273	926	259	667	2,078	52	26,065	26,338	99,727	795	1,002
14	28,152	28,364	212	989	305	684	2,061	35	28,152	28,364	99,788	837	1,107
15	30,241	30,390	149	1,051	357	694	2,051	25	30,241	30,390	99,851	882	1,214
16	32,330	32,416	86	1,113	416	697	2,048	22	32,330	32,416	99,914	929	1,323
17	34,416	34,442	26	1,174	484	690	2,055	29	34,416	34,442	99,974	977	1,432
18	36,496	36,468	-0-	1,238	561	677	2,068	42	36,496	36,496	100,000	1,027	1,546
19	38,567	38,494	-0-	1,300	649	651	2,094	68	38,567	38,567	100,000	1,079	1,660
20	40,627	40,520	-0-	1,362	747	615	2,130	104	40,627	40,627	100,000	1,133	1,776
25	50,650	50,650	-0-	1,573	1,441	132	2,613	587	50,650	50,650	100,000	1,430	2,284

(a) Column represents the successive additions of the employer's annual level contribution of $2,026. This annual level contribution equals one-twenty-fifth of the cash value at the end of the 25th policy year.
(b) The amount of one-year term insurance purchased equals the terminal cash value for the current year.
(c) The employer's death benefit equals the greater of employer contributions or the cash value of the policy.
(d) The employee's death benefit equals the difference between the total of the policy's face amount plus the term additions, and the amount payable to the employer.
(e) $719 is the employee's total contribution to the gross premium, including both his out-of-pocket contribution (Col. 8) and the amount of the dividend applied (Col. 6)

DIVIDENDS ARE BASED ON THE CURRENT SCALE AND ARE NEITHER GUARANTEED NOR ESTIMATES FOR THE FUTURE. The 25th policy year is the last year the current dividend is sufficient to purchase one-year term addition equal to the full cash value.

Policy Ownership

A key employee purchases a life insurance policy on his or her own life. The employee endorses the death benefit over to his or her employer, making the employer the beneficiary of the policy and a subowner of the policy. Note that the death benefit is endorsed, not collaterally assigned, which, in the opinion of the proponents of reverse split-dollar plans, frees the employer from tax liability problems in the accumulated earnings tax and the alternative minimum tax areas.

The employee, as the owner of the policy, is entitled to any cash value buildup in the policy. If the employee dies while the plan is in effect, the employer receives the agreed-upon death benefit tax-free plus a refund of any prepaid premiums. Any additional death benefits go to the beneficiary named by the employee.

The employer relinquishes his or her rights in the contract at the agreed-upon termination date of the agreement—usually the employee's retirement date. On that date, the retired employee is the full owner of the policy and has access to the accumulated cash value of the life insurance policy. Because of its preferred status over the period of the agreement (i.e., through P.S. 58 rate structures versus the high earnings of the policy), the policy is expected to have a high cash value at the employee's retirement date.

The Taxation Issues

For many agents, reverse split-dollar is another creative split-dollar idea that represents the cutting edge of advanced sales. Others are not so confident about the reverse split-dollar concept. However, it should be kept clearly in mind that neither the reverse split-dollar proponents nor the reverse split-dollar critics can point to a single revenue ruling, statute, court case or other clear legal authority for either position. The answers simply are not available.

Proponents of reverse split-dollar plans say that at the employee's retirement date, the cash value will not be taxable because:

1. no deductions have been claimed for premium payments made;

2. employer-paid premiums were based on government P.S. 58 tables;

3. there was no transfer of property between employer and employee; and

4. the employee is really the sole owner of the policy.

The proponents of this premise also state that the cash values involved are funds from the corporation not deemed to be the employee's compensation. Neither is the cash value a dividend.

The opposing view holds that an aggressive marketing of a reverse split-dollar plan based on a premise of tax-free dollars for both the employer and the employee is, at best, speculative. At worst, both employer and employee might find themselves involved in a variety of federal tax and legal liability issues.

The taxation issue involving reverse split-dollar plans can be divided into two parts: those affecting the company and those affecting the employee.

From the company's standpoint, a reverse split-dollar plan can make its impact in the areas of the accumulated earnings tax, in the alternative minimum tax and in the transfer-for-value rule.

With regards to the employee, a reverse split-dollar plan will affect his or her annual federal income tax, retirement planning and estate taxation.

Life Insurance Product Choices

With the introduction of variable and flexible premium life insurance products, the possibilities offered by the split-dollar insurance plan have increased significantly. These products have made possible the early cessation of required premiums, earlier policy rollouts and more favorable premium splits. Let's look at how these products manage these favorable outcomes.

Earlier cessation of required premiums results from the greater cash values (when compared to traditional whole life policies) that may build under variable, universal and universal variable policies. Instead of relying on a traditional premium offset, flexible premium policies permit the stop and go of premium payments, limited only by the sufficiency of cash value and the objectives of the policyowner. Similarly, these potentially greater early cash values can permit earlier split-dollar policy rollouts as cash values more rapidly equal cumulative employer premium payments.

More favorable premium splits are possible under universal, variable and universal variable policies for precisely the same reason that they permit earlier rollouts and the ability to stop making premium payments: potentially higher early cash values. You will recall in out discussion of the basic split-dollar plan with which we began this chapter that the employer pays that part of the premium that equals the annual increase in the cash value of the policy. Since the employer's portion of the premium is equal to the cash value increase, the insured's (or third-party owner's) portion of the premium is the balance of the policy's annual premium. When the premium is less than the cash value increase, the employer pays all of it.

In the front-end loaded traditional whole life policy, cash values often do not accrue until the end of the second or third year, and annual cash value increases typically do not exceed the annual premium for several years. There are two unfortunate premium-split results of this delayed cash value crediting in the basic split-dollar plan:

- high required first (and, possibly, second) year employee premium contributions, often equal to the entire annual premium; and

- continued premium payments required by the employee, possible extending for twenty or more years.

As a result of these unfavorable (for the non-employer) premium splits, a number of split-dollar variations have appeared including the level-contribution plan and other methods designed to mitigate the employee's problem of the large first year premium. Using universal life, variable life or universal variable life policies can go a long way to solving the problem without resorting to these more exotic splits. The reason for this is due to these policies' providing for an earlier crediting of cash values and their having potentially greater cash value accumulations than traditional whole life policies.

Since these non-traditional life insurance policies provide for earlier cash value crediting, the employer's share of the premium starts earlier, often beginning in the first policy year. Furthermore, because the cash values under these policies may accumulate faster than under a traditional whole life policy, the employer's share of the premium can increase substantially and may equal more quickly the entire premium. As a result of these potentially higher cash values, the employee's total premium share may be considerably lower than under a traditional whole life policy for the face amount.

These possible results are accompanied by some uncertainty with respect to cash value accumulations. While the earlier cash value crediting found in universal life, variable life and universal variable life insurance policies is a matter of contract design and can be relied upon to reduce the employee's first-year premium share, the higher long-term cash value accumulations in these policies may not materialize. A universal life insurance policy's interest-crediting rate may decline to the point where the policy's cash value accumulation would be less than that provided by a whole life policy. Similarly, the investment performance of the separate account underlying a variable life or universal variable life policy may result in only modest gains or even losses, causing the cash values to be less than comparable whole life policy cash values.

■ TAX CONSIDERATIONS

Tax considerations pertaining to split-dollar plans should be explained to business owners, as well as to the employees covered.

Income Taxation

Because it is directly or indirectly a beneficiary of the proceeds, the employer does not receive a deduction for its premium contributions under the plan. Likewise, the employee cannot deduct any portion of his or her portion of premiums paid.

Additionally, a portion of the value of the policy may be treated as a taxable benefit to the employee each year. To illustrate the taxable amount, if any, let's discuss how to compute the amount. It involves a three-step process.

1. Value of Basic Insurance Protection

The first step is to compute the value of the insurance protection payable to the insured's beneficiary under the basic split-dollar policy. This is done on a year-to-year basis, using the lower of the government's "P.S. 58" rates (reproduced in Ill. 13.3) or the insurance company's published rates for individual one-year term policies (not "fifth dividend option" rates). The selected rate is

ILL 13.3 ■ "P.S. 58" Table of One-Year Term Rates

Age	Premium	Age	Premium
15	$1.27	49	$ 8.53
16	1.38	50	9.22
17	1.48	51	9.97
18	1.52	52	10.79
19	1.56	53	11.69
20	1.61	54	12.67
21	1.67	55	13.74
22	1.73	56	14.91
23	1.79	57	16.18
24	1.86	58	17.56
25	1.93	59	19.08
26	2.02	60	20.73
27	2.11	61	22.53
28	2.20	62	24.50
29	2.31	63	26.63
30	2.43	64	28.98
31	2.57	65	31.51
32	2.70	66	34.28
33	2.86	67	37.31
34	3.02	68	40.59
35	3.21	69	44.17
36	3.41	70	48.06
37	3.63	71	52.29
38	3.87	72	56.89
39	4.14	73	61.89
40	4.42	74	67.33
41	4.73	75	73.23
42	5.07	76	79.63
43	5.44	77	86.57
44	5.85	78	94.09
45	6.30	79	102.23
46	6.78	80	111.04
47	7.32	81	120.57
48	7.89		

applied only to the amount at risk payable to the insured's beneficiary under the basic policy and, with one exception, not to any additional amounts payable under one of the dividend options.

The exception is that when dividends on a participating policy are used to buy paid-up additions *and the employer controls the cash value of such additions,* the amount at risk is lumped with such amount under the basic policy, with the lower of the P.S. 58 rate or company rate applied to the sum total.

2. Value of Dividends

In the next step, the dollar value of any dividends used for the insured-employee's benefit is added to the value of the basic insurance protection determined in the first step. This includes any dividends paid to the employee in cash, applied to pay the employee's share of the premium or accumulated for the employee's benefit. It also includes the amount of dividend used to purchase term insurance under the fifth dividend option or paid-up additions when the employee controls the cash value in them. Note that the reportable amount is the amount of dividend used to purchase any additional insurance and not the P.S. 58 cost of this insurance.

3. Employee's Premium Contribution

The final step is to subtract the employee's share of the gross premium from the total value of the basic life insurance protection and the dollar value of dividends used for the employee's benefit (the sum of steps one and two above). The difference, if any, is the amount the employee must report as income.

The employee's share of the gross premium should include both the employee's out-of-pocket contribution and the amount of any dividend applied to his or her share.

Examples. The tax treatment of a split-dollar plan can be understood best by referring to the two tables noted earlier in our discussion. First, refer to Ill. 13.1. This is a basic plan, using a $100,000 nonparticipating policy. Note that the taxable amount is computed yearly, based on a decreasing death benefit. Because this is a nonparticipating policy, the insurance protection is the only taxable benefit the employee receives under the plan. The employee's contribution in the first two years is sufficient to eliminate the insurance cost; however, the excess of $627 in the first year (column 3 less column 6) is not carried over to reduce reportable income in subsequent years.

In Ill. 13.2, provision is made for a level employer premium contribution and an approximately level employee death benefit through the use of the fifth dividend option. Note here that the P.S. 58 rate is applied only to the amount at risk payable to the insured's beneficiary under the basic policy—the difference between $100,000 and column 10. Further, because the dividend is reportable in full by the employee, the employee's total contribution to the gross premium is $719—the employee's out-of-pocket contribution plus the amount of dividend applied to reduce the employee's share.

Equity Split-Dollar Concerns

Certain split-dollar arrangements are characterized as *equity split-dollar plans*, and these plans may result in additional employee income taxation, according to an IRS technical advice memorandum (TAM). A TAM is issued to IRS personnel by the national office of the IRS to assist with application of the Internal Revenue Code, regulations and other precedents. Although TAMs do not provide binding precedent, courts have considered them n reaching decisions. The TAM addressing this additional employee income taxation is TAM 9604001.

Equity split dollar plans are those in which the employer's interest in the cash value and death benefit of the split-dollar life insurance policy is limited to a return of its cumulative contributions. Since life insurance policy cash values often eventually exceed the employer's total premiums, cash values in excess of those premiums—in a sense, the *equity*—accumulate to the benefit of the employee. It is this benefit that is the subject of TAM 9604001.

In the early years of an equity split-dollar plan, there would generally be no tax consequences because the cash values usually will be less than or equal to the employer's premium payments. As the cash values grow beyond the employer's total premium payments and begin to accumulate for the employee, the tax questions to answer are:

1. Will the insured employee need to recognize taxable income each year as cash value increases exceed the corporation's annual premium payments?

2. If the cash value growth inuring to the employee escapes income taxation in the year of increase, will the employee be taxed on the lump sum, minus basis, upon policy rollout or surrender or upon the employee's termination of employment?

A number of theories can —and possibly, will — be advanced in support of both current taxability and tax deferral when this material is settled. For now, it is important for the life insurance practitioner to realize that the tax status of equity split dollar plans is unsettled. In those cases in which an equity split dollar approach is indicated for a particular and recommended, the prudent practitioner will ensure that the client fully understands the tax issues and possible consequences.

Level Contributions

Mention already has been made of the practical effect of leveling contributions in the manner illustrated in Ill. 13.2 (namely, by reducing the employee's first-year premium commitment). Instead of paying a large portion in the first year and considerably less in later years (to a point where he or she eventually may make no contribution), the employee remains as a modest premium-payer throughout the period covered by the plan.

This procedure also may be beneficial from a tax standpoint, in that the insured employee has an offset each year against the amount he or she must otherwise report as income. The employee does not make a substantially higher contribution—from an offset standpoint—in the first year; instead, the employee spreads this excess throughout the period of the plan and has an offset each year against the amount otherwise taxable.

Employer-Pay-All Plan

A split-dollar plan in which the employer pays the first and all subsequent premiums was discussed earlier under the heading "First-Year Premium Problem." Although not specifically covered, the "economic benefit" principle for taxing the employee provides a guide for determining how such a plan *might* be taxed.

Under this arrangement, the employer owns the policy, but names the employee's beneficiary for the difference between the face amount of the policy and the total premiums paid by the employer (or the cash value, if greater). The value of this economic benefit, namely one-year term insurance protection, should be determined by reference to the P.S. 58 table (or to the insurance company's published rates, if lower). This, then, should be the amount the employee reports as income currently, together with any dividends used for his or her benefit. No other portion of the employer's contribution should be reportable, because the employee has no rights in the policy beyond naming a beneficiary for the previously mentioned amount.

The effect of this arrangement is to provide insurance for the employee at the lowest possible cost; namely, the tax the employee must pay on the P.S. 58 cost and taxable dividends the employee includes in income. Caution should be exercised in this area. Many decisions regarding implementation of an employer-pay-all plan should be based only on advice of counsel.

Collateral Assignment Method

Under a collateral assignment split-dollar plan, the same general tax rules apply. Though premium amount is loaned to the employee, the IRS has ruled that the debtor-creditor relationship exists only in form and not in substance. The IRS concludes that a loan does not actually exist because the employee is not expected to repay the loan; instead, the amounts are repaid eventually out of proceeds or a policy loan.

Employer's Deduction

The IRS specifically denies any employer deduction for its premium contributions, because it "is directly or indirectly a beneficiary" of a portion of the policy proceeds.

Stockholder-Employees

In general the law and subsequent rulings make no distinction between employee-stockholders and other employees in a split-dollar plan. There may be problems, however, when controlling stockholder-employees are involved with the possible applicability of the accumulated earnings tax.

The Accumulated Earnings Tax

An accumulated earnings tax is imposed when a corporation—to aid its shareholders in avoiding income tax consequences—accumulates earnings and profits instead of distributing them as dividends. If the accumulations are for a proper business need or purpose, then the tax is not applied.

The issue of an accumulated earnings tax could arise in a split-dollar plan with a substantial shareholder. The IRS might determine that the investment of corporate earnings in life insurance cash values or in the secured loans of the split-dollar plan is an unreasonable accumulation. However, if the IRS could be convinced that the accumulations are for reasonable business needs and not the needs of the shareholder, then an accumulated earnings tax could be avoided. No case has yet been decided on this issue. Nevertheless, it seems only reasonable that, to the extent the policy indemnifies an employer for the economic loss the employee's death would cause, the policy should be looked upon as a reasonable business need.

"Private" Split-Dollar Plans

Revenue rulings cover only split-dollar arrangements between an employer and an employee. No mention is made of so-called private split-dollar plans. Apparently, then, if a father and son, for instance, entered into a split-dollar insurance arrangement, there would be no income tax consequences. On the other hand, if an employer-employee relationship exists between the father and the son, it would no longer be a private split-dollar plan and the son would be in receipt of an economic benefit in some tax years. There are some authorities who contend that the father has made a *gift* to his son, measured by the P.S. 58 economic benefit. This issue has not been definitively resolved.

Estate Taxation

Under the general rule, life insurance is included in the gross estate of the insured when the insured has an incident of ownership in the policy at the time of death. Because the right to name a beneficiary is an incident of ownership, the portion of death proceeds payable to the employee's beneficiary under a conventional split-dollar plan presumably will be in the employee's gross estate.

Excluding Proceeds from Estate

Can split-dollar proceeds be excluded from the insured employee's estate? The answer to this one, although far from certain, depends upon who owns the policy at the outset.

Under the *employer-owned* split-dollar plan, the employee's only right is to name a personal beneficiary for the amount at risk. While use of the unlimited marital deduction may provide the most simple approach for avoiding estate taxes for many individuals, the client's attorney may recommend a more detailed estate plan. In that event, questions arise. If the employee absolutely assigns this right to his or her spouse, for example, would the employee thereby effectively divest himself or herself of any incident of ownership? Possibly so, but keep in mind that the split-dollar arrangement typically is dependent upon the employee's continued employment. Thus, even though the employee gives up the right to name a beneficiary, the employee would remain in control of the situation; should the employee terminate employment, the spouse's right to name a beneficiary also would terminate. If the employee is a sole or controlling stockholder in the employer's corporation, an incident of ownership problem arises. In such a case, the employer's incidents of ownership would pass through to the employee-stockholder and the proceeds would be includable in his or her estate except to the extent paid to the corporation. Of course, the portion of the proceeds paid to the corporation would increase the value of the employee-stockholder's stock for estate tax purposes.

Collateral Assignment Method

If the insured employee's spouse applies for and owns the policy in the first instance and then collaterally assigns it to the employer under a split-dollar insurance plan, this could remove the proceeds from the insured's estate. However, such action is generally unnecessary, because use of the unlimited marital deduction usually will accomplish the initial estate planning objective. Then additional planning can be done with the estate of the surviving spouse. Finally, if the spouse paid the insurance-at-risk portion of the insurance premium personally, the possibility of exclusion from the insured's estate would be more certain.

Majority Shareholders

If the employee is a sole or controlling stockholder in the corporation, however, the mere possession of incidents of ownership by the corporation is sufficient to include the proceeds in the shareholder's estate. The method by which the corporation acquired such incidents is not relevant.

The sole or controlling shareholder-employee can achieve a desirable tax result with a little extra planning. The shareholder's spouse or some other third party should be the applicant for and owner of the policy. The spouse and the employer enter into a collateral assignment split-dollar arrangement. In this situation, the shareholder holds no direct incidents of ownership and the corporation is merely a collateral assignee and has no incidents that can be attributed to the shareholder.

It is important to note that the corporation must not possess *any* incidents of ownership in the policy—not even the right to borrow on the cash values.

Otherwise, those incidents of ownership will be attributable to the controlling shareholder-insured, and the proceeds will be includable in the insured-shareholder's estate. We should point out that even when the proceeds are includable in the insured's estate, if the "owner" who collaterally assigned the policy to the corporation is the spouse of the controlling shareholder-insured, any estate tax resulting from the inclusion of the proceeds can be neutralized by the unlimited marital deduction.

While the mechanics of the premium payments are important for income tax purposes, they are not relevant for estate tax purposes. In the words of the Internal Revenue Service, "the same Federal estate tax consequences would obtain regardless of the source or purpose of payment of policy premiums."

Note that in the above situation, only the proceeds paid to the personal beneficiary were includable. Some observers had feared that, if a decedent held any incidents of ownership, the entire proceeds would be includable. This apparently is not the case.

Caution should be exercised when the corporation's incidents of ownership are restricted. One case has held that, when the corporation could exercise its incidents only with the consent of the majority shareholder's daughter, the incidents would be passed through to the majority shareholder.

However, ownership is pretty much a gray area, subject to interpretation of the IRS in its rulings. The results depend on how ownership is arranged between the insured, the corporation and the beneficiary. Simply be aware that there is a potential problem with a majority shareholder in terms of estate taxation. The best advice is to work closely with your or the client's attorney.

Split-Dollar Plans and ERISA

Although ERISA includes split-dollar as an employee welfare benefit and thus subject to its jurisdiction, these plans are not generally subject to the full array of statutory compliances which apply to other benefit programs. In fact, the Department of Labor has issued regulations that largely exempt split-dollar plans from the reporting and disclosure requirements of the law.

Split-dollar plans that cover only a select group of managerial or highly compensated employees require no reporting or disclosure. Further, all split-dollar plans with less than 100 participants are exempt from the reporting requirements, apparently even when the plan is contributory. However, in the "under 100" plan, disclosure in the form of a summary plan description must be made.

MAJOR USES OF SPLIT-DOLLAR

There are many potential uses of split-dollar insurance. It may be used to provide an employee benefit for key employees, to help a key employee who receives a rated insurance policy or as deferred compensation. Split-dollar has been used as part of a proprietorship purchase agreement, as well as partnership and corporate buy-sell agreements. Others have used it to shift the cost of present personally owned insurance to the corporation, for intrafamily gifts, as an executive bonus plan or to provide a cash accumulation fund in a professional corporation.

Employee Benefit for Key Employees

Split-dollar insurance may be used as an employee benefit for any key individuals of a business. Split-dollar insurance is an excellent incentive plan, especially when used with younger executives and key employees. The employer can help these valuable persons purchase a substantial amount of insurance—more than they personally could afford on their present income.

The employer's benefit from purchasing split-dollar for selected key individuals is the increased loyalty and heightened morale of those key individuals. By selecting them for the extra insurance benefits provided by split-dollar policies, the employer has indicated his or her interest in them as valuable assets to the company.

Not only has the company greatly aided the employee, but a split-dollar policy costs the company nothing other than the net after-tax loss of earnings if the money had been invested elsewhere.

Deferred Compensation Plans

A third use of split-dollar insurance in the employee benefit area is as deferred compensation. The typical insured deferred compensation plan calls for the life insurance to be owned by the company. When the employee dies, the company uses the insurance proceeds it receives from the policy to pay a death benefit to the employee's beneficiaries.

Suppose, however, that the company had split-dollared the insurance with the employee. When the life insurance company pays the insurance benefit directly to the beneficiary of the employee, the beneficiary takes the proceeds tax free—just as the beneficiary would take the proceeds of any other insurance on the decedent tax free. The reason is that when the death benefit was established under the split-dollar arrangement, the deceased employee personally purchased the insurance benefit (or at least paid tax on the economic benefit), in the same manner that the employee purchased any other personal insurance. Conversely, when a death benefit is paid by an employer under a deferred compensation arrangement, the payment represents deferred salary. The payment is deductible by the employer and taxable income to the employee's beneficiary.

When split-dollar is part of a deferred compensation plan, the employee's beneficiary receives more because the benefit is not subject to income tax. At the same time, the employer has retained the cash value of the policy; this cash value may be the source of the funds the company uses at retirement to pay the deferred compensation benefits.

The employer benefits, too, in that it has not paid the full premium for the life insurance. Through split-dollar, the employer has reduced its cost of funding its obligation under the deferred compensation agreement.

Proprietorship Purchase Agreement

A fourth use of split-dollar insurance is the proprietor purchase agreement. The term *proprietor,* in the context of this chapter, means not only the unincorporated sole owner of a business, but also the stockholder who owns all the stock of a corporation. Such a person might have operated a business for a number of years. No children are in the business with the owner. However, there is a bright young man or woman, employed by the owner, who might be interested in buying the business someday.

In this situation, it is possible for the proprietor and this employee to enter into a proprietorship purchase agreement. Under the agreement, the employee would purchase the owner's business at death, and possibly at retirement. All the employee has to do is to buy an insurance policy on the business owner's life. The life insurance policy funds a binding buy-sell agreement at a predetermined price.

However, this is not as easy as it sounds. In most cases, the employee will not have any extra money to pay premiums for a substantial amount of insurance on an older person. Of course, the proprietor could lend the employee the money for the premiums or increase the employee's salary. But the problem also could be solved with split-dollar insurance. The proprietor could put up the portion of the premium that equals the increase in cash value each year. The employee then is responsible only for the balance of the premium. Perhaps the employee's part of the premium could be paid through payroll deduction.

If the employee still would have difficulty meeting the first few years' premiums, the employee and the employer could work out one of the split-dollar variations discussed earlier under the heading, "First-Year Premium Problem." The employer could make a level contribution to the plan or pay all the first few years' premiums. Any way they arrange the proprietor purchase agreement, there is a split-dollar variation to set up the insurance funding. Furthermore, should the key employee quit, the proprietor can recover his or her investment in the insurance contract, because the proprietor owns the insurance cash values at all times.

Buy-Sell Agreement

A fifth use of split-dollar insurance is to fund buy-sell agreements between partners and their partnerships, or stockholders and their corporations.

There are at least two business situations in which it may not be advisable to use the entity plan. In both situations, a cross-purchase plan combined with split-dollar insurance might be used effectively.

Desire to Control Firm

The first situation is one in which the purchase of the deceased associate's interest by the partnership or corporation might affect the control of the firm. For example, take the case of the ABC Corporation. The corporation has three stockholders: A, who owns 40 of the 100 shares outstanding; B, with 20 shares; and C, with 40 shares. C does not get along with A and B; however, as long as A and B together own the majority interest, they have no control problems.

But if the stockholders were to enter into a stock redemption agreement with the corporation in which the corporation bought a stockholder's shares at death or withdrawal and A died first, the chance would exist for C to gain control of the corporation. C then would own 40 of the 60 shares outstanding.

On the other hand, A and B could agree to a cross-purchase agreement between themselves; the survivor would be assured of a majority interest and control of the corporation. And split-dollar insurance would permit them to afford the insurance they would need on each other's lives to fund the agreement.

While C may not be pleased that company funds were used at no effective interest to keep him from getting control, A and B hold the majority interest in the corporation. Barring fraud, they can make reasonable business decisions in the absence of C. C, as a minority shareholder, has few remedies. However, should C be upset, perhaps C can be made to feel better by the firm installing a split-dollar plan for C outside of the one for A and B. Also, other benefits such as a salary continuation plan would be added, thus providing C with adequate income to take early retirement.

Buyout in a Family Corporation

A second situation in which split-dollar insurance might be used effectively in a buy-sell agreement is in the family corporation. In this context, the term *family corporation* means a corporation in which all the stockholders are lineal heirs. For this chapter's purposes, a corporation in which the stockholders are siblings or cousins is not considered a family corporation.

From a tax viewpoint, it can be dangerous for the corporation to agree to redeem or purchase the stock of a family member at the family member's death or withdrawal from the business. The amount distributed to a withdrawing stockholder or to the decedent's estate in return for his or her shares could be taxed as ordinary income. This is because a partial redemption of a stockholder's shares must reduce the stockholder's interest in the corporation to certain minimums; otherwise, the amounts distributed to the stockholder in the redemption will be the equivalent of a dividend and ordinary income. In the family corporation, the law assumes that for purposes of redemption each family member constructively owns the stock of the other family members. Thus the minimums are not met.

Take the case of a father-daughter corporation—each owning half the shares. The daughter dies and the corporation redeems her shares from her estate. In this case, the amount received by the estate will be taxed to it as ordinary income. The reason is that the father is a possible heir of the daughter, so the estate is considered to own the stock the father owned, as well as what it actually owned. Thus, after the redemption, the estate still constructively owned 100 percent of the stock of the corporation.

There are a number of ways that attorneys can arrange buy-sell agreements to reduce or negate the possibility of the adverse tax effect described. One method is to arrange a cross-purchase agreement among the family members. This way does not involve corporate funds, so there is no possibility of ordinary income tax treatment of amounts received for transferred stock. Of course, split-dollar insurance can ease the burden to the family members of the cost of carrying insurance on each other's lives.

Split-Dollar Section 303 Redemption

A conventional Section 303 redemption has two drawbacks: (1) any insurance the corporation purchases to fund the redemption may increase the value of the stock for estate tax purposes; and (2) Section 303 is available only for the immediate cash needs of the estate, not for the continuing security of the surviving spouse and children. These problems can be mitigated, however. The stockholder-employee's spouse purchases an insurance policy on the life of the stockholder. He or she enters into a split-dollar agreement with the employer, whereby the corporation agrees to loan to him or her each year an amount equal to the annual increase in the cash value. In return, he or she collaterally assigns the policy to the corporation to secure the loans. Upon the stockholder's death, the corporation receives only an amount equal to the cash value immediately before death or the aggregate premiums paid, whichever is greater. The spouse receives the balance of the proceeds but loans them to the corporation, receiving interest-bearing notes in exchange. The employer then carries out the Section 303 redemption with the proceeds. The employer retires the notes as they fall due and deducts the interest it pays to the widow or widower.

In addition to mitigating the two problems presented earlier, the parties have avoided an estate tax problem for the majority shareholder. By using a third-party owner (the spouse), the shareholder avoids holding any direct incidents of ownership, and because the corporation is only a collateral assignee, it has no incidents of ownership that can be attributed to a majority shareholder. The P.S. 58 cost still is charged to the employee each year for income tax purposes, but this sum can be "bonused out" to the employee each year (assuming there's no problem with "reasonable compensation"). The employee may make a gift of the P.S. 58 cost to the spouse if necessary to help pay premiums. Gifts to a spouse generally qualify for an unlimited marital deduction, so the gift of the P.S. 58 costs should incur no gift taxes.

Shifting Cost of Present Insurance

A seventh use of split-dollar insurance is as a means of transferring the major cost of personally owned insurance to the corporation. Insurance agents often face the problem of the corporate key executive who needs additional personally owned life insurance, but cannot afford the additional premium.

A possible solution is, first, to have the key executive arrange with his or her employer to borrow from the employer each year a sum equal to the increase in cash values on the executive's present insurance. These loans would bear no interest. In return, the employee collaterally assigns the policies to the employer.

If the existing policies split-dollared by the executive are old enough, the loan from the employer will pay most of the premium each year. This split-dollar plan thus frees premium money, which allows the key executive to take the second step—the purchase of needed additional insurance. Of course, the employee will continue to have some expense from the policy he or she split-dollars with his or her employer; the executive will have the premium cost in excess of the increase in cash value each year, as well as the income tax on the P.S. 58 costs.

Intrafamily Gifts

An eighth use of split-dollar insurance is intrafamily gifts. A father could split-dollar an insurance policy with his son, for instance. Either father or son could be the insured; the choice of which one would depend upon the purposes of the insurance. If the insurance was intended to provide the cash to buy out the father's business interest or to pay the costs and taxes in his estate, the father would be the insured. On the other hand, if the insurance was intended to build the son's insurance program at a low cost to him, the son would be the insured. Split-dollar insurance also has been used between a grandparent and a grandchild—to help the grandchild pay the early premiums and get his or her insurance program started.

Another example of an intrafamily application of a split-dollar plan is that of a mother-in-law who insures the son-in-law for the protection of the mother-in-law's daughter and grandchildren. In this situation, it might be desirable for the beneficiary to be the owner, for control reasons, in the event of marital problems.

In these intrafamily split-dollar plans, apparently there is no problem with a family member being in receipt of an economic benefit. However, this problem would exist if the family member is also an employee of the parent or grandparent.

In the usual gift of split-dollar insurance, the family member's cost would be limited to the insurance-at-risk portion of the premium. The insurance benefit might be offered as a gift, which could be measured by the P.S. 58 rates. In most cases, the value of the gift will be small and well within the donor's annual $10,000 gift tax exclusion.

Cash Accumulation Fund in a Professional Corporation

A ninth use of split-dollar insurance is that in which a closely held or professional corporation with one shareholder desires to accumulate cash in a tax-favored manner. For example, it may need cash to fund a living buy-out. Or, an individual may need a creditor-proof supplemental retirement plan. The reverse split-dollar concept works especially well in these situations.

Reverse split-dollar is, as its name indicates, a reversal of the traditional split-dollar plan. The employee is the applicant for the insurance. One employee owns the full cash value. The employee endorses the policy so that the employer has the right to name the company as the beneficiary of the death benefit. The employer pays the P.S. 58 rate, which decreases the employee's premium.

With a reverse split-dollar plan, the corporation receives nothing back should the plan ever be terminated. Thus, a typical prospect for a reverse split-dollar plan would be a professional corporation or close corporation with the sole stockholder as the insured employee.

SUMMARY

This chapter discussed the basic structure of split dollar plans and various modifications to that structure, including different premiums, cash value and death benefit splits, as well as various policy-ownership arrangements. It examined the advantages of the split-dollar method of life insurance policy purchase that inure to employers—selectivity and simplicity at no direct cost—and to covered employees, including its low employee cost.

The use of the split-dollar method to purchase flexible premium and equity-based products was addressed also. The special advantages resulting from the greater flexibility and higher early accumulated values of these policies were consider.

Income and estate tax issues with respect to split-dollar plans were discussed, including the non-deductibility of employer and employee premiums and the income tax-free nature of death benefits. The unsettled income tax area of equity split-dollar and TAM 9604001 also were considered.

The chapter concludes by addressing the principal uses of split-dollar, including its use as an employee benefit for key employees, as an informal funding vehicle for deferred compensation plans and as a funding vehicle for proprietorship purchase and certain buy-sell agreements. Sample split-dollar agreements were included for reference purposes.

SAMPLE SPLIT-DOLLAR INSURANCE AGREEMENTS

The following agreements illustrate some of the various split-dollar plans. Each particular approach used, of course, will require an agreement unique to that method. As with all agreements in this course, only the client's attorney actually should prepare the necessary documents. These samples are included here for illustrative purposes only. Finally, the American Bankers Association Form 10 is included for your reference.

ILL 13.4 ▪ *Sample Split-Dollar Agreement*

(Corporation-Owned Policy; Basic Split-Dollar Plans)

CAUTION: This is a specimen agreement. The actual agreement used in any particular case must be prepared by a qualified attorney.

INTRODUCTION AND PARTIES

This Agreement, made this _____ day of _____, 20_____, between Company, Inc., a _____ corporation (hereinafter called *the Employer*), and _____ (hereinafter called *the Employee*):

WITNESSETH:

PURPOSES OF THE AGREEMENT

Whereas the Employer has purchased and owns a certain policy of life insurance on the life of the Employee, being Policy No. _____ issued by _____ Insurance Company in a face amount of $_____ (said policy being hereinafter called *the Policy*); and

Whereas the parties hereto have agreed upon a plan for payment of the premiums due or to become due on the Policy, and mode of payment of death benefits thereunder, and for the protection of their mutual interests do desire and intend to set forth such plan and their agreements relating thereto herein:

Now, Therefore, in consideration of the premises, it is mutually agreed by and between the parties hereto as follows:

PAYMENT OF PREMIUMS

1. Premiums on the Policy shall be paid each year while the Policy and this Agreement remain in force, in accordance with and subject to the following terms and conditions:

   (a) Premiums on the Policy shall be payable annually or more frequently, as the Employer may elect; provided, however, that the Employer shall cause all premiums to be billed to it on a net basis (i.e., gross premium less dividend, if any).

   (b) The premium or premiums due on the Policy for the first policy year shall be paid by the Employer from funds contributed by the Employee for that purpose and to the full amount of such premiums, unless otherwise agreed in writing by the parties.

   (c) Each net premium due on the Policy after the first year shall be paid by the Employer out of a fund which shall consist of:

   (i) Amounts to be contributed by the Employer during each policy year after the first equaling but not exceeding the amount of the increase in the cash surrender value of the Policy for the forthcoming policy year over the amount of the cash surrender value for the preceding policy year, as shown and provided in the Policy; and

ILL 13.4 ▪ *Sample Split-Dollar Agreement (Cont.)*

(ii) An amount to be contributed by the Employee during each policy year after the first equaling but not exceeding the difference, if any, between the amount of the Employer's contribution, as above-described, for such policy year, and the total net premium(s) due for such year; and

(iii) Provided, however, that if for any policy year the total net premium(s) due for such year shall be less than the said increase in the cash surrender value, the Employer shall contribute only an amount equal to said total net premium(s) due, and the Employee shall contribute nothing.

(d) Except as may be agreed upon by the parties hereto and as provided herein, the Employee shall have no right, title or interest in or to the Policy, and any insurance company issuing any policy referred to herein need take no cognizance of this agreement and may conclusively rely on the authority of the Employer to deal with such policy as sole and complete owner thereof.

BENEFICIARY DESIGNATION

2. So long as this agreement remains in effect, the parties agree that the beneficiary designation under the Policy shall provide that upon the death of the Employee the proceeds of the Policy will be payable in two (2) parts, as follows:

(a) One such part shall be payable to the Employer, and shall be in the amount of the cash surrender value of the Policy at the end of the period for which premiums have been paid at the date of the Employee's death, less any policy loan and interest then due; and

(b) The other such part shall consist of the entire balance of the proceeds payable, in excess of the part provided under (a) above, and shall be payable to the person or persons last named in writing to the Employer by the Employee as his (her) beneficiaries, and so designated upon the Policy by the Employer at the written request of the Employee. If the Employee requests the Employer in writing to make such part payable under a mode of settlement other than lump sum, the Employer will make prompt and reasonable effort to have the Policy endorsed accordingly. The Employer agrees to make no changes in the beneficiaries entitled to such part of the proceeds except upon the written request of the Employee.

(c) If the Policy be assigned or encumbered in any way on the date of the Employee's death, other than by policy loan, as above provided, the Employer shall promptly take all necessary steps to procure a release or discharge of such assignment or encumbrance, and to effect and ensure prompt payment to the beneficiaries designated by the Employee of the entire sum otherwise due them under the Policy in the absence of such assignment or encumbrance.

PROCEDURE AT EMPLOYEE'S DEATH

3. Upon the death of the Employee while the Policy and this Agreement are in force, the Employer shall promptly take all necessary steps, including rendering of such assistance as may reasonably be required by the Employee's beneficiaries, to obtain payment from the insurance company of the amounts payable under the Policy to the respective parties, as provided under Paragraph 2 above.

TERMINATION OF AGREEMENT

4. This Agreement will terminate upon the first to occur of any one of the following events:

(a) Failure by the Employer or the Employee for any reason to make the contribution due toward any premiums payable on the Policy;

(b) Termination of the Employee's employment with the Employer;

ILL 13.4 ■ *Sample Split-Dollar Agreement (Cont.)*

(c) Performance of its terms, following death of the Employee; or

(d) The written agreement of the Employer and Employee to that effect.

Upon such termination, for any reason other than (c) above, the Employee shall have a 30-day option to purchase the Policy with all the Employer's rights therein, for and in consideration of the payment by the Employee to the Employer of an amount equal to the cash surrender value existing in the policy at the end of the period for which premiums have been paid. If the Policy shall then be encumbered by assignment, policy loan, or otherwise, the Employer shall either remove such encumbrance, or reduce the sales price to the Employee by the amount of indebtedness (including interest then due or accrued thereon) outstanding against the policy. If the Employee exercises such option to purchase, the Employer shall execute all necessary documents required by the insurance company to effect a transfer of ownership, or absolute assignment, of the Policy over to and in favor of him.

CONCLUSION

In Witness Whereof, The Employee has hereunder set his (her) hand and seal, and the Employer has caused this instrument to be executed in its corporate name and under its corporate seal by an officer duly authorized, the day and year first above written.

Witness (SEAL)

_____
Employee

_____ COMPANY, INC. (SEAL)

by_____

_____
Employer

ILL 13.5 ■ *Sample Split-Dollar Agreement*

**(Corporation-Owned policy;
dividends purchase one-year term, balance reduce premiums)**

**CAUTION: This is a specimen agreement. The actual agreement used
in any particular case must be prepared by a qualified attorney.**

INTRODUCTION AND PARTIES

This Agreement, made this _____ day of _____, 20_____, between Company, Inc., a _____ corporation (hereinafter called *the Employer*), and _____ (hereinafter called *the Employee*):

WITNESSETH:

PURPOSES OF THE AGREEMENT

Whereas the Employer has purchased and owns a certain policy of life insurance on the life of the Employee, being Policy No. _____ issued by _____ Insurance Company in a face amount of $_____ (said policy being hereinafter called *the Policy*); and

Whereas the parties hereto have agreed upon a plan for payment of the premiums due or to become due on the Policy, and mode of payment of death benefits thereunder, and for the protection of their mutual interests do desire and intend to set forth such plan and their agreements relating thereto herein:

Now, Therefore, in consideration of the premises, it is mutually agreed by and between the parties hereto as follows:

PAYMENT OF PREMIUMS

1. Premiums on the Policy shall be paid each year while the Policy and this Agreement remain in force, in accordance with and subject to the following terms and conditions:

   (a) Premiums on the Policy shall be payable annually or more frequently, as the Employer may elect; provided, however, that the Employer shall cause all premiums to be billed to it on a gross basis with dividends, if any, used to purchase one-year term insurance equal to the terminal cash value for the current policy year and the balance, if any, used to reduce the gross premium.

   (b) The premium or premiums due on the Policy for the first policy year shall be paid by the Employer from funds contributed by the Employee for that purpose and to the full amount of such premiums, unless otherwise agreed in writing by the parties.

   (c) Each gross premium due on the Policy after the first policy year shall be paid by the Employer out of a fund which shall consist of:

   (i) Amounts to be contributed by the Employer during each policy year after the first equaling but not exceeding the amount of the increase in the cash surrender value of the Policy for the forthcoming policy year over the amount of the cash surrender value for the preceding policy year, as shown and provided in the Policy; and

   (ii) An amount to be contributed by the Employee during each policy year after the first equaling but not exceeding the difference, if any, between the amount of the Employer's contribution, as above-described, for such policy year, and the total gross premium(s) due for such year; and

ILL 13.5 ▪ *Sample Split-Dollar Agreement (Cont.)*

    (iii) Provided, however, that if for any policy year the total gross premium(s) due for such year shall be less than the said increase in the cash surrender value, the Employer shall contribute only an amount equal to said total gross premium(s) due, and the Employee shall contribute nothing.

(d) Except as may be agreed upon by the parties hereto and as provided herein, the Employee shall have no right, title or interest in or to the Policy, and any insurance company issuing any policy referred to herein need take no cognizance of this agreement and may conclusively rely on the authority of the Employer to deal with such policy as sole and complete owner thereof.

BENEFICIARY DESIGNATION

2. So long as this agreement remains in effect, the parties agree that the beneficiary designation under the Policy shall provide that upon the death of the Employee the proceeds of the Policy will be payable in two (2) parts, as follows:

(a) One such part shall be payable to the Employer, and shall be the greater of Employer contributions or the cash surrender value of the Policy at the end of the period for which premiums have been paid at the date of the Employee's death, less any policy loan and interest then due; and

(b) The other such part shall consist of the entire balance of the proceeds payable, in excess of the part provided under (a) above, and shall be payable to the person or persons last named in writing to the Employer by the Employee as his (her) beneficiaries, and so designated upon the Policy by the Employer at the written request of the Employee. If the Employee requests the Employer in writing to make such part payable under a mode of settlement other than lump sum, the Employer will make prompt and reasonable effort to have the Policy endorsed accordingly. The Employer agrees to make no changes in the beneficiaries entitled to such part of the proceeds except upon the written request of the Employee.

(c) If the Policy be assigned or encumbered in any way on the date of the Employee's death, other than by policy loan, as above provided, the Employer shall promptly take all necessary steps to procure a release or discharge of such assignment or encumbrance, and to effect and ensure prompt payment to the beneficiaries designated by the Employee of the entire sum otherwise due them under the Policy in the absence of such assignment or encumbrance.

PROCEDURE AT EMPLOYEE'S DEATH

3. Upon the death of the Employee while the Policy and this Agreement are in force, the Employer shall promptly take all necessary steps, including rendering of such assistance as may reasonably be required by the Employee's beneficiaries, to obtain payment from the insurance company of the amounts payable under the Policy to the respective parties, as provided under Paragraph 2 above.

TERMINATION OF AGREEMENT

4. This Agreement will terminate upon the first to occur of any one of the following events:

(a) Failure by the Employer or the Employee for any reason to make the contribution due toward any premiums payable on the Policy;

(b) Termination of the Employee's employment with the Employer;

(c) Performance of its terms, following death of the Employee; or

(d) The written agreement of the Employer and Employee to that effect.

ILL 13.5 ▪ *Sample Split-Dollar Agreement (Cont.)*

Upon such termination, for any reason other than (c) above, the Employee shall have a 30-day option to purchase the Policy with all the Employer's rights therein, for and in consideration of the payment by the Employee to the Employer of an amount equal to the cash surrender value existing in the policy at the end of the period for which premiums have been paid. If the Policy shall then be encumbered by assignment, policy loan, or otherwise, the Employer shall either remove such encumbrance, or reduce the sales price to the Employee by the amount of indebtedness (including interest then due or accrued thereon) outstanding against the policy. If the Employee exercises such option to purchase, the Employer shall execute all necessary documents required by the insurance company to effect a transfer of ownership, or absolute assignment, of the Policy over to and in favor of him.

CONCLUSION

In Witness Whereof, the Employee has hereunder set his (her) hand and seal, and the Employer has caused this instrument to be executed in its corporate name and under its corporate seal by an officer duly authorized, the day and year first above written.

Witness: (SEAL)

_____

"Employee"

_____ COMPANY, INC. (SEAL)

by_____

_____

"Employer"

ILL 13.6 ▪ *Sample Policy Endorsement*

CAUTION: This is a specimen endorsement. The actual endorsement used in any particular case must be prepared by a qualified attorney.

Application No. or Policy No. _____
 Date this form is signed is signed _____
 Insured_____
 Place _____

The XYZ Life Insurance Company is hereby requested and directed to make the provisions of this form a part of the policy. Attachment by the Company of a copy of this form to the policy will constitute proper endorsement of the policy.

All previous designations of payees and elections of settlement options pertaining to death proceeds are hereby revoked including the Monthly Income Settlement of any Increased Protection Benefit or Family Income Policy or Supplementary Term Benefit Agreement. It is hereby requested and directed that:

BENEFICIARIES

(1) _____ a corporation with its principal place of business at _____, _____, or its successors shall be the direct beneficiary of an amount of the proceeds equal to the cash value of the policy as of the date of death of the Insured less any indebtedness to the Insurance Company.

(2) The beneficiaries of any remaining proceeds including the amount of any Increased Protection Benefit, Convertible Protection Benefit, Accidental Death Benefit and Decreasing Term Insurance Benefit shall be designated by the Insured or his Transferee.

OWNERSHIP

(Employer)

(3) The Owner of the policy shall be _____. The Owner alone may exercise all the rights and privileges specified in the policy, including but not limited to the right to assign or borrow on the policy except that (a) the Owner shall not have the right to designate and change direct and contingent beneficiaries of the portion of the proceeds described in Paragraph (2) above, or to elect and change a settlement option for such beneficiaries; (b) the Owner shall not have the right to exercise the Conversion Privilege of any Increased Protection Benefit, Convertible Protection Benefit or Decreasing Term Insurance Benefit; and (c) while the Split-Dollar Insurance Agreement referred to in Paragraph 4(c) below is in effect, the Owner shall not have the right to surrender or cancel the policy.

(4) The Insured or his Transferee shall have the right to (a) designate and change direct and contingent beneficiaries of that portion of the proceeds described in Paragraph (2) and to elect and change a settlement option for such beneficiaries, it being understood and agreed that for the sole purpose of such designation and election and change, the Insured or his Transferee shall be considered the "Owner" under the BENEFICIARY AND SETTLEMENT PROVISIONS of the policy applicable to the portion of the proceeds described in Paragraph (2); (b) exercise the Conversion Privilege of any Increased Protection Benefit, Convertible Protection Benefit or Decreasing Term Insurance Benefit and shall be the Owner of any new policy issued in lieu of such Benefit; and (c) surrender or cancel the policy in accordance with Paragraph 6 of Split-Dollar Insurance Agreement [Endorsement Method] dated _____ while such Agreement is in effect. This Paragraph shall not limit the rights of the Owner as specified in Paragraph (3) above.

ILL 13.7 ▪ *Modification of Assignment Provisions of the Policy*

CAUTION: This is a specimen document. The actual document used in any particular case must be prepared by a qualified attorney.

Upon the death of the Insured the interest of any collateral assignee of the Owner of the policy designated in Paragraph (3) above shall be limited to the portion of the proceeds described in Paragraph (1) above.

OWNER

By _____

I accept and agree to the foregoing and subject to the rights of the Owner as stated above, designate _____, my_____, as direct beneficiary of that portion of the proceeds described in Paragraph (2).

The contingent beneficiaries thereof shall be the payees designated in one of the following captions marked with "X":

☐ (a) _____, my children and any (other) children of mine, in equal shares, or the survivors or survivor of them.

☐ (b) _____, my children and any (other) children of mine, in equal shares, or the survivors or survivor of them, except that any amount (or the withdrawal value thereof if a settlement option is in effect) a deceased contingent beneficiary would have received, if living, shall be payable when due in one sum in equal shares to his or her then living children.

☐ (c) _____, my_____, in equal shares, or the survivors or survivor of them.

Under captions (a) and (b), "children" includes any legally adopted child, and decisions made by the Insurance Company upon evidence satisfactory to it shall be conclusive and shall fully protect it.

If all direct and contingent beneficiaries and further payees of the portion of the proceeds described in Paragraph (2) die before receiving full payment, the remainder shall be paid to.

_____   _____
              Witness   Insured

_____

_____

For   ENDORSED ATTACHMENT   THE XYZ Life Insurance Company
Home Office
Use Only   Date_____   By_____

ILL 13.8 ▪ *Sample Collateral Assignment Agreement*

CAUTION: This is a specimen agreement. The actual agreement used in any particular case must be prepared by a qualified attorney.

THIS AGREEMENT made the _____ day of _____, 20____, between a corporation (hereinafter called "the Corporation") and _____ (hereinafter called *the Employee*).

WITNESSETH

WHEREAS, the Employee desires to insure his (her) life for the benefit and protection of his (her) family, in the face amount of $_____ under a policy to be issued by _____ Insurance Company; and

WHEREAS, the Corporation is willing to make loans to the Employee from time to time without interest thereon, in amounts which shall not exceed the cash surrender value of such policy at any given time, and

WHEREAS, the Employee will collaterally assign such policy to the Corporation as security to guarantee the repayment of such loans.

NOW, THEREFORE, in consideration of the mutual covenants and agreements set forth below, the Corporation, for itself and its successors, and the Employee for him- (her-)self, his (her) executors, administrators, and assigns agree as follows:

1. The Employee will apply for a policy of life insurance on his (her) life and do everything necessary to cause _____ Insurance Company to issue a policy of life insurance in the face amount of $_____, naming the said Employee as owner thereof, and designating as beneficiaries thereunder such individuals as are named by the Employee subject to change by him (her) from time to time.

2. The Employee agrees to execute a collateral assignment of the policy to the Corporation as security for the payment of any indebtedness of the Employee to the Corporation as hereinafter set forth in Paragraph 5.

3. The Employee agrees to pay to the Corporation an amount equal to the first annual premium on such policy less the amount of the guaranteed cash value of said policy on its first anniversary. On or before the due date of the second and each subsequent annual premium, the Employee shall pay to the Corporation an amount determined as follows: Subtract the guaranteed cash value of the policy as of the premium due date from the guaranteed cash value as of the next policy anniversary and such difference to be subtracted from the net premium to be paid.

4. The Corporation agrees that upon receipt of the amount (if any) required to be paid by the Employee as set forth in Paragraph 3, it will pay to _____ Insurance Company the net annual premium on or before the due date.

5. All amounts paid to _____ Insurance Company by the Corporation less the sum of (1) amounts paid to the Corporation by the Employee in accordance with Paragraphs 2, 3 and 4 above, and (2) amount of any outstanding insurance company loans against the policy made by the Corporation, shall constitute an indebtedness of the Employee to the Corporation without interest.

6. The Corporation shall have possession of the policy during the period of indebtedness but it shall make the same available to the _____ Insurance Company when it is necessary to endorse changes of beneficiary thereon.

7. Upon the death of the Employee while this Agreement is in force, the Corporation shall satisfy the entire indebtedness under this Agreement from the policy proceeds and shall take all steps required to release all interest in the balance of such proceeds which are to be paid under the terms and provisions of the policy to the beneficiaries named by the Employee.

ILL 13.8 ■ *Sample Collateral Assignment Agreement (Cont.)*

8. The Corporation, during the lifetime of the Employee and the continuance in force of this Agreement, will not exercise any of its rights as collateral assignee without the consent of the Employee.

9. This Agreement shall terminate upon the first to occur of any one of the following events:

    (a) The written agreement of the Employer and the Employee to that effect.

    (b) Termination of the Employee's employment with the Employer.

    (c) The bankruptcy of the Corporation.

    (d) Payment in full of the indebtedness by the Employee and release of the collateral assignment by the Corporation.

10. In the event of termination under (a), (b), or (c) of Paragraph 9 above, the indebtedness shall become due and payable except that the Employee shall have 30 days in which to pay such indebtedness before the Corporation shall avail itself of its rights as collateral assignee under the policy.

11. _____ Insurance Company (1) shall not be deemed to be a party to this Agreement for any purpose nor in any way responsible for its validity; (2) shall not be obligated to inquire as to the distribution or application of any monies payable or paid by it under any such policy or policies issued on the life of the Employee; (3) payment or other performance of its contract obligations in accordance with the terms of such policy or policies shall fully discharge the Company from any and all liability under the terms of said policy or policies.

12. This Agreement shall not be modified or amended except by a writing signed by the parties, and (b) that the Agreement is binding upon the heirs, administrators or executors and assigns of each party.

13. This Agreement shall be subject to and construed by the laws of the State of _____.

IN WITNESS WHEREOF, the parties hereto have executed this Agreement the day and year above written.

_____
"Corporation"

_____
"Employee"

ILL 13.9 ■ *Assignment of Life Insurance Policy as Collateral*

(The Standard American Bankers Association Form 10)

CAUTION: This is a specimen agreement. The actual agreement used in any particular case must be prepared by a qualified attorney.

A. For Value Received the undersigned hereby assign, transfer and set over to _____ of _____ its successors and assigns, (herein called the *Assignee*) Policy No. _____ issued by the contracts issued in connection therewith (said policy and contracts being herein called the *Policy*), upon the life of _____ of _____ and all claims, options, privileges, rights, title and interest therein and thereunder (except as provided in Paragraph C hereof), subject to all the terms and conditions of the Policy and to all superior liens, if any, which the Insurer may have against the Policy. The undersigned by this instrument jointly and severally agree and the Assignee by the acceptance of this assignment agrees to the conditions and provisions herein set forth.

B. It is expressly agreed that, without detracting from the generality of the foregoing, the following specific rights are included in this assignment and pass by virtue hereof;

   1. The sole right to collect from the Insurer the net proceeds of the Policy when it becomes a claim by death or maturity;

   2. The sole right to surrender the Policy and receive the surrender value thereof at any time provided by the terms of the Policy and at such other times as the Insurer may allow;

   3. The sole right to obtain one or more loans or advances on the Policy, either from the Insurer or, at any time, from other persons, and to pledge or assign the Policy as security for such loans or advances;

   4. The sole right to collect and receive distributions or shares of surplus, dividend deposits or additions to the Policy now or hereafter made or apportioned thereto, and to exercise any and all options contained in the Policy with respect thereto; provided, that unless and until the Assignee notifies the Insurer in writing to the contrary, the distributions or shares of surplus, dividend deposits and additions shall continue on the plan in force at the time of this assignment;

   5. The sole right to exercise all nonforfeiture rights permitted by the terms of the Policy or allowed by the Insurer and to receive all benefits and advantages derived therefrom; and

   6. The sole right to the value of any funds held by the Insurer for the purpose of paying future premiums under the Policy as determined by the premium agreement applicable thereto.

C. It is expressly agreed that the following specific rights, so long as the Policy has not been surrendered, are reserved and excluded from this assignment and do not pass by virtue hereof;

   1. The right to collect from the Insurer any disability benefit payable in cash that does not reduce the amount of insurance;

   2. The right to designate and change the beneficiary;

   3. The right to elect any optional mode of settlement permitted by the Policy or allowed by the Insurer; but the reservation of these rights shall in no way impair the right of the Assignee to Insurer; but the reservation of these rights shall in no way impair the right of the Assignee to surrender the Policy completely with all its incidents or impair any other right of the Assignee hereunder, and any designation or change of beneficiary or election of a mode of settlement shall be made subject to this assignment and to the rights of the Assignee hereunder.

ILL 13.9 ▪ *Assignment of Life Insurance Policy as Collateral (Cont.)*

D. This assignment is made and the Policy is to be held as collateral security for any and all liabilities of the undersigned, or any of them, to the Assignee, either now existing or that may hereafter arise in the ordinary course of business between any of the undersigned and the Assignee (all of which liabilities secured or to become secured are herein called *Liabilities*).

E. The assignee covenants and agrees with the undersigned as follows:

  1. That any balance of sums received hereunder from the Insurer remaining after payment of the then existing Liabilities, matured or unmatured, shall be paid by the Assignee to the persons entitled thereto under the terms of the Policy had this assignment not been executed;

  2. That the Assignee will not exercise the right to surrender the Policy or (except for the purpose of paying premiums) the right to obtain policy loans from the Insurer, until there is default in the Liabilities or a failure to pay a premium when due, nor until 20 days after the Assignee has mailed, by first-class mail, to the undersigned at the addresses last supplied in writing to the Assignee specifically referring to this assignment, notice of intention to exercise such right; and

  3. That the Assignee will upon request forward without unreasonable delay to the Insurer the Policy for endorsement of any designation or change of beneficiary or any election of an optional mode of settlement.

F. The Insurer is hereby authorized to recognize the Assignee's claims to rights hereunder without investigating the reason for any action taken by the Assignee, or the validity or the amount of the Liabilities or the existence of any default therein, or the giving of any notice under Paragraph E (2) above or otherwise, or the application to be made by the Assignee of any amounts to be paid to the Assignee. The sole signature of the Assignee shall be sufficient for the exercise of any rights under the Policy assigned hereby and the sole receipt of the Assignee for any sums received shall be a full discharge and release therefor to the Insurer. Checks for all or any part of the sums payable under the Policy and assigned herein, shall be drawn to the exclusive order of the Assignee if, when, and in such amounts as may be, requested by the Assignee.

G. The Assignee shall be under no obligation to pay the premium, or the principal of or interest on any loans or advances on the Policy whether or not obtained by the Assignee, or any other charges on the Policy, but any such amounts so paid by the Assignee from its own funds, shall become a part of the Liabilities hereby secured, shall be due immediately, and shall draw interest at a rate fixed by the Assignee from time to time not exceeding 6 percent per annum.

H. The exercise of any right, option, privilege or power given herein to the Assignee shall be at the option of the Assignee, but (except as restricted by Paragraph E(2) above) the Assignee may exercise any such right, option, privilege or power without notice to, or assent by, or affecting the liability of, or releasing any interest hereby assigned by the undersigned, or any of them.

I. The Assignee may take or release other security, may release any party primarily or secondarily liable for any of the Liabilities, may grant extensions, renewals or indulgences with respect to the Liabilities, or may apply to the Liabilities in such order as the Assignee shall determine, the proceeds of the Policy hereby assigned or any amount received on account of the Policy by the exercise of any right permitted under this assignment, without resorting or regard to other security.

J. In the event of any conflict between the provisions of this assignment and provisions of the note or other evidence of any Liability with respect to the Policy or rights of collateral security therein, the provisions of this assignment shall prevail, as to the Insurer, and the provisions of agreement dated _____ shall prevail as between the parties thereto.

K. Each of the undersigned declares that no proceedings in bankruptcy are pending against him (her) and that his (her) property is not subject to any assignment for the benefit of creditors.

ILL 13.9 ▪ *Assignment of Life Insurance Policy as Collateral (Cont.)*

Signed and sealed this _____ day of _____, 20_____.

_____ _____
Witness   Insured or owner

_____ _____
Address   Address

_____ _____
Witness   Witness

_____ _____
Address   Address

(NOTARIAL ACKNOWLEDGMENTS SHOULD BE ADDED TO ANY ACTUAL ASSIGNMENT)

QUESTIONS FOR REVIEW

1. All the following statements about basic split-dollar plans are true EXCEPT

   A. an attorney should prepare the necessary agreements for the split-dollar arrangement

   B. the employee is the applicant and the owner of the insurance

   C. the death benefit received by the beneficiary has tax advantages over payments received under a conventional deferred compensation plan

   D. upon termination or death of the employee, the business is entitled to the policy's cash values unless there is a written agreement to the contrary

2. When the insured employee dies, the personal beneficiary receives the

   A. policy's cash surrender value

   B. difference between the face amount and the cash surrender value

   C. face amount of the policy

   D. face amount of the policy, plus the cash value

3. Sales situations that might call for the use of split-dollar insurance include

   A. employee benefit for key employees

   B. deferred compensation plans

   C. funding for buy-sell agreements

   D. all of the above

4. An advantage of the fifth dividend option split-dollar plan is

   A. the employer's cash value grows more rapidly

   B. the employer has the potential to receive significantly more than its premium contributions

   C. the employee's death benefit remains approximately level

   D. all of the above

5. Which of the following statements describes an executive bonus plan?

   A. The executive collaterally assigns the insurance policy to the employer.

   B. The bonus is income tax deductible to the employer.

   C. Amounts are tax deferred to the employee.

   D. None of the above

14

Group Term Life Insurance

Because of its low cost and tax advantages, group term life insurance has mushroomed in recent years. Qualifying requirements for group term life insurance are examined, as well as current taxation of employees, conversion privileges and group term insurance documents. Special attention is given to group insurance and buy-sell agreements and group life insurance on less than 10 lives.

Since the first group term life contract was issued in the early 20th century, there has been a tremendous growth in the popularity of the group life concept. In a recent year, group insurance accounted for 41 percent of all life insurance in force in the United States, with a total face amount of $4.2 trillion. More significantly, the average policy size per insured under employer-sponsored plans is about $30,000. In short, for many men and women in this country, group life is a valuable benefit and source of protection. It is also highly valued by employers due primarily to its low cost and its tax advantages. Because of group underwriting economies, premiums for group term life insurance contain less expense loading than conventional policies, resulting in a lower cost per $1,000 of protection. In this chapter, we will look at what group term is and its tax advantages.

As an insurance professional, you will find that group term life has become an almost universally expected employment benefit. It is a fairly simple sale to explain and present to the employer. Also, one group term life sale can lead to a wealth of additional business: as you enroll and work with employees under the plan, you will find numerous other opportunities to meet additional, personal needs for the employees and their families.

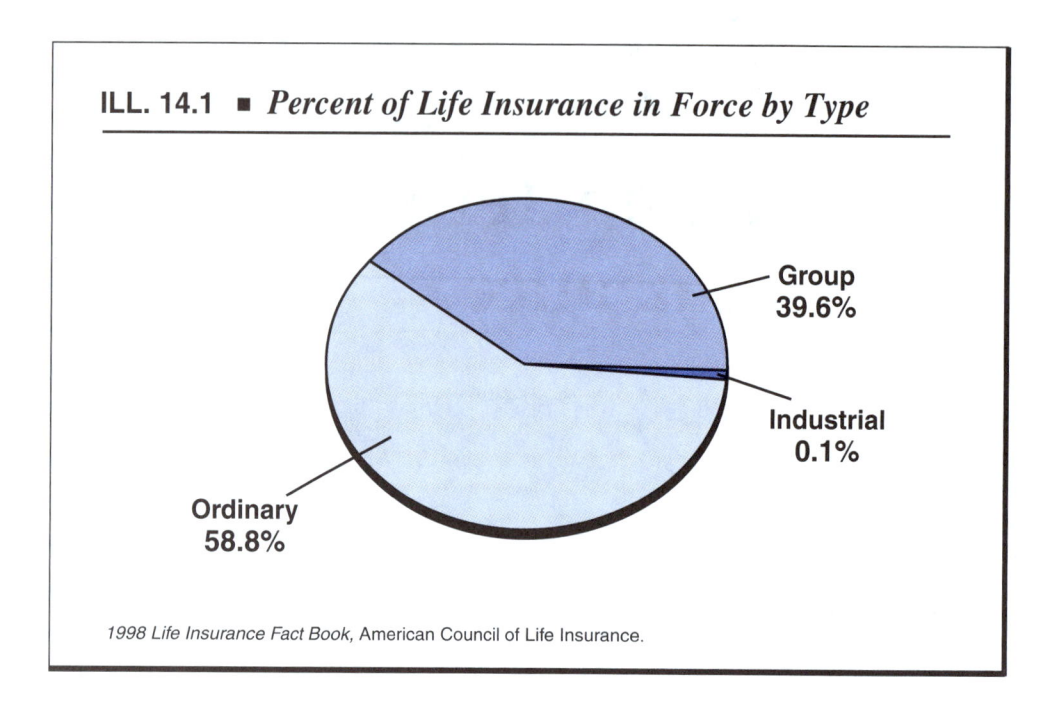

ILL. 14.1 ■ *Percent of Life Insurance in Force by Type*

- Group 39.6%
- Industrial 0.1%
- Ordinary 58.8%

1998 Life Insurance Fact Book, American Council of Life Insurance.

■ OVERVIEW OF GROUP TERM LIFE

Group term life insurance is defined by the limits described under Section 79 of the Internal Revenue Code. If a plan meets the qualifications, the employer can deduct the cost of coverage for its covered employees.

Group term life insurance, for the purposes of qualifying under Section 79, is term life insurance that:

1. provides a general death benefit excludable from gross income;

2. provides coverage to a "group of employees";

3. is provided under a policy "carried directly or indirectly" by the employer; and

4. provides an amount of insurance to each covered employee based upon factors that preclude individual selection.

A group of employees is defined as either all employees or less than all employees if eligibility is determined solely on the basis of age, marital status or factors related to employment. Such factors include union membership, duties performed, compensation received and length of service. Shareholders who also are employees may be a part of the group so long as their stock ownership is not the basis for their membership in the group. Moreover, participation in an employer's pension, profit-sharing or accident and health plan is also a factor related to employment.

An employee is a person who:

1. performs services in the legal relationship of employer-employee;

2. is a full-time life insurance salesperson; or

3. is a former employee.

Therefore, although self-employed persons may set up group term plans for themselves and their employees, only the employees can secure the tax benefits of Section 79. Independent contractors are not eligible for Section 79 unless their coverage is based upon former service for the employer.

ELIGIBILITY AND AMOUNT OF COVERAGE

There are two sets of rules for group term life. One set applies to plans covering 10 employees or more. Another applies to plans covering under 10 employees.

Groups of 10 or More

Under Section 79, a group term plan covering 10 or more employees is not considered discriminatory (and therefore qualifies for favorable tax treatment) if both of the following conditions are met:

1. the plan does not discriminate in favor of key employees as to eligibility to participate; and

2. the type and amount of benefits available under the plan do not discriminate in favor of participants who are key employees.

A plan, however, will not be judged discriminatory merely because the amount of life insurance provided to employees bears a uniform relationship to compensation.

Eligibility Classification

An employer-provided group term life insurance plan does not discriminate in favor of key employees as to eligibility to participate if:

1. the program benefits at least 70 percent of all employees;

2. at least 85 percent of all participating employees are *not* key employees;

3. the program benefits employees who qualify under a classification set up by the employer and found by the Secretary of the Treasury not to discriminate in favor of key employees; and

4. as part of a cafeteria plan, the plan will not be considered discriminatory if the eligibility requirements of Section 125 are satisfied.

For purposes of Section 79 discrimination testing, employees of related employers are generally treated as if employed by a single employer. The following employees, however, may be excluded from consideration when applying the eligibility-to-participate standard:

- those who have not completed three years of service with the employer;

- part-time and seasonal employees; and

- nonresident aliens who receive no U.S. source income from the employer.

Definition of Key Employee

Key employee generally has the same meaning as in the pension context. A key employee is a plan participant who, during the year or any four preceding plan years, is (or was):

1. an officer earning more than 50 percent of the defined benefit plan dollar limit for the current year;

2. an officer of the company who owns both more than a ½ percent interest and one of the 10 largest interests in the company and to whom the employer pays annual compensation exceeding the current defined contribution dollar limitation under code Section 415;

3. an owner of 5 percent or more of the employer; or

4. a 1 percent or greater owner of the employer having an annual compensation of more than $150,000.

If a group term life plan fails to satisfy the nondiscrimination rules, the cost of the first $50,000 of group term life coverage, normally excludable from gross income, will be included in a key employee's gross income. The rank-and-file employees will not be so penalized.

Groups Under 10

Groups of fewer than 10 employees may obtain Section 79 tax treatment when certain requirements are met:

1. The insurance must be provided to *all* full-time employees of the employer or, if evidence of insurability affects eligibility, to all full-time employees who provide evidence of insurability satisfactory to the insurer.

2. The amount of insurance provided must be computed either as a uniform percentage of compensation or on the basis of coverage brackets established by the insurer. In general, no bracket may exceed 2½ times the next lower bracket, and the lowest bracket must be at least 10 percent of the highest bracket. However, the insurer may establish a separate schedule of coverage brackets for employees who are over age 65, but

no bracket in the over-65 schedule may exceed 2½ times the next lower bracket. The lowest bracket in the over-65 schedule must be at least 10 percent of the highest bracket in the basic schedule.

Deductibility of Premiums

An employer may deduct premiums for group term life insurance as a business expense as long as there is no reasonable compensation problem. The employer will lose the deduction when it directly or indirectly is a beneficiary of the group policy. It should be noted that the laws of some states prohibit the employer from being the beneficiary of group life insurance on employees. Thus, you must check the state law where your client resides if he or she wishes to benefit from the insurance. All employee-paid premiums are nondeductible.

CURRENT TAXATION OF EMPLOYEES

When the group term plan qualifies under Section 79, an employee (or retired employee) does not have to report the employer-paid premiums as income if the insurance coverage is $50,000 or less. If the plan fails to qualify under Section 79, the employee's allocable share of premiums paid by the employer will be additional compensation to the employee.

In a *noncontributory* plan, the employee will be taxed on the cost of coverage in excess of $50,000. However, the cost of the insurance in excess of $50,000 will not be taxed to the employee if:

1. the employer is the beneficiary;

2. a qualified charity is the sole beneficiary for the entire period for which the cost otherwise would be taxed to the employee;

3. the employee has terminated employment due to disability; or

4. the group term insurance is provided through a Section 401(a) qualified plan.

The $50,000 exemption must be reduced if the applicable state law imposes a lower maximum on group coverage on one life. Only a few states have a lower limit. If an employee has group term coverage with more than one employer, the $50,000 exemption applies to the aggregate coverage. For example, suppose an employee is covered by a $30,000 group term policy and another $35,000 group term policy. The employee is taxable annually on the cost of $15,000 of protection (less any contributions he or she makes).

In a *contributory* plan, the employee may subtract the entire contribution from the cost of the coverage over $50,000 that otherwise would be taxable to the employee. In other words, the employee's contributions can be allocated entirely to the cost of excess coverage (over $50,000) to reduce or eliminate any current tax cost to the employee. He or she may not carry over until the subsequent year any unused portion of contributions.

ILL. 14.2 ▪ Uniform Premiums for $1,000 of Group Term Life Insurance Protection [Reg. Section 1.79-3(d)(2)]

5-year age* bracket	Cost per $1,000 of protection for 1-month period
Under 30	8 cents
30 to 34	9 cents
35 to 39	11 cents
40 to 44	17 cents
45 to 49	29 cents
50 to 54	48 cents
55 to 59	75 cents
60 to 64	$1.17
65 to 69	2.17
70 and above	3.76

*The employee's age for purposes of this table is his or her attained age on the last day of the taxable year.

In the typical situation, in which the employee has excess coverage and designates a personal beneficiary, the cost of the coverage over $50,000 is taxable in accordance with Ill. 14.2. The cost generally is based on the protection the employee receives during the year, not the premiums paid by the employer.

For example, suppose an employee, age 56, is provided with $100,000 of group term life insurance coverage. The employee contributes $6 per $1,000 annually. Under Ill. 14.2, the amount includable in the employee's gross income is computed as follows:

Excess coverage ($100,000 less $50,000)	$50,000.00
Annual cost per $1,000 of excess coverage ($0.75 × 12 months)	9.00
Annual cost of excess coverage ($50,000 × $9 per $1,000)	450.00
Cost of insurance attributable to employee's contribution ($100,000 × $6 per $1,000)	600.00
Amount included in employee's gross income ($450 − $600)	$ 0

If the insurance protection provided to an employee exceeds the maximum statutory limit permitted under the applicable state law, the actual premium paid for the coverage in excess of the maximum is includable in the employee's income, rather than the Ill. 14.2 cost. "Applicable state law" means the state whose laws govern the terms and conditions of the policy.

When the employee has assigned his or her group insurance, premiums for coverage in excess of $50,000 are not taxed to the employee if paid by the assignee. But if the cost of the excess coverage is shared by the employer and the assignee, the employer's portion of the excess cost is includable in the employee's gross income.

When the employer reserves the right to change the method of paying death proceeds to some method other than a lump sum, and the employer can make this selection at each employee's death, the qualification of the plan for Section 79 tax treatment is not affected at all.

Dependent Coverage

Although the cost of dependent coverage is not group term life insurance, it is not taxable to the employee if it is "incidental." The cost of dependent coverage is incidental if the amount of insurance payable upon the death of a spouse or child does not exceed $2,000. If the amount of insurance does exceed $2,000, the entire cost of the dependent coverage will be taxable to the employee. This taxable cost is determined under Ill. 14.2.

Income Taxation of Proceeds

Group term proceeds are income tax-exempt if they are paid in a lump sum and if the group insurance is not part of a qualified plan. If the proceeds are paid in installments, the interest portion is taxed at ordinary income rates.

Estate Taxation of Proceeds

Group term proceeds will be includable in the deceased employee's gross estate if he or she possessed any incidents of ownership, or if the proceeds are payable to his or her estate. The common incident of ownership that an employee possesses is the right to change the beneficiary. There are others, however. The IRS has ruled that the employee's conversion privilege upon termination of employment is not an incident of ownership. The employee's right to select a settlement option is a gray area. The employee's power to cancel his or her group coverage by terminating his or her employment is not an incident of ownership.

The constructive incidents of ownership rules for majority shareholders carve out a special exception for group insurance. The corporation's power to surrender or cancel a group term policy will not be attributed to a sole or controlling shareholder. Typically, this will be the only incident the corporation possesses; if there are others, the majority shareholder clearly has an estate tax problem.

The insured employee can be rid of all direct incidents of ownership by absolutely assigning his or her rights to a third party, including any conversion privilege, provided the policy and state law permit the assignment. It is not necessary that state law specifically authorize the assignment, as long as it does not prohibit it. Group life assignments now appear to be permissible in all 50 states and the District of Columbia. Even if state law permits assignments, policy terms to the contrary will control. An assignment is invalid if the assignment is specifically prohibited by the master policy. However, an assignment is valid if it is permitted by the master policy but prohibited by the individual certificates.

ILL 14.3 ▪ *Assignment of Group Insurance (To Spouse)*

CAUTION: This is a specimen assignment. The actual assignment used in any particular case must be prepared by a qualified attorney.

I, Richard Roe, of Chicago, Illinois, do hereby transfer and assign unto my wife, Mary Roe, all of my right, title and interest in and to group life insurance policy No. _____ issued by the XYZ Life Insurance Company to my employer, Acme Mfg., Inc., as master contract holder.

IN WITNESS WHEREOF, I have executed this assignment this _____ day of _____, 20_____.

_____
Richard Roe

ASSIGNMENT OF GROUP INSURANCE
(To Trust)

I, Richard Roe, of Chicago, Illinois, do hereby transfer and assign unto the Reliable Trust Company, as trustee under a trust agreement executed by me on _____, 20____, all of my right, title and interest in and to group life insurance policy No. _____ issued by the XYZ Life Insurance Company to my employer, Acme Mfg., Inc., as master contract holder. The Reliable Trust Company shall hold this interest and exercise all rights incident thereto pursuant to the terms of the above-described trust agreement. The XYZ Life Insurance Company shall have no obligations with respect to the validity of this assignment, nor with the execution of the provisions of the above-described trust agreement.

IN WITNESS WHEREOF, I have executed this assignment this _____ day of _____, 20____.

_____
Richard Roe

SAMPLE ANTICIPATORY ASSIGNMENT OF GROUP INSURANCE

The undersigned employee of _____, the employer, and as such an insured under master contract group life insurance Policy No. _____ of the _____ Insurance Company, does hereby assign all of his right title and interest in and to such group life insurance to _____; and the undersigned also assigns all other rights or interests or other benefits growing out of this or any other master contract policy of group life insurance held by his employer, including (but not limited to) any increases in amount or type of coverage, or change of insurer, or any other alteration or modification of the group life insurance plan of the employer.

Dated:_____

_____
Employee-Assignor

Accepted and filed:

_____

Employer
by _____
its _____

Group Term Versus Qualified Plan

An employer of 10 wonders whether employee death benefits should be provided as an incidental benefit in a qualified retirement plan or through a separate group term plan. Cost quotes will, of course, play a major role in the decision. From a tax standpoint, the group term plan seems to have a slight advantage, as the table below indicates. Bear in mind that the P.S. 58 rates are somewhat higher than the Ill. 14.2 rates.

	Group Term	Qualified Plan
Employer's deduction	Generally deductible in full	Generally deductible in full
Current taxation of employee or retired employee	First $50,000 coverage exempt; Table 14.1 for excess	P.S. 58 applies from first dollar of coverage
Income taxation of proceeds	Fully exempt	Only the pure insurance portion is exempt
Estate taxation of proceeds	Generally must be assigned more than three years before death to escape estate tax	Generally includable
Gift taxation of assignment	Employer premiums treated as gifts by employee	Employer-funded portion is exempt

Of course, there still can be estate tax problems after the assignment if the insured employee dies within three years. Assignments of incidents of ownership in group policies made within three years of death will be includable.

Illustrative Group Insurance Assignment Forms

The three forms of assignment that appear below may be used to assign group life insurance out of the gross estate (assuming no three-year problem). Many insurance companies recommend particular language to carry out assignments, beneficiary changes, etc., with respect to policies issued by them, and that their agents should be contacted in particular cases.

The first form that follows may not be needed in many instances because of the unlimited marital deduction. The unlimited marital deduction allows the full estate of the first spouse to die to pass to the surviving spouse free of estate taxes. However, the form is presented as an illustration of what may be used, as well as a teaching aid in the event that the client's attorney recommends more sophisticated estate planning.

Accidental Death and Disability Benefits

Group term policies often provide ancillary benefits in the form of accidental death and disability protection. Payments made for disability benefits provided under a group term policy are considered payments made for accident and health insurance. As such, employer contributions to provide such benefits are

Advantages of Group Term Life Insurance

To the employer:

1. The employer provides the benefit at low cost on an impartial and predetermined basis to virtually all his or her employees.

2. The coverage is desirable in that it helps the employer hire and retain quality employees.

3. Probably the most important advantage is that, under current tax laws and regulations, the employer's contributions are deductible as a business expense for income tax purposes.

To the employee:

1. For many employees, it is the only life insurance they have, because they either cannot qualify for individual life insurance or simply have not purchased any other insurance.

2. It provides peace of mind to the employee in that he or she has some insurance in case of premature death.

3. When the employee contributes toward the cost, the premiums are automatically withheld from wages, thus reducing the chance of lapse.

4. With the possible exception of split-dollar insurance, it provides the greatest amount of insurance at the lowest cost.

5. The death benefit usually is not considered taxable income to the beneficiary, despite the fact that the employer's contributions are not taxable as income to the employee.

6. The conversion privilege enables a terminated employee to convert his or her group coverage to an individual policy without medical examination.

Limitations of Group Term Life Insurance

1. There is no assurance for the employee that the master group policy will be continued in force from year to year. However, very few businesses do discontinue their group life except in extreme instances such as business failure.

2. Group term life does not have portability, thus it cannot be carried over to the next employer by an employee.

3. Group term life insurance often obscures the need for proper insurance purchases and planning by the employee. Many employees are surprised to discover that while they had insurance protection no cash or paid-up values were purchased.

4. At age 65, or other retirement age, group term either will be reduced or eliminated. Furthermore, the high cost of converting group insurance makes that an impractical solution.

---

deductible by the employer and nontaxable to the employee. Disability benefits received by an employee may be taxed in whole or in part.

Section 79 does not apply to travel insurance or accidental death insurance, including amounts paid under a double indemnity clause or rider. However, employer contributions to provide such benefits are still deductible by the employer and nontaxable to the employee. Accidental death proceeds are treated as life insurance for income tax and estate tax purposes.

CONVERSION PRIVILEGE

An insured employee usually has the right to convert the group term coverage to an individual policy of permanent insurance if he or she exercises this privilege within 31 days of the termination of his or her employment (or the master contract). During this 31-day grace period, the employee usually remains insured under the group term plan. Generally, the insured need not submit evidence of insurability to exercise the conversion privilege; the permanent policy will be issued at standard rates for the insured's attained age. Thus, the conversion privilege can be of great importance to the health-impaired or uninsurable individual. The experience of most insurers is that only about 1 to 2 percent of terminating employees exercise their conversion privilege.

GROUP INSURANCE AND BUY-SELL AGREEMENTS

Generally, group term life insurance is not a sound way to fund a buy-sell agreement.

For example, under a stock redemption agreement, the corporation would have to be either beneficiary of the insurance or assignee of the shareholder's group certificate to obtain the monies to make the redemption. But here, the corporation would not be able to deduct the premiums it pays for group insurance coverage, because the employer would be a direct or indirect beneficiary. Thus, the main advantage of Section 79 group term life insurance would be made meaningless.

Even if the shareholders are willing to lose the deduction, some states do not allow an employer to be beneficiary of group insurance on employees.

In a cross-purchase buy-sell situation, group term life insurance also would not be practical. The "Century" ruling (a private letter ruling issued June 28, 1962) indicated that, when group term insurance proceeds are used to fund a cross-purchase agreement among principal shareholders, the corporation may not deduct the premiums it pays for the group coverage. Also, the premiums might be considered constructive dividends in such cases.

Even if the shareholders were willing to forego the corporate deductions in the cross-purchase situation, the shareholders might find themselves as transferees for value, because of the reciprocal transfers. Thus, the proceeds would be taxed as ordinary income upon receipt.

Thus, as you can see, the use of group term life as a funding agent is fraught with problems and should not be contemplated.

GROUP LIFE INSURANCE ON LESS THAN TEN LIVES

Normally, Section 79 is available only when group coverage is provided to at least ten full-time employees who are in the "group of employees." However, when special requirements are met, groups of less than ten employees may secure Section 79 tax treatment. These special requirements were discussed earlier in this chapter; here we would like to show how some insurance companies apply the requirements. Two types of insurance policies currently being written qualify as group term life insurance for less than ten lives. One type is wholesale, or franchise, life insurance. The other type is group insurance written through an employers or association trust.

Wholesale or Franchise Insurance

Wholesale, or *franchise*, insurance had its beginnings years ago when the minimum group size for group term life insurance was 50 lives. As group-writing insurance companies reduced their minimum group requirements down to ten lives, the market for wholesale insurance became the smaller employee groups of generally four to nine lives.

When wholesale insurance is used to insure an employer-employee group, each insured receives an individual policy with standard policy provisions. The policy is often yearly renewable term, and waiver of premium and double indemnity are included.

The insurance is provided on a formula basis, both to adhere to the Treasury regulation and to minimize selection against the insurer. Each proposed insured must sign an application, which includes health questions and is subject to individual underwriting. Again, to adhere to Treasury regulations, no medical examination can be required. An individual who has an impairment may be accepted at standard premium rates as far as physical condition is concerned (either for the amount of insurance requested or for a reduced amount) or he may be declined altogether.

The main advantage of wholesale life insurance from the employer's viewpoint is the fact that it is available at a premium rate less than that charged for a regular individual policy. The advantage to the employee is nonincludability of the employer's insurance cost in his or her gross income. Of course, the particular wholesale life plan must qualify as "group term life insurance" in order for the employee to exclude the premium cost from his or her income.

It is also advantageous for the insurance agent to sell wholesale life insurance. Insurance companies often offer it to or through associations or groups of employers. Once an insurance company gets permission or backing of a particular employer association, it can have its agents call on the individual employers and get them to adopt the association-sponsored plan. Thus, the individual insurance agent has a tremendous sales advantage—the backing of the association—when he or she talks to each employer.

Group Insurance Through a Multi-Employer Trust

Some group-writing insurance companies are using the vehicle of a multi-employer trust to underwrite employers who have fewer than ten employees. Most often the group term life insurance coverage is combined with disability income, basic hospital and major medical coverage into one rather comprehensive group plan. To reduce the administration problem, the employer is given a choice of, perhaps, six plans. The chief difference from one plan to the next is the daily room and board benefit the employer desires to purchase in the hospital plan. For example, the minimum plan may have a $25 daily benefit, while the maximum may be $75.

The advantage of multi-employer trust group life plans for the small employer is that the business purchases life insurance coverage for its employees at a price that approximates the regular group rate. The insurance companies that sell these plans also claim that their premium rates are competitive for 10 to 24 employee groups.

The advantage to the covered employee is that this life insurance is considered to be group term life insurance. Therefore, the employer-paid cost of coverage for $50,000 or less is not includable in the employee's gross income. The portion of employer-paid cost in excess of $50,000 coverage, however, is includable unless the beneficiary is an eligible charity.

The agent also benefits from the multi-employer trust approach to group insurance. The insurance is made available to a group of employers. If the agent has the endorsement or the active promotion of the employers association or franchise behind him or her, he or she has considerable sales leverage in approaching individual employees.

Group Permanent Life Insurance Plans

For some years, attempts to offer some type of permanent life protection to key employees under the provisions of Section 79 were popular; however, successive tax reform restrictions have lessened the attractiveness of these ideas. Such programs as Retired Lives Reserve and other group permanent coverages no longer have the tax-sheltered umbrella they once enjoyed under former, more liberal regulations.

Some insurers still offer such plans, particularly in the area of group universal and variable life, but the loss of former tax advantages limits their appeal.

SUMMARY

In this chapter we examined the nature and requirements of group term life insurance and found that term life insurance that qualifies as group insurance has certain tax advantages. Those tax advantages generally include income-tax deduction of the premium by the employer and the avoidance by covered employees of income tax consequences on the first $50,000 of coverage. In addition, the death benefits generally are received income tax-free. Qualifying as group insurance requires that the policy provide death benefits to an employee group under an employer-purchased policy whose benefit amounts are not based on individual selection.

Group term life insurance is differentiated on the basis of number of employees. One set of rules applies to those groups of 10 or more employees, while another set applies to groups of less than 10. Groups of 10 or more employees have generally greater latitude than smaller groups with respect to participation requirements and the levels of insurance provided to employees in different classifications. Insurer approaches to the under-10-life marketplace include wholesale (franchise) life insurance, in which each employee receives an individual life insurance policy, and multiple employer trusts.

In addition to the income tax advantages that apply to group insurance, group insurance also offers certain non-tax advantages. Those non-tax advantages include:

- generally lower coverage cost;

- group underwriting that usually precludes individual selection (thereby providing the possibility of coverage to otherwise uninsurable employees); and

- a conversion privilege that permits a terminated employee to obtain an individual life insurance policy without underwriting.

GROUP TERM INSURANCE DOCUMENTS

On the following pages are the board resolution authorizing the adoption of a plan of group life insurance, and the plan document. Also included is a sample preapproach letter.

The board resolution and plan document should be prepared only by the client's attorney. These sample documents are presented here only for teaching purposes.

In the event that a true group plan is installed, as opposed to a grouping of individual insurance policies, it is important to be certain that the group master policy and the plan document do not conflict. In your interaction with the client's attorney, therefore, it will be imperative that you provide a current copy of the group master contract, if applicable. If, instead, the plan established combines individual policies into a group, the attorney will need sample individual policies. As an insurance professional, you can perform a service to clients by determining that the attorney has all the necessary relevant information regarding the plan to be installed.

ILL. 14.4 ▪ *Sample Resolution of the Board of Directors of Employer, Inc.*

CAUTION: This is a specimen resolution. The actual resolution used in any particular case must be prepared by a qualified attorney.

The undersigned, being all of the members of the Board of Directors of EMPLOYER, Inc., hereby signify their consent to adoption of the following resolutions and acknowledge their approval of the following actions of the President and Secretary of the corporation:

Whereas, the corporation desires to provide additional employee benefits for all of its full-time employees, and thereby provide additional incentives for their continued efforts on behalf of the corporation; and

Whereas, there has been presented to the Directors a proposed plan of Group Insurance with ABC Company;

Now, Therefore, be it,

Resolved: That the corporation adopt a Plan of Group-Term Life Insurance, as presented by the Secretary, said Plan to be executed, marked Exhibit A, attached to these minutes and incorporated herein by this reference;

Be It Further Resolved: That the President and Secretary be, and they hereby are, authorized and directed to take all necessary steps to acquire Group-Term Insurance for the corporation's employees with ABC Company in accordance with the Group-Term Life Insurance Plan; and

Be It Further Resolved: That Don Jones be and he hereby is appointed as Plan Administrator and the Named Fiduciary.

DATED this _____ day of _____, 20 _____.

_____
Director

_____
Director

_____
Director

ILL 14.5 ▪ *Sample Group-Term Life Insurance Plan*

CAUTION: This is a specimen plan. The actual plan used in any particular case must be prepared by a qualified attorney.

EMPLOYER, INC., a ( ) corporation, hereinafter the *Employer*, hereby establishes for the benefit of its employees as defined in paragraph 1.3 thereof, a "Group-Term Life Insurance Plan."

WITNESSETH:

Whereas, a suggested Group-Term Life Insurance program has been very favorably received by its employees, Employer has determined to adopt a plan providing group-term life benefits for its employees; and

Whereas, the corporation has agreed to contract for group-term life insurance with ABC Company, hereinafter the *Insurer* and has agreed to pay the entire term premium including any rating, plus supplemental benefits established by the Insurer for covered employees;

Now, Therefore, the following Plan is hereby adopted by the Employer effective upon the _____ day of _____, 20___.

ARTICLE I

Definitions

1.1 "Compensation" shall mean a participant's basic salary as it is in effect on the first day of each Plan Year but not including pay for work in excess of 40 hours per week, overtime and bonuses, and any amounts contributed to this Plan or amounts contributed to any other employee benefit plan for which a deduction is permitted to the Employer under Section 404 of the Internal Revenue Code.

1.2 "Continuous Service" shall mean and include the period since the last date on which a participant, whether an eligible employee or otherwise, entered the employ of the Employer and since which there has been no termination of employment by the Employer and no loss of qualification as an eligible employee.

1.3 "Participants" as used in this Plan, includes a group of employees consisting of all personnel employed full-time by the Employer. An individual shall be considered to be employed full-time if he customarily works at least five (5) months per calendar year and at least twenty (20) hours per week.

1.4 "Permanent Disability" shall mean disability as defined by Section 72(m)(7) and paragraph (f) of the Regulation Section 1.72-17.

1.5 "Plan Year" shall mean the period corresponding to the Employer's fiscal year for federal income tax reporting purposes.

1.6 All code references are to the Internal Revenue Code of 1986, as amended, or any subsequent statute of similar import. The masculine pronoun shall include the feminine and the singular form shall include the plural as necessary for proper interpretation of this Plan.

ILL 14.5 ▪ *Sample Group-Term Life Insurance Plan (Cont.)*

ARTICLE II

Participation

2.1 Eligibility. Each participant shall be eligible for personal Group-Term Life Insurance under the Employer's Group-Term Insurance Plan as of the first day of the Plan Year coinciding with or next following the employee's completion of six (6) months of consecutive and continuous service.

2.2 Change of Status. A participant whose service with the Employer has been terminated or who has been terminated or who has ceased to be an eligible employee and who was or later rehired by the Employer or becomes again an eligible employee, shall be deemed to be a new employee for all purposes under this Plan and his previous periods of service shall not be included in determining the period of his continuous service hereunder.

2.3 Underwriting Required. Eligible employees are not automatically insured. Each eligible employee must satisfy each Insurer's rules and requirements for insurability. No insurance or additions will be provided for any employee who is rated more than three times the standard rates.

ARTICLE III

Benefits

3.1 Amounts. The Employer shall provide the following amounts of Group-Term Life Insurance on the life of each participant:

3.2 Coverage. The amounts of insurance will be provided under Insurer's master policy No._____.

3.3 Funding Policy. For all classes the Employer shall pay the entire cost of the term insurance, including any rating. Premium payments shall be made within 31 days of the due date. Payments shall be made from the general assets of Employer directly to ABC Company. Any dividends or rate credits shall be applied against future premium obligations within three months of receipt by Employer.

3.4 Additions. Any participant may become eligible for additional insurance coverage according to the schedule set forth in paragraph 3.1. Such additional coverage shall be provided as of the first day of the following Plan Year. Any addition must be for at least $2,000 of insurance.

ARTICLE IV

Retirement and Disability

4.1 Retirement. If a participant retires at age 65 after ten years of continuous and consecutive service, Employer shall continue his term insurance provided by the ABC Company Group Policy on the basis it was established immediately prior to his retirement. Insurance provided under the standard policy terminates at 65.

4.2 Disability. Upon termination of employment by reason of a participant's permanent disability, the Employer shall, based on the participant's length of service, continue to pay all or a portion of the term premium on such participant's life as set out in the following schedule, to the extent such premium is not covered by a waiver of premium rider for disability.

ILL 14.5 ■ *Sample Group-Term Life Insurance Plan (Cont.)*

Completed Years of Continuous Participation	Percentage of Premium To Be Paid
1	5%
2	10%
3	15%
4	20%
5	25%
6	35%
7	50%
8	65%
9	80%
10 and over	100%

4.3 Temporary Disability. Notwithstanding paragraph 4.2, the Employer shall continue to pay the term premium in the event of disability for at least six (6) months prior to making a determination as to whether the employee is permanently disabled.

4.4 Partial Coverage. In the event of the retirement or permanent disability of a participant prior to completing that number of years of continuous service which would require the Employer to continue to pay the full term premiums for the coverage on such employee's life, said participant or his assigns shall be entitled to pay directly to the Insurer the balance of the term premium.

4.5 Competition. The Employer is not required to continue to pay term premiums for a retired or disabled employee who engages in any occupation or business, which, in the opinion of the Employer, is a competing business.

ARTICLE V
Policy Interests

5.1 Beneficiary Designation. In the event of the death of a participant, his designated beneficiaries shall be entitled to receive the entire proceeds. If any participant fails to designate a beneficiary, or if all designated beneficiaries shall have predeceased the participant, for the purpose of the Agreement the Plan Administrator shall be empowered to direct the Insurer to distribute such benefits in the order named: (1) the participant's spouse, (2) the issue of a participant by right of representation, or (3) the estate of the participant.

5.2 Plan Benefits. Payments of benefits under this Plan shall only be in accordance with the insurance contracts. Any person claiming benefits under this Plan may appeal in writing to the Plan Administrator in the event benefits are denied. Upon receiving the appeal, the Plan Administrator shall make a prompt full review of the claim, and if they deem it appropriate shall request the Insurer to reconsider its determination.

5.3 Ownership. The insured participant may assign all or any part of his interest in the policy(s) insuring his life. The insured may also designate a person to own his interest in the insurance. The owner or his assignee shall have the sole right to exercise any policy rights affecting the policy.

5.4 Right to Convert. In the event the participant's employment terminates prior to retirement or permanent disability or this Plan is terminated, the participant or his assignee shall have the right, pursuant to the terms of the policy, to convert the insurance provided by the Employer into an individual term or ordinary policy.

ILL 14.5 ■ *Sample Group-Term Life Insurance Plan (Cont.)*

5.5 Right to Drop or Decline Permanent Benefit. A participant has a right at any time to decline to purchase a permanent benefit if offered to him, and a right to drop such benefit if he has such coverage, provided however, the amount of group-term benefit cannot be reduced if such election is made.

ARTICLE VI

Termination and Amendments

6.1 Amendments. The employer may, by appropriate resolution of the Board of Directors, amend this plan in any particular.

6.2 Termination. The Employer reserves the right to terminate or partially terminate, this Plan in its entirety at any time by an affirmative vote of the Board of Directors.

6.3 Effect of Amendment or Termination. Any amendment or termination shall be prospective only and shall not retroactively reduce or modify Plan benefits for a participant. Prior to termination or partial termination, each participant will be notified by the Plan Administrator of his conversion privilege, if any, at least 30 days prior to lapse of the Group-Term Insurance.

ARTICLE VII

Plan Administration

7.1 Named Fiduciary. The Plan Administrator shall be designated by the Board of Directors of Employer and shall act until his successor is appointed. The Plan Administrator shall be the Named Fiduciary.

7.2 Powers and Duties. The Plan Administrator shall have the primary responsibility for the administration and operation of the Plan and shall have all powers necessary to carry out the provisions of the Plan, including the following:

- To determine all questions arising in the administration, interpretation and appreciation of the Plan, but he shall not be responsible for the selection of the insurance carrier or the terms of the insurance contract. Responsibility for these decisions is reserved to the Board of Directors.
- To determine the eligibility and class of each employee for participation in the Plan.
- To set down uniform and nondiscriminatory rules of interpretation and administration which may be modified from time to time in light of the Plan Administrator's experience.
- To publish and file or cause to be published and filed or disclosed all reports and disclosures required by federal or state law.

7.3 Records and Reports. The Plan Administrator shall keep a record of all its proceedings and acts, and shall keep all such books of account, records and other data as may be necessary for the proper administration of the Plan. The Plan Administrator shall maintain records with respect to each participant sufficient to determine the benefits due or which may become due to such participant. The Plan Administrator shall report to each participant with respect to benefits due or which may become due if such participant requests such a report or terminates his participation.

7.4 Payment of Expenses. The Plan Administrator shall serve without compensation for his services but all expenses of the Plan Administrator shall be paid by Employer.

7.5 Indemnity of Plan Administrator. Employer shall indemnify the Plan Administrator against any and all claims, loss, damage, expense or liability arising from any action or failure to act, except when the same is determined to be due to the gross negligence or willful misconduct of the Plan Administrator.

7.6 Agent for Service of Process. The Plan Administrator shall be the agent for service of legal process.

ILL 14.5 ■ *Sample Group-Term Life Insurance Plan (Cont.)*

ARTICLE VIII

Claims Procedure

8.1 Claim. If an Employee is denied participation or a participant or his beneficiary (hereinafter referred to as a "Claimant") is denied all or a portion of an expected Plan benefit for any reason, he may file a claim with the Plan Administrator. The Plan Administrator shall notify the Claimant within 60 days of allowance or denial of the claim. The notice shall be in writing, sent by mail to Claimant's last known address, and must contain the following information:

- The specific reasons for the denial;
- Specific reference to pertinent Plan or insurance contract provisions on which the denial is based;
- If applicable, a description of any additional information or material necessary to perfect the claim, and an explanation of why such information or material is necessary; and an explanation of the claims review procedure.

8.2 Review Procedure

- A Claimant is entitled to request a review of any denial of his claim by the Plan Administrator. The request for review must be submitted in writing within 60 days of mailing of notice of the denial. Absent a request for review within the 60-day period, the claim will be deemed to be conclusively denied. The Claimant or his representative shall be entitled to review all pertinent documents, and to submit issues and comments in writing.
- If the request for a review by a Claimant concerns the interpretation of an insurance contract, the issuing company shall review the claim and render the final decision.
- If the request for review by a Claimant concerns the interpretation and application of the provisions of this Plan and Employer's obligations, then the Board of Directors of Employer shall review the claim and render the final decision.

8.3 Final Decision. Within 60 days of mailing of a request for review, the insurance company or Board of Directors of Employer shall allow or deny the claim. The decision shall be made in writing to the Claimant. The decision shall recite the facts and reasons for denial, with specific reference to pertinent Plan provisions.

ARTICLE IX

Miscellaneous

9.1 Employment Obligations. The establishment of this Plan shall not be construed as creating any contract of employment between the Employer and the employee. Nothing herein contained shall give any employee the right to inspect the books of the Employer or to interfere with the right of the Employer to discharge any employee or the right of an employee to terminate his employment at any time.

9.2 Insurance Contract. The Insurer shall not be considered a party to this Plan, or any supplement of or amendment thereto. The Plan or any supplement or amendment thereto shall in no way enlarge, change or vary the Insurer's obligations as specifically set forth in any policy issued by it. Upon payment by the Insurer of the death benefit under a policy issued by it, the Insurer shall be fully discharged as to said policy. The provisions of this Plan with regard to eligibility, participation and amounts shall be applied regardless of any inconsistent provisions in any insurance contract.

ILL 14.5 ▪ *Sample Group-Term Life Insurance Plan (Cont.)*

9.3 Conflicts of Law. All matters respecting the validity, effect, interpretation and administration of this Plan shall be determined in accordance with the laws of the state of _____. All matters respecting the validity, effect, interpretation and administration of any insurance policy shall be determined in accordance with the laws of the state in which the group policy is delivered.

9.4 Interpretation. This Plan, the Trust and Group-Term Contract shall be construed to comply with Section 79, and its accompanying regulations.

EMPLOYER, INC.

By _____
President

By _____
Secretary

CHAPTER 14 QUESTIONS FOR REVIEW

1. By definition, group term life insurance provides a benefit that

    A. favors key employees

    B. is sponsored by the employees themselves

    C. provides a general death benefit includable in the employee's gross income

    D. none of the above

2. Which of the following are considered to be eligible for Section 79 tax benefits?

    A. A sole proprietor sponsoring a plan for his or her employees

    B. A former full-time employee

    C. An independent contractor performing services for the employer

    D. None of the above

3. Employees who may be excluded in determining the eligibility-to-participate standard are

    A. those who have not completed at least three years of service

    B. part-time employees

    C. seasonal full-time employees

    D. all of the above

4. Which of the following is considered to be a key employee for group term insurance purposes?

    A. The company president, who has no ownership interest but earns $50,000 a year

    B. The receptionist earning $12,000 a year, who has received a 7 percent ownership interest in the company in reward for her years of loyal service

    C. The CEO, who owns 3 percent of the stock and earns $160,000 a year

    D. All of the above

5. Under a group term plan, premiums for coverage up to $50,000 are

    A. deductible by the employer but reportable as income by the employee

    B. deductible by the employer and not reportable as income by the employee

    C. not deductible by the employer but reportable as income by the employee

    D. not deductible by the employer and not reportable as income by the employee

Answer Key to Questions for Review

Chapter 1
1. D
2. A
3. D
4. A
5. D

Chapter 2
1. C
2. A
3. D
4. C
5. A

Chapter 3
1. B
2. C
3. A
4. B
5. C

Chapter 4
1. C
2. C
3. A
4. B
5. D

Chapter 5
1. D
2. B
3. D
4. C
5. A

Chapter 6
1. C
2. C
3. D
4. C
5. D

Chapter 7
1. C
2. B
3. A
4. B
5. A

Chapter 8
1. D
2. A
3. D
4. D
5. C

Chapter 9
1. B
2. A
3. D
4. B
5. B

Chapter 10
1. C
2. C
3. D
4. C
5. C

Chapter 11
1. C
2. B
3. A
4. B
5. A

Chapter 12
1. D
2. B
3. B
4. D
5. B

Chapter 13
1. B
2. B
3. D
4. C
5. B

Chapter 14
1. D
2. B
3. D
4. D
5. B